radiation and a chemical carcinogen lead to apparent synergy in the induction of tumors, an observation that invoked comments from Dr. Reif. A similar effect involving radiation exposure and smoking is described by Dr. Reif in his book. Subsequently, we have attempted, as yet unsuccessfully, to identify markers of early lung cancer. We are currently trying to determine if cigarette smoke exposure damages the stem cells of the lung and inhibits repair processes. In this situation, one option would be to provide a cell source from outside the lung. Unfortunately, we think that smoking may damage stem cell populations throughout the body and thereby decrease their ability to repair accumulating tissue damage with age. Consequently, we are just starting a National Institute on Aging study of the quality of stem cells with aging. A major focus will be the effect of lifestyle factors, including smoking, on the quality of stem cells as individuals age.

On a personal note, my wife's father began smoking as a young man in the Navy in World War II. The family, as Dr. Reif suggests, persuaded him to quit, in part by indicating we did not want him to expose our children (his grandchildren). He did quit after many attempts, interestingly, with acupuncture treatment, which Dr. Reif suggests is not very effective. Unfortunately, 17 years later he succumbed to lung cancer, having smoked at least one too many camels so many years ago. If this book can prevent one such death, it will be worthwhile. However, I think its impact and benefits will be much, much greater than saving just one life. It presents facts that even the most battle-hardened politicians will find hard to ignore and I look forward to reading and gifting the print version.

J. Graham Sharp, Ph.D.

T0243371

ENDORSEMENT

The book "Fighting Smoking" by Arnold E. Reif, D.Sc., is a tour de force. Although its primary focus is to inform and educate the public about the dangers of smoking and to offer strategies for smokers to quit, this book is so much more. As noted by Dr. Sporn, it will be "a most valuable resource" and is "a superb catalogue of the scientific details of the consequences of smoking and its resultant societal ills." The book integrates the health risks with the advocacy and legislative attempts to reduce these risks (or at least warn the public about their magnitude). It outlines tobacco industry responses to regulations and their attempts to maintain a lucrative market. Dr. Reif lays out the socio-political environment that provides a fertile soil for the recruitment of new, young nicotone-addicted smokers. He then provides advice and strategies to help smokers to quit and suggests further governmental actions that might reduce the worldwide social, health and economic burden of smoking.

The book is easy to read and manages to cleverly incorporate many statistics without being overwhelming. Although its overall message is sober, the book is interesting and should only be scary for smokers with no interest in quitting. In fact, the book is a must read for smokers who wish to quit since it will surely motivate them. It is a necessary read for teachers, school administrators, advocates of all positions and legislators. As suggested on page 245, this book should be required reading for all medical students and highly recommended reading for physicians, surgeons, dentists and other health professionals.

The book reaches out to a wide array of targets, not least of which is the tobacco industry which might be tempted to buy up all the copies of this book before it is widely distributed because it powerful message will likely cause them further, future headaches. The book is well suited for the general public because it covers, in a most interesting fashion, not only all aspects of smoking, but also such topics of concern as marijuana, asbestos and airborne radiation from radon, nuclear reactor meltdowns and atomic bombs. The risks that are outlined regarding the smoking of marijuana might prove useful ammunition for parents counseling their children about sensible choices of behavior. The section on airborne radiation hazards should be useful to counter-terrorism planners and will serve as a caution to first responders who smoke.

My colleague, Dr. Stephen Rennard, a pulmonologist, notes that smoking should not be regarded as a "habit" but rather as a primary disease and should be treated as such. For example, for those who feel they cannot quit, the book discusses harm reduction or "safer cigarettes" in a reasonable and balanced way, but concludes that stopping smoking must be the real goal. The book addresses an important topic and currently no other book appears to exist that covers this area so comprehensively.

I strongly recommend this book and I sincerely hope that it is published in a timely fashion so that its benefits will become widely available to readers, not only in the USA, but worldwide. Indeed, I think this is a health, educational and social imperative. This book was reviewed on the basis of 35 years of experience in cell biology. Dr. Reif and his work came to my attention about 15 years ago when we published a study that showed exposure to

FIGHTING SMKING

FIGHTING SM🚭KING

AND OTHER CAUSES
OF LUNG CANCER

ARNOLD E. REIF

TATE PUBLISHING
AND ENTERPRISES, LLC

Published by Tate Publishing & Enterprises, LLC
127 E. Trade Center Terrace | Mustang, Oklahoma 73064 USA
1.888.361.9473 | www.tatepublishing.com

Tate Publishing is committed to excellence in the publishing industry. The company reflects the philosophy established by the founders, based on Psalm 68:11,
"The Lord gave the word and great was the company of those who published it."

Book design copyright © 2016 by Tate Publishing, LLC. All rights reserved.
Cover design by Rodrigo Adolfo
Interior design by Angelo Moralde

Published in the United States of America

ISBN: 978-1-63122-613-7
1. Self-Help / Substance Abuse & Addictions / Tobacco
2. Self-Help / Chemical Dependence
16.05.24

For my beloved father
Heinrich Reif, D.Jur.
Who died prematurely of
a smoking-caused cancer

HARVARD MEDICAL SCHOOL
DEPARTMENT OF SOCIAL MEDICINE

JULIUS B. RICHMOND, M.D.
John D. MacArthur
Professor of Health Policy, Emeritus

641 Huntington Avenue
Boston, MA 02115
617-432-1410
Fax: 617-432-2565
julius_richmond@hms.harvard.edu

July 26, 2005

Arnold E. Reif, D.Sc.
39 College Road
Wellesley, MA 02482

Dear Dr. Reif.

Congratulations on the manuscript.

This is a virtual encyclopedia on the health effects of smoking which constitute the greatest man-made epidemic in history. In addition to many strategies for controlling the epidemic, it has an appropriate emphasis on public health education – especially in the early years – including the Head Start program. This is a useful and timely book for all who work to improve the health of our people.

Julius B. Richmond, M.D.
Assistant Secretary for Health and
Surgeon-General 1977-81.
Founding Director, National Head Start
Program 1965-66

John R. Seffrin, PhD
Chief Executive Officer

August 23, 2005

Arnold E. Reif, D.Sc.
Research Professor of Pathology, Emeritus
Boston University School of Medicine
39 College Road
Wellesley, MA 02482

Dear Dr. Reif:

Thank you so much for forwarding your manuscript "Smoking" to me for review and comment. As you know, I have asked a member of my staff to do this review, although I have also had the opportunity to briefly peruse the manuscript.

You have produced a manuscript of great breadth, which covers the full range of topics involved in our fight against tobacco - from basic science, to clinical treatment, to policy change. You have also brought your own perspective to this manuscript - as a groundbreaking cancer immunologist, you bring scientific standing to an issue that has often been clouded in political, rather than scientific, discussion.

In your note, you asked about the possibility of an ACS-generated comment for the dust cover of the publication that may derive from this manuscript. I have asked a member of my staff, Tom Glynn, to coordinate this with you. Dr. Glynn is on e-mail at tom.glynn@cancer.org or may be reached at our Washington, DC office (901 E Street, NW, Washington, DC. 20004).

Again, thank you for bringing this work to our attention. The American Cancer Society is, of course, thankful to you for all of your contributions to the ACS and its mission over the years.

With best regards,

John R. Seffrin, PhD

JRS/jn

cc: Tom Glynn

National Home Office
1599 Clifton Road NE, Atlanta, GA 30329-4251 t) 404 329 7601 f) 404 329 7530
Cancer Information 1.800. ACS.2345 www.cancer.org

American Heart
Association®

Learn and Live ℠

National Center
7272 Greenville Avenue
Dallas, Texas 75231-4596
Tel 214.373.6300
americanheart.org

July 28, 2005

Arnold E. Reif, D.Sc
39 College Road
Wellesley, MA 02482

Dear Dr. Reif:

I am so pleased to have had the opportunity to read your manuscript, which provides a remarkable resource in this area so critically important to the public's health.

I am delighted to comment on it for the purpose of aiding your potential publishers in determining the appropriate market or markets, although I must confess to a lack of expertise in this area. My own experience with books is limited to those aimed specifically and only at the physician-scientist group, and more recently, and indirectly, with the consumer publications of the American Heart Association, so you and they will have to recognize my limitations. I must also say that my comments must be taken as those of an individual, since the Association, by policy, does not review or endorse books.

That said, I believe that your manuscript makes a very important contribution to the area of tobacco control and smoking cessation. Because of your own distinguished scientific career, your review of the consequences of smoking and the underlying reasons carries great weight. In addition, this sets the stage for the subsequent sections of the work. Perhaps the greatest benefit is the fact that you provide in one place so much information about so many aspects of this problem, not otherwise easily obtainable. It would seem to me that many different kinds of individuals might want to have this material available as a reference work. Libraries, as well, might not only use it to guide students of many levels for research in this area, but to aid those interested in community action to benefit both schools and their broader communities. I would certainly want our staff scientists to have it available for reference as they work.

One further comment. I wonder if there are sections of the text that might be useful as stand-alone smaller pieces aimed at focused markets. This is certainly an area in which I have no experience, but simply raise it for consideration.

Again, thank you for the privilege of reviewing your work. I believe it will be recognized as a critical piece in the enormously important ongoing struggle against this nation's leading preventable cause of death.

With warm best wishes,

Rose Marie Robertson, MD, FAHA, FACC, FESC
Chief Science Officer

Richard A. Daynard
President

Tobacco Control Resource Center
102 The Fenway, 117 Cushing Hall
Boston, Massachusetts 02115-5000

Phone: 617.373.2026
Facsimile: 617.373.3672
E-mail: www.tobacco.neu.edu

S CHOOL OF L AW

July 29, 2005

Dear Editor:

Please feel free to use the following in promoting Dr. Reif's book:

Dr. Reif has written a must-read book for anyone interested in knowing what tobacco products and the tobacco industry can do to the human body, and what we can do to stop the carnage. The book deals expertly with the relevant biology, history and politics, while at the same time being both succinct and perfectly accessible to the nonprofessional reader. In addition the book covers virtually all types of tobacco use, and all substances that cause cancer when inhaled. A truly impressive accomplishment!

Sincerely,

Richard A. Daynard, JD, Ph.D.
Professor of Law
Northeastern University School of Law
President, Tobacco Control Resource Center

FOREWORD

––––––––

With this volume, the eminent cancer researcher, Arnold E. Reif, has given the reader a badly-needed overview of the totality of the smoking problem, and the manner in which the tobacco habit envelops our society in such a detrimental manner. Dr. Reif has spent a lifetime in cancer research, and his passion for a critical, but constructive overview of the smoking problem clearly stems from some touching, personal experiences that he recounts about his father's smoking and terminal illness with cancer. Interestingly, he notes that it was not lung cancer that was the cause of his father's death, but rather bladder cancer. This is just a small comment on the extent and breadth of the damage that the carcinogens and co-carcinogens in tobacco are capable of causing, and indeed, the cardiovascular and respiratory complications of tobacco are just as serious as those which result in malignancy.

The book is divided into four sections, which deal first with health effects of tobacco, secondly with the manner in which the tobacco industry maintains its market of addicts, thirdly with approaches to kicking the tobacco habit, and finally with the world-wide implications of the endemic use of tobacco. The entire book gives ample documentation of the biological extent of the human wreckage left by the tobacco industry, as well as the societal costs of the use of nicotine as an addicting drug.

So where do we stand now with the tobacco problem? In spite of a vast wealth of information that smoking has terrible long-term consequences, we still see very large numbers of young people being drawn into the pool of new addicts, who are fodder for the tobacco industry. Here in my bucolic college town, one only has to see the extremely large number of students who are still smoking away, in public on the college green, to realize that in many respects, we have not made enough progress. These students surely know that smoking has extremely dangerous long-term consequences for their future health, but somehow, they do not heed this information. I believe that reading this volume would be of great benefit to many of them, as well as to people of all ages, and that it will also be a valuable resource for professionals engaged in the fight against smoking.

The book ends with a meaningful final challenge to readers: "to engage their emotions in the fight- not only against tobacco, but also against poverty and poor education, for success in that goal is crucial for reducing smoking as well as many other social ills." Perhaps those young people who are capable of overcoming their own personal weakness and addiction to tobacco will be motivated to use this personal triumph as an inspiration to help others who may not be quite as strong or successful. I believe that is the ultimate message that Arnold Reif provides his readers. This book is a superb catalog of the scientific details of the consequences of smoking and its resultant societal ills. Hopefully, it will also provide inspiration in an even broader sense to tackle many other problems that afflict all of us.

Michael B. Sporn, M.D.
Professor of Pharmacology and Medicine
Dartmouth Medical School, NH

ACKNOWLEDGMENT

Best thanks for being a wonderful friend - as well as a distinguished medical scientist - especially to Dr. J. Graham Sharp – who is doing potentially life-saving work on markers in incipient lung cancer – for his detailed review.

CONTENTS

Part II: Battling a Deceptive Industry

Part III: Strategies for Quitting

Part IV: Societal and Global Problems

Part V: Airborne Causes of Chronic Diseases

INTRODUCTION

WHERE THERE'S SMOKE, THERE'S FIRE

In 2014, precisely half a century after publication of the land-mark Surgeon General's Report on Smoking and Health, Science magazine of February 7, 2014 published an article by Charles Schmidt entitled "A former surgeon general lends support to e-cigarettes." Richard Carmona, a past Surgeon General, is reported to have joined the board of an electronic cigarette manufacturer, NJOY. By calling its cigarettes by a name that includes joy, the manufacturers claim that the act of smoking is joyful. But as with opium or heroin, decades later, any euphoria from smoking is followed by an extended pay-back period of suffering. Is it possible that Carmona has succumbed to the lure of generous remuneration? If so, it need not surprise us, for according to St. Paul, money is the root of all evil.

Also in 2014, the U.S. Department of Health and Human Services published the report "The Health Consequence of Smoking – 50 Years of Progress." This report summarizes the progress made in the 50 years since the publication of the first Surgeon General's Report on Smoking and Health in 1964, in understanding the damage that smoking causes to multiple organs, and in the success achieved in reducing smoking by warning the public about the dangers of smoking. Since the first report of 1964, 31 subsequent Surgeon General's reports have used the best available evidence to expand our understanding of the health consequences of smoking, and of involuntary exposure to tobacco smoke.

Further in 2014, smoking-connected issues continued to be headlined in newspapers and journals. In the Boston Globe of April 4, Brady Dennis wrote the article, Poison centers get rise in e-cigarette calls. According to the Centers for Disease Control and Prevention (CDC) the volume of calls from people seeking help from nicotine poisoning while smoking e-cigarettes rose drastically to 215 per month. This proves that liquid nicotine, inhaled after being heated into a vapor by a smoker of an e-cigarette, is a highly toxic substance. Still, e-cigarettes are readily available for sale to anyone in pharmacies.

Another article in the Boston Globe of February 10, 2014 by Mike Stobbe was headlined "Tobacco nearing last gasp in US, some say." Also, the National Geographic magazine of August, 2014 devoted a page to an article entitled "Smoked Out." It said in part, "We've come a long way, baby. In 1931 doctors promoted cigarettes (photo). In 1965, the year after Surgeon General Luther Terry's landmark report linked smoking to lung cancer and heart disease, 42% of U.S. adults puffed daily. By 2012, just 18% were lighting up." As of August 2014, federal legislation on the marketing of e-cigarettes was pending. So it seems that antismoking crusaders have been steadily making progress since 1965.

An additional concern that surfaced in 2014 was whether some cigarette brands are more addictive, because they contain a higher quantity of nicotine that will give them more "kick" than other brands. As reported in the Boston Globe of January 20, 2014, a federal law allows the FDA to regulate the nicotine content of cigarettes, but the FDA has not done so yet, perhaps waiting for nicotine to be banned altogether. In fairness, I must report that an article in Discover magazine of March, 2014 addressed the positive properties of nicotine. The author, Dan Hurley, suggested that nicotine may enhance learning and help to treat Parkinson's, schizophrenia, and other neurological diseases. But because nicotine is present in cigarettes and is so firmly associated with harm, people find it hard to credit nicotine with beneficial effects. Is it possible to endorse a drug linked to the greatest preventable health scourge that humanity has ever known? Still, after just 45 minutes with a nicotine patch, nonsmoking ADH (attention deficit hyperactive) patients were better than they had been at inhibiting an impulse, delaying a reward and remembering an image. As regards the addictiveness of nicotine, in 2009 a French team found that combining nicotine with five other chemicals found in tobacco smoke – nornicotine, anabasine, anatabine, cotinine, myosmine, and acetaldehyde – significantly increased its addictiveness. Since there is no good long-term safety data about nicotine use, it is too early to recommend it.

As of 2014, smoking was still the leading preventable cause of premature disease and death in the United States. No wonder that U.S. health agencies have expended tremendous efforts on trying to reduce smoking in our population, with considerable success. The admirable goal of Surgeon General Lushniak is to eventually eliminate smoking altogether, so that in 50 years' time another Surgeon General's Report on Smoking will no longer be necessary. I hate to be pessimistic, but I doubt that people who are dissatisfied with their station in life and are searching for something to give them a kick, will ever stop smoking. Still, smoking is preferable to use of opium or heroin, which can be acutely fatal.

For me, the fight against smoking is personal, because my loving father died of bladder cancer, which is a type of cancer typically caused by his 2-pack-a-day smoking habit. So the motto of my fight against smoking has been, "take no prisoners."

In 2013, the U.S. acting surgeon general, Dr. Boris D. Luchniak, expanded the list of illnesses that cigarette smoking has been scientifically proven to cause. The illnesses that his report named are vision loss, tuberculosis, rheumatoid arthritis, impaired immune function, and cleft palate in the infants of women who smoke. Previously, it was known that these illnesses were associated with smoking, but Lushniak's report was the first time the federal government concluded that smoking causes them.

It is noteworthy that e-cigarettes are far from harmless, and their use among adolescents is exploding. According to a study published in March, 2014 in JAMA Pediatrics, e-cigarette users are likely to progress from e-cigarettes to tobacco smoking more often than nonsmokers. Thus e-cigarettes put youths on the first rung of the ladder that leads them to smoking tobacco.

According to an article by Matt Richtel in the Boston Globe of March 24, 2014, the nicotine that vaporizes in e-cigarettes can poison. In most brands of e-cigarettes, its level is between 1.8% and 2.4%, but levels as high as 10% are available in cigarettes for sale on the internet; these are highly dangerous.

Unfortunately, e-cigarette use is rising. According to CDC (Centers for Disease Control and Prevention), the percentage of youths in grades 6 to 12 who tried e-cigarettes doubled from 3.3% to 6.8% between 2011 and 2013. Further, dual use among youths was extremely high in 2012, with 76% of e-cigarette users also smoking tobacco cigarettes. As of March 2014, over 100 U.S. cities had some degree of restriction against e-cigarettes.

In November 2013, the acting U.S. Surgeon General, Dr. Boris D. Lushniak, significantly expanded the list of illnesses that smoking has been scientifically proven to cause, by adding to this list the following: vision loss, tuberculosis, rheumatoid arthritis, impaired immune function, and cleft palates in children of women who smoke. Smoking had been known to be associated with these illnesses, but in this report the federal government for the first time concluded that smoking caused them. Also, the list of the organs that smoking damages keeps growing.

This book covers the medical, social and legal aspects of common airborne contaminants that demand attention, because they cause serious chronic diseases. *The primary focus is on smoking, since it kills more people worldwide than any other preventable cause of death.* However, the book also covers other causes of lung diseases, namely marijuana, asbestos, atmospheric pollution, radon, and radioactive materials produced by a nuclear reactor meltdown and by "dirty bombs."

Because smoking is a major problem for one quarter of the patients seen by physicians and dentists in the United States, this book is written for health and public health practitioners, teachers, and for researchers in diseases caused by smoking. Since smoking also raises issues that affect the environment, legislation, economics and bioethics, students and lay advocates will find it useful to have this book, for it summarizes the principal health hazards of smoking as well as of other airborne toxins. Family members and friends of smokers may wish to give them this book to motivate them to quit. To make this book accessible to such a diverse group of readers, the goal has been to present the vital facts clearly and concisely.

Since this book covers a large variety of airborne toxins, it is intended to be a resource that is dipped into, rather than read cover to cover. To help the reader decide which chapters are of interest, this Introduction provides an overview of each chapter. In addition, the book ends with a more detailed summary of each chapter.

In the United States, smoking is the major cause of heart disease, cancer and chronic bronchitis, COPD (chronic obstructive pulmonary disease), and emphysema. It is also the primary cause of one-fifth of all deaths, for smoking and other forms of tobacco use produce the large variety of diseases that are discussed in the twenty two chapters of Part I. These chapters cover the history, mechanism, heredity, detection, and therapy of the diseases that smoking causes, as well as the addictive power of nicotine, the dangers of environmental tobacco smoke, the search for a safer cigarette, the effect of diet, and the dangers of smoking marijuana.

Part II deals with the problems posed by the tobacco industry itself. Like certain other industries, it has tried to maximize its profits by deceptive advertising. Big Tobacco is exceptional, because its sales product is very harmful. Since tobacco contains the highly addictive nicotine, tobacco companies have become fabulously wealthy as the legalized pushers of this drug. They have used their wealth to fund extensive propaganda campaigns to rebut health warnings and defeat legislation aimed at safeguarding smokers from addiction. The four chapters of Part II cover the many attempts to prevent smoking with health warnings, legislation, lawsuits, and damages awarded against the industry.

Part III includes five chapters on quitting for use by smokers, and by professionals who wish to advise smokers on how to quit. To identify the best strategies for quitting, the success rates achieved by different methods of attack are documented, and a comprehensive step-by-step approach to quitting is included. Part I of the book documents that smoking causes so many deadly diseases, that quitting is the only rational choice, even for inveterate smokers. While rationality may not affect long-term smokers, perhaps the nefarious practices of tobacco companies will rile them sufficiently that they will wish to quit, to stop making these companies rich.

Part IV discusses smoking as a global social problem. It pinpoints the close link between smoking, poverty, and lack of education. Thus, the inevitable conclusion is that to curtail smoking, education and living standards must be upgraded. Both these goals are ones that public-minded politicians of all stripes can agree on. If youths from poor neighborhoods are to become successful and productive citizens, there needs to be much more generous support for programs such as Head Start and (a reformed) No Child Left Behind, and for other recreational and work programs. Part IV also deals with the international marketing of cigarettes, which produces a worldwide epidemic of smoking-related diseases. After years of hesitation, the United States supported the

Global Tobacco Treaty of the UN World Health Organization (WHO), which was ratified in 2004 by 40 countries. The Global Tobacco Treaty in effect today has the potential to eventually reduce smoking even in underdeveloped nations.

Part V deals with airborne hazards that cause lung cancer, which have invariably been found to be more dangerous for smokers than for nonsmokers. They include air pollution, inhalation of asbestos and of radioactive gases such as radon, and of finely dispersed radioactive dust that is produced by the explosion of "dirty bombs"–fiendish devices that terrorists might use to cause panic. Some of these substances have been found synergistic with smoking, causing more damage than if their effects were merely addictive. While other airborne causes of lung cancer have not been investigated for synergism with smoking, they have been proven to be more dangerous for smokers than for nonsmokers.

The underlying theme of this book is that "prevention is better than cure." This concept holds true for a large variety of ill consequences, whether the result of diseases, accidents, or acts of terrorism. But prevention requires dedicated action based on past experience to marshal the effort, often large and costly, to prevent such events. Failure to protect us from poisons that contaminate the air we breathe will lead to serious consequences. Here is an overview of individual chapters.

Chapter 1 summarizes the main health effects of smoking. Long-continued smoking is the major cause of heart disease, cancer, and chronic obstructive pulmonary disease (COPD–which includes emphysema and chronic bronchitis). Smoking is also the primary cause of one-fifth of all deaths in the United States.

Chapter 2 explains how chemicals cause cancer. A normal cell cannot multiply, unless ordered to do so by the genetic blueprint of the body. But if a carcinogen causes a cell to lose its ability to respond to that blueprint and now fails to obey the body's command to stop multiplying, then it becomes a tumor cell. The genetic instructions in the DNA of normal cells do not permit them to grow in organs other than their own, and this is also true for tumor cells. Since the change from a normal cell to a tumor cell gives it genetic instability, its daughter cells may undergo a change in DNA that frees it from that restriction. Then the tumor cell has become a true cancer cell that can metastasize (seed out to other organs) and there start new growths.

Chapter 3 summarizes the history of smoking. Tobacco was introduced into Europe in 1585. Cigarette smoking only began late in the nineteenth century, and then received a huge boost during World War I. Women began to smoke in large numbers about two decades later. While cigarette smoking peaked in the United States in 1963, lung cancer did not peak until 30 years later–because of three decades of time-lag between long-term exposure to tobacco smoke and the resulting development of cancer. *Many smokers fated to an eventual tragic death fail to quit, because the consequences of smoking occur long after the act of smoking.*

Chapter 4 describes the chemical constituents of tobacco smoke, which include dozens of carcinogens. These are present in the inhaled gas, and are also attached to the minute smoke particles. The carcinogens present in these particles tend to be more concentrated and are therefore more dangerous than those in the gaseous phase.

Chapter 5 deals with heart disease caused by smoking. Perhaps surprisingly, heart disease kills more than three times as many smokers as cancer, for the immediate effect of smoking tobacco is to increase the blood pressure and heart rate. This stimulation, repeated many times a day for decades, makes the heart work harder, wearing it out faster and causing premature death.

Chapter 6 documents that smoking advances the incidence of vascular disease throughout the body, including the brain. As a result, more than 50% of the deaths from stroke in people less than 65 years old are caused by smoking.

Chapter 7 focuses on lung cancer, which is responsible for two-thirds of the deaths from the various types of cancer that smoking causes; these are discussed in chapter 11. Lung cancer is the most common deadly cancer in the United States, responsible for 29% of all cancer deaths. Smoking two or more packs a day increases the risk of lung cancer twentyfold relative to the risk for nonsmokers. Quitting reduces that risk greatly over time, and has other benefits, irrespective of how long one has smoked.

Chapter 8 documents the effect of heredity on the likelihood that long-continued smoking will eventually cause lung cancer. Ten percent of the U.S. population possesses a gene that reduces their risk of developing lung cancer, while a different ten percent carries a gene that confers a higher risk of lung cancer. Hopefully, some day it will become routine to test smokers for these genes—for they predict whether the risk of contracting lung cancer that one assumes by smoking is low, average, or high.

Chapter 9 concludes that screening of long-term smokers to detect early lung cancer may be worthwhile, for if cancer is discovered at this stage, the five-year survival rate is 50%, contrasted with 15% for all lung cancer cases. Still, there are both *pros* and *cons* on the benefits of screening, and these are the subjects of a spirited debate. The American Cancer Society leaves physicians free to decide whether screening will help their patients. Up to date information on the benefits and limitations of testing for lung cancer is available at state of the art cancer centers.

Chapter 10 focuses on the therapy of lung cancer. A type of lung cancer called "non-small-cell lung cancer" makes up over 75% of all cases. Thirty percent of these cases are diagnosed early enough so that they can receive surgery, which allows 42% of that 30%—or nearly 13% of all patients—to survive for five years after diagnosis. Without surgery, only 5% are alive at that time. New methods of therapy are now available, that auger well for further improvements in survival rates.

Chapter 11 shows that once the carcinogens in tobacco smoke enter the body, they can eventually cause cancer at the sites where they have been deposited, or to which they have been transported.

Cancers of the mouth, larynx, bronchi and lung result from the direct impingement of inhaled smoke particles, while cancers of the esophagus, stomach, and intestines result from absorption of the swallowed carcinogens from the gastrointestinal tract into the blood stream, where they have access to body organs> As a result, the incidence of cancer in many organs is higher in smokers than in nonsmokers. Organs especially at risk include the kidneys, pancreas, bladder, female breast, bone marrow, skin, liver, cervix, uterus and nasal sinus.

Chapter 12 reports that there are differences between males and females in the incidence of certain types of cancer that result from smoking. A group of women who have a deficiency in an enzyme that detoxifies lung carcinogens as a result develop lung cancer four times more frequently than men if they smoke. Women also have a higher risk of bladder cancer than men who smoke as many cigarettes. Most important, if a woman smokes during pregnancy, she may sow the seed for cancer in her fetus, which may strike when it has developed into a youth or an adult.

Chapter 13 deals with chronic obstructive pulmonary disease (COPD), which includes three separate diseases: emphysema, chronic bronchitis, and chronic obstructive bronchitis. Smoking is the major cause of all three diseases. While most patients have all three diseases, their relative severities vary for different patients, but those with an advanced stage of COPD must fight for every breath. The best defense against COPD is to quit.

Chapter 14 discusses additional health effects of tobacco. Because tobacco smoke damages the lung's ability to ward off bacteria, four times as many smokers as nonsmokers contract pneumonia. Compared to nonsmokers, smokers are about twice as likely to lose all their teeth and hearing, and to develop serious eye pathology: macular degeneration and blindness. Most important, habitual smokers age faster than nonsmokers. On average, smokers lose five years of their natural lifespan.

Chapter 15 documents accidental deaths and injuries. Each year, about 1,000 Americans die from fires ignited by cigarettes, often due to falling asleep while smoking in bed. Cigarette manufacturers have developed self-extinguishing cigarettes. While there are local laws that mandate this safety feature for cigarettes, a federal law is needed to protect the entire United States. As of 2004, Sweden has such a law on its books.

Chapter 16 concludes that the addictive power of nicotine equals that of cocaine or heroin. For all three drugs, addiction causes changes in the brain that hijack pleasure pathways. While these changes are reversible, it can take more than two months after quitting before the brain's chemistry returns to normal.

Chapter 17 relates smoking to mental problems. Mentally ill people are twice as likely to smoke as the general population, and they smoke nearly half of all cigarettes sold in the United States. Thus, it is not surprising that some of those who become smokers are more likely than nonsmokers to have an inborn tendency to develop depression or schizophrenia late in life. *Chapter 18* reports that compared to nonsmokers, cigar smokers have severalfold higher risks of cancer of the mouth, larynx, lung, pancreas and bladder–and their risks of COPD and heart disease are similar to those of cigarette smokers. Pipe smoking is declining in the U.S., while smoking the more dangerous kreteks (clove cigarettes) and bidis (mini-cigarettes) is increasing. Both chewing tobacco and taking snuff increase the risks of cancer of the mouth, throat, larynx and esophagus.

Chapter 19 presents the evidence that environmental tobacco smoke (ETS) causes lung cancer, heart disease, and exacerbates allergies–especially in asthmatic children. The reason for an earlier lack of consensus on whether ETS causes lung cancer was that not incidentally, the authors of three-quarters of negative reviews on this topic were affiliated with the tobacco industry. Now there is a consensus that nonsmokers married to a smoker, or else constantly exposed to tobacco smoke at work, face a 30%

increase in risk of lung cancer. For children, the increase in the risk of cancer is higher than 30%.

Chapter 20 summarizes the results of the search for a safer cigarette. Smoking cannot be safe, because all carcinogens cannot be eliminated from tobacco smoke, nor all the tar that causes COPD, nor all the nicotine that makes smoking addictive, and also causes heart disease and stroke. While low-yield brands cause less COPD, smokers of "light" brands compensate by smoking more cigarettes, and so quitting is incomparably more beneficial.

Chapter 21 asks whether dieting is helpful. A diet low in fat and high in fruit and vegetables may reduce a smoker's risk of lung cancer by as much as 50%, whereas so far there is no evidence that supplements can do so. But in comparison the reduction in risk from quitting is roughly forty times higher than the reduction achieved by a change to a wholesome diet.

Chapter 22 deals with smoking marijuana. This weed can cause immediate reactions that range from none to feeling relaxed, high, anxious, or paranoid. Also, marijuana can cause distortion of sight, sound, time, and touch; loss of coordination; an increase in heart rate; and not bothering with safeguards when having sex. About 40% of long-term consistent marijuana smokers experience some loss of short-term memory, lessening of learning aptitude, loss of motivation, and lung damage similar to that of smokers. While occasional marijuana smoking is less harmful than heavy use of alcohol and tobacco, pot can be a gateway to addictive drugs.

Part II of the book is entitled "Battling a Deceptive Industry." It begins with *chapter 23* on the prevention of smoking by children, adolescents, and young adults. This is a vital task, for 80% of smokers start before age 18, and tobacco companies employ many tricks to lure youths to start. Arrayed against the industry are government and state agencies, the majority of legislators, private foundations, the families and friends of smokers, and a strong coalition of educators and health professionals. Health education in schools should be supported by strict measures such as enforcing the laws against sales to minors, raising the taxes on tobacco, and youth-oriented media campaigns based on modern social marketing principles.

In 1998, a suit between U.S. states and the tobacco industry was settled. It required tobacco companies to continue to make substantial payments to the 50 states and some territories while tobacco sales continued – meaning "for the foreseeable future." Although the tobacco companies undertook to warn youths not to smoke, many of their antismoking advertisements included subliminal messages that turned them into incitements for starting to smoke. So much for hiring foxes to police the chickens. But during the 1980s, Surgeon General C. Everett Koop was a highly effective crusader against smoking.

Chapter 24 deals with health warnings, advertisements, and legislation. A year after the landmark Surgeon General's Report on Smoking and Health of 1964, Congress required cigarette packages to carry the mild warning "CAUTION: CIGARETTE SMOKING MAY BE HAZARDOUS TO YOUR HEALTH." Today, all cigarette advertising on TV or radio is banned, and all cigarette packages and advertisements must carry prominent health warnings. The United States would do well to follow Canada's lead, and require half the space on cigarette packs to display dramatic pictures with powerful antismoking messages in large contrasting type.

Chapter 25 is entitled industry deception, handouts, regulation, and lawsuits. Historically, the temptation to accept money from an immensely wealthy tobacco industry has overcome the scruples of many individuals, institutions, businesses, and media personalities. Even when medical researchers accept a grant from the industry that is unrelated to tobacco, the industry benefits from the implication that it is sincerely interested in the health of the public. If true, the industry should fold.

While FDA commissioner David Kessler lost his battle to establish FDA control over tobacco in the 1990s, whistle-blowers from the tobacco industry revealed to him that its executives had known for years what they were vigorously denying: that smoking endangers smokers and nonsmokers, that nicotine is highly addictive, and that the prime targets of their advertisements were teenagers. These revelations led states to file lawsuits that accused the industry of racketeering during the last half century, by misleading smokers about the addictive power and health effects of smoking. This suit was won, and resulted in multi-billion dollar settlements by the industry to U.S. states.

Chapter 26 describes the use, misuse, and effects of the tobacco settlement funds. The Centers for Disease Control and Prevention (CDC) suggested that states spend over 20% of these massive annual awards to support comprehensive antismoking programs and media campaigns. Unfortunately, most of the states soon used the funds almost exclusively as a source of revenue. Still, since the price of cigarettes increased dramatically, the CDC reported that smoking among high school students declined.

Part III of the book deals with strategies for quitting. Smokers should be ready to quit after reading part I on the health risks of smoking, and part II on the deceptions the industry has used to retain its customers. Part III includes a step-by-step guide on how to quit, written both for smokers and for those who wish to guide them to success in that tough task.

Chapter 27 compares the effectiveness of common strategies that are used to quit. These include willpower, seeking the advice of a health professional, joining a group of people who are planning to quit with the help of a professional, or acting on antismoking messages from the telephone, radio, TV, or CD.

Chapter 28 describes the success of antismoking programs in motivating people to quit. The best community education campaigns succeed in preventing or postponing smoking in 20% to 40% of youths. The least effective ways to quit smoking are cold turkey, on one's own, or with acupuncture. Compared to people who use these methods, those that use nicotine gum are 50% more successful. Use of the nicotine patch, antismoking medication, or else even brief counseling help twice as many people to succeed. Even more effective is having more than 8 hours of counseling, or the employment of a nicotine inhaler. Research has shown that a switch to low-tar cigarettes is useless, because the slack is taken up by smoking more.

Chapter 29 presents a composite guide for quitting. The smoker can choose a strategy to follow, then prepare for zero hour on the quitting date by assembling physical tools, such as nicotine replacements and low-calorie foods, and psychological resources to help overcome future crises. Although over 50 million Americans have succeeded in quitting, achieving success requires a strong conviction that quitting is vital, and the resolve never again to sneak even a single cigarette.

Chapter 30 asks if genetics is involved in addiction. Acting together, nature (genetics), nurture (environment) and our will power determine almost everything about us, including whether or not we are likely to become addicted to smoking–or else overpowered by alcoholism, substance abuse, or compulsive gambling.

Genetics loads the gun, but it is the environment that can pull the trigger. Our brains tend to recognize a reward stimulus as a reward, whether it comes from the brain's own molecules, from chemicals supplied externally, or from stimulating experiences. While the strength of the genetic predisposition to smoke varies greatly from person to person, for most people it is relatively mild, and thus can be resisted. Nonsmokers harvest magnificent highs from great sex, loving relationships within our families, having stout friends, success in achieving our various goals in life, in our profession and in sports, sufficiently good health and wealth to satisfy us, lofty enough societal status, and achievement of our very own goals.

Chapter 31 describes the important role that physicians can play, for their advice above all is usually followed. When physicians tell their patients "You really must stop smoking" and explain the reasons, patients tend to respond more positively than to any other warning. While medical schools have been slow to teach their students to fight smoking, this problem is gradually being remedied. Hopefully, eventually all physicians will be trained to caution youths not to start smoking, and to motivate smokers to quit.

Part IV begins with *chapter 32*, which focuses on societal problems and their solutions. Most commonly, poverty and scant education are inversely related to smoking: the poorer and less educated people are, the higher the chance that they will smoke. Only if poverty is reduced and education for poor children is greatly improved will there be a large drop in smoking–as well as in drug use, and in gangs and crime. The programs advocated here are the same as those recommended by every U.S. president.

The lack of discipline in schools situated in low-income districts often forces teachers to spend most of their time in trying to keep order in their classrooms – really–hard as this may be to believe for the middle and upper-middle class people who are likely to read this book. One possible solution for this problem is the federal Head Start program, which aims to prepare young children from poverty-stricken families to become good students, and grow up into adults who can hold down well-paying jobs. Head Start serves only 60% of the 3- to 5-year olds from families with incomes below the poverty level. The "No Child Left Behind" program serves older children, but is as underfunded as after-school and vacation recreational programs in the poverty-stricken areas where they are most needed.

Work Start programs fund student work in after school hours and during the summer vacations. They serve to keep youths off the streets, and accustom them to a working life. Again, the need far outstrips availability–as applies to the funds needed by disadvantaged college-bound students to receive special coaching. To reach U.S. national goals for the reduction in smoking,[4] government funding for all these programs should be greatly increased, for the needs of impoverished children are vastly more important than putting a man on Mars. Also, state legislators must honor their responsibility to use funds from the tobacco Master Settlement Agreement for intense antismoking education.

Chapter 33 deals with smoking as a worldwide problem. To compensate for the loss of sales in developed countries, tobacco companies formed multinational corporations that have rapidly expanded worldwide. In 1998, Philip Morris' profits from developing countries, where 80% of the world's more than 1 billion smokers lived, were five times as high as from domestic sales. Today, that figure is even higher.

In most European countries, the percentage of smokers is higher than in the United States, for some of the laws needed to decrease cigarette consumption have not been passed, or are not enforced, and tobacco companies work hard to discourage interference. In the Czech Republic, Philip Morris argued the government should be happy, since the premature death of Czech smokers was saving almost $30 million a year in old age benefits!

Smoking rates are especially high in Asia. In China, Japan and Vietnam, the percentage of male smokers is respectively 63%, 54%, and 73%. Because women are subordinated, the percentage of women smokers is in the single digits. In this unusual case, *Asian women have benefited by being deprived of equality in smoking—and of its eventually associated intense suffering.*

The key to eradicating the worldwide tobacco epidemic is the adoption of a comprehensive tobacco control campaign, as embodied in the Framework Convention on Tobacco Control (FCTC) of the World Health Assembly of the World Health Organization (WHO). This treaty was signed in 2003 by the 168 participating nations, and it was put into effect when 40 nations – but not the United States–ratified it in 2004. The treaty asks for real commitment: higher taxation of cigarettes; bans on tobacco advertising, sponsorship, and promotion; restrictions on smoking in workplaces and public spaces; and boosting cessation therapy. Presently, the United States is acting ethically in response to HIV, malaria, and some other worldwide scourges. But a similar response in concert with United Nations resolutions is needed on environmental issues such as pollution, greenhouse gases, global warming, renewable energy, preservation of flora and fauna, sustainable agriculture – and of course, smoking.

These and many other issues should all be part of a humane, fully integrated United States global ethical strategy, not disparate entities. If the United States pursued all of these issues, humanity would benefit, and the United States would gain respect and soften the ire of its critics and enemies. While the United States supports the FCTC treaty, as of early 2012, more than 150 nations had ratified it, while 25 nations *including the United States* had not done so as yet.[1] In July 2014, Vera Luiza da Costa e Silva of Brazil took office as the head of the busily active secretariat of the FCTC, and smoking was one of its concerns.

Part V deals with airborne hazards that cause lung cancer and are especially dangerous for smokers, namely air pollution, asbestos, silica and some other dusts, radon, and radioactive materials that nuclear reactors can emit, and that can be blown into the air by the explosion of a "dirty bomb." Asbestos, radon and certain radioactive substances have been proven to be synergistic with smoking.[2] This makes them especially dangerous when inhaled by smokers.

Chapter 34 focuses on air pollution. The air sacs of the lung are protected against all but the tiniest of particles, less than 5 micra (millionth of a meter) in diameter. When the United Kingdom (UK) still had intense air pollution in the 1960s, nonsmokers in urban areas had twice the incidence of lung cancer as those in rural areas. Today, UK cities have far less air pollution. On average for the whole of the United States, urban living increases the risk of death from lung cancer by roughly 11%. In huge cities such as Los Angeles, where the driving of millions of cars frequently causes smog, the consequences of air pollution are more serious.

Chapter 35 focuses on the diseases caused by asbestos, silica, wood, and other types of dust. Since asbestos is strong and fire-resistant, the United States used nearly a million tons per year by 1973. But very fine asbestos fibers can penetrate deep into the lung where they can cause mesothelioma, a malignant lung cancer. Today, EPA only permits asbestos to be used for specialty applications, and a vast program of removing or encasing it is ongoing—as are over 200,000 suits against asbestos companies.

Chapter 36 discusses the hazard of radioactive gases and of radioactive atoms bound to fine particles. Radon is a radioactive gas emitted by uranium-228, which is present in trace amounts throughout the earth's crust. Radon is unstable and changes into the radioactive element polonium, which is a dangerous lung carcinogen. Radon levels in houses and buildings vary widely, depending on how much uranium-228 is present in the rock or earth on which they are built, and whether their basements are sealed sufficiently well to prevent the seepage of radon gas into them. Most often owners are unaware that their homes are built on rocks with a high content of uranium-228. In the United States radon inhalation is estimated to cause between 4,000 and 20,000 lung cancer deaths per year. But testing for radon is inexpensive, and if its level exceeds the tolerable limit set by EPA, installation of a basement fan will usually correct its level. Like asbestos, radon acts in synergism with smoking to produce lung cancer, and thus is far more dangerous for smokers than for nonsmokers.

Chapter 37 discusses the risk of cancer from inhaling radioactive gases and particles emitted during and after the meltdown of a nuclear reactor, by the explosion of a "dirty bomb," and (very briefly) by an atomic bomb. The meltdown that occurred at the nuclear power plant at Three Mile Island raises the question of whether completely safe nuclear reactors can be built. Readers will be challenged to draw their own conclusion by evaluating the long list of *pros* and *cons* for nuclear reactors.

As yet, terrorists have not exploded a "dirty bomb"–one that contains dangerous radioactive material which is dispersed by the explosion of a conventional explosive such as dynamite. Such a weapon is intended to terrorize the population. Western nations would be well advised to be prepared to deal with the effects of the explosion of a dirty bomb in a city. The public should know how to decontaminate themselves, and at what level the radiation is sufficiently low to be harmless – a knowledge that could avoid needless panic.

Last, the effects of an atomic bomb explosion are summarized. It is conceivable that terrorists could be sufficiently crazed not to realize that the high toll of innocent civilians from such an explosion, especially of women and children, would besmirch their cause indelibly for ever after. Although explosion of an atomic bomb is a very unlikely event, it would be wise to stockpile pills of sodium iodide, so that people exposed to radioactive iodine from the explosion could take them to block the uptake of inhaled radioactive iodine by their thyroid glands. A thick book would be needed to deal adequately with the effects of the explosion of an atomic bomb, but there is space here to summarize these effects only briefly.

The *Afterword* suggests worthwhile humane challenges that are greatly in need of more support. It is followed by a *Summary* with a detailed overview of chapters, and by an *Appendix* and *Endnotes*.

Finally, I should mention that I have a personal account to settle with smoking, for it killed my father at a premature age.

But slowly, our society is winning the fight against smoking.

In 1965 the percentage of Americans who smoked peaked at 42%.

Since then it has almost steadily declined to 19% as of 2011.

The National Geographic Magazine of August 2014 reported this change and entitled its page of statistics "Smoked Out." We need to remember that while smokeless cigarettes avoid most of the risks of cancer, they still pose the risk of inhaling nicotine.

PART I

THE HEALTH EFFECTS OF SMOKING

Smoking in this world could be as sickening as in the next

ONE

OVERVIEW OF THE HEALTH EFFECTS
OF SMOKING

On April 6, 2005, the New York Times and most newspapers in the United States headlined the story that ABC's popular newscast anchor Peter Jennings had contracted lung cancer, from which he died later that year. He had smoked heavily and quit in the 1980's, but even in later years, he was known to sneak a cigarette or two. After the terrorist attack in 2001 he began to smoke regularly again, but soon after quit for good.

The majority of the 50 million smokers in the United States may have read this story avidly, and concluded that the struggle to quit smoking might not be worthwhile, for they could already be fated to develop lung cancer. To counter that conclusion, here is the most important message of this book: *quitting at any stage in life rapidly decreases the risk of heart disease (chapter 5), greatly reduces the risk of lung cancer, and provides some benefit for people with emphysema and chronic bronchitis (chapter 13).* The sooner smokers quit, the larger the benefits.

In America and Europe, smoking is by far the most common cause of death from heart disease, stroke, cancer, emphysema, and chronic bronchitis. In the United States population, smoking is responsible for almost one-third of all deaths from heart disease and cancer. Equally sad, half of all long-term smokers die of a smoking-connected disease, and smoking is the cause for one in every five deaths in the United States.

The full impact of cigarette smoking is spelled out in the 28th United States Surgeon General's report of 2004 entitled "The Health Consequences of Smoking." For the year 2008, the American Cancer Society estimated that it would kill 470,000 people.[3] For those who die from smoking-caused diseases, the loss in lifespan is 13.2 years for men, and 14.5 years for women. Smoking costs the United States economy $157 billion a year–$75 billion in direct medical costs and $82 billion in lost productivity.[4]

Obesity and physical inactivity have become an increasingly serious health hazard in the United States, but they do not cause as many premature deaths as smoking. U.S. Surgeon General Carmona has called tobacco the only consumer product that can kill you when used as directed.

As for adolescents, they can successfully resist the pressure of role models who smoke and of tobacco advertisements, and choose not to smoke. Adults who smoke can succeed in quitting, and thereby avoid much future suffering. Since the nicotine content of tobacco is a powerful addictive, once a smoker is addicted, quitting becomes a major challenge. While alcohol and drug abuse have sometimes immediate consequences, the most serious effects of smoking are cumulative and often begin only decades after smoking is begun. *So smokers are lulled into a false sense of security, because the bomb that is silently building within their bodies has a long delayed-action fuse. But eventually it is likely to explode.*

Worldwide, smoking causes 4.8 million deaths a year, and is the most dangerous of widespread habits. The driving force behind these deaths is the proliferation of tobacco companies that target developing countries, where they can use the old effective advertising ploys that are now outlawed in the United States and in most Western countries. As a result, the number of deaths caused by smoking in the whole world is expected to keep rising.

Smoking not only causes the major diseases mentioned above, but also damages health in other serious ways. Because smoking impairs the lung's defenses against bacteria, smokers have a much higher risk of developing pneumonia, and convalesce more slowly from surgical procedures. For women, smoking during pregnancy is particularly dangerous, because it increases the risk of having a spontaneous abortion and of giving birth to an under-weight baby.

Tobacco smoke is also a dangerous contaminant of indoor air, for its long-term inhalation can cause lung cancer in nonsmokers. This has grave social consequences for smokers, for nonsmokers resent being exposed to tobacco smoke, and a tiny minority is extremely allergic to smoke. As a result, states and cities in the United States prohibit smoking in schools, restaurants, offices, and indoor public spaces. Further, smokers are unwelcome in the homes of nonsmokers, and at parties hosted by nonsmokers.

Finally, smoking damages the beauty of people and of the environment. Smoking causes wrinkled facial skin, and stains the teeth and fingers, and the clothes of smokers; also, their breath smells of tobacco smoke. Indoor smoking not only pollutes the air, it causes littering from butts, and burn marks on furniture and clothes. Worst of all, nearly half of all domestic fires in the United States are started by a smoldering cigarette that was carelessly discarded. Following successful lawsuits by the states against tobacco companies, cigarettes have become very expensive, for smokers have to pay for the huge fines that the industry has to keep paying indefinitely after conviction for its deceptive advertising.

A variety of programs is now available to help smokers quit. *But prevention is far better than cure, and resisting the temptation to start is far easier than trying to quit.* Cancer Centers throughout the United States make cancer prevention their primary focus – and their first and most important rule for cancer prevention is "No Smoking."[5] While quitting slowly reduces the risk of lung cancer, it rapidly reduces the risk of heart disease, so that it returns to normal within five years.

TWO

HOW CHEMICALS CAUSE CANCER[6],[7]

The goal of this book is not only to look at the damage that cancer-causing chemicals produce, but far more importantly, at how to prevent that damage. Therefore, only an overview of the mechanism by which chemicals cause cancer is needed, to understand what follows. On the one hand, the essence of what is really important about the development of cancer is simple and easy to understand. On the other hand, we now know that the *details* of the different ways in which cancer can develop are highly complicated. It is not surprising that on this very subject, many dozens of books have been written, and hundreds of papers (including one of mine) are being published every year.

Early in modern cancer research, the development of cancer of most common types was found to be a multistage process, and this still remains our present view. In the 1970s, Alfred Knudson found that retinoblastoma (a pediatric tumor of the eye) arises after two DNA mutations (changes). He proposed that people with the heritable form of the disease had inherited one of the DNA mutations required to turn them into tumor cells. Thus, they needed only one other properly targeted "hit" to their DNA to develop this cancer. In contrast, people without the heritable mutation required two hits, and were therefore far less at risk of developing retinoblastoma.[8] Four decades after this discovery, this explanation of the origin of the two forms of retinoblastoma has been proven correct, and its mechanism has been discovered: the great majority of human beings carry two copies of the ret-inoblastoma gene *Rb*, which produces the *Rb* protein that acts as a powerful tumor suppressor. Both copies of the *Rb* gene must be lost before the *RB* protein is no longer produced. The tiny minor-ity of people at high risk of developing the heritable form of retinoblastoma are already born lacking one copy of the *Rb* gene. Those born with the normal two copies of the *RB* gene are far less susceptible to retinoblastoma, since they require two "hits" that delete a copy of this gene before they develop this type of cancer. Later work established that the *Rb* protein is lost or inactivated in more than 70% of all human tumors of this type. Hence the *RB* protein that the *Rb* gene produces is of vital importance in preventing the development of retinoblastomas.[9]

Another potent protein that suppresses tumor development is the *p53* tumor-suppressor protein that is produced by the *p53* gene. In the majority of human cancer *p53* is either mutated, or one of the genes that regulates it–such as *p14*–is mutated. The *p53* tumor-suppressor protein performs its vital function by act-ing through several different specific molecular pathways.[10]

Irrespective of the molecular mechanism by with tumors develop, the vital step in the formation of a tumor cell consists of a mutation in the genetic structure of a cell that gives it an advan-tage in its ability to divide, and causes an instability in its DNA that makes it easier for subsequent mutations to occur. Even after a second mutation that causes the loss of a vital tumor suppressor gene such as *rb+* or *p53*, the daughter cells of the mutated cell may need to go through several stages of further enhancement in aggressive ability before they can grow as primary tumors within the organ in which they originated. Yet by no means do all cells with that initial mutation progress to become cancer cells:[11] for another mutation is required to enable tumor cells to metasta-size – to seed out from their primary site to other organs of the body[12]–which is the hallmark of cancer. Further, different types of cancers vary widely in the rate at which they grow, and in the aggressiveness with which they metastasize.

Another set of genes provide angiogenesis: the stimulation of the growth of blood vessels toward nodules of metastasized tumor – *i.e.* tumors that have seeded out from the organ in which they originated to other organs. Angiogenesis is essential to free tumors to grow larger in size than about 1 cm. Modern cancer treatments are being designed to frustrate the changes in genes that lead to the formation and growth of cancer cells.

During the early 1980's, the discovery of oncogenes (cancer genes) that change a normal cell into a cancer cell when these oncogenes are activated (switched on) suggested that the path from a normal to a cancer cell was very simple. Then cancer researchers discovered the first complication: there are suppressor genes that function in keeping oncogenes inactive (switched off). If a suppressor gene is missing or damaged, then the oncogene which it suppressed is switched on, and the cell that contained it becomes a tumor cell.

How does a tumor cell differ from a normal cell? A normal cell becomes a tumor cell when it acquires a heritable change that increases its ability to divide into daughter cells, and make it irresponsive to the limits to cell division that a normal cell of its type should possess. All carcinogens produce this fundamental genetic change in the cells that they target.

But there are "incomplete" and "complete" carcinogens. The former can "initiate" tumor cells – set them onto the first stage of their change into tumor cells–but cannot stimulate them to divide further into many daughter cells. This latter process is known as "promotion," and often is performed by hormones. In contrast, complete carcinogens can initiate cancer cells and also promote the growth of daughter cells, and thus produce cancer directly. Most types of carcinogens are both initiators and promoters, but are more effective in one or another of these two categories. For instance, X-rays are powerful initiators but very weak promoters. As a result the latent period between irradiation and the appearance of a human tumor is often one or more decades.

Today, we know that the process that begins with an organ that contains normal cells and ends with a cancer in that organ is complicated at several different levels.[13] At the molecular level, it is still true that a single active oncogene[14] or an inactive suppressor gene—one of the most important of which is *p53*—may be the precondition for the development of cancer. Still, the interaction of literally hundreds of genes both with the oncogene and with each other are implicated in whether or not a tumor develops. Also important are the local conditions under which the potential tumor cell is situated within its organ, especially whether it has access to growth hormones that will stimulate its daughter cells to grow.

Even for a single variety of tumor, while there may be one or several genetic changes that must occur to produce it, yet a tumor of that particular type which occurs in a given person is genetically slightly different from the same type of tumor in any other person. We now know that there exist a large variety of other genes that are major players in the pathway that leads to a tumor cell. For instance, there are genes involved in the process of apoptosis (programmed cell death) which ensure that a cell dies when the normal genetic blueprint – normal DNA – requires it to do so. If one of these suppressor genes essential for normal development is turned off or lost, then the cell type that it should prevent from uncontrolled cell division has acquired this property that is essential to turn it into a tumor cell.

The initial mutation that occurs in cells on the path to become tumor cells frequently induces instability in their DNA, so that further mutations that increase the aggressiveness of the tumor cell are more easily accomplished. This process is known as tumor progression.

Three of the vital constituents of a cell are its DNA, RNA, and protein. The DNA is located within the center of the cell, its nucleus; this contains nearly all of the cell's genetic material. The RNA transfers genetic information from DNA to the cell's machinery for protein synthesis in the plasma of the cell, its cytoplasm, which surrounds the nucleus. The proteins are the workhorses of the cell, many of which act as enzymes: biological catalysts that perform tasks such as synthesizing or degrading molecules.

The interactions of carcinogenic chemicals with cells can cause cancer directly, if the carcinogens bind to the DNA of the cell and thereby mutate it, giving it the characteristics of a pre-tumor cell or of a tumor cell, depending on whether the carcinogen is an incomplete or a complete carcinogen. Chemicals can also act by binding to the RNA of a cell and mutating it. The RNA can then transfer these changes to the DNA of the cell and make them heritable, with an enzyme called reverse transcriptase.

There are several other ways in which carcinogens can cause cancer. For instance, cells possess a mechanism for repairing DNA damage. But some carcinogenic chemicals can damage this vital repair mechanism, and thereby increase the risk of cancer.

Many different factors contribute to the final outcome of a contact between a carcinogen and a human being. Most important are the type of carcinogen, the size of its cumulative dose, the route by which it enters the body, its target organ or organs, and the susceptibility of the person exposed to it, that can vary widely. Additional relevant factors include the time over which the carcinogen is delivered, and the time intervals between different exposures. Further, previous environmental exposures to other carcinogens that target the same organ are very important.

Most carcinogens affect only a fraction of the people exposed to them, because people differ greatly in their inherited likelihood of developing cancer of a particular organ. Their genetics affects the possession of enzymes that interact with the carcinogen under consideration. Most chemical carcinogens are only weakly active or even inactive, unless they are metabolized–changed chemically within the body–to their active form, the "ultimate carcinogen." This change is catalyzed by enzymes within our bodies, and people with low levels of these enzymes have a low susceptibility to particular classes of carcinogens.

In addition, other types of enzymes inactivate certain carcinogens. Therefore, people who have inherited high levels of an enzyme that inactivates a given carcinogen have a low risk of developing cancer from it. Chapter 9 describes the discovery of genes that lower the risk that smokers will develop lung cancer, and also of different genes that increase this risk.

The best clue as to the type of cancer to which we might be susceptible is provided by the kinds of cancer (if any) that our close relatives have developed. Since my father was a chain-smoker who died from a smoking-caused cancer, I would be very unwise to smoke. But I should not overemphasize the role of genetics, since for the majority of people, exposure to carcinogens is far more decisive than genetics, in determining whether or not they will contract cancer.

THREE

HISTORY

Tobacco was first discovered by two men in Columbus' crew during his maiden voyage to the New World in 1492. Sent to explore the area upriver in a land that would later be named San Salvador, the men saw natives breathing through strange, glowing sticks, which contained tobacco wrapped in cigar-like fashion. But not until 1561 was tobacco *imported* into Europe, where it was first used in Paris. Ralph Lane, Governor of the Virginia colony, brought back tobacco to Sir Walter Raleigh in 1585. Raleigh lit up, and tobacco soon became a staple in English society.[15] As a result, Chief Pocahontas eventually got his revenge in spades. But the British evened the score by introducing him to alcohol.

French tobacco firms began to market tobacco rolled into paper-encased tubes in 1843, and gave them a French name, *cigarettes*. But for several decades, most smokers bought tobacco and paper separately and rolled their own cigarettes. However, in 1881 a machine was patented that could make 120,000 cigarettes a day, and by 1900 there were already more than 160 brands. The stage was now set for a dramatic expansion of cigarette sales.

Cigarette smoking received a big boost during the First World War, when long periods of watching and waiting separated brief flashes of intense action. Even today, "hurry up and

---

wait" is widely accepted in England as the norm during army service. In fact, soldiers the world over are sorely tempted to relieve the dreariness of long periods of inaction by lighting a cigarette.

Soldiers returning from World War I spread the habit of smoking among men during the 1920s. Women started smoking in large numbers roughly two decades later, in the early 1940s. The average number of cigarettes smoked per year by a United States citizen increased from 50 in 1900 to a maximum of 4,300 in 1963. After publication of the first Surgeon General's Report on Smoking and Health in 1964, consumption gradually fell to 2300 by 1998, when it leveled off.[16]

When I was a little boy, my chain-smoking father showed me how neatly cigarettes were arranged in a pack of cigarettes—a work of art, no less. During the 1930's, smoking was associated with being adult and male. As yet, there was no evidence that smoking might be bad for one's health, and in many developed countries the majority of males smoked.

The first report in the English-speaking world that linked smoking to disease was published by F. E. Tylecote in the medical journal *The Lancet*: in almost every case of lung cancer he had seen or known about, the patient had smoked. This theme was first incorporated into a public health campaign in Nazi Germany in the 1930s, and the first conference on Tobacco Hazards Research was held there in 1941, and some restrictions on smoking indoors were imposed. This need not be surprising, for there was no problem in imposing restrictions in Nazi Germany, and Hitler did not smoke. Indeed for decades, Germany and Austria-Hungary had been one of the world's leaders in medicine and public health.[17]

It was not until 1950 that epidemiologists Doll and Hill in England[18] and Wynder and Graham in the United States[19] reported on a link between smoking and lung cancer almost simultaneously. Their reports were followed by other landmark studies published in 1954 and 1956 by Doll and Hill in England,[20] and in 1958 and 1959 by Hammond and Horn in the United States.[21]

Nevertheless, when the International Cancer Congress opened in London in 1958, there was by no means as yet a consensus on the question of whether smoking causes cancer. When I reported on this Congress for Science magazine, I focused on epidemiological studies on the effect of cigarette smoking on lung cancer incidence.[22] The data presented by Wynder, by Doll, and by Horn were especially convincing, and only one study reporting at the Congress did not conclude that smoking was the main cause of lung cancer.

It took several years to recognize that a consensus was building that smoking causes cancer. This led to the first groundbreaking *official* reports that smoking causes cancer. In Britain, it was the report of 1962.[23] In the United States, it required publication of 7,000 articles on smoking and health, before Luther Terry released the first Surgeon General's Report on Smoking and Health in 1964.[24]

But not until 2003 did I find that documents used in suits against the tobacco industry were freely available at the website www.tobaccodocuments.org. There I discovered that Paul Kotin, the UCLA professor who presented the only report that denied the link between smoking and cancer at the 1958 International Cancer Congress, had close ties to the tobacco industry. In January 1959, he wrote a letter to the Executive Secretary of the Tobacco Industry Research Committee, in which he castigated me for the conclusions I had drawn in my report in *Science*, and talked about launching a multi-signature protest against my article. In deciding against that course, he said, "In all candor, I think Reif has his critics over a barrel in that the only people reporting epidemiological studies at the meeting were of the group that would agree with his broad conclusions."

When the first Surgeon General's report was finally published in 1964 – with potent lobbying by advocates such as Ernst Wynder–it was able to conclude not only that "cigarette smoking is causally related to lung cancer," but that "the magnitude of its effect far outweighs all other factors." The report stated that the risk of developing lung cancer increased with duration of smoking and was reduced by quitting. The available data for women were less extensive, since at the time far fewer women were smoking, but pointed in the same direction. Cigarette smoking was also a cause of cancer of the larynx, and the most important of the causes of chronic bronchitis. Further, pipe smoking was a cause of lip cancer. The report also found a statistically significant relation between smoking and cancer of the esophagus and cancer of the urinary bladder, heart disease, emphysema, peptic ulcer, and low birth weight for pregnant women who smoked. However at that point in time, the evidence was insufficient to call these relationships "causal."

For many years after 1967, Surgeon General's Reports were issued annually or biannually, and most reports addressed just one aspect of the health effects of tobacco.[25] By bringing in new data, these reports converted most of the "significant associations" of the 1964 report into "causal relationships," and highlighted dangers not even previously suspected. These included the causation of cancer in many other organs,[26] the hazards of involuntary smoking[27] and of nicotine addiction.[28]

Because the health hazards of smoking were so serious, the 1964 report concluded that remedial action was necessary.[24] In response, Congress passed an act in 1965 that required the placement of health warnings on cigarette packs. This law was updated in 1970[25] and since then, many other laws to regulate smoking have been passed by Congress and by state legislatures.

In retrospect, it seems amazing that we were so slow to recognize the dangers of smoking; but then, hindsight is 100% accurate. I believe that the reason was, the disarmingly long lag time between cause and effect. On average, it takes roughly 27 years from the start of habitual smoking for lung cancer to develop in those susceptible to it. This explains why even by 1930, the death rate of United States men from lung cancer was only 5 per

100,000. Though 1963 saw the peak consumption of cigarettes in the United States, it took until 1990 for the lung cancer death rate to increase fifteenfold, to reach its peak of 76 per 100,000.[5]

It is difficult to pick out one particular antismoking advocate among the many who have fought against smoking with great success, but Alan M. Blum is one of the most outstanding. In 1977, aware that Medical Schools and Schools of Public Health were extremely remiss in teaching their students about smoking, he started DOC (Doctors Ought To Care), which has more than 150 chapters in the United States and in 27 other countries. Its mission is to organize physicians and medical students to promote healthy lifestyles through talks in the clinic, classroom and local community. The focus is not only on prevention of smoking, but on a wide variety of health issues, even including alternatives to violence.[29] Blum single-handedly revolutionized antismoking advocacy by changing it from a focus on health effects to an attack against the devious tobacco industry, and he used counter-advertising in all types of media.

While Blum was editor of the *New York State Journal of Medicine* and of the *Medical Journal of Australia*, he published the very first single-theme issue on any subject in 1983 – in his case, on smoking. Since then, single-theme issues on a variety of subjects have become commonplace, and in following years, before the prevalence of smoking begun to decline, JAMA published many single-theme issues on smoking.

Alan Blum has been highly energetic in holding the tobacco industry accountable, has given over 1,700 invited talks on tobacco prevention and control around the globe, and earned several awards. Presently, he is a professor of family medicine and director of the University of Alabama Center for the Study of Tobacco and Society.[30] The Centers of Disease Control and Prevention (CDC) state that as of 2014, nearly one-third of all cancer deaths are directly linked to smoking. Even as early as 1959, tobacco use in the United

States caused approximately 430,000 deaths each year, including an estimated 3,000 deaths from lung cancer among nonsmokers. Nonsmokers also suffered an estimated 62,000 annual deaths from heart disease as a result of exposure to tobacco smoke in their environment.[31] Compared to nonsmokers, smokers tend to drink too much, exercise too little, and to eat less fruit and green vegetables–and this also contributes to their high cancer death rate.

Regarding the prevalence of smoking, the CDC and the Office on Smoking and Health of the United States publish annual data on the smoking habits of adolescents and adults. During the years 1991 to 1999, smoking among high school students increased from 27.5% to 34.8%, although late in the decade, smoking may have leveled off. But there were bright spots. In Florida, where comprehensive tobacco-control programs had been initiated, smoking declined 40% among middle school students and 20% among high school students.[32]

As regards smoking among adults, there was a steady decline in smoking between the mid-1960s and the early 1990's, when the prevalence of smoking stabilized. In 1999, 23% of adults smoked, namely 24% of men and 21% of women.[317] CDC statistics of May, 2003 showed that 23% of United States citizens over 18 smoked in 2001. The latest figures available in early 2007 were valid for 2004, when the number of U.S. smokers over 18 had dropped to 21%; this included 23% of men and 19% of women.[33] The CDC statistics for 1998 reported that adults with 16 or more years of education had a much lower level of smoking (11%) than those with only 9–11 years of schooling (37%).[34]

Sad to report, a lavishly illustrated multi-authored 2005 book entitled "Smoke: A Global History of Smoking" has been written to delight tobacco manufacturers and smokers – a strong indication that it was planned and underwritten by the tobacco industry. The book is largely an apology for smoking, which it glorifies as a universal human need. Even a fine chapter by Allan Brandt is insufficient to redeem its overall pro-smoking message. Brandt argues that tobacco executives recognized the possibility of creating the desire for its product long ago, and were first to devise such advertising techniques as sky-writing, movie implants, and large photo-billboards.[35] In 2014, the only items of these adverts still in use seem to be movie implants.

FOUR

TOBACCO SMOKE CONSTITUENTS

Cigarettes contain only about 50% of unprocessed tobacco. Another 30% contains reconstituted tobacco, and 20% consists of expanded tobacco. The last two ingredients contain a variety of chemicals, flavorings and food products such as sweeteners, which are intended to reduce the harshness of the smoke, improve its aroma, and intensify the absorption of nicotine.

Tobacco smoke consists of two main elements: a particulate phase which we see as smoke, and an invisible gaseous phase. Most chemicals are either in one phase or the other, but a few are present in both phases.

Reviewers have estimated that a burning cigarette releases between 6,800 (Ernst Wynder, 1979)[36] and 4,000 (Howard Koh and coworkers, 2001)[37] different chemicals. The most recent reviews have favored a value under 5,000, but all these numbers represent estimates rather than firm figures. Only well under 400 of these chemicals have been quantified in cigarette smoke, and well-documented toxicological data exists for a much smaller number.[38]

Recent advances in analyzing traces of chemicals have made it possible to detect many of these carcinogens in human fluids, swabs, or tissues obtained at autopsies. Other chemicals also have been identified by finding their metabolic breakdown products. In 2005, the International Agency for Research on Cancer (IARC) expanded its list of chemicals in tobacco smoke that fall into its Group 1 category, "proven to be carcinogenic to humans," to 60 different compounds.[39, 40]

While it is certain that both the particulate and the gaseous phases of tobacco smoke contain many carcinogens, it is difficult to prove which are the most dangerous. Further, the carcinogenic hazard that a constituent in tobacco smoke poses to human beings depends not only on its carcinogenicity but also on its concentration. New Zealanders Fowles and Bates have taken this factor into consideration in prioritizing the carcinogens in cigarette smoke that cause the most risk. In addition, they have prioritized the relative toxicity of smoke constituents for reproduction and growth, and for the heart, eyes, nerves, liver, and kidney of smokers. Further, they have estimated which of the chemicals inhaled in secondhand smoke are the most dangerous.[38]

While polonium-210,[41] dioxins, free radicals,[42] and co-carcinogens (substances that assist the action of carcinogens) such as phenol and catechol are present in tobacco smoke, it is difficult to determine the quantitative deleterious effect of each of these substances. Since nicotine inhibits the apoptosis (self-destruction) of lung cancer cells, it has been labeled a co-carcinogen.[43] Because it is inherently difficult to rank the relative contributions of individual carcinogens and co-carcinogens in a complex mixture, it is also difficult to prioritize their removal from tobacco smoke. However, some reviewers believe that nitrosamines are the most potent lung carcinogens and therefore most dangerous.[42]

The carcinogens in cigarette smoke can be classified into nine different classes, of which only three – namely aromatic amines, N-heterocyclic amines and N-nitrosamines—are not radically different.[44] Fowles and Bates report that 89% of the carcinogenicity of cigarette sidestream (passively inhaled) smoke is contributed by 1,3-butadiene, acrylonitrile and NNN (N'-nitrosonornicotine).[38] NNN is of special interest, since it is the first carcinogen discovered in raw (unburned) tobacco. As early as 1975, it was suspected to cause mouth cancer in people who chewed tobacco, or else betel nut quid wrapped in tobacco leaf.[45]

It is also important to know that NNK is just one of several nitrosamines that so far have been discovered only in tobacco smoke. All of these tobacco-specific nitrosamines are highly potent in producing lung cancer in animal experiments.

Lung cancer is by no means the only cancer induced by the carcinogens in tobacco smoke, although lung cancer constitutes two-thirds of all cancer caused by smoking cigarettes,[25] many other organs are also affected. For instance 2-naphthylamine, which causes bladder cancer and is recognized by the IARC as a human carcinogen[20] is present at a low concentration in tobacco smoke. But as noted in Chapter 11 which discusses cancer in other organs, bladder cancer is one of the many organs where the risk of cancer is several times higher for smokers than for nonsmokers. 2-naphthylamine may be merely one of many carcinogens in smoke that target the bladder.

Because tobacco smoke contains so many different carcinogens, it is not feasible to describe all their different modes of action at the molecular level. But benzopyrene is of special interest, although it is present at a very small concentration (20 to 40 nanograms per cigarette). Benzopyrene was the first carcinogen to be identified, is one of the most potent carcinogens known, and is recognized as a human carcinogen by the IARC.[39] It seems to cause cancer by binding to and thereby inactivating the p53 suppressor gene, which when active prevents uncontrolled cell division. The p53 gene is mutated and thus inactive in 60% of lung cancer cases,[46] and in 58% of people who smoke cigarettes and drink alcohol—but only in 17% of people who neither smoke nor drink.[47]

The long-term cumulative effect of the many carcinogens in tobacco smoke is insidious. The danger is that smokers remain unaware that carcinogens may have started cellular changes that may take decades to develop into a cancer. By the time detectable symptoms are present it may be too late to prevent a bad outcome.

In addition to carcinogens, tobacco smoke contains many potent toxins. Nicotine is not only highly addictive, but at slightly higher concentrations than in smoke, it is a potent poison (see chapter 16). Another constituent, acrolein, is a powerful irritant responsible for 97% of the acute (near-term) respiratory effects of mainstream smoke, and 99% of its eye irritation.[38] In much higher concentrations than present in tobacco smoke, inhalation of methanol causes headaches, dizziness, and visual disturbances.[48] Nitrobenzene inactivates hemoglobin by binding tightly to it.[49] Carbon monoxide is roughly a thosuandfold more concentrated than any other biologically active substance in tobacco smoke.[44] Thus, it is by far the main reason why smoking a cigarette temporarily lowers the oxygen carrying ability of the blood.[50] Hydrogen cyanide has the same effect as carbon monoxide, but is present in vastly smaller quantities, and its mechanism of action is quite different. It prevents tissues from utilizing oxygen, because it inhibits the enzyme cytochrome oxidase. In higher amounts, hydrogen cyanide asphyxiates very rapidly,[51] while hydrogen sulfide causes coughing and irritates the throat,[52] but this occurs only when it is tested alone at higher concentrations than are found in smoke.

The toxic substances in tobacco smoke other than carcinogens injure a variety of organs and body functions that include the heart, lung, reproduction, development, nerves, liver, and kidney. The harmful effects of smoke on the heart and the lung are described in chapters 5, 7 and 13. Of the other effects of smoke, eye irritation poses a serious problem,[38] but the effect on reproduction is the most worrisome. Further, the Mayo Clinic reports that the sperm of men who smoke one to two packs a day may become misshapen and move slower than that of non-smoker. Even smokeless tobacco reduces the quantity and quality of sperm. Men who drink and smoke have significantly lower sperm counts than men who only drink.[53] Women who smoke 16 to 20 cigarettes per day are 20% less likely to become pregnant in their first year of trying, and almost 50% less likely during the subsequent two years.[54]

Massachusetts was the first state in the nation to pass a law that requires tobacco companies to disclose the ingredients in all their brands and products. However, the tobacco companies contested this law, and in 2002 a United States Court of Appeals struck it down. While the tobacco companies argued that the law would force them to reveal trade secrets, one cannot help but wonder what else they need to hide.

FIVE

HEART DISEASE AND NICOTINE

Most of us believe that the major health consequence of smoking is cancer.[55, 56] But recent evidence shows that more than three times as many smokers die early as a result of heart disease than of cancer. Perhaps people underestimate the life-robbing effect of heart disease, because they tend to dread cancer far more. In *Time* of April 28, 2003, science reporter Christine Gorman branded heart disease the no. 1 killer of women, killing more women than all cancers combined, and identified smoking as the top risk factor for heart disease for both sexes.

The Surgeon General's report on cardiovascular disease says that cigarette smoking is the most important preventable risk factor for coronary heart disease in the United States, and together with other risk factors greatly increases the risk of contracting it. Depending upon the amount that they smoke, smokers have between two and four times the risk of sudden cardiac death compared to nonsmokers.

Smoking also contributes to development of arteriosclerotic blood vessel disease both in the aorta that feeds the heart, and in the arteries that feed the limbs, and it also causes abdominal aortic aneurysms (AAA). The death risk due to the bursting of blood vessels is two to three times higher in smokers as compared to never smokers.[57] Also, for women who smoke cigarettes and also use oral contraceptives, the risk of coronary artery disease and of a form of stroke called subarachnoid hemorrhage is greatly increased.[55]

Nicotine is rapidly absorbed from the lungs into the blood stream. Unlike larger molecules that cannot cross the blood-brain barrier, nicotine readily enters the brain, where it produces the stimulation that makes it a powerful addictive.[58] But it also causes a rapid rise in blood pressure and heart rate. These changes, together with long-term increases in blood cholesterol and "bad" LDL (low density lipoprotein) and a drop in the "good" HDL (high density lipoprotein) markedly accelerate the tendency to form atherosclerotic plaques in blood vessels. It is often from the site of such plaques that blood clots develop, which then become the main cause of heart attacks and strokes.[55]

Carbon monoxide, the other major constituent of the gases in cigarette smoke, binds tightly to the hemoglobin in red blood cells, displacing oxygen. To compensate for the resulting loss in the ability of red cells to deliver oxygen to body tissues, the body is forced to produce more red cells. These, together with an increased number of white cells and increased fibrinogen content, promote the process of thrombosis[59]–blood clotting–within a blood vessel, especially at the site of a plaque.

The Framingham Heart Study began approximately 60 years ago and is the longest ongoing medical study in history.[60] Its first findings in the 1950s, twelve years after it began, was that a high blood pressure, high cholesterol and smoking were risk factors for heart disease, heart attacks and stroke. Diabetes was soon added to this list. The Framingham Heart Study found that in almost two thirds of men and women, heart disease can hide for decades, with none or only the slightest of signs, then suddenly produce a massive heart attack, cardiac death, or stroke. Women most fear breast cancer. In fact, their risk of dying of a heart attack is 10 times as high as dying of breast cancer.

Medical researchers found that any damage to the heart is irreparable. The solution for a heart damaged so badly that it may soon stop working is a heart transplant. During 2007, 60,000 people needed a heart transplant in the United States, but only 2,000 received one. Since heart disease cannot be mended, it must be prevented from developing in the first place. The preventative that the Framingham Heart Study found capable of lowering the risk of a heart attack was lowering the blood pressure. As detailed below, this could be achieved by a low-fat diet, exercise, and eventually a group of drugs called *statins*.

Another key player in the development of heart disease was cholesterol. The body synthesizes all the cholesterol it needs for itself, but fatty meals provide an overload. The danger comes from "bad" LDL: it binds to other substances in blood to form plaques in the arteries of the body, including those that lead to the heart and the brain. It is held to acceptable levels in the body by binding to receptors in the liver, from which it is then excreted from the body. Statins act by helping the liver to clear LDL from the body, thereby lowering the blood LDL level and reducing plaque formation. Happily, statins also act to lower inflammation, which is another major factor in plaque formation.

The latest findings of the Framingham Heart Study are that the risk for coronary heart disease in men who are current smokers is double (207%) that of nonsmokers. For current women smokers, the risk is between double and triple (265%) the risk of non-smokers.[61] In women under the age of 50, smoking is the dominant identified risk factor causing myocardial infarction (heart attack). The next smaller risk factor is a high level of LDL and total plasma cholesterol, together with a low level of HDL (High Density Lipoprotein).[62] Unfortunately, there are 246 other risk factors other than cholesterol that have been identified for heart disease. One of the most important is inflammation, for which C-reactive protein (CRP) is a marker, and this may be a better predictor of heart attacks than the cholesterol level.[63] So it is not

ARNOLD E. REIF

surprising that merely having a low cholesterol level does not by itself protect against smoking-related heart disease.[64] Additional major risk factors include a sedentary lifestyle, obesity, diabetes, uncontrolled high blood pressure, psychological stress,[65] a strong family history of heart disease, and bacterial infections of the heart muscle. However, by far the highest risk factor is smoking: even smoking as few as 1 to 4 cigarettes a day can give women a twofold to threefold increase in the risk of fatal coronary heart disease and of nonfatal heart attack.[66] This result is supported by a recent equally dramatic finding regarding the increase in risk from as little exposure to environmental smoke as 30 minutes per day (see chapter 19). On the other hand, quitting results in a dramatic and relatively rapid reduction in the risks of fatal and nonfatal heart attacks, and of fatal strokes.[67] Smoking also causes a serious increase in the risk of developing an abdominal aortic aneurysm, which could rupture with fatal results.[68]

For people who already suffer from coronary heart disease (CHD) and who smoke, quitting results in more than a one-third (36%) reduction in the risk of death from CHD. Quitting is especially important for women who use oral contraceptives, since smoking greatly increases their risk of a heart attack. These conclusions were arrived at in 2003 from review of 20 different studies that met strict criteria for scientific validity.[69]

The *Journal of the American Medical Association (JAMA)* of August 20, 2003 devoted four articles to vital new results: 80% to 90% of people who develop coronary heart disease and 95% of those who have a fatal heart attack have *at least one of four major risk factors:* smoking, diabetes, hypertension (high blood pressure) and either high cholesterol, or abnormally high LDL and low HDL. Smoking was the most serious risk factor, and most urgently needed change. Other risk factors can be reduced by regular aerobic exercise, reducing body weight if overweight, and using appropriate medication. This includes low-dose aspirin to prevent blood clots, cholesterol-lowering drugs, blood pressure medication, and statins–because they lower C-reactive protein. Exercise strengthens hearts and lungs, helps to keep the weight down, is a potent escape valve from psychological stress, and has been shown to sharpen the brain and substantially retard age-related brain deterioration.[70] Merely active participation in everyday social activities helps in attaining these objectives.[71]

As of 2008, cardiovascular research had proven that angiograms were valuable in revealing the degree to which coronary arteries were blocked, but failed to reveal plaques hidden inside the walls of the arteries. These plaques can be fatal, for when one splits, then the bloodstream has access to the walls of the artery and a blood clot forms at that site. This is the cause of approximately 70% of all heart attacks. Now tiny ultrasound probes have been developed, which can be threaded into coronary arteries and detect plaques inside artery walls. Then bypass surgery can avoid the risk that coronary arteries might become blocked.

Genetics is an underlying factor in most diseases, and coronary heart disease is no exception. A genetic disease called Familial Hyperlipidemia (FHL) has now been discovered, in which the liver's ability to rid the body of LDL is almost eliminated. As a result, people who have inherited FHL develop plaques in their arteries in their forties or fifties. To survive, they require frequent surgery to bypass blocked coronary arteries.

This is a rare disease, but a study of twins in the population at large has shown that death from heart disease at relatively young ages is strongly influenced by genetic factors.[72] But while as yet we cannot change our inheritance, we do have the option to adopt a healthful lifestyle. The vital first step is to quit smoking–and incidentally thereby save a great deal of money. Other steps that are also very important include exercising on a regular basis, dieting to reach normal weight if overweight, and eating a diet plentiful in fruits and vegetables but low in saturated and monounsaturated fats. If these measures have failed to normalize abnormal blood lipid levels, high blood pressure, or the presence of diabetes, then drugs should be taken to reduce the risk of heart disease and of a heart attack.[73]

As of 2008, the most common way to predict the risk of a heart attack is the "Framingham Score." By assessing age, sex, total cholesterol level, LDL level, smoking status, and systolic blood pressure, the risk of experiencing a heart attack during the next 10 years can be calculated. The likelihood that this assessment is correct (the discrimination ability) is 75%.[74]

The American Heart Association warns the public that chest discomfort felt as pain, pressure or squeezing is not the only warning sign of a heart attack. Symptoms for most heart attacks include back, neck or jaw pain, or shortness of breath. Other signs can be nausea, dizziness or lightheadedness, weakness, numbness or tingling in the arm, hand or jaw, or sweating. If one experiences these symptoms, calling 911 could save one's life.

A wealth of excellent up-to-date information about smoking and heart disease is available from the American Heart Association (800-242-8721; www.americanheart.org), the National Heart, Lung and Blood Institute (www.nhibi.nih.gov/health), the U.S. Centers for Disease Control and Prevention (CDC)–Heart Disease (www.cdc.gov/HearDisease), and from the American Lung Association (212-315-8700; www.lungusa.org).

SIX

STROKE

Smoking causes vascular disease throughout the body, not merely limited to the blood vessels of the heart. Thus, it is not surprising that smoking increases the risk of cerebrovascular disease- disease related to the blood vessels of the brain—which can result in stroke.[4] Research by the Heart and Stroke Foundation of Ontario has shown that cigarette smoking causes more than 50% of the deaths from cerebrovascular disease in men and women under 65 years in age. Fortunately, this excess risk diminishes with increasing age.[75] Still, compared to nonsmokers, the risk of stroke for smokers is 72% higher for men, and 43% higher for women.[76] However, because stroke is a far less common cause of death than heart disease, the number of excess deaths from stroke that are caused by smoking are also far fewer.

Because there are two different types of stroke, the prevention of stroke is similar to but not identical with the prevention of heart disease. Hemorrhagic strokes account for 20% of strokes, and occur when a blood vessel ruptures, causing blood to leak into brain tissue, thereby damaging it. Ischemic strokes comprise 80% of strokes, and occur when blood vessels within the brain are blocked, thereby killing the tissues which those blood vessels normally supply with oxygen. Therefore, preventive programs must address both types of stroke.[77] Further, strokes can range from "massive" to "silent" (without symptoms). Indeed, silent strokes may be one of the reasons for the gradual diminution of brain power in old age. But if silent strokes occur frequently, that increases the risk that a large stroke may occur.[78] Happily, there is new evidence for the efficacy of stroke prevention.[79, 80]

Heart disease is also connected to stroke, because atrial fibrillation, a common heart rhythm disturbance in which the upper chambers of the heart quiver rapidly rather than contract forcefully, increases the risk that clots may form in the heart. Should such clots break loose and lodge in the brain, they can cause a stroke. But therapy for atrial fibrillation with low doses of warfarin and other medications reduces the risk of clot formation by approximately 50%.[81]

Additional information is provided by the American Stroke Association, which is an arm of the American Heart Association (888-4-STROKE: 888-478-7653], www.StrokeAssociation. org).

SEVEN

LUNG CANCER

Yul Brynner, then one of the world's most famous actors, was diagnosed with lung cancer in 1983, 15 years after he quit smoking, following 36 years of heavy smoking. Early in 1985, already weak from radiation treatments and chemotherapy, he told a television audience that he wanted to film a commercial that would air after he was gone, in which he would say "Now that I'm gone I tell you: Don't smoke, whatever you do, just don't smoke."

He made these remarks with complete conviction and high intensity on the "Good Morning America" show. After he died, they were incorporated into a moving American Cancer Society commercial that caused thousands of smokers to quit.[82]

Chapter 3 on the history of smoking highlights the importance of the scientists who first proved that smoking causes cancer. Each decade after their groundbreaking report of 1954, Richard Doll and his coworkers published an update of that study, which was based on answers to a questionnaire sent to all male physicians who resided in the United Kingdom in 1951, to which two-thirds responded. In 2004, Doll and coworkers published their 50-year update, which is uniquely important, because they had followed nearly 90% of their physician subjects to the end of their lives.[83]

The 2004 report proves that the risks for life-long smokers are even larger than we knew previously, because they continue to increase until the end of life. Approximately one quarter of all persistent smokers are killed by their habit while still middle aged (35–69 years old). Eventually, about half of persistent smokers die from diseases caused by smoking, on average losing a whole decade of their natural life-span. So the hidden price of smoking is vastly higher than the high monetary price that smokers resent when they buy cigarettes.

But that 2004 report also had some good news: the earlier a smoker quits, the greater the gain in life-span. At age 30, quitting prolongs life by about 10 years; at age 40, about 9 years; at age 50, about 6 years; at age 60, about 3 years. Even quitting at any time later in life was shown to be beneficial. An accompanying editorial quoted Doll's collaborator Richard Peto as estimating that *the current worldwide patterns of smoking will cause about one billion tobacco deaths in the current century – unless there is widespread cessation.*[84]

Today, leaders in epidemiological research the world over agree that tobacco smoking causes by far the most cases of cancer than any other carcinogen in our environment, namely predominantly causing lung cancer.[85] Currently, the American Cancer Society attributes 87% of all lung cancer to smoking,[86] while a Surgeon General's report has estimated this figure to be about 90% for women,[87] a value previously estimated for both genders.[85]

The figures on lung cancer released by the National Cancer Institute in June, 2001 indicated that relative to all other cancers, lung cancer incidence stood at 13%, while lung cancer deaths amounted to 29%, or nearly one third of cancer deaths of all types.[88] This large disparity between the percentages of incidence and of death exists, because lung cancer is far harder to cure than most other types of cancer. Because men began to reduce their smoking in the late 1960s, lung cancer mortality in men has now begun to decrease at a rate of nearly 3% per year.

But because women lagged about two decades behind men in starting to smoke and in quitting, lung cancer mortality in women has not yet reached its peak, and is increasing at almost 1% per year.[88]

The Surgeon General's report on Smoking and Health for 2001 is entitled "Women and Smoking." It documents in excruciating detail the vast harm that women have suffered from smoking–and the situation is not very different for men who smoke cigarettes. Here is a summary of some of the highlights of the report:[87]

- Since 1980, approximately 3 million United States women have died prematurely from all smoking-related diseases, as well as from fires started by cigarettes.

- During each year between 1990 and 2000, United States women lost over 2 million years of life due to smoking.

- The risk of dying of lung cancer is 20 times as high for women who smoke two of more packs a day than for women nonsmokers.

- The risk of contracting lung cancer increases in step with the number of cigarettes smoked per day, the number of years a woman has smoked, and the intensity of smoke inhalation.

- Women nonsmokers who are regularly exposed to tobacco smoke have an increased risk of lung cancer and coronary heart disease.

- Women who stop smoking greatly reduce their risk of dying prematurely, and quitting is beneficial at any age.

- Smoking is harmful to the fetus during pregnancy, to newborn babies, and to children,[89] and is a major public health problem.

- Tobacco industry advertising is effective in motivating girls to start smoking.

Most of the above statistics that relate to men are very similar for women. But in North America, men began to smoke in large numbers about 25 years before women did. As a result, the incidence of lung cancer when standardized for age is 72% higher for men than for women.[90]

As to the mechanism by which smoking causes lung cancer, it usually starts in the stem cells that underlie the cells that line the passages of the lung. These stem cells serve to replace damaged epithelial cells, and are therefore programmed for cell division, which makes them susceptible to conversion into cancer cells when exposed to carcinogens. This exposure is most intense where tobacco smoke deposits the most tar, namely at the points where the air vessels of the respiratory tree bifurcate (subdivide).[91, 92] Recently, the most common type of lung cancer in smokers has changed to adenocarcinoma, a shift that may be due to changes in the carcinogens present in modern cigarettes.[87]

The development of lung cancer may include the following symptoms[93]–although it is important to note that many of these symptoms have several other unrelated causes:

- a persistent cough (but see chapter 13),
- constant chest pain
- fatigue (which has very many other causes)
- recurrent pneumonia (but see chapter 13)
- swelling of neck and face
- coughing up blood

In addition to smoking, there are other causes of lung cancer. Particularly important are environmental tobacco smoke (chapter 19), marijuana (chapter 22), air pollution (chapter 34), asbestos (chapter 35), and airborne radioactivity such as radon (chapter 36). In addition, the IARC (International Agency for Research on Cancer) notes that the following occupations are hazardous, because they increase the risk of lung cancers, particularly for smokers:

OCCUPATION	CARCINOGEN ENCOUNTERED
Construction and building	Asbestos, wood dust
Textile industry	Benzidine
Coloring and dyeing	Benzidine
Petroleum and oil products	Shale, mineral oils and soot
Metal Casting and steel furnaces	Coke, coal tars, and soot
Carpentry and joinery	Wood dusts

Soot is carcinogenic, because it contains polycyclic aromatic hydrocarbons such as benzopyrene, which are potent carcinogens. A study performed in Greece and reported by Christos Chatzis and coworkers in 1999 concluded that on average, employment in one of the above occupations that trebled the already high risk of lung cancer that smokers incurred, even if they had none of the above occupational exposures.

Jyoti Patel and coauthors, writing in JAMA of April 15, 2004, have concluded that at present there is a lung cancer epidemic in United States women. Further, they cite evidence that women may be more susceptible to the carcinogenic properties of tobacco smoke than are men. Despite all that is known about the devastating effects of cigarettes, one quarter of U.S. women continue to smoke. The authors conclude that publicizing data about this epidemic may prevent similar epidemics in other parts of the world where women are just becoming addicted to tobacco.

A vast amount of definitive up-to-date information about all aspects of lung cancer is available at the American Cancer Society website www.cancer.org. Similar information can be found at the websites of the American Lung Association and the National Cancer Institute. Several excellent pamphlets that include information on various facets of lung cancer can also be obtained directly from all three of these sources (see Appendix).

EIGHT

SCREENING FOR LUNG CANCER

The usefulness of screening for any type of cancer is often measured by the increase in the five-year survival rate- the percentage of patients still living five years after diagnosis of cancer. Unfortunately in the case of lung cancer, mass screening of smokers, or of people involved in industrial exposure to lung carcinogens, so far has not resulted in an increase in the five-year survival rate. But that is by no means the end of the story.

For all patients with lung cancer, the five-year survival rate is only 14%. But it is so low only because by the time the cancer is detected, it is usually at an advanced stage. Only about 15% of lung cancers are diagnosed at a stage where surgery is judged capable of removing the cancer completely, but the five year survival for such patients is much higher, roughly 50%.[94]

At first sight, the above evidence seems to indicate that a powerful diagnostic method will greatly increase the cure rate of lung cancer. But the same data exaggerate the benefit of early diagnosis, because they inevitably lengthen the time to death, relative to patients diagnosed at a later stage of their disease and therefore already much closer to death. Consequently, both the American Cancer Society (ACS)[95] and the National Cancer Institute (NCI)[96] summarize their careful analyses of available studies as indicating that there is no good evidence, that screening for lung cancer can reduce lung cancer mortality.

Typical of such studies on the benefits of screening is the Mayo Lung Project reported by Pamela Marcus and colleagues in the August 16, 2000 issue of the Journal of the National Cancer Institute. This large, 20-year long study found that X-rays taken at frequent intervals do not decrease the death rate from lung cancer. A troubling aspect of this study was that a substantial number of the tumors uncovered by screening proved to be of a type that did not cause serious illness or death. However, positive X-ray findings necessitated surgery for their biopsy or excision, and entailed what eventually proved to be unnecessary worry, risk, and cost.[97]

Screening with sputum cytology (microscopic examination of the sputum to determine if it contains lung cancer cells) has been studied extensively, but has failed to produce a reduction in lung cancer deaths. Even when sputum cytology is performed in addition to the taking of conventional chest X-rays, an article from the National Cancer Institute (NCI) published on its web site (www.cancer.gov) in February, 2003, concluded that at present, there was little if any evidence of the efficacy of this technique. But attempts to improve and automate the technology for sputum cytology are continuing.[95]

Because of uncertainty in the medical community on how the available data from past studies should be interpreted, there is no consensus on the issue of screening for lung cancer. This has motivated the National Cancer Institute to launch a very large study, in which 37,000 men are being screened for lung, colorectal, and prostate cancers, while an equal number of women are screened for lung, colorectal and ovarian cancers. But this important study is not scheduled to be completed until 2015.[96]

One of the most promising methods for diagnosing lung cancer is Low-radiation dose Computed Tomography (LCT, also called spiral CF or helical CT). In this process, the patient lies still on a table inside the hole of the donut-shaped LCT machine for about 15 seconds, while the machine rotates around the patient and takes X-rays of sections of the lung that are 5 mm apart. The digital data are fed into a computer, which then uses it to create a 3-dimensional model of the lung. LCT permits the use of lower doses of radiation (similar to those required for a mammogram) than are required for a conventional X-ray of the lung, which records images only on 2-dimensional films. Early trials suggest that LCT can detect up to 6 times as many small lung cancers as a conventional X-ray. But because its ability to save lives has not yet been proven,[98] NCI has begun a study to compare LCT to conventional chest X-rays. While its benefits are still unproven, restraint is advisable in the use of direct-to-consumer marketed LCT scans for lung cancer screening,[99] LCT scans cost $300 to $1,000, and usually are not covered by health plans, although about half the hospitals in the United States own LCT machines.[100]

Most recently, Integrated Positron-Emission Tomography (PET) scans used in conjunction with CT have been found to be more effective than either PET or CT scans used alone. By combining the two techniques, cancer nodules smaller than 1 cm in size can be identified, thereby significantly improving the diagnostic accuracy of staging lung cancer of the non-small cell lung cancer type.[101] Another promising method for the early detection of lung cancer is fluorescence bronchoscopy.

While molecular techniques are still in an early stage of development, they promise to greatly improve the early detection of lung cancer. Various methods that assess the extent of genetic damage in bronchial epithelial cells (the cells that cover the air passages of the lung's bronchi) are under study. One such method employs the polymerase chain reaction,[102] while another looks for the types of mutations that often occur in cancer cells–for instance, mutations of the suppressor gene p53.[95]

While ACS does not recommend lung cancer screening for people at risk of lung cancer, it does not discourage them from having early detection tests, and leaves that decision up to them and their physicians. Although new, promising techniques are now available, ACS makes it clear that none have been validated to produce a decrease in death rate. While research on these new techniques is in progress, ACS encourages those at risk to enquire at institutions with state-of-the-art capabilities, as to the possible benefits, risks, and limitations of testing for early detection of lung cancer.[95] Some physicians believe that even the conventional lung X-ray technique, while less sensitive in detecting cancer, could still be useful, because it tends to give fewer false positive results.[103]

Finally, there is every reason to justify thorough future trials of new techniques.[104,105] More sensitive techniques could be useful not only for routine screening, but for testing people at high risk of lung cancer, and for the accurate staging of lung cancer once it has been detected. Still, whatever benefits are derived by developing more effective diagnostic procedures, smokers would benefit far more from quitting permanently, thereby greatly reducing the likelihood that they would develop cancer.

NINE

HEREDITY AND SUSCEPTIBILITY TO LUNG CANCER

The interplay between nature and nurture that occurs in the development of disease was well expressed by Archibald Garrod in 1931,[106] though for clarity's sake his words are paraphrased here:

"In every case of every illness, two sets of factors are at work in its development: internal constitutional factors inherited by the sufferer, and external factors that fire the train."

Since lung cancer is no exception to this rule, it is important to clarify the role of inheritance in its inception.

In 1959, Sir Ronald Fisher, a brilliant statistician but unschooled in biology and a smoker, suggested that genetic predisposition to lung cancer is a more important factor than cigarette smoking, and that therefore one may smoke![107] He was right in that genetic predisposition is indeed a factor, but wrong in concluding it was more important than whether or not one smoked. He came to his fallacious conclusion because he was unaware of the decades-long time lag between starting to smoke and the development of lung cancer. Also, he did not know that pipe and cigar smokers had a smaller risk of developing lung cancer than cigarette smokers.[108]

Fisher's thesis was later taken up by Burch,[109] who also defended a second thesis advanced by Fisher. This maintained that the very people who are genetically fated to develop lung cancer are also genetically fated to take up smoking. During this period, I seemed to be alone in taking Burch's work sufficiently seriously, to publish evidence against it and against Fisher's two theses.[108]

- Smokers who quit greatly reduce their risk of lung cancer.
- There is a very close parallel between the f cigarettes smoked daily and the risk of lung cancer.[110]
- Reduction in the amount of tar inhaled reduces the risk of lung cancer.
- The earlier in life smoking becomes habitual, the higher the risk of lung cancer.
- After lagging two or three decades behind men in starting to smoke in large numbers, women were catching up to men in lung cancer incidence.
- Members of religious sects that forbid smoking have drastically lower rates of lung cancer.
- Smokers also have much higher rates of cancers of many organs other than the lung.

Merely to explain the last point, Fisher's thesis would have to be broadened to say, "those genetically fated to develop cancers of a large variety of organs are also genetically fated to take up smoking"- which makes no sense at all. The data that most clearly disprove Fisher's theses are the effect that quitting has on the lung cancer death rate. Compared to a nonsmoker, a current smoker has roughly twenty times the risk of dying from lung cancer. But ten years after quitting, the risk of lung cancer has dropped by more than 80%, to four times the risk of a nonsmoker. Twenty years after quitting, the risk has dropped over 90%, to less than twice that of a nonsmoker. These decreases in risk would not be possible if Fisher's two theses were true...[108]

The battle against the dangerous theory that genetic tendency to develop lung was all that mattered, not whether one smoked, was won[111] long before we were able to determine the function of specific genes. Since then, the discovery of genes that govern our susceptibility to the development of lung cancer has given us a deep insight into the link between nature and nurture in that context.

At this point, it should be mentioned that irrespective of the scientific topic, there is usually a small group of scientists who are ready to defend an opposing point of view- especially if it accords with that of an industry that rewards those who do its bidding. But as rewards are never publicized, one can never be certain whether or not dissention is motivated purely by honest dissention, or by greed. It is gratifying that the last time a serious objection was voiced against the evidence that smoking causes cancer was in 1986, in the book "The Smoking Scare De-Bunked" by William Whitby. This book merely reiterated the contrary opinions that mostly honest scientists had voiced in the distant past, long before the extensive evidence that smoking causes cancer was known.

In 1990, Caporaso and coworkers published their discovery of a gene that increases the risk of lung cancer, and is carried by 90% of the United States population. Since most people carry this gene, possessing it is the normal situation. But the 10% of people who do not have this gene are exceptional, in that they have an unusually low susceptibility to develop lung cancer.[112]

Also in 1990, Sellers and coworkers described a different gene that in contrast increases the risk of lung cancer in the 9.9% of people who carry it in single copy (heterozygous) form; if these people smoke, they are apt to develop lung cancer at a relatively early age. But for the 0.3% of the population who carry the gene in its full complement of two copies (the "homozygous" form), the risk of lung cancer even if they do not smoke is dramatically higher, and people in this tiny minority develop 10% of all lung cancers.[113]

Both the above reports were published in the same issue of the Journal of the National Cancer Institute (JNCI), together with an editorial by Bonney, in which he suggested that the genes discovered by the two groups were identical.[114] Because I had worked on susceptibility to lung cancer, JNCI published my letter in which I expressed concern that these findings were being misunderstood in the popular press. For an article in *The Boston Globe* had called the chance that smoking would cause cancer "a crapshoot… And what determines that is something genetic, not the level of exposure." Smokers would seize on this thought to excuse keeping on smoking, while ignoring the preceding sentence, "The more you smoke, the more likely you are to get lung cancer."[115]

I also said it was unlikely that the above two lung cancer susceptibility genes were the same. Also, except for the 0.3% of our population who inherited two copies of Seller's gene and with them a strong predisposition to develop lung cancer, smoking is the principal hazard, not genetics. I was happy that both Caporaso's and Sellers' group responded, and agreed with me on my interpretation of their data.[115]

Cancer statistics prove that for the 90% of our population who possess Caporaso's gene, smoking poses a grave risk of lung cancer. That risk is greater for the 9.9% of our population who carry Seller's gene in single copy. But the 0.3% who carry two copies of Sellers' gene are at even greater risk, and are likely to be highly susceptible to carcinogenesis by *environmental* tobacco smoke. Thus, the development of methodology that will allow smokers to be tested both for Caporaso's and for Sellers' gene seems urgently needed.

TEN

———

THERAPY OF LUNG CANCER

Before launching into the technicalities of lung cancer, it is important to address the problem that many patients with lung cancer have a feeling of guilt, that this is their punishment for disregarding advice about quitting, whether from family, friends or health warnings. They should be reassured that their guilt is minute. compared to that of the tobacco companies, which portrayed smoking as sexy, cool and harmless, and enticed their friends and role models to become ensnared by a seemingly benign but addicting drug habit, that is as hard to quit than cocaine.

The types of lung cancer likely to develop in heavy smokers are of two types- small ("oat") cell carcinoma, and squamous cell carcinoma. Other types of lung cancer, namely adenocarcinoma and large-cell carcinoma, are more common in nonsmokers and former smokers. The types of cancer that are not small cell carcinoma account for 75–80% of new cases of lung cancer, and are called "non-small-cell lung cancer".[116]

In order to decide on treatment, it is necessary to "stage" the cancer. This is done at or very soon after diagnosis. Not only is CT (computed tomography) used to locate metastases, but also such metabolic staging methods as positron-emission tomography (PET), which is superior, are used (see chapter 7).[117]

———

The international TNM staging system, with separate gradings for T (tumor size), N (lymph node involvement), and M (metastasis) has been in use since 1986. Tumors 3 cm or smaller without the presence of lymph node or any other metastases are T1 tumors (MU), while those larger but without the p8resence of metastases are T2 tumors. Stage III tumors have grown extensively at their site of origin and metastasized to local lymph nodes and other tissues. Stage III is subdivided between IIIA where the disease is viewed as operable, and stage IIIB where it is viewed as inoperable.[116] Stage IV tumors are similar to those in stage IIIB, but also have metastases to distant organs.[118]

Of patients diagnosed with non-small-cell lung cancer, only about 30% have their cancers caught at an early enough stage (I, II and IIIA) that surgery is likely to cure or benefit them. Analysis of data from two large national data bases regarding stage I and II patients who underwent surgery showed that their 5-year survival rate was 42%, while for those who did not have surgery, it was 5%.[119] Another 30% of the patients in whom lung cancer is diagnosed have locally advanced disease viewed as inoperable (stage IIIB). Of the remaining 40% of patients who have distant metastases (stage IV), the majority do not survive one year.[116] However, a 2002 study of four different combination (multi-drug) chemotherapies showed that all of these drug treatments allowed one-third of the patients to live more than one year, and are therefore worth considering.[120]

Despite the wide use of chemotherapy in patients with non-small-cell lung cancer, two recent evaluations of combination chemotherapy produced disappointing results: the mere possibility of a gain in survival of two to three months,[121] But for T1 and T2 patients who have adenocarcinoma—which does not usually occur in smokers—a study in the NEJM (New England Journal of Medicine) of April 15, 2004 reported that survival was improved significantly, when surgical excision of the cancer was followed by chemotherapy with a combination of uracil and tegafur.

Thus, chemotherapy comes into consideration after surgery of stage I and II disease, and preoperatively for patients with locally advanced but operable stage IIIA disease. For patients with inoperable stage IIIB disease, a combination of chemotherapy and radiotherapy may be proposed. For patients with stage IV disease, chemotherapy alone may be recommended.[116]

In general, chemotherapy seems to be most effective when combined with radiation treatment. Thus, a study from the Hoag Cancer Center in California reported that the 5-year survival was 17% for those who received the combined therapy, compared to 6% for those who had radiation only.[122] However, the effects of the combined therapy on long-term survival and cure rates are less certain.[116] But combination therapy with surgery and radiation (rather than with surgery and chemotherapy) is sometimes used for stage IIIA patients.[123]

In many types of cancers, the presence of certain genes can predict the response to chemotherapy. At the 14th European Cancer Conference in November 2007, Rafael Rosell reported that the degree of expression of the BRCA1 gene in the tumors of people with non-small cell lung cancer correlates inversely with their response to cisplatinum: the higher the expression of this gene (which is also associated with aggressive breast cancer), the lower the response to cisplatin-based therapy. Rosell's report[124] confirms earlier studies that obtained the same result.

While without chemotherapy half the patients with metastases survive no more than half a year, even with treatment, cures are almost unheard of. Therefore, before chemotherapy is begun, its effect on the quality of life must be considered.[116] Old age is not a contraindication to treatment, since the age of the patient does not influence either response to treatment or survival.[125]

The biomedical community is continually researching new methods of therapy. One radical approach is lung transplantation. In the years between 1988 and 1997, about 1,000 lung transplants had been done in the United States, and had produced a 5-year survival rate above 40%.[126] Further, in the 30 years between 1960 and 1990, the five year survival rate for lung cancer doubled,[127] and new avenues of research promise great progress in the future.

A very exciting advance was reported by Lynch and coauthors in the May 20, 2004 issue of NEJM, with an accompanying editorial by Mark Green. About 10% of patients with non-small-cell lung cancer have *a rapid and often dramatic shrinkage of their cancer in response to the drug gefitinib.* The reason for this response is that they have a mutation in gene EGFR (epidermal growth factor receptor) which makes their cancer cells highly vulnerable to this drug. Because of this mutation, they appear unable to make their own epidermal growth factor (EGR), which is apparently essential for their growth, and must rely on receiving it from other cells. *Gefitinib* binds to and thus blocks the receptor (binding site) for EGR on the cancer cells, thus preventing their growth.

ELEVEN

OTHER TYPES OF CANCER

Those harmless-looking wisps of tobacco smoke deposit a veritable witches brew of potent carcinogens where ever they impinge–the mouth, larynx, bronchi and lung–or where they make contact with cells after being swallowed along with saliva–the esophagus, stomach, and intestines. Also, various carcinogens are absorbed into the blood stream and cause cancer in the kidney and pancreas, while carcinogens excreted into urine are stored in the bladder, and there cause bladder cancer.

In 1976, tobacco smoke was only known to cause cancer of the lung, larynx, mouth, esophagus, kidneys, pancreas, and bladder. In the case of lung and larynx, respectively 92% and 94% of the cancers of those organs were attributable to smoking.[85] The Surgeon General's report of 2004 accepted the inclusion of cancers of 12 organs as definitely proven to be at higher risk because of smoking. However, there is also evidence that 6 additional organs are at higher risk of cancer (see below).

A 1994 study found that compared to nonsmokers, people who had smoked for 40 or more years had 2.1 times the risk of pancreatic cancer. If everyone stopped smoking, that would eliminate 27% of all pancreatic cancers that occur in the United States.[128] As compared to nonsmokers, people who smoked more than 25 years had 4.5 times the risk of contracting kidney cancer.[129]

Besides dramatically higher rates of lung cancer, smoking also produces a much smaller increase in cancer incidence for organs other than those listed in the 1976 report. In the case of stomach cancer, my abstract for a cancer meeting in 1956, in which I claimed that cigarette smoking increased its risk, was rejected for insufficient evidence. This blow to my self-esteem was probably well justified—but it took another 30 years before a Japanese study produced statistically significant data on the association between smoking and stomach cancer.[130] This link was then confirmed by several other studies.[131, 132, 133]

Regarding colorectal cancer, early studies did not take into account other risk factors, such as a diet low in fruits and vegetables and high in fat, getting too little exercise, and being overweight.[134] After correcting for these factors, ACS epidemiologists found that current smokers had a statistically significant increase in colorectal cancer. Its rates were lowest among people who had never smoked, intermediate among smokers who had quit, and highest among current smokers. The risks of dying of colorectal cancer increased, the earlier smoking was begun, the larger the number of cigarettes smoked per day, and the higher the number of years smoking continued.[135]

As for hematopoietic cancer, a large, prospective study of United States veterans concluded that smokers have 1.93 times the risk of myeloid (bone marrow) leukemia as do nonsmokers.[136] Further, a CDC study of 1993 indicted smoking as the leading cause of myeloid leukemia, and estimated that 22% of all cases in the United States are caused by smoking.

The only good news is that tobacco smoke has anti-estrogenic effects.[137] But a 1996 report identified a group of postmenopausal women who had a low concentration of an acetylation enzyme (an enzyme that attaches acetyl groups to proteins) that is needed to help detoxify tobacco carcinogens that reach the lung. For these women, smoking was reported to increase the risk of lung cancer fourfold.[138] Some studies of large groups of women failed to show that smoking increases the risk of breast cancer.[139, 140] But a very large, well-controlled study in 2004 found that active smoking increases the risk by 25% relative to women who had never smoked and also were not exposed to secondhand smoke in their homes.[141]

This study was probably published too late to be considered in the Surgeon General's report.[4] With respect to the risk of skin cancer, a 2001 study at Leiden University Medical Center in the Netherlands found that smoking 1 to 10 cigarettes a day doubled the risk, while smoking 11 to 20 cigarettes trebled it.

In June, 2002, the International Agency for Research on Cancer, a branch of the World Health Organization (WHO), reported that for types of cancer already known to be caused by smoking, the risk of cancer is even higher than previously noted. For example, it was previously thought that smokers had three or four times the risk of tumors of the bladder and of the renal pelvis as nonsmokers. Now, there was evidence that these risks are five or six times higher. The report also mentioned types of cancer newly confirmed to have risks that are increased by smoking: cancers of liver, cervix, uterus, and nasal sinus.

PET scans show that all organs of the body are potentially at risk of cancer, from absorption of cigarette smoke carcinogens from the lung into the bloodstream that feeds all organs.[142] As more powerful epidemiological studies are done, more organs affected by tobacco carcinogens are being discovered. In the Surgeon General's report of May 2004, the following organs were accepted as having been proven to be at risk from smoking.

ORGANS AT RISK OF CANCER FROM ACTIVE SMOKING[4]

- Lung and larynx
- Oral cavity, pharynx and esophagus
- Pancreas
- Kidneys

- Bladder
- Cervix
- Ovary
- Uterus
- Stomach
- Marrow, causing myeloid leukemia

The Surgeon General's report of 2004 also concluded that smokers may have a higher mortality rate from prostate cancer, but that smoking does not seem to cause breast cancer.[4] *Still, as mentioned above, there is evidence for a causal link between smoking and cancer of the skin, nasal sinuses, colon and rectum, liver, and breast* – in the latter case, especially for a specific subgroup of women.[138] Further, a possible link to prostate cancer is discussed below.

TWELVE

MALE/FEMALE DIFFERENCES IN CANCERS LINKED TO SMOKING

Differences between males and females in the development of smoking-related cancers were discussed in the Surgeon General's report of 2001, "The Health Consequences of Smoking. Women and Smoking."[87] When men and women smoke the same number of coffin nails per day, women are at higher risk of lung cancer and of bladder cancer.[143,144] One possible reason, other than differences in possession of sex hormones, is that women tend to have smaller bodies and lower body weights than men. Thus, carcinogens from a given number of cigarettes act on a smaller mass of tissue, and achieve a higher concentration in proportion to it.

Further, the study by Jyoti Patel and coworkers in JAMA of April 2004 referred to in chapter 7 reports that there are distinct differences in the DNA of lung cancer of females and males. From these differences the authors inferred that women are more susceptible than men to cancer induction by cigarette smoke.

Tobacco smoke also promotes some types of cancer that arise in female sex organs. There is consistent evidence that a woman's smoking history parallels the risk of cancer of the uterine cervix. However, this need not be understood to prove that smoking causes cervical cancer, for there is a complication: human papillomavirus (HPV) is the main risk factor for cervical cancer. Since women who smoke tend to have more sexual partners than non-smokers (perhaps because they are less averse to risks), they have a greater chance to become infected with HPV.[145] A study in Latin America showed that for women infected with HPV there is a close parallel between cervical cancer and the number of cigarettes smoked.[146] Thus, the carcinogens contributed by smoking may augment the carcinogenic effect of HPV. Precisely the same considerations apply to the association between smoking and vulvar cancer, for in this case HPV infection is also the major causative factor.[145] On the positive side, women who smoke may have a *decreased* risk of thyroid cancer and of endometrial cancer-but this effect is probably limited to women who have passed the menopause.[87]

It used to be thought that there was no definitive evidence that smoking or exposure to secondhand smoke raises the risk of breast cancer.[141] But a group of postmenopausal women who lack an enzyme that detoxifies tobacco carcinogens are at very high risk of breast cancer if they smoke (see chapter 11).[138] Although data is lacking on this issue, one might expect this group of women also to be highly sensitive to secondhand smoke.

A Harvard Medical School study concluded that compared to nonsmokers, women who smoke heavily have nearly double the risk of having an early menopause. This deficit increases, depending on how early smoking became a habit, how long smoking continued, and the lifetime total of all the cigarettes smoked.[147] Further, the Surgeon General's report of 2004 concluded that women who smoke have reduced fertility.[4] But as seen in chapter 14, smoking also does not allow male sexuality to get off Scot-free.

When a woman is pregnant, cigarette smoking has been claimed to be a much greater public health problem than use of crack.[148] Happily, public health agencies and physicians have been getting out the message that smoking during pregnancy harms the fetus, and this has had a strong positive impact. According to a CDC release in 2000, during the 10-year period of 1987 to 1996 the percentage of current smokers decreased for non-pregnant women from 27% to 24%, and for pregnant women from 16% to 12%.[149]

We used to think that babies born to smokers are more than twice as likely to have very low birth weights than those born to nonsmokers,[150] and this was recently confirmed.[151] But the true relationship between low birth weights and smoking may be smaller, because in infants born to African-Americans as compared to whites the incidence of very low birth weights is threefold higher.[152] Sadly, on average African-Americans are poorer and receive less health care than whites. Further, certain genes seem to influence the extent to which smoking reduces birth weight.[151]

There are other harmful effects of smoking during pregnancy, since it exposes the fetus to smoke. These effects include almost a doubling of the risk of spontaneous abortion,[153, 154] and increases in the risks of malformations and stillbirths,[155] and of lung disorders later in life. Animal studies have supported these findings by showing that nicotine is teratogenic (a cause of abnormal development).[156] Finally, smoking during maternity doubles the child's risk of attention deficit disorder (ADD).[157] As a result, the Food and Drug Administration (FDA) has labeled smoking during pregnancy "a substantial risk to the fetus".[158]

There are many reasons for the above deleterious effects on the fetus, for tobacco smoke contains many toxic constituents, and their individual effects on the embryo are unknown. But we do know that carbon monoxide decreases the transfer of oxygen, and that nicotine causes constriction of arteries, including those in the uterus, thereby creating the potential for hypoxia (lack of oxygen) in the fetus,[159]–thereby accentuating hypoxia caused by natural problems of pregnancy and childbirth. Finally, children born to mothers who smoke have an increased risk of smoking during adolescence, perhaps because as babies they became accustomed to the smell and taste of tobacco in their mother's breast milk, which are both quite noticeable.[160] Also, children become accustomed to the smell and taste of tobacco smoke in their home, and tend to pick up the habits of their parents.

For men, a study in California found that smokers had a 90% increase in prostate cancer risk as compared to nonsmokers. While the cause for this increase is still unknown, there are several possibilities that could explain it. First, some carcinogens from smoke inhalation are absorbed into the blood stream and thus have access to all body organs. Second, another risk factor for prostate cancer is an early age at first sexual intercourse.[161] But this is also a risk factor for cervical cancer, because it increases the chance that a woman is infected by the human papillomavirus (HPV), which is the main risk factor for this cancer. While it is conceivable that venereal transmission of HPV might also be a risk factor for men, there is no evidence in support of this possibility at present. A far more likely explanation is that early sexual activity and smoking are both common behaviors of people who are willing to take high risks.

For smokers of both sexes, even when they have finished a meal, many taste not the taste of the last food that they ate, but the taste of tobacco. More important, when a nonsmoker kisses a smoker, they can smell the ugly aroma of tobacco. Does a nonsmoker really want to marry a smoker, a person who always reeks of tobacco, fills the air with smoke, and litters the house with smelly butts? When it comes to the choice of a lifetime partner, would not a nonsmoker prefer a mate of the same ilk?

In most instances, the persons who smokes restrict their partners to the steadily decreasing minority of people who also smoke

THIRTEEN

CHRONIC OBSTRUCTIVE PULMONARY DISEASE (COPD)

COPD consists of two separate diseases: emphysema, and chronic bronchitis. In addition, chronic bronchitis includes chronic obstructive bronchitis as a separate and distinct subdivision. Each of these diseases obstructs the flow of air into the lung, and can cause irreversible damage.

In 1964 the first Surgeon General's Report on Smoking and Health singled out smoking as the most important cause of chronic bronchitis in the United States. In 1989, the updated issue of that report warned that there was now abundant evidence that cigarette smoking has "overwhelming importance" as a cause of COPD, and that if people did not smoke at all, COPD would be uncommon.[162] Presently, COPD is the sixth most common cause of death worldwide, and is the only cause of death in the United States that has become more frequent during the past two decades.[163]

The mortality of smokers from heart disease, lung cancer, and COPD is roughly in the ratio 3:1:1. People are generally unaware that death from heart disease is the principal risk of smoking, that the number of deaths from COPD is just as high as from lung cancer, and that the threat of COPD is as deadly as the threat of cancer. COPD develops in approximately 14% of white

American males who smoke, but only in 3% of nonsmokers; both figures are lower for white females and for African-Americans. However, 40% more people die from COPD than 15 years ago, and its cost in medical bills is $31 billion dollars a year.[164]

According to the American Lung Association on its internet site www.lungusa.org, COPD affects roughly 13 million Americans. It is the fourth leading cause of death in America that claims 120,000 deaths a year, of which over 80% are caused by smoking.[165] The other 20% are attributed to air pollution from many sources: burning carbon-based fuels (coal, oil, coke and charcoal, wood, crop residues), volcanic eruptions, secondhand smoke, childhood respiratory infections, genetics, and industrial pollution—most especially of workers at the places of origin of the pollution.[166]

Indeed, living in an area with a high level of air pollution just for one year has a highly significant effect in lowering the forced expiratory volume.[167]

To understand how COPD develops we need to understand how the normal lung functions. When fresh air is inhaled into the alveoli (terminal air sacs) of the lung, oxygen diffuses across their thin membranes into the blood-stream, where it is bound within red blood cells to the protein hemoglobin that they contain. The organs of the body then divide up the oxygen according to their need, and burn it to carbon dioxide. This binds to the hemoglobin molecules that are free to accept it, now that they have delivered their oxygen. When the carbon dioxide -rich blood returns to the lung, carbon dioxide diffuses back into the alveoli, from which it is expelled when the air is exhaled.[165]

Most patients with COPD have both emphysema and chronic bronchitis, but the relative proportion of these two diseases differs from patient to patient. Their characteristics are as follows:[168, 162]

Chronic bronchitis develops because minute tar particles from cigarette smoke form permanent deposits on the lining of the air passages. These deposits are especially heavy at the points of their bifurcation: the forks at which large air passages subdivide into smaller ones. Chronic bronchitis consists of an inflammation of the lining of the bronchial tubes that direct air into the upper reaches of the lung, which eventually scars these linings. People with chronic bronchitis have an overabundance of mucus secretion—so they must cough and clear their throat frequently, and are short of breath.[165] The bronchi become thickened because their cellular constituents are stimulated to divide, while the structural component cartilage degenerates. The criteria that physicians use to diagnose chronic bronchitis are, that it includes a cough that produces sputum, and that it lasts more than three months in more than two successive years.

Chronic obstructive bronchitis (obstructive bronchiolitis) occurs when the small airways of the lung become inflamed. Many of the same symptoms occur as in chronic bronchitis – increased secretion of mucus, excessive growth of goblet (mucus secreting) cells and smooth muscle cells, and inflammation with formation of fibrous tissue. But its additional feature is the collapse of the central lumen, the passageway for air, which sets the stage for the early closure of the airway during expiration.

Emphysema is derived from the Greek word meaning inflation. The type of emphysema usually found in cigarette smokers involves destruction and changes in structure of the fine subdivisions of the bronchial tree, the bronchioles. The inhaled toxins irritate the cells lining the bronchioles, and in some people this leads to their collapse and the obstruction of air flow. But in advanced emphysema the alveolar tissue tend to thin out, and the alveoli tend to stiffen in their expanded form, and to break. Also, loss of elasticity reduces the ability of alveoli to expand and to contract, reducing the volume or air that can be inhaled and exhaled. As a result, the amount of oxygen that each breath delivers to the blood is reduced, so the rate of breathing must be increased. The heavier and more long-continued the smoking, the higher is the risk of permanent damage to the lung.

COPD can be diagnosed and assessed by several methods, the most common of which is spirometry. The subject fills the lungs to maximum capacity and then exhales into a spirometer that can measure the volume expired in a given amount of time. This allows the determination of two lung characteristics, namely the forced expiratory volume in 1 second, FEV_1, and the forced vital capacity, FVC. In 1 second, a normal person can forcibly expire about 81% of all the air that can be exhaled. In contrast, a subject with severe COPD can only exhale 22% in 1 second. Both spirometry results, 81% and 22%, are the ratios of FEV_1 to FVC, which are usually called FEV_1/FVC ratios and expressed as percentages ($100 \times FEV_1/FVC$) rather than as fractions. They are still widely used to classify the stage of COPD (see Table 1).[169]

TABLE 1. GOLD CLASSIFICATION OF COPD[169]		
DISEASE STAGE		CHARACTERISTICS
0	At risk	Normal spirometer record Chronic symptoms (cough, sputum production)
I	Mild COPD	FEV_1/FVC less than 70%, FEV_1 greater than 80% of the predicted with or without chronic symptoms (see above)
II	Moderate COPD	FEV_1/FVC less than 70% FEV_1 between 30% and 80% of the predicted
III	Severe COPD	FEV_1/FVC less than 70% FEV_1 less than 30% of the predicted or FEV_1 less than 50% of the predicted plus:

| | | respiratory failure or |
| | | clinical signs of right heart failure |

Even in aging nonsmokers, the forced expiratory volume FEV_1 becomes smaller by approximately 20 ml per year. In patients with COPD, the loss in lung function averages 50 ml per year. Coupled with the other pathological changes that occur in COPD, this progressive reduction produces increasing shortness of breath in response to exertion, which can advance to respiratory failure.[170]

In the future, laboratory tests may supplement or replace respiratory tests. Ito and coworkers have reported that as the severity of COPD progresses, it is paralleled by a reduction in the activity of the enzyme histone deacetylase (HDAC).[171] Thus, its measurement could be used to determine the severity of COPD.

Physicians are beginning to assess the status of the disease in their COPD patients with a new grading system, the BODE index. This index combines four components: body-mass index, airflow obstruction, dyspnea (shortness of breath) and exercise capacity. Because it is simple to evaluate in a physician's office, BODE promises to become a valuable tool in optimizing the treatment for patients with COPD.[162]

In emphysema, the walls of the alveoli of the lung become broken down. Normally, the macrophages of the lung are white cells that protect it by disposing of foreign particles and debris. But in genetically susceptible people, the oxidants in cigarette smoke act as irritants that inactivate the HDAC enzymes of the macrophages of the lung, which normally protect their chromatin from unwinding.[172] Once the chromatin unwinds, the macrophages produce cytokines (cell signaling molecules) that draw neutrophils (a type of white cells) to the lung. These are the cells which are thought to be the main cause of the damage to alveoli, because they produce the enzyme elastase, a protein that degrades the matrix (the ground substance) of the alveoli.

But macrophages also produce proteins called "MMPs" that have some elastase activity. Thus, both macrophages and neutrophils release proteases (protein degrading enzymes), that break down the connective tissue of the lung and progressively destroy it.[164] In addition, a third type of white cells, cytotoxic T-lymphocytes (tissue-destroying thymus-derived white cells) directly attacks alveolar cells. The breakdown of alveoli is the result of the combined action of cells, enzymes and cytokines. Together these produce the changes seen in emphysema.[171],[173]

Chronic bronchitis is due to long-continued irritation of the respiratory tract. This causes the goblet cells that bound on the lumen (the open inner portion) of the air passageways to overproduce their normal secretion of mucus, and also stimulates the submucosal glands (those below the mucosa, the uppermost layer of cells) to hypersecrete.[174] These excessive secretions are part of an inflammatory process caused in the air passageways of people susceptible to contact with the tar in cigarette smoke.

Hogg and coauthors have concluded that the pathological changes responsible for the obstruction of small airways in COPD are caused by the accumulation of inflammatory cells both in the lumen of the small airways and in the walls of the lumen, which the body then attempts to repair. The result is a thickening of the wall of the airways, which narrows the airways.[175]

In COPD, chronic bronchitis and emphysema combine to a degree that varies from person to person. Overall, chronic bronchitis produces inflammation that obstructs small airways, while emphysema causes the loss of alveolar attachments. The combined result of these two pathologic processes leads to a premature closure of the airway on expiration. This results in air trapping and over-inflation of alveoli. As a result, people with COPD have the shortness of breath that is the single most characteristic symptom of COPD.[176]

People tend to dread lung cancer far more than COPD, although COPD is a very devastating disease in its own right.

The symptoms of COPD usually begin gradually in middle age after years of smoking. The first major complaints are coughing and shortness of breath. People with chronic bronchitis have recurrent coughs that brings up thick phlegm, while people with emphysema have coughs that are dry and less prominent, but their shortness of breath is more severe.

Eventually, many COPD sufferers have to fight hard for every breath. In addition, episodes of acute distress can occur. These may require visits to hospital emergency rooms, where the first line of therapy involves the use of bronchodilators.[177] Therapies that prolong life and minimize the worsening of COPD include anti-inflammation medications, supplemental oxygen,[178] and use of a multivalent pneumococcal vaccine that reduces the risk of pneumonia (see chapter 14).

Because COPD is progressive, it is essential to stop smoking, and to avoid exposure to secondhand smoke. While this will not reverse the damage, it does slow down the progression of the disease.[164] People who continue to smoke once they have developed COPD risk suffering the same fate as the 40% of people with COPD who slowly suffocate, breath by breath, over many years,[179] eventually dying from respiratory failure.[180]

In severe cases of COPD, treatments do little to improve its progression. Glucocorticoid medications are only effective if smoking is discontinued,[181] and then only slightly,[182, 183, 184] Use of the retinoid all-*trans*-retinoic acid (ATRA) seems rational, since it activates genes that promote alveolar growth, at least in the prenatal and immediate postnatal period. Two separate studies showed that in a rat model of emphysema induced by instillation of elastase, a 12-day treatment with ATRA results in significant regeneration of damaged lung tissue. But no significant positive changes were found in a carefully controlled study, when ATRA was given to 20 patients with severe emphysema for 12 weeks. But further trials to evaluate higher doses or longer treatment are likely.[185]

Since emphysema destroys the ability to breathe and to exercise, surgeons have devised operations aimed at reversing these devastating effects. The most favored operation is lung-volume reduction surgery, which aims to give the most viable parts of the lung room to expand, which patients lack since the weakened alveoli are swollen in size.[186]

Because earlier work questioned whether mortality is reduced by lung-volume reduction surgery,[187, 188] a large National Emphysema Treatment Trial was undertaken, and its results were reported in 2003. Its goals were to evaluate the effectiveness of this surgery, and to discover which patients it would benefit and which it would harm. The investigators excluded one in eight patients, because they judged them to be at much greater risk of death from surgical rather than medical treatment. Even with this exclusion, the operation failed to significantly increase the life span of all patients. However, for patients with emphysema localized mainly in the upper lobe of the lung and with a low exercise capacity, there were modest benefits in physiological function, quality of life, and length of survival.[189, 190]

The first of two reviews of the treatment of COPD emphasized the benefit of long-acting bronchodilators and inhaled corticosteroids in reducing periods of distress in patients with moderate-to-severe COPD. It also found that oxygen therapy was beneficial in a defined group of patients.[191] The second review said, "the single most important known causative factor of COPD is cigarette smoking. Smoking cessation, therefore, remains the mainstay of COPD therapy."[192] Part III of this book focuses on how to succeed in this challenging task.

While the benefits from therapy in advanced stages of COPD are presently modest, the development of new drugs to benefit patients is progressing at a rapid rate.[168] Even quitting smoking does not prevent the progression of COPD completely,[193] although the sooner one quits smoking, the better the eventual outcome. Bacterial infections worsen the symptoms of COPD, but antibiotics can eliminate them.[194]

New treatments for COPD are greatly needed, for preventing and quitting smoking is very difficult for the majority of patients. Also, other atmospheric pollutants need to be minimized or eliminated altogether. Once the genes have been identified which can explain why only a minority of smokers are predisposed to develop COPD, then these genes will provide novel targets for therapy. Finally, more basic research on COPD is needed,[195] to aid the logical development of new therapies.[168]

Since COPD reduces the lung's ability to fight against infections, smokers also have an increased death rate from pneumonia and influenza.[196] Therefore, it is not surprising that Richard Peto and coworkers have reported that smoking greatly increases the risk that infections with tuberculosis bacteria will escape the control of the immune system and cause active tuberculosis. This explains why in India, where TB is still widespread, men who smoke are approximately four times as likely to die from TB as nonsmokers. Worldwide, TB infects 1 billion people, and it kills about 1.0 million people in Asia, 400,000 in Africa, and 100,000 in the Americas and Europe. At least half of these TB deaths are attributed to smoking.[197]

The most useful resource for information for COPD sufferers is the American Lung Association (ALA), which can be reached at its internet site, by phone, or by letter (see Appendix). The ALA website gives detailed data on COPD, and includes an interactive "COPD Lung Profiler." This program asks patients with COPD (or their physicians) to answer specific questions, and the answers produce responses with information on choosing the most effective treatment. There are also tips on how to quit smoking.

In addition, a search for "COPD" at the National Institutes of Health site www.nim.nih.gov/medlineplus gives very useful information. A free brochure on COPD is available from the NHLBI Health Information Center, P.O. Box 30105, Bethesda,

MD 20824-0105 (301-592-8573), and a 2003 report on COPD can be purchased from the Harvard Health Publications of Harvard Medical School.

A Google search for "COPD" is also very productive. Many COPD sites carry wonderful human stories written by victims of COPD, who have found ways to live full and satisfying lives despite their disease. Typical is the story of an easy rider on the web site "Living with COPD." This 50-year old man carries an oxygen tank when he rides his motor cycle. He believes that to live with COPD, "one must *accept, adapt, and adjust*." While he knows he cannot overcome the disease itself, he has found a response to it that works for him – and may also work for those for whom it is too late to accept the message of his book, which is to quit smoking.

FOURTEEN

OTHER HEALTH EFFECTS

The only vigorous sport in which smoking is allowed in baseball–though Babe Ruth paid dearly for his love of tobacco. In other sports, such as football, soccer, hockey, track, swimming or basketball, coaches make "no smoking" a condition for being on their teams, for smoking is incompatible with the achievement of top physical fitness. Indeed, smoking can produce mild airway obstruction even in adolescents (see chapter 23).

Prolonged contact with tobacco leaves causes green tobacco sickness, with symptoms of nausea, vomiting, and dizziness. Among the migrant workers picking tobacco in North Carolina in 1999, 41% contracted green tobacco sickness,[198] and many cases of such poisoning have also been reported from Mexico: even unlit, tobacco is toxic. Also, tobacco growing requires heavy use of pesticides, and traces of their residues remain on tobacco leaves.[199]

Endotoxin is a bacterial toxin that can cause chronic bronchitis. According to a 1999 article by Jeffrey Hasday of the University of Maryland, nearly half a milligram of endotoxin
is present in every pack of cigarettes.

Tobacco Mosaic Virus (TMV) is a virus that commonly infects tobacco plants. While it is unknown whether it has any effect on human beings, it seems preferable to steer clear of viruses.

Pneumonia, most commonly caused by the invasive bacterium *Streptococcus pneumoniae*, is over four times as common in smokers as in nonsmokers, and smoking is the strongest risk factor for catching pneumonia.[200] However, it is only smokers who have already developed COPD who are at risk.[4] The probable reason is that the accumulation of tobacco tar particles in the lung reduces the number and mobility of phagocytes (natural defense cells) that protect the lung from infection. Pneumonia is a disease that causes approximately 500,000 hospitalizations and 40,000 deaths per year in the United States. Therefore, experts in infectious diseases have urged physicians to redouble their efforts to promote smoking cessation.[201] The link between smoking and pneumonia was graphically demonstrated, when 9 of the 19 U.S. soldiers who developed severe pneumonia in Iraq in a brief period during the fall of 2003 had started to smoke recently.[202] The fact that smoking is most prevalent in families with low income and that these families have less intensive health care than families with high income is an important reason why smoking is more common in families with a low income. A letter in the March 3, 2004 issue of JAMA suggests that smokers–especially those over 65 years old – are far more liable to catch pneumonia than nonsmokers, and should be protected against it by inoculation with a polyvalent pneumococcal vaccine.

Loss of teeth results mostly from periodontal (gum) disease–and smoking is a serious risk factor for both. Periodontitis is advanced gum disease that destroys the tissue and bone that surround the teeth, and is generally caused by bacteria that find shelter in plaque buildup. According to a CDC study headed by Scott Tornar published in 2000, the risk of total loss of teeth for current smokers is nearly four times as high as for nonsmokers. The ill effects of tobacco smoke on the teeth are so severe, that merely exposing children to tobacco smoke in their home doubles their risk of developing dental caries.[203]

Loss of Hearing is another of the risks of smoking. In 1998, a carefully executed study by Karen Cruickshanks and coworkers found that smokers were 70% more likely to suffer hearing loss than nonsmokers. Household members of smokers were also more likely to lose their hearing.[204]

Age-related macular degeneration consists of progressive damage to the retina that impairs vision and can lead to blindness. In two different studies reported in the same issue of JAMA in 1996, the risk for developing this disease was found to be between 2.4[205] and 2.5[206] times as high for smokers of either sex as compared to nonsmokers. To date there are no proven medical interventions that prevent or delay the progression of this dreaded disease of advanced old age.[207]

Deterioration in neuromuscular function can also be the end result of smoking. In their large and well-controlled study of 1994, Nelson and coworkers found that smokers were deficient in agility, strength, and integrative physical function. Although this study was limited to women, other data indicate that that the situation for men is similar. Smoking advances the deterioration of physical performance of elderly smokers by roughly five years beyond their actual age. The higher the total number of cigarettes smoked, the greater the deterioration. A possible reason for this decline is that nicotine directly affects the central nervous system.[208]

As for the overall loss of life from all causes, according to the Surgeon General's Report of 2001 on "Women and Smoking," for every woman who died from a cause connected with smoking, an average of 14 years of life are lost.[87] This may be the real context for the years of life lost that are reported in the Surgeon General's Report of 2004.[4] The situation is even worse for male smokers.[209]

Because of the close agreement between the years of physical performance that smoking steals and the overall loss of life, one would expect a variety of age-related changes to occur at much earlier ages in smokers. Some of these changes are listed below.

Wrinkling of skin due to loss of skin elasticity is so pronounced in old smokers that it produces features that clinicians call "smoker's face."[210] It is most unattractive.[211]

Early loss of male sexuality leading to sexual impotence is yet another possibility for smokers. Men who smoke have been reported to be almost twice as likely to develop erectile dysfunction as nonsmokers,[212] but the Surgeon General's Report of 2004 did not find this evidence persuasive.[4] Still, many men have quit smoking, motivated by wanting to preserve their sex lives.[213] But it should be noted that the adverse effects of obesity are similar to some of the health effects of smoking.

Rupturing of the abdominal aorta is the thirteenth most frequent cause of death in the U.S. A 2001 paper by Tony Dajer of New York University's Downtown Hospital concludes that smokers have between 4 and 8 times a nonsmoker's risk of this deadly event. Each cigarette produces a cycle of contraction due to nicotine infusion, followed by relaxation as nicotine fades from the blood stream. This additional work for arteries, repeated thousands of times, increases the risk of rupturing.

Inflammatory bowel disease is also more likely in smokers than in nonsmokers.[214]

Wound healing is delayed by smoking. Surgeons believe that the effect of smoking is sufficiently strong, that they tend to advise smokers to stop smoking prior to surgery.[215]

Absences from work are more frequent for smokers. A study from Australia found that male smokers are 66% more absent from work than male nonsmokers. The corresponding differential for females is only 23%.

Appetite reduction is one of the physiological effects of nicotine that causes an inverse relationship between smoking and body weight.[216] Smoking appears to lower the "set point" of body weight; when smoking stops, that set point returns to normal,[217] and ex-smokers may gain ten pounds. But if their weight increases beyond this arbitrary limit, ex-smokers should make a determined effort to keep their weight down. The ill effects of overweight are considerable and should not be underestimated.

Changes in brain function, such as impairment of cognitive function, are associated with smoking. When men averaging 75 years of age were given tests of mental status over a 3-year period, smokers made 20% more errors than men who had never smoked.[218]

Development of Alzheimer's disease may be twice as frequent in smokers as in nonsmokers. But the mechanism of this disease is not clear, irrespective of whether it occurs in nonsmokers or in smokers.[219]

Allergy to tobacco smoke can be so severe that it can be fatal. According to the New York Times of February 25, 2004, the U.S. Supreme Court upheld the award of $1.4 million to the widow of a physician who died on a plane from an acute allergic reaction to tobacco smoke. The widow had sued the airline for failing to move her husband away from smokers.

At life's end many smokers face disability and helplessness. This is one of the messages of the book of 2003 by Frank Sloan and coauthors entitled "The Smoking Puzzle: Information, Risk Perception, and Choice." The message that the end of life may not come quickly to smokers, but might entail a long period of disability and helplessness, seems to worry some smokers sufficiently that it can motivate them to quit.

FIFTEEN

ACCIDENTAL DEATHS AND INJURIES

Cigarette smoking is one of the many causes of fires, car accidents, and also random types of accidents.

Fires kill their victims in an excruciatingly painful way. I recall stopping on a highway at the sight of a house engulfed in flames on my way to a ski vacation in Maine. I got out to look at the fire, but the heat was so incredibly intense, that I could not get close to it. It was scary.

Newspapers frequently report stories of people killed because they fell asleep while smoking in bed, which can allow a lighted cigarette to roll under the bed and set it ablaze. This, for instance, was how the 43 year old Rev. Paul O'Brien was killed on November 8, 1999, while visiting a Catholic shrine in Massachusetts. The incident was reported in the press, because the fire also destroyed a historic building at that site.[220]

Each year, roughly 1,000 Americans die in fires ignited by cigarettes.[221] But smoking causes vastly more fires, for the rate of *injury* of people involved in fires is only 6 100 fires, which is equivalent to one injury for every 17 fires.[222] Intoxication, as confirmed by a blood alcohol level above 22 mmol/L, has been shown to be a factor in starting the blaze in approximately half of all residential fires.[223] These data leave no doubt that the combination of smoking and drinking in bed can have deadly consequences. Further, fires result in 1.4 million injuries a year in the United States,[224] and a significant number of these are started by smoldering cigarettes.

To counteract the danger of fires started inadvertently by burning cigarettes, cigarette manufacturers have experimented with designs for less hazardous cigarettes: wrapping the tobacco in paper with banded "speed bumps" reduces its porosity and thereby slows its burning. Because the tobacco industry has been slow to utilize this and other more effective improvements, the late Congressman Joseph Moakley of Massachusetts supported a Federal bill that would require manufacturers to produce safe cigarettes.[221] As of 2004, only New York City had passed a law that requires the sale of self-extinguishing cigarettes (see chapter 20). Contributions from tobacco lobbyists to key legislators are highly effective in derailing such vital bills.

Car accidents are 50% more likely for smokers than for non-smokers.[225] The reasons for this include "the act of smoking," which can involve fumbling, be it to find a pack, to light a cigarette, or to brush ashes off clothing. But it can also involve a premature deterioration in physical coordination and understanding. Still, elderly drivers can adopt the preventive strategy of avoiding driving under challenging conditions, such as at night, in heavy traffic, or in inclement weather.

Various other accidents are also more common for smokers than for nonsmokers. Some of the reasons for such accidents are the same as those mentioned above. Another reason is that smoking can eventually cause a host of medical conditions, some of which increase the risk of accidents.[225]

SIXTEEN

NICOTINE ADDICTION

The 1988 Surgeon General's report on the Health Consequences of Smoking was entitled "Nicotine Addiction." This 639-page report documented its conclusions with a vast amount of evidence-which tobacco companies immediately tried to refute. The major conclusions were as follows.[28]

- Cigarettes and other forms of tobacco are addicting, and the drug in tobacco that causes addiction is nicotine.

- The mechanisms of tobacco addiction are similar to those that cause addiction to drugs such as heroin and cocaine.

The 1988 report lists the three most important criteria that indicate that a drug is addictive as follows:

1. It causes highly controlled (regulated) or compulsive use.

2. It has psychoactive effects–it is capable of altering mood, tension or behavior.

3. Its use reinforces (makes more desirable) continued use.

But the report also listed additional criteria for addictive behavior: it generally involves a constant pattern of drug use that continues despite harmful effects, there are recurrent cravings for the drug, and an attempt to quit is often followed by a relapse.

Further, addictive drugs often produce pleasant (euphoric) effects as well as tolerance to them. Unfortunately, nicotine qualifies as an addictive drug on all these counts.

In 1988, Surgeon General Everett Koop warned the 51 million smokers in the United States that tobacco products are as addictive as cocaine or heroin.[226] Regarding the claim that nicotine is *more* addictive than cocaine, a 1991 report concluded that while both drugs are highly addicting, nicotine is not more addictive than cocaine. But in case of both drugs, their patterns of use and the development of addiction to them was strongly influenced by their availability, price, regulation, and by social pressures.[227]

Nicotine and cocaine cause similar changes in brain chemistry that produce addiction. When studied in rats, both drugs produce patterns of brain activation, some of which are specific for each drug, while others overlap.[228] Nicotine snares smokers twice: not only does it raise the level of dopamine, a chemical linked to addictive behavior, but it also inhibits the enzyme that destroys dopamine, thereby prolonging nicotine's grip on the smoker.[229]

Recent research shows that drugs are addicting because they hijack memory and motivation, as well as pleasure pathways. More than two months after undergoing detox, the dopamine system of a former abuser has not yet recovered to normal levels.[230] The real question is, how we can use our new-found knowledge of addiction to treat compulsive behaviors. That was the focus of an article by Eric Nestler and Robert Malenka in the Scientific American of March, 2004,[231] and this is also a theme in Part III of this book.

SEVENTEEN

MENTAL DIFFICULTIES AND SMOKING

The facts on the link between mental problems and smoking are so startling that it is essential to start by saying that it is unlikely that there is any human being alive today, who does not have some mental problems. These include worries small and large, anxieties, fears, suspicions, confusion, sadness, grief, hopelessness, depression, and so on. All these problems can be perfectly normal; but if they deepen and are frequent or even constant, then they might constitute mental illness. However, the boundary line between normal and abnormal feelings and behavior needs to be drawn by a psychiatrist, not by self-diagnosis.

If we keep the great difficulty in drawing that line firmly in mind, we shall be better prepared to face the findings of a study at the Harvard School of Public Health in 2000, which otherwise may greatly disturb smokers. It concluded that mentally ill people smoke nearly half (44%) of the cigarettes marketed in the United States, and that the mentally ill are about twice as likely to smoke as other people, although they have substantial quit rates. This study employed standard psychiatric definitions of common mental illness, such as major depression, bipolar disorder, phobias, anxiety and conduct disorders, schizophrenia, alcohol abuse and dependence, and antisocial personality.[232]

The authors of the above study commented that mentally ill smokers are equally at high risk of smoking-related deaths as are all smokers. Further, smoking complicates the treatment of some mental disorders by decreasing the blood levels of anti-psychotic drugs. Another study concluded in 2000 that cigarette smoking is linked to anxiety disorders during adolescence and early adulthood, and may increase their risk.[233] But it seems more likely that the opposite explanation holds, namely that people who are anxious choose to smoke to relieve their anxiety. Irrespective of which explanation is correct, the fact is that taking up smoking makes it more likely that depression,[234] panic attacks,[235] or schizophrenia[236] may develop later.

A small study has shown that nicotine, administered through a skin patch, can help children with attention deficit disorder to focus sufficiently, to block distractions. This may explain why people on medication for psychoses tend to crave the nicotine that smoking delivers. However, researchers investigating the possible benefits of nicotine patches in people who have early symptoms of Alzheimer's warn that healthy people should not consider using nicotine even in patch form, for it has been difficult to show reliably that any agent enhances normal performance.[237]

The authoritative Epidemiologic Catchment Area (ECA) survey of 1997 provided data for the conclusion that the frequent occurrence of either major depression or of nicotine dependence predicts a high occurrence rate of the other. Since there is a genetic component to the predisposition to develop major depression, and since this is tied to a predisposition to nicotine dependence, it follows that addiction to nicotine must also have a genetic link. This has been confirmed by the publication of a Swedish study of 25,000 same-sex twins followed since 1986, which showed that some people do indeed have a strong genetic predisposition for tobacco use.

The above facts are disturbing, for once we have accepted these dismal data to be factual–and unfortunately, that is what they are—we may view smokers in a new light. It is disconcerting to know that a little under half of all smokers may have serious underlying problems, which if not apparent at present may surface at some future time.

EIGHTEEN

CIGARS, PIPES, SNUFF, CHEWING TOBACCO, AND MORE

In Henry Thoreau's day, cigarettes were not yet available, so smokers had to content themselves with pipes, cigars, and chewing tobacco. Never one to mince his words, Thoreau said in his book *Cape Cod*,[238] "I was glad... to have left behind me for a season the bar-rooms of Massachusetts, where the full-grown are not weaned from savage and filthy habits–still sucking a cigar."

In 1920, ordinary cigars cost 5 cents,[239] but in 2004 they cost about $3, and one could pay $20 for a fine Cuban cigar. Winston Churchill and by Celtics coach Red Auerbach used cigars, or stogies as they are also called, as their trademark. Because of their expense, they were regarded as status symbols and smoked chiefly by well-heeled men. In the late twentieth century, cigar smoking declined. But since 1993, thanks to an aggressive advertising campaign by the tobacco industry, cigar use has increased more than 50%. While it has continued to decline in males over 65, most new cigar smokers have been young men aged 18 to 24, and surprisingly, women.[240]

In the June 2005 issue of the journal *Addiction*, researchers led by Carrie Carpenter reported that tobacco companies studied why women smoked, and then designed "slim" and "light" brands, which appealed to women's desire to appear thin, glamorous and healthy. The researchers found that women are very concerned not to hurt their families by damaging their health. So they manage to compromise by smoking low-tar brands.

Cigarettes are generally fairly uniform in size, contain under 1 gram of tobacco, and take less than 10 minutes to smoke. In contrast, cigars vary widely in size and shape. Large cigars typically contain 5 to 17 grams of tobacco, and take on hour or two to smoke. Since smoke from both cigarettes and cigars derives chiefly from tobacco, it contains very similar toxic substances and carcinogens. As a result, the health risks are equally dependent on the frequency of use, the amount of tobacco smoked each time, and the depth of inhalation.[240]

Most cigarette smokers smoke daily and inhale. In contrast, perhaps three-quarters of cigar smokers smoke only occasionally, and the majority do not inhale. But even so, both cigarette and cigar smokers directly expose their lips, mouth, tongue, throat, and larynx to tobacco smoke and its carcinogens. Further, even when smoke is not consciously inhaled, the act of drawing on lighted tobacco still insures that some smoke is sucked into the upper reaches of the lung. In addition, the place where smoke first contacts the body is the mouth, and the saliva that coats its surfaces absorbs its constituents. Saliva then transfers carcinogens to the tissues of the mouth, and after it is swallowed, to the esophagus and then to the entire GI tract.[240] Consequently, the risks of cigar smoking are only somewhat less severe than those of cigarette smoking.

In June, 1998, the American Cancer Society held a conference on the health risks of cigars. Its findings were as follows:[241]

1. Rates of cigar smoking are rising among both adults and adolescents.

2. Smoking cigars instead of cigarettes does not reduce the risk of nicotine addiction.

3. As the number of cigars smoked and the amount of smoke inhaled increases, the risk of death related to cigar smoking approaches that of cigarette smoking.

4. Cigar smoke contains higher concentrations of toxic and carcinogenic compounds than cigarette smoke and is a major source of indoor air pollution where cigars are smoked.

In the year 2000, ACS completed a study of cigar smoking that included 127,000 United States male cigar smokers. Compared to nonsmokers, cigar smokers incurred the following risks:[242]

- Their lung cancer risk is fivefold higher than for nonsmokers.

- For men who smoke 3 or more cigars a day, their risk is eightfold.

- For men who inhale the smoke, the risk is elevenfold.

- Their risk of cancer of the larynx is tenfold higher.

- Their risk of cancer of the oral cavity is fourfold higher.

- For current cigar smokers who inhale, the risk of pancreatic cancer is 2.7-fold higher, and of bladder cancer 3.6-fold higher.

The nicotine content of cigarettes averages approximately 8 mg, but popular brands of cigars contain between 100 and 200 mg of nicotine, and some even contain 400 mg. Because so many cigar smokers do not smoke daily, the percentage who becomes addicted is somewhat smaller than in the case of cigarette smokers. But cigar smokers are twice as likely to take up cigarette smoking, as people who have never smoked cigars.[240]

Similar to cigarette smokers, cigar smokers have increased risks of heart disease (see chapter 5) and of COPD (see chapter 13). As for cigarette smokers, there are many benefits to quitting. Soon after quitting, blood pressure, pulse rate, and breathing patterns begin to return to normal. With time, the risks of cancer,[239] heart disease and COPD begin to decline, and there is an improvement in the quality of life–not only for the former smokers, but also for their families and friends. The National Cancer Institute published a monograph on cigars in 1998 that gives further detailed information on their health effects.

Pipes were very popular among English college students in the early 1940's, when I was a student at Cambridge University. Not to be left out, I started to smoke a pipe, but quit half a year later, when I joined a religious society that disapproved not only of smoking but alas, of other frivolous pursuits. At the time, the public did not know that there could be serious consequences to smoking a pipe. But years later, the headmaster of the school I had attended in Yorkshire developed lung cancer and subsequently died. I can still see him walking on the front lawn of his house with his two Irish setters, always puffing on a pipe that he held rakishly between clenched teeth. He certainly was addicted. There is a sad end to this story. He eventually developed lung cancer, and until he died, he lived with the vice-principal and his wife close to the school. Not until many years later was a firm connection between pipe smoking and lung cancer established.

Even as late as 1976, our knowledge of the mortality ratios (the risk a smoker has of dying of a particular type of cancer, relative to the risk that a nonsmoker has to die of that cancer) was still quite limited for male pipe smokers:[85]

MORTALITY RATIOS OF PIPE SMOKERS FOR CERTAIN CANCERS	
TYPE OF CANCER	MORTALITY RATIO
Lung cancer	4.2
Laryngeal cancer	3.5
Oral cancer	3.3
Esophageal cancer	2.7

Both the Surgeon General's reports and publicity campaigns by the American Cancer Society focused media attention on the health effects of smoking a pipe, and thereby helped to outmode pipe smoking. Between 1955 and 1997, the sale of pipe tobacco declined from 59 to 7 million pounds; by 1998, only about 1% of Americans still smoked pipes.[243] Now that even Castro has long died,[244] pipe smoking has also died—and public health workers are happy to serve as its pallbearers.

Bidis are a form of cigarette used for centuries in India. They are about half the size of an ordinary cigarette, hand-rolled with a greenish-brown leaf, and filled with tobacco flakes. Though they contain less tobacco than a conventional cigarette, Samira Asma of CDC (Centers for Disease Control) says that bidis produce three times as much nicotine and five times as much tar. Nationwide, 2% to 5% of teens have lighted up a bidi at least once. Bidis come in flavors such as grape, chocolate, and root beer- a marketing strategy apparently aimed directly at youths. While they seem harmless, CDC characterizes them as "dangerous mini-cigarettes with a maxi-punch," and researchers from the National Institute of Drug Abuse (NIDA) agree.[245]

Kreteks represent another import, which comes mainly from Indonesia. As of 2005, Philip Morris was trying to buy a local tobacco company that manufactures these pungent cigarettes, which contain about 60% tobacco and 40% ground cloves. They deliver more tar than ordinary cigarettes, and are just as addictive.[246] They contain eugenol (the active ingredient of cloves) that can cause severe lung injury in susceptible persons who have a respiratory infection.[247]

Student crazes have a long and hallowed tradition. In the 1960s, it was "pot." Later, and happily localized at UCLA in Los Angeles, it was smoking the hookah, the ancient Middle Eastern water pipe. It seems to have remained localize4d there, or even to have died out.[248]

Chewing tobacco and snuff are forms of smokeless tobacco, and both increase the risk of cancer of the mouth, as documented in the 1995 publication "Spit Tobacco and Youth," published by the Department of Health and Human Services (HHS). According to a 1998 release from the National Cancer Institute, smokeless tobacco contains 28 carcinogens, of which nitrosamines are the most harmful. Nitrosamines are formed during the curing, fermenting, and aging of tobacco, and result in levels 100 times higher than those of other nitrosamines that are legally permitted to be present in bacon or beer. Additional carcinogens include arsenic, benzopyrene, and tiny amounts of radioactive polonium-210. As a result, users of smokeless tobacco have increased risks of cancer of the mouth, throat, larynx, and esophagus.[249] Some rural Indians have long chewed betel nuts mixed with a little lime and rolled in tobacco leaf, and this habit has proven to be a potent producer of cancer of the mouth.

Because the number of smokeless tobacco users is vastly less than the number of cigarette smokers, it is difficult to obtain accurate statistical data on cancer incidence. However, studies from areas of Asia where the habit of chewing tobacco is common has shown that people who chew quids that contain tobacco have a much higher incidence of oral cancer than those who chew quids that do not contain tobacco. In areas where quids do contain tobacco, the most common type of cancer is cancer of the mouth.[250]

As for the use of snuff, a study in North Carolina found that women snuff users develop cancer at over four times the rate of women who do not use any form of tobacco. Although not enough men were studied to perform a valid comparison, it is likely that similar statistics apply to men.

Traditionally, many professional baseball players and rodeo performers used to chew tobacco. A 1988 survey found 36% of major-league baseball players used smokeless tobacco, 31% were past users who had quit, and 33% reported that they had never used it.[251] Regrettably, the use of spit tobacco is presently on use by young Southerners. Users who munch on 8 to 10 chews a day, each of about one-quarter of an ounce of tobacco, receive a dose of nicotine equal to that of a heavy smoker (30 to 40 cigarettes daily), and have equivalent blood levels of nicotine. Because nicotine is addicting irrespective of its mode of absorption into the body, users who quit chewing tobacco experience the same withdrawal symptoms as cigarette smokers who quit.[252] The most famous baseball player of all time, Babe Ruth, was a heavy snuff dipper, tobacco chewer, and cigar smoker[252]- and sadly, died of throat cancer at age 53.

The US Smokeless Tobacco company, which makes snuff, pitches its products as a safer option for those who can't quit smoking. But Gregory Connolly, who heads the Tobacco Control Program for the state of Massachusetts, was quoted in the Boston Globe of June 5, 2002 as saying, while snuff users have a much lower risk of heart disease or lung cancer than smokers, they do have the same high risk of mouth cancer, so "the last thing we want is kids taking up these products because they think they are safe."

There are many resources available on this topic. The American Cancer Society (800-ACS-2345) has a free pamphlet, "Quitting Spitting" on this topic, and other pamphlets with tips for smokeless tobacco users who want to quit. The American Lung Association (800-586-4872) provides referrals to local smoke-less tobacco cessation programs, and their Nicotine Anonymous World Service (415-750-0328) has a 12-step program for quitting. Also, the federal Office on Smoking and Health (770-488-5705) provides brochures on tobacco, its health effects, and on quitting.

The bottom line is, there is no such thing as the safe use of a tobacco product of any type- not even smokeless tobacco.

NINETEEN

———

ENVIRONMENTAL TOBACCO SMOKE (SECONDHAND SMOKE)

In 1986, the United States Surgeon General issued a detailed report on "The Health Consequences of Involuntary Smoking," which marshaled all the evidence then available on secondhand smoke,[27] and was updated in the National Cancer Institute's "Smoking and Tobacco Control Monograph no. 10" of 1999. In 2001, the landmark Surgeon General's report on "Women and Smoking" definitively summarized the many relevant studies performed up to that time.[87] By then, the evidence for the harmful consequences of the exposure of nonsmokers to "passive exposure", "secondhand smoke", or else "Environmental Tobacco Smoke" (ETS), was so ironclad, that the Tobacco Industry and its lobbyists toned down and then abandoned their earlier campaign, to discredit all the evidence for it.

The reason why all review articles did not agree that exposure to ETS is harmful was carefully researched in 1998 by Deborah Barnes, a Public Health specialist at the University of California, and coauthor Lisa Bero. After examining over 100 reviews on the effects of ETS, they found that nearly two-thirds concluded that it causes serious health effects. But of the one-third of reviews which found that ETS had no harmful effects, *nearly three-quarters (74%) were written by authors affiliated with the tobacco indus-*

try. The odds that a study *failed to find harmful effects were 88 times higher if its author (or authors) had a gainful connection to the tobacco industry,* than if there was no such connection.[253] In his article "Payola Profs" in the July 2005 issue of Reader's Digest, Michael Crowley confirmed that medical school professors were willing to prostitute themselves professionally and conclude falsely that ETS is innocuous: during the 1990s thirteen scientists were secretly paid over $150,000 for letters and articles disputing the dangers of secondhand smoke.

These startling results document what is, unfortunately, a general phenomenon for all types of research. It has long been common knowledge that if researchers have a financial connection to a firm that stands to gain or lose from their research, this can affect the way data are included or excluded from their study, how the data are analyzed, and how the results are interpreted. For instance, in May 2004, Pfizer was fined $430 million for the promotion of the drug neurontin for non-approved uses, in which they succeeded by such ruses as hiring physicians as consultants in clinical trials for these uses.[254]

For this reason, today first rate scientific and medical journals insist that authors disclose any financial connection that bears on the subject matter of their manuscript at the time that it is submitted for publication. This is not an entirely satisfactory solution, for financial connections are relegated to footnotes set in small print, and tend to escape the notice of many readers. A more effective policy would be to acknowledge all financial connections with for-profit organizations within a specified number of past years, such as two years, in a bracket immediately following that author's name. Since there is strong evidence that in some cases such connections have slanted either the selection of data or their interpretation, or both, such a policy would highlight gainful connections, and thus provide valuable insight that readers could use to judge the credibility of the report.

Regarding the effect of ETS on the risk of lung cancer, nonsmokers can experience exposure to ETS in three different places: the home, the workplace, and smoke-filled public rooms or spaces. In all three environments, the Surgeon General's Report of 2001 found that there was a trend for the risk to increase significantly with increase in the intensity of the smoke pollution experienced, and with the total time over which ETS had to be inhaled. Some (but not all) studies found that the risk was highest, if exposure began during childhood.[87]

The effect of ETS exposure in the home is difficult to summarize, because the various available studies differ in important details. It may be more meaningful to present the details of one carefully executed study that is representative of many others. The study of Fontham and colleagues of 1994 meets these requirements.[255]

Their five-year multi-center study in the United States was controlled for age, race, study area, education, intake of fruits and vegetables, vitamin supplements, dietary cholesterol, family history, and employment. It found that women nonsmokers who lived with a spouse who smoked had an approximately 30% higher risk of contracting lung cancer. For women nonsmokers whose husbands smoked at the highest level, the excess risk was 80%.

The first large multi-center study of ETS in Europe was published by Boffetta and coworkers in 1998. Among women who were or had been married, husbands who smoked increased the risk that their nonsmoking wives would contract lung cancer by 20%. But at the highest exposure level, computed as hours per day multiplied by the years of exposure, the excess risk for wives was 70%.[256]

A pooled analysis of two large studies was published in 2003 by Paul Brennan and others of the International Agency for Cancer Research, and encompassed data from the United States and seven European countries. The analysis concluded that long-term exposure to ETS increased the risk of lung cancer of nonsmokers by 27%. Similar results were obtained for ETS exposure in various social settings and for exposure to combined sources of ETS.[257]

Regarding exposure to ETS in the workplace, the 1991 report by the National Institute for Occupational Safety and Health on this topic summarized data for 21 separate studies. The report concluded that long-continued ETS increased the risk of lung cancer of nonsmokers by 30%. There was a dose-response effect, and ETS was most harmful when exposure began as a child.[258]

As for exposure to tobacco smoke elsewhere than at home or in the workplace, it used to be very hard to avoid smoke-filled public spaces. Thanks to the passage of laws against ETS, smoke-filled rooms have become increasingly confined to private spaces, such as the homes of smokers. Smokers have been exiled from their place of work to the street, and nowadays they are even asked to move away from the entrance of their buildings, which adds to their discomfort and feeling of isolation.[259]

ETS also increases the risk of chronic heart disease. The 2001 Surgeon General's Report on Women and Smoking cites 16 separate investigations and 10 reviews on this topic undertaken between 1984 and 1999, that address both sexes. The conclusion arrived at is that nonsmokers with long-term exposure to ETS suffer a 30% increase in their risk of developing coronary heart disease.[87]

There is convincing evidence which explains why nonsmokers exposed to ETS have an increased risk of chronic cardiac events, as distinct from its acute effects that are discussed below. ETS reduces the body's ability to deliver oxygen to the heart, and thereby reduces exercise capability. ETS also increases platelet activity (which makes the formation of blood clots more likely), and accelerates formation of atherosclerotic lesions.[260] A study focused on the rate of progression of atherosclerosis concluded that exposure of nonsmokers to ETS increased atherosclerosis by 20%.[261]

ETS can be acutely dangerous to people who have existing heart disease. In 2001, an editorial in *JAMA* was entitled "Even a little secondhand smoke is dangerous."[262] Further, the CDC (Centers for Disease Control and Prevention) disclosed in a commentary to a study published in the *British Medical Journal* of April 24, 2004, that for people with heart problems, as little as 30 minutes of exposure to ETS can have a serious and even lethal effect. The explanation is that that ETS rapidly increases the tendency of blood to clot–and this could lead to acute reactions in people whose arteries have narrowed and contain potentially dangerous plaques.

The smoking gun that connects ETS to lung cancer is provided by laboratory studies which prove that people exposed to ETS absorb a carcinogen present exclusively in tobacco smoke. It is a complex molecule called NNAL[263] that includes the potent carcinogen nitrosamine as one of its constituents. NNAL is detected by measuring its breakdown products that appear in the urine of nonsmokers after exposure to ETS.[264, 265]

Regarding the effect of ETS on reproduction, a 1988 study found a positive dose-response relationship between the levels of smoking-related DNA damage in the placenta, and the extent of maternal exposure to cigarette smoke during pregnancy.[266] But this result cannot yet be interpreted to signify significant harm to the fetus. More relevantly, the Surgeon General's Report of 2001 concludes that"infants born to women who are exposed to ETS during pregnancy may have a small decrement in birth weight and a slightly increased risk for intrauterine growth retardation compared with infants born to women who are not exposed; both effects are quite variable across studies."[87] Since these issues are still unsettled, NIH (the National Institute of Health) recently funded a study to investigate the lifelong consequences of fetal exposure to tobacco smoke.

Sensitivities and allergies to ETS pose a major problem for those who suffer from them. Asthma is the most common chronic lung disease in children, and affects approximately 2 million children in the United States. Measurement of a tobacco-specific compound (cotinine) in children with asthma showed that their exposure to ETS paralleled acute exacerbation of their asthma, as witnessed by reduced lung function and an increased number of visits to hospital emergency rooms for treatment of acute asthma. The authors who reported these results concluded that children with asthma should be strenuously guarded from exposure to ETS.[267]

Adults can be highly sensitive to ETS. My friend Gordon Wilson, an MIT professor, was so sensitive to ETS that to protect himself from extreme respiratory distress in smoke-filled rooms, he had to wear a gas-mask.[268] The legislation against smoking in public places vastly improved the quality of his life.

As for the status of smoking in private homes, wives who are non-smokers tend to protect their home from smoke pollution. Thus, a survey in California in 1993 found that 52% of nonsmoking women insisted on a complete ban on smoking in their homes, while 21% had a partial ban in place. A 1994 survey found that 13% of women nonsmokers reported being exposed to ETS at home.[87] Of course, most nonsmoking spouses implore their partners to quit, hoping to protect themselves and their children from the risks of smoke.

As of April, 2003, New York City outlawed smoking in all public establishments, workplaces, places of entertainment, restaurants and bars. The latter are now coping with the law by providing outdoor seating for smoking patrons, and according to its Commissioner of Finance, business is up 12% for the year. As of May 1, 2004, the same ban was in force in the entire state of New York and in five other states, and smokefree workplace legislation had been passed in four other states. It seems only a matter of time before similar bans becomes nation-wide.

As to whether protection from ETS improves health, Mark Eisner and coworkers recorded in *JAMA* that establishment of smoke-free bars and taverns produced a rapid improvement of respiratory health for their workers. This was documented by improved lung function- increases in expiratory volume and vital capacity- and a lessening of symptoms of lung irritation.[269]

Plants other than tobacco contain nicotine, although in much smaller amounts. This includes vegetables such as eggplant and tomato, and explains why minute amounts of nicotine are even found in the bodies of people who have not been exposed to ETS.[270]

To protect ourselves against environmental smoke, the American Medical Association advises us as follows: *Do not permit smoking either in your home, at work, and in your car, and try to minimize the time spent in smoky environments.*[271]

Further information on ETS is available from the American Cancer, Lung, and Heart Associations, from the National Cancer Institute, CDC, and the site Joe@smokefree.org. For scientists and teachers, the Surgeon General's Report of 2001 on "Women and Smoking" is an excellent reference.[87] But the National Academy book of 2000, "Clearing the Smoke: Assessing the Science Base for Tobacco Harm Reduction" is only useful for researchers.[272]

TWENTY

SEARCH FOR A SAFER CIGARETTE

While smoking tobacco could be safer, it could never be safe. A puff from a burning cigarette contains tar and vapor, both of which contain carcinogens. Some of the tar remains deposited within the lung, and the vapor contains carbon monoxide and addictive nicotine.[273] Also, a burning cigarette poses a fire hazard. Still, making a safer cigarette is a laudable objective, as long as such cigarettes are not used as an alternative to quitting, which is a vastly more user-friendly goal.

The three main goals for manufacture of a safer cigarette are reductions in tar (and with it, of carcinogens), in nicotine, and in fire hazard. Historically, the most important step in reducing tar and nicotine yields was the addition of a filter tip that selectively removed these components. Unfortunately, Kent's Micronite filter of 1952 contained asbestos, which is a potent lung carcinogen. Studies commissioned by Kent's manufacturers Lorillard showed that asbestos fibers did get into the smoke, but kept that secret. Even though asbestos was removed from the Micronite filter in 1955, the type of lung cancer caused almost exclusively by asbestos, mesothelioma, began to show up in recent years. Today, filter cigarettes no longer contain asbestos.[274]

Between 1955 and 1987, the average tar yield of American cigarettes declined almost one-third, from 34 to 23 mg, and the average nicotine yield fell by one-half, from 2 to 0.9 mg. Thus, the cigarette industry did work to reduce harmful constituents, at least according to testing machines that perform standardized puffing. Unfortunately, smokers compensate for lower tar and nicotine content by puffing harder and breathing the smoke more deeply, as well as by smoking more cigarettes.[274, 275] At least the tobacco companies were pleased, for "ultra light" cigarettes forced smokers to buy more cigarettes, and thus boosted sales.

Regarding the question whether reducing the yield of nicotine and carbon monoxide of cigarettes would reduce the risk of a non-fatal heart attack, an epidemiological study in women concluded that this is not true. However, women who quit smoking reduced their risk to one-third. This study proved that for avoiding a fatal heart attack, switching to a low-yield brand is not a viable alternative to quitting.[276]

However, epidemiological data do suggest that low-yield cigarettes are less hazardous for development of cancer of various types, including lung cancer. Some studies on chronic lung diseases also suggest that low-yield cigarettes slightly reduce coughing, phlegm, the impairment of lung function, as well as deaths from emphysema.[274] Still, these mild improvements are but a pale shadow of the health benefits of quitting.

Canada's ban of 'light' or 'mild' labels on cigarette packages provides a "reality rub-in" on the health benefits of low-yield cigarettes. Speaking in 2001 at a meeting of the Canadian Medical Association, the Canadian Health Minister Allan Rock said "There is nothing light or mild about the lies of big tobacco. Cigarettes branded as light or mild are as lethal as regular cigarettes. The industry knew this when they introduced the terms, but they continued to mislead the public for decades." Industry documents show that it has long known, that low-tar cigarettes may keep smokers from quitting. This is one of the major objectives of the industry.[277] A class-action suit has accused Philip Morris (sanitized by adopting the name Altria Group) of deceiving consumers, by suggesting that Marlboro Lights and Cambridge

Lights were less hazardous. As of 2004, the $10 billion suit had been appealed to the Supreme Court.

Vector Tobacco recently introduced Quest cigarettes, which come in three flavors: 17% less nicotine than a typical "light" cigarette, 58% less nicotine, and close to zero nicotine. The idea is, that smokers can embark on a quest of weaning themselves off cigarettes, by advancing progressively to the last of the three flavors, and then quitting. That is an admirable concept- as long as smokers commit (a) not to compensate for low nicotine content by smoking more cigarettes, (b) not to stay on each of the three flavors for more than six weeks, and (c) then to quit.

In the year 2000, the Federal Trade Commission stopped the advertisement of herbal cigarettes as being healthier than regular cigarettes. Herbal cigarettes must now carry health warnings, since the FTC has found that their smoke contains the same levels of carcinogens as regular tobacco smoke. Similarly, tests in 2000 by the Massachusetts Department of Public Health of R. J. Reynolds' "non-burning" Eclipse cigarette, which was said to have an 80% lower level of carcinogens, found the claims to be "blatantly false." These claims were also disputed by Michael Thun and Thomas Glynn of ACS in a letter written to *The Journal of the American Medical Association (JAMA)* in December of 2000. At the end of 2003, J. R. Reynolds introduced a new cigarette that again flirted with that 80% figure: this time the smoker was promised 80% less secondhand smoke, as well as no lingering odor.

In 2001, a panel from the National Academy of Sciences reported on the safety of cigarettes modified with the intention of reducing their health risks, and concluded that it is feasible to manufacture less harmful cigarettes. But since tobacco is not federally regulated, new brands are not independently evaluated, so the public has no unbiased information about their safety. While some new brands do claim reduced health risks, there was no evidence to support those claims. An editorial in the May/ June 2004 issue of the ACS journal *CA* quoted evidence that "less lethal smoking is still a pipe dream." The lung cancer risk is the same for smokers of very low-tar cigarettes as for smokers of medium-tar brands. While cigarettes have changed, the risk of lung cancer for smokers has not changed.[4]

Because of the high price of cigarettes, the home rolling of cigarettes and the sale of cigarette rolling machines (which permit the making of filtered cigarettes) has been booming.[278] Although home-made cigarettes are sure to be less uniform than commercial ones, they are still likely to be as dangerous.

As regards the fire hazard, the National Fire Protection Association says that cigarettes are the leading cause of fatal fires in the nation, and in one year, cigarette-related fires cause more than 900 deaths, 2,500 injuries, and $400 million in property damage (see chapter 15). These fires are particularly dangerous, because they often erupt in the middle of the night, when a smoker went to sleep while a cigarette was still burning.

There are fire retardants that can be added to cigarettes to make them self-extinguishing if they are not drawn on. But by 2004, the tobacco industry had lobbied successfully for over two decades against federal legislation introduced to mandate the addition of fire retardants to all cigarettes sold in the United States The industry argues that a self-extinguishing cigarette may add yet more toxicity to cigarettes. But in March 2004, Canada became the first country in the world to pass a bill that requires all cigarettes sold there to self-extinguish if left burning but not being actively smoked.

In the United States, industry lobbyists had been equally successful in defeating similar bills proposed in individual states—until New York State lawmakers defied them, and passed a law that required all cigarettes sold in the state after June 28, 2004, to meet a self-extinguishing standard set by the American Society of Testing and Materials (ASTM). This is feasible, for cigarettes can be wrapped in paper that has banded "speed bumps." These are thickened bands of paper, which reduce the access of oxygen to the burning tobacco, thereby snuffing it out.[279]

TWENTY ONE

CAN DIET HELP?

During the early 1990's, a high (as compared to a low) level of consumption of fruits and vegetables was found almost to halve the risk of lung cancer in smokers.[280] But when the expectation that this beneficial effect might be due to the beta-carotene content of fruits and vegetables was tested, beta-carotene supplements were found to increase rather than decrease the risk of lung cancer in smokers, and should therefore be avoided by smokers.[281] These results were confirmed in the July 23, 2003 issue of the Journal of the American Medical Society.

Regarding the effect of dietary supplements of vitamin E, the risk of lung cancer has been found to be over threefold lower for nonsmokers with the highest as compared to the lowest levels of vitamin E intake. Unfortunately, the risk of lung cancer did not change significantly for smokers, irrespective of the level of their intake of vitamin E.[282] To date, studies have failed to find evidence, that any dietary supplements could decrease the risk of lung cancer for cigarette smokers.[283]

In contrast, there is definitive evidence that a diet low in fat and very high in fruits and vegetables (11 servings per day) halves the risk of lung cancer for smokers.[284, 285] Therefore, eating such a diet can only have a beneficial effect for cigarette smokers.[283] But smokers should not use the excuse that they eat a wholesome diet to justify continued smoking. For the best of diets can only drop their risk by 50%, while quitting and staying off cigarettes for twenty years or more will reduce their risk of lung cancer by 90%. Even more important, the beneficial effects of quitting on the risk of a heart attack are equally spectacular, but occur vastly more rapidly.

TWENTY TWO

MARIJUANA

Since societal opinions about smoking cannabis (marijuana, pot) are strongly divided, it is a challenge to present both sides of the picture fairly. To place the situation in America in a wider context, it will be of interest first to describe the situation in various European countries.

Prince Harry, 17 and third in line to the British throne, made Time Magazine early in 2002 for smoking pot and indulging in underage drinking at a pub. Subsequently, he was duly admonished by his father, Prince Charles, and sent to spend an eye-opening day at a rehab clinic. But Harry's problems provided a welcome opportunity not only for British parents to talk to their own teens about marijuana, but also for European parents to do so, for nearly 40% Europeans aged 15 to 34 have tried pot.[286]

Most countries of the European Union keeps laws against marijuana possession on their books, but enforcement tends to be lenient. In the English city of Brixton, the police have begun to experiment with cautioning users on the spot and confiscating their pot, rather than prosecuting them. In France and Germany, authorities–police, prosecutors and judges–are given the discretion to be tolerant. In Belgium, users are arrested only if smoking occurs in the presence of minors. In Spain, recreational drug use including heroin is no longer prosecuted. In Portugal, first-time

149

users of any drug are given a suspended sentence, while those hooked on drugs are called "patients" and offered treatment at drug-dependency clinics; if they refuse, they can be fined or sentenced to community service, but not jailed. In Holland, where the sale of soft drugs including cannabis is allowed, popular opinion may be beginning to swing back toward banning sales.[287]

As for Canada, federal legislation was introduced there in May, 2003, to remove criminal penalties for possessing small amounts of marijuana. At the time, White House officials warned that decriminalization would result in an increase in smuggling powerful hydroponically grown Canadian marijuana into the United States, and increase cannabis use among Americans. For even then, an underground Canadian marijuana-growing industry was selling $4 billion worth of the weed to dealers in the United States.[287] In any case, in December, 2003, Canada's Supreme Court endorsed criminal penalties for smoking marijuana, but left open the possibility that the Canadian Parliament at a later time could legalize the casual use of the drug and the possession of half an ounce of marijuana.[288]

Regarding smuggling marijuana originating from other countries than Canada, *Time* of December 13, 1999 reported that the drug business dominates life on the Southern border of the United States. Like the Columbian drug cartels, Mexican drug lords make clandestine shipments of cocaine and marijuana to the United States. But although the recent emphasis on home defense is focused on reducing illicit immigration across United States frontiers, it has also helped to impede illicit drug shipments.

In the United States, marijuana is the most widely used illicit drug, and already by 1979, roughly 50 million people had smoked marijuana at least once.[289] The liberalization of the sale of cannabis in Europe and Canada did not sway President Bush, who held that legalization would be a social catastrophe. Despite a rising number of arrests, as of 2006 federal law prohibits the possession of marijuana. Still, Eric Schlosser reported in the New York

Times of April 26, 2004 that eleven states had decriminalized the possession of marijuana; in Ohio, possession of up to three ounces has been decriminalized for many years. In contrast, most states have tough laws against selling marijuana. For instance, selling any amount in Washington State brings a recommended prison sentence of five years. Roughly 700,000 people were arrested in the United States in 2002 for disobeying laws relating to marijuana, and 90% of arrests were for possessing rather than selling it. Still, even a misdemeanor can lead to jail, suspension of a driver's license and job loss—so conviction for a marijuana offense is not a light matter.

The medical use of marijuana is another topic on which there is heated controversy. This has not lessened since 1996, when California voters approved the Medical Marijuana Initiative (Proposition 215) by a vote of 56 to 44 percent. The act entitled Californians to possess and to cultivate marijuana for medical purposes "where that medical use is deemed appropriate and has been recommended by a physician who has determined that the person's health would benefit from the use of marijuana in the treatment of cancer, anorexia, AIDS, chronic pain, spasticity, glaucoma, arthritis, migraine, or any other illness for which marijuana provides relief."[290]

Since marijuana is not approved for drug use by the Food and Drug Administration (FDA), the California act violated the policy not to permit the use of an unapproved drug. Its passage sparked several studies aimed at evaluating both the beneficial and the harmful effects of marijuana. The controversy was resolved by the United States Supreme Court in May, 2001, when it ruled that since federal law does not recognize medical benefits from marijuana, doctors may not prescribe it. While this ruling did not explicitly overturn the laws already passed by nine states that permitted the medical use of marijuana, it did restrict it to research projects tightly controlled by the federal government.[291] Still, most "pot" infractions fall under state and local jurisdiction, and an increasing number of law-enforcement officers are refusing to prosecute "medipot" cases.[292] Further, in February 2004, a Federal appeals court in California upheld the right of Calif44s approved by California voters in 1996.

Unfortunately, there are many highly qualified experts on both sides of the debate over the medical use of marijuana, and neither side is shy of accusing the other side of prejudice. For instance, the 1997 book "Marijuana: The Forbidden Medicine," by Lester Grinspoon and James Bakalar argues strongly for its use, while the 1998 book "Marijuana and Medicine," edited by Gabriel Nahas and his colleagues concludes that neither marijuana nor THC (delta-9-tetrahydrocannabinol, which is the active chemical in marijuana) qualify as safe and effective medications, and have no place in modern pharmacology. The book "The Science of Marijuana" of 2000 by Leslie Iversen, who contributed to a British House of Lords select committee report on cannabis, is very even-handed. Iversen not only summarizes the potential advantages and side effects of marijuana for each of the proposed therapeutic uses of the drug, but also gives therapeutic alternatives and discusses the *pros* and *cons* of the choices. Also published in 2000, "Marijuana as Medicine. The Science beyond the Controversy" by Alison Mack and Janet Joy provides patients and caregivers with sound science and good advice. Early in 2004, the drug Sativex, a liquid extract of marijuana that contains all its components, seemed poised for approval in Europe for people suffering from multiple sclerosis and severe pain.

Regarding Canadian use of marijuana for medicinal purposes, in July 2001 Canada became the first country to permit people who suffered from long-term debilitating or terminal illnesses to grow and smoke their own marijuana. But a spokesperson for the Canadian Medical Association, which represents tens of thousands of Canadian doctors, said that there was no solid research anywhere in the world to show that marijuana is a good treatment for pain management, and that the new law ignored fundamental medical issues of quality, effectiveness, and patient safety.[293] But in 2002 a Canadian Senate committee found that there were "clear, though not definitive" benefits for using marijuana to treat chronic pain. Then in July, 2003, Canada allowed patients who suffered chronic pain or nausea to buy high-grade marijuana grown under government contract–despite objections from Canadian medical organizations that routine clinical trials to test the efficacy and safety of marijuana had not been done. In December, 2003, Canada amended its Marijuana Medical Access Regulations, to provide for reasonable access to a legal source of marijuana for medical purposes.[294] In the fall of 2004, a pilot project devised by Canada's National Health Service was begun, which allowed pharmacies in British Columbia to sell marijuana for medicinal purposes without a prescription. This allows pharmacists to decide whether a potential buyer needs medication.

Regarding the health effects of marijuana, the United States Surgeon General report of 1982 listed some of the known or suspected chronic effects of marijuana.[295] These include:

- Short-term memory loss and slowing of learning ability

- After extended use, impairment of lung function similar to that in cigarette smokers, indications of cancer and COPD.

- Children and adolescents are particularly vulnerable to the drug's behavioral and psychological effects.

- Prolonged marijuana use by youths can create the "amotivational syndrome" characterized by energy loss, diminished school performance and deterioration of relationships with parents.

- Decreased sperm count and sperm motility.

- Interference with ovulation and pre-natal development.

- Impairment of immune response.

- Possible adverse effects on heart function.

- Roughly 40% of heavy users have some or all of these symptoms.

- Byproducts of marijuana remain in body fat for several weeks.

A 1988 report in the New England Medical Journal stated that compared to smoking tobacco, smoking marijuana results in an approximately threefold increase in the tar inhaled and a fourfold higher binding of carbon monoxide to the hemoglobin in red cells. Thereby, it reduces their oxygen carrying capacity. Compared to cigarette smokers, marijuana smokers caused these differences by using a larger puff volume, a greater depth of inhalation, and a fourfold longer breath-holding time.[296]

With regard to mental flexibility and learning ability, a 1996 study in JAMA found that heavy users of marijuana had a significantly greater impairment of cognitive functions, compared to light users. Heavy use of marijuana has residual adverse neuropsychological effects even after a day of abstinence from the drug;[297] these findings extend those of a similar 1993 study.[298] When the lead author of the 1996 JAMA report, Harrison Pope, was interviewed for Harvard Magazine, he said that his study showed that heavy users were impaired in their ability to pay attention rather than to remember. His study confirmed the previous finding "that it is unwise to take a calculus exam or fly a 747 airplane the morning after you get stoned."[299]

A pamphlet from the National Institute on Drug Abuse (NIDA) entitled *Marijuana: Facts for Teens* updated in 1998 answers the most frequently asked questions about the effects of marijuana use, and summarizes our present state of knowledge:[300]

- People differ in their reaction to marijuana, which also depends on the strength of its THC content, what is expected to happen, where and how it is taken, and whether alcohol or other drugs are used as well. Reactions can range from feeling nothing to feeling relaxed or high, and some users of strong marijuana can become anxious or have paranoid thoughts.

- The short-term effects of marijuana can include problems with memory, thinking, and learning; distorted perceptions of sights, sounds, time, and touch; loss of coordination; increased heart rate; and anxiety.

- These short-term effects can affect a variety of activities. Athletes could have their performance degraded by poor timing and coordination. Since judgment is affected, users can forget to take safety precautions when having sex, and thereby expose themselves to the AIDS virus, HIV.

- Regarding cancer as a possible end-result of long-continued marijuana smoking, smoking five joints (cigarettes) of marijuana a week may expose one to the same quantity of carcinogens as smoking a pack of cigarettes a day.

In view of the above findings, it is worrisome that a CDC survey in 1991 found that nearly half (46%) of marijuana users reported having driven while high on marijuana. Further, more than one-quarter (27%) had been high on at least one occasion while at home and engaged in caring for their family.[301]

Further, a study by Murray Mittleman published in June, 2001 in the journal *Circulation* indicates that for the first hour after smoking marijuana, the risk of a heart attack is five times greater than normal. This finding adds marijuana smoking to a growing list of temporary pleasures- such as having sex or eating a very big meal–that might trigger heart attacks. For healthy young people, this is of very little concern, since their risk of a heart attack is extremely low. But for older people who already possess risk factors such as coronary heart disease, high blood pressure, or diabetes, an additional risk is a matter of concern.

Still, there is evidence that the health consequences of marijuana use are less than those of alcohol and of tobacco. Although that claim was made in a highly partisan book,[302] it is also made by Eric Schlosser in his 2004 article mentioned above. Alcohol is directly linked to one-quarter of the suicides in the United States, almost half the violent crime, and two-thirds the domestic abuse. Drinking too much alcohol can be instantly lethal for a healthy young person, and American children are four times more likely to drink alcohol than to smoke pot.

My only experience with marijuana came during a weekend trip with two of my sons. One of my sons befriended three girls at the inn we were staying on Cape Cod, and invited them to go on a walk with us to smoke a "joint", assuring me that my worries about his smoking would be eased. In a meadow away from our inn, the five young people sat down in a circle, and my son produced a joint, lit it, took a puff, and passed it around. As I watched, each youngster took a slow puff, then passed it on. Not a word was spoken until it was consumed. I must admit that this seemingly innocuous experience did calm my fears. My son continued to smoke one or two joints a week for a few years, then quit permanently.

However, there is a huge difference between the number of people who have experimented with marijuana for a short while—roughly half of all American youths—and the number who become steady users. According to Wilson Compton and coauthors writing in the May 5, 2004 issue of JAMA, approximately 4.0% of the adult United States population uses marijuana. This percentage has remained constant over the decade between 1992 and 2002. But disorders associated with marijuana use affected one-third of all those who had used marijuana for more than a year, and increased by 25% over this decade, from 1.2% to 1.5% of the population. In this study, "disorders" were defined as including either abuse of or dependence on (*i.e.* addiction to) marijuana. To be diagnosed as abusing marijuana, at least 1 of the following 4 criteria of abuse within the year prior to the interview had to be reported: failing to fulfill major role obligations, recurrent marijuana use in physically hazardous situations, recurrent marijuana-related legal problems, and continued marijuana use despite having persistent or recurrent social or interpersonal problems caused by or exacerbated by use. To be classified as dependent upon marijuana required that at least 3 of 6 criteria commonly used to indicate dependence on a drug had to be met.

That smoking marijuana may act as a gateway drug for use of strongly addicting, career-destroying hard drugs such as cocaine is perhaps the most serious charge against pot. While a 2002 study by the nonprofit RAND Drug Policy Research Center published in the journal *Addiction* disagreed with this conclusion, a study by Michael Lynskey and coauthors in the January 22, 2003 issue of *JAMA* seemed crafted perfectly to settle this issue. It included more than 300 sets of same-sex twins, of whom nearly half were identical twins. But it only included a set of twins, if one twin—and only one twin—had smoked marijuana before age 17. The study found that the twins who smoked marijuana before the age of 17 were twice as likely to use opiates such as heroin, and five times more likely to use hallucinogens such as LSD, compared to their twins who had not used marijuana prior to age 17. The results were similar whether or not the twins were identical. These results show that inheritance plays little if any role in deciding whether early users of marijuana later switch to more potent drugs. The researchers concluded that twins who had started to smoke marijuana early experienced social and peer pressures that reduced their resistance to switch to harder drugs later on.[303] But an accompanying editorial by Denise Kandel suggested that these results do not unequivocally prove that marijuana is a gateway drug—for even identical twins may not share the same environment during adolescence.[304] But there is such a large difference in the eventual use of hard drugs between twins who began to smoke pot early as compared to their twins who did not do so, that Kandel's suggestion seems very far-fetched.

However, neither the authors nor the editorial commented on a striking finding: the lifetime prevalence of drug abuse or dependence among these twins was 54% for early marijuana users, and 43% for the twins who switched to marijuana later. These percentages are so much higher than for the general population, that they confirm the thesis that *people who smoke marijuana have a high risk of future drug abuse or dependence.* Further, the younger the age at which marijuana use is begun, the higher the risk of later addiction to more potent illicit drugs. Also, this study showed that marijuana use predicts a high lifetime risk of alcohol dependence (47% for early marijuana users, 34% for their twins who switched to marijuana later but still became alcoholics). Lastly, the results of this landmark study confirm that marijuana is indeed a *"marker"* (suggested as less controversial than a *"gateway drug"*) for a later switch to more potent drugs or to alcohol abuse.

Regarding the mechanism of addiction to marijuana, since its active principle THC is slowly metabolized and thus leaves the body slowly, withdrawal symptoms are muted or nonexistent. In 1997, it was argued that 9% of individuals who have ever (even once) used marijuana meet criteria of dependence. But this figure goes up to 20 to 30% for people who have used it at least a few times,[305] and increases to 33% for those who have smoked marijuana for at least a year.[303] These facts are enlightening. Every year, roughly 100,000 people seek treatment for marijuana dependence in the United States. Some of these may be coerced to do so by their employers or the courts, and many are addicted to marijuana.[306]

The mode of action of marijuana has been the subject of much debate. Prior to 1997, there was little evidence that it can addict. Then Di Chiara reported in *Science* that THC produces a key biochemical event that also seems to reinforce dependence on other drugs, including nicotine and heroin: a release of dopamine in part of the brain's reward pathway.[307] In the same issue of *Science*, de Fonesca and coworkers reported that the chemical CRF (corticotropin-releasing factor), which had already been linked to anxiety during withdrawal from opiates and alcohol, had the same function during marijuana withdrawal. Together, the two sets of data indicate that marijuana manipulates the brain's stress and reward systems very much like more potent drugs.[231] These results were interpreted as a strong message that marijuana use is dangerous, and is fully capable of causing addiction.[308]

When Leslie Iversen published his even-handed book *The Science of Marijuana* in the year 2000, a central puzzle related to the mode of action of "the weed" was still unanswered: why the mammalian brain needed extremely high levels of THC to bind to CB_1 the lock (or "receptor") in brain tissue, into which the THC molecule fits like a key, thereby unlocking the latent activity of CB_1.[309] The answer was provided in March, 2001 by lead authors Rachel Wilson and Anatol Kreitzer, writing respectively in the journals *Nature* and *Neuron*: the fit of the THC molecule key within its lock CB_1 was rather loose, while more strongly addicting opioids such as heroin bind far more tightly to CB_1. Further evidence that the action of THC is closely allied to that of hard drugs was provided by Marilyn Huestis and coworkers. They showed that blocking the binding of THC to the CB_1 cannabinoid receptor with a specific inhibitor named SR141716 made the action of THC ineffective. Since SR141716 also blocked the action of cocaine and heroin, Huestis and coworkers proved that these two drugs and THC act on the same receptor.[311]

But while *natural* brain chemicals called cannabinoids stimulate the brain merely for tens of seconds, marijuana floods the brain with THC for much longer periods of time. Thereby THC eliminates the natural control systems of the brain that fine-tunes the brain's control of memory, and its coordination of movements—just as spilling a bottle of ink across a page obliterates the words that are written there.[310] Later reports convincingly confirm the above conclusions.[311,312] Further, an article in 2002 concluded that long-term heavy cannabis users show impairments in memory and attention that endure beyond the period of marijuana intoxication and worsens with increasing years of regular marijuana use.[313] Nevertheless, an accompanying editorial contradicted this conclusion, and suggested instead that the cognitive defects persist merely for hours or days after acute intoxication with marijuana has subsided.[314]

High school students are at risk of experimenting with marijuana use. According to a 1990 survey conducted by CDC, an average of 12% of United States high school students reported that they had smoked marijuana at least once.[315] A survey done in 1997 that comprised over 16,000 questionnaires that was completed in 151 schools showed a dramatic rise in marijuana use. 47% of all students had smoked marijuana at least once during their lifetime, and the percentage increased from 9th graders (39%) to 12th graders (52%). In addition, 26% of all students had used marijuana at least once during the 30 days preceding the survey.[316] However according to a survey performed by the nonprofit Partnership for a Drug-Free America, the use of marijuana by teenagers declined by 4% between 1997 and 2000. This decline was a hollow victory, for it came at the cost of a substantial increase in the use of ecstasy, which doubled between 1995 and 2000, when approximately 10% of teens had tried this "club drug" at least once.[317]

To turn off youths from experimenting with marijuana, the role of parents is critical. According to a 1999 statement by the Office of National Drug Control Policy/Partnership for a Drug-Free America, "kids who learn about the risks of drugs from their parents are 36% less likely to smoke marijuana than kids who learn nothing from them." The reduction in drug use is even higher for parents who talk to their children about the use of inhalants, of LSD, and of cocaine. But even if the parents themselves smoked pot in their younger days, the benefit of talking to their children to discourage drug usage is still great.[318] When the parents were young, the ill effects of marijuana were almost unknown, and the marijuana contained far less THC. Because the marijuana sold today is much stronger, the National Education Association has suggested a number of measures that public schools can employ to stem the use of marijuana:[319]

- School policies should be clear, consistently enforced, fair, and appropriate.

- Kids who seem to have problems with drugs need counseling.

- Only drug curricula rigorously proven effective should be used.

- Students should be fully engaged in finding solutions.

The National Commission for Drug-Free Schools has issued an excellent report, "Preventing Drug Abuse among Children and Adolescents: A Research-Based Guide" that includes suggestions on how to adopt an effective curriculum. It can be obtained from the National Clearinghouse for Alcohol and Drug Information (800-729-6686), or downloaded from the web site www.health. org. Other resources for fighting drug abuse include the National Council on Alcohol and Other Drug Dependence (NCADD), which can be reached at 800-622-2255 or 800-475-4673, or at www.ncadd.org. Also helpful is the information provided by the federal Substance Abuse and Mental Health Services Administration at the site www.samhsa.gov.

In conclusion, marijuana is a "marker" for the future use of strongly addicting drugs or addiction to alcohol. Former long-term marijuana smokers have a seventeenfold higher risk than nonusers of turning to heroin use later.[320] The need to buy marijuana brings its users into contact with sellers of hard drugs, who are often willing to give them away free in order to snare new addicts. Marijuana dependency is most likely for those with behavioral and emotional problems,[321] and it is they who are most likely to suffer ill effects from its long-term use. To prevent them from starting to smoke marijuana, schools should make an effort to identify youths with such problems and then provide them with help and treatment.

PART II

BATTLING A DECEPTIVE INDUSTRY

A lie runs until truth overtakes it

TWENTY THREE

PREVENTION: CHILDREN, ADOLESCENTS, AND YOUNG PEOPLE

According to the National Cancer Institute, every day another 3,000 children begin to smoke. The average age at which teenagers begin to smoke is 13½ years, when they are in eighth grade. This means that many children start smoking much earlier.

Regarding the health effects of starting to smoke early in life, in chapter 7 we saw that the earlier smoking is begun, the higher the risk of lung cancer. A study by John Wiencke in the Journal of the National Cancer Institute of 1999 supports these results with findings from molecular biology: the earlier teenagers start to smoke, the worse the damage to the DNA of their lung cells. This is true even if they smoke fewer cigarettes than those who started smoking later in life.[322]

Not all health effects of smoking as a teenager are deferred until later years. A study by Diane Gold and coworkers has shown that even in adolescents, cigarette smoking produces mild airway obstruction and retards the growth of lung functions.[323] This explains why most coaches drop smokers from their teams if they refuse their request to quit. But the most insidious effect of tobacco smoking is addiction, and young smokers become as rapidly addicted to nicotine as adults.

Numerous issues tilt adolescents toward or away from taking up smoking.[324] Richard Lowry and coworkers demonstrated that the likelihood that a teenager will indulge in risky behavior (such as smoking) increases with factors related to the parent or the responsible adult, namely low socioeconomic status, low income, and low educational status. But the lifestyle of each individual is also an important factor. The chance that smoking will become a habit is higher for youths who have a sedentary lifestyle, a low consumption of fruits and vegetables, a high consumption of foods high in fat, and episodes of alcohol drinking.[325]

In addition, Robert Anda and colleagues found in 1999 that the tendency to take up smoking was also closely tied to adverse childhood experiences: verbal, physical or sexual abuse, having a battered or divorced mother, and living with someone who abused alcohol or drugs, or had mental illness, or had been jailed.[326] Further, numerous studies have shown that if one or both parents smoke, the risk that their children will take up smoking is greatly increased. According to *Time* of March 20, 2000, 75% of the 4 million teens who smoke come from homes where a parent smokes. A report in *Pediatrics* in 2001 states that parents have more influence on their teens than they realize and suggests they tell them "that you expect them never to smoke, that they will be punished if they do, and not to befriend kids who smoke."[327]

Indeed, peer pressure may be most important of all. According to a report by the American Lung Association, the majority of adolescents smoked for the first time when they were with a friend who smoked.[328] In November 2003, the Time website www.time.com/time/2003/kids said that kids whose friends smoke are nine times more likely to try smoking than those with nonsmoking friends. It is very hard to remain a nonsmoker if one chooses a group of friends who all smoke.

As regards the statistics of adolescent smoking, a 1999 report by the United States Centers for Disease Control (CDC) reported that approximately 80% of smokers start to smoke before they turn 18. Between 1991 and 1997, current cigarette smoking (defined as smoking more than 1 cigarette per month) in the 11 states surveyed increased by roughly 25%, while frequent smoking (more than 20 cigarettes per month) increased by roughly 30%; but there was a great deal of variation between states.[329] According to the American Cancer Society, smoking among high school students has been falling: while in 1997, 28% said that they were frequent smokers, by in 2001 that figure had fallen to 14%.[330]

A CDC report in *JAMA* of February 18, 2004 that covered the period 1999–2001 documented large variations in the prevalence of smoking among racial/ethnic minority population in the United States. The percentage of youths who smoked was 28% for American Indians and Alaska Natives, and 16% for non-Hispanic whites (15% for males and 17% for females). For other non-whites, the percentage of smokers was lower. Thus, for non-Hispanic African-American youths it was 7% (8% for males and 6% for females).

In some states, aggressive tobacco prevention and education programs have had a very beneficial effect. For instance in Oregon, the residents approved a ballot measure that increased the state cigarette tax by 30 cents and stipulated that 10% of this new tax be allocated to the Oregon Health Division to develop and implement a tobacco-use prevention program. After the program was started, tobacco consumption declined by 11%, and smoking among adults declined by 6%.[331]

Similarly, when the legislature of Florida allocated $70 million for aggressive antismoking programs in 1998, the percentage of middle school smokers dropped from 18.5 to 15% within a year, and in high schools smoking decreased from 27.4 to 25.2%.[332] In Massachusetts, the Department of Public Health has conducted a long-term vigorous educational campaign. The state's Youth Tobacco Report of 2001 concluded that the number of students who smoked at least once during the month that preceded its survey decreased from 36% in 1995 to 26% in 2001.[333] For the nation as a whole, ACS reported that the number of high school students who smoked on one or more days in the month before its survey dropped from 36% in 1997 to 28% in 2001.[334]

On the other hand, the economic depression of 2002 and 2003 caused large budget deficits in most states, and legislators, encouraged by tobacco industry lobbyists, eliminated tobacco control funds. For instance, while in Massachusetts the budget contained $50 million for antismoking programs for the year FY2002 (fiscal year 2002, July 2002-June 2003), that was cut to $5 million for FY2003, then halved to $2.5 million for FY2004. As a result, cigarette sales to teenagers rose sharply in 2003, and by 2004, illegal cigarette sales to minors had tripled.[335]

To dupe youths into becoming smokers, tobacco companies- or rather the innovative advertising agencies that their deep pockets can afford- employ an unending variety of tricks. Perhaps the best known advertising creation is Joe the Camel- an unforgettably grotesque camel-like chain-smoking motorcyclist he-man with vast appeal to young males. By 1994, when Camel's 80th anniversary celebration was staged, the brand was so successful that there were six different varieties of Camel cigarettes. Their contents of tar and nicotine ranged stepwise from "Ultra Lights" (6 mg tar and 0.5 mg nicotine) to "Regular" (22 mg tar and 1.5 mg nicotine). The packs contained "C-notes" that could be exchanged for so many different Camel-embossed items, that a 12-page brochure was needed to list them all. Eventually, the makers were forced to eliminate Joe the Camel from their advertisements.

A constant motive in tobacco ads aimed at youngsters is the use of startlingly beautiful young girls bursting with vitality.[336] Cigarette giant Philip Morris even launched its own record label to snare the young.[337] In 1998, a joint study headed by Charles King, which included Harvard University, Boston University, and the Massachusetts Department of Health, found that tobacco advertising was heaviest in magazines read by youths and young adults- an obvious effort to target youngsters.[338] Another study in the same issue of JAMA proved that tobacco advertising is indeed effective in persuading people to start smoking.[339]

That the tobacco industry continues to target youths is proved by a $20 million fine assessed against R. J. Reynolds in June, 2002, for ads in magazines with large teenage readerships such as Vibe, Spin and Rolling Stone. Although Reynolds attempted to justify its action by claiming that the ads targeted adults, a California Superior Court Judge concluded that Reynolds contravened the Master Settlement Agreement between the industry and states, which bars tobacco companies from taking any action, directly or indirectly, to target youths (see chapter 23 and 25).

Newport is by no means alone in showing young handsome men and beautiful girls in their ads, living a rich, fun-filled life. But other approaches encourage smokers to think of themselves as brave souls rebelling against repressive orthodoxy, as implied by the brand name Back Alley Blend cigarette, or picturing smokers as recreating the days when smoking was fashionable.[340]

One way for citizens to deal with the problem of cigarette advertising in print is to send a letter to the editor, asking that tobacco advertisements not be accepted, perhaps threatening to cancel if they continue to be run. Such campaigns can be effective: as of April 29, 1999, the New York Times dropped all tobacco advertising. But this ban does not apply to the Boston Globe and 20 other newspapers owned by the parent company of the Times, nor is it a policy among other major newspapers, such as The Washington Post, USA Today, the Wall Street Journal, and the Los Angeles Times.[341] If citizens and health-conscious legislators continue to protest against cigarette advertisements in printed media, there is sure to be progress on this front.

In Massachusetts, a 1999 law banned the placement of tobacco advertisements within 1,000 feet of schools, playgrounds, and parks, in order to protect children. The tobacco industry rolled out its high-powered legal team to fight these state limits, on the grounds that they infringed on their rights for freedom of speech. Unfortunately, even though the United States Justice Department filed a brief defending the state law, and the United States secretary of Health and Human Services wrote that "there is no constitutional right to infringe on children,"[342] in June, 2001 the state Supreme Court overturned a law that was intended to protect children.[343]

Another major avenue used by the industry to promote smoking among kids is to show the use of tobacco (and, incidentally also of alcohol) in G-rated animated films for children. According to a 1999 study in JAMA, more than two-thirds of such films feature tobacco or alcohol in story plots- of course, without a clear verbal message of any negative long-term health effect associated with their use.[344] More recently, use of cigarettes in feature-length films has made a strong comeback. According to a Time magazine report of 2002, behind this recent renaissance of on-screen tobacco promotions are underhand money contributions from the tobacco industry. This is a serious problem, for a 2001 study by James Sargent and coworkers at Dartmouth-Hitchcock Medical Center in New Hampshire showed that teens were strongly influenced to take up smoking if their favorite actors smoked. The study proved that movies exert a powerful influence. Here are some its findings:[345]

- Today's movies include about 50% more smoking than between 1960 and 1990, although today far fewer Americans smoke.

- In 2001, most smoking in films occurred in those rated G, PG, or PG-13- and not incidentally, most smokers begin to smoke when they are children or teenagers, as documented above.

- On screen, smoking is associated with glamour, rebelliousness, and independence. Negative reactions to it are almost never seen.

- Many movies even show specific brands, most often Marlboros, which were prominently chain-smoked by Sissy Spacek in the film "In the Bedroom." The underlying message is that a girl who smokes is sexually liberated and an easy mark. It is easy to guess which tobacco company achieved that coup and how it did it.

- In addition, it is hard to avoid seeing tobacco money behind a film such as "Thank You for Smoking," which portrays a lobbyist for Big Tobacco very sympathetically.[346]

In 2003, the same team at Dartmouth Medical School published the results of a study that involved 2,600 children aged 10 to 14, who had never smoked a cigarette when recruited in 1999. Within two years, roughly 10% of the children had started to experiment with smoking or had begun to smoke. The researchers concluded that for 52% of those who started smoking, it was entirely because they saw movie stars smoke on screen.[347] The latest figures available early in 2007 gave figures collected in 2003: in the U.S. about 26% of middle school students and 52% of high school students had tried cigarette smoking, and 22% of high school students were current smokers, defined as having smoked one or more cigarettes in the month preceding the survey.33Stanton Glantz, a professor of medicine at UC San Francisco, has an excellent web site (www.SmokeFreeMovies.ucsf.edu) which asks the industry to follow the following rules voluntarily:[348]

- Certify in film credits that nobody got paid or was given any gift for using or displaying tobacco.

- Require antismoking ads before a film in which people smoke.

- Stop identifying brands.

- Rate movies that feature smoking with "R" to keep kids out.

But it seems futile to expect the film industry to have the self-control and public spirit it would need to refuse to accept well-hidden contributions from tobacco companies. While in the past the film industry has been notoriously deaf to pleas to reduce the violence in its films, there are indications that in order to receive a lower rating than R, moviemakers are beginning to reduce violence, sex, nudity, drug use and profanity. So, Glantz' suggestion that smoking should be added to this list is highly cogent. Smoking is as much a risk for children and adolescents as the other items on his list. In order to safeguard children, vigorous lobbying to actuate Glantz' suggestion is badly needed. When in 1992 the United States Supreme Court gave the green light to suits against tobacco companies, it took another six years before the threat of suits by 46 states extracted a settlement: the industry will pay $10 billion per year forever to the 50 states and some territories. The entire story of the battle is told in a book by Michael Orey, published in 1999.[349] As part of the settlement the industry undertook to educate youths by warning them not to smoke- but it soon developed that the industry was succeeding in reversing the court-ordered mandate, and using covert psychology to turn it into a prime opportunity for motivating teenagers to smoke.

Here is the action of a tobacco industry spot "against" smoking that I watched on TV in May, 2000. The setting is a drug store, and the camera focuses on a repulsive middle-aged man, standing behind a counter that prominently displays the sign "No tobacco sales to anyone under 18." In comes a wedding party, complete with a lovely young bride in an ethereal wedding dress, a groom and best man in white tie and tails, and merry friends, all attractive and vivaciously alive. When the couch-potato behind the counter tells them he cannot sell them cigarettes, they turn on their heels and storm out angrily. It is not hard to guess with whom teenage viewers will identify, and feel that they themselves have been abused. This is merely one example of how the tobacco industry spikes its "antismoking" ads with carefully crafted subliminal messages, which turn them into *powerful pro-smoking* ads. Big Tobacco's venture into antismoking education employs the strategy of a fox, which puts on a coat of chicken feathers before it enters the chicken-coop.

In April, 1999, 17 states asked Philip Morris to replace its ineffective youth-targeted tobacco ads, all of which fail to mention the health impact of smoking. In May 2000, the Massachusetts Department of Health severely criticized cigarette makers for using these ads to lure youths to start smoking, and also for their more conventional ads.[350] In the Boston Globe of June 5, 2002, an editorial excoriated the slick Philip Morris campaign built around the slogan, "Think, don't smoke," which supposedly was against teenage smoking; but its real message was, it is useless to tell teenagers that cigarettes are "uncool"- because they are cool.

As of 2002, there was every indication that the tobacco industry continued to flaunt the terms of the 1998 court-approved agreement in the suit by 46 states, to end the targeting of youths. The agreement called for the companies not to "take any action, directly or indirectly, to target youth…" Unfortunately, the agreement did not define what is meant by "targeting." As a result, the FDA, ACS and CDC have called for a new and wide range of actions to reduce the impact of tobacco on public health:[351]

- Strong regulation of tobacco by the FDA.

- Effective national clean indoor air laws and restrictions on smoking in public places.

- Congressional passage of the Medicare, Medicaid, Maternal and Child Health (MCH) Smoking Cessation Act, to expand Medicare and Medicaid coverage for smoking-cessation materials and service.

Protests by the American Legacy Foundation in 2002 caused Philip Morris to cut its annual youth prevention budget by 50%. But with evidence of the industry's deception in hand, the attorney generals of the states that secured the Master Settlement from the industry should sue offending tobacco companies, and use the money from punitive damages to fund ad campaigns directed against smoking by their own Departments of Public Health. Then the ad campaigns will not be controlled by the foxes, but by the hunters.

As of 2002, Philip Morris adopted a startling new strategy. It mailed out an honest, outspoken brochure on the health effects of smoking, a message currently expanded on its website under "Health." Given Philip Morris' past record, it is unavoidable to ask, what does this complete break with past denial do for the company? First, given the huge settlements assessed against it, Philip Morris had to acknowledge the health effects of smoking clearly, to guard against new future lawsuits. Second, the number of their ads touting their website that features material on youth smoking prevention, quitting smoking, and responsible marketing peaked in June 2005, around the time the judge in the U.S. suit against the industry was due to hand out her decision.[352] Third, confirmed smokers who read their admission that smoking is dangerous were encouraged to say, "we have long known all those bad things that are supposed to happen to us, but we are tough enough to take that risk." Nor does this new strategy prevent Philip Morris from continuing to use its other sales strategies.

While some states forbid the sale of tobacco products to youths under the age of 18, other states have raised the limit to age 21, in line with laws on buying alcohol. While not uniformly enforced, these statutes have proven effective in making it more difficult for youths to procure cigarettes. Also, they force teenagers and cigarette salespeople to think about just why these laws were enacted.[353]

The initiatives that are in place in many states to fight against adolescent smoking are an indication of how much the public resents the hawking of cigarettes to children. So the tobacco industry has found a target which is practically unprotected: college students, and against this target, industry ad campaigns have been very successful. Henry Wechsler and coworkers reported in *JAMA* that between 1993 and 1997, current cigarette smoking rose from 22% to 28% in 99 of the 116 colleges that they monitored, a relative increase of 27%. The authors were very concerned about these findings, and recommended strongly that the national efforts to reduce smoking be extended to college students.[354] As of early 2006, the Core Institute of Southern Illinois University Carbondale had published the results of their 2004 Survey of a sample of 68,000 students from more than 130 colleges in the United States: 32% reported smoking at least once during the month prior to completing the survey, and 24% reported smoking at least three times per week.[355]

As of 2007, there was every indication that Tobacco companies are fully engaged in continuing to entice nonsmokers—of course including college students – to start smoking. This is proven by their efforts to recruit bright psychology and journalism majors at many universities, especially those in tobacco growing states. What other purpose would employees trained in these skills serve for tobacco companies?

Unfortunately and with questionable ethical justification, the recruiters for tobacco companies are given a warm welcome at employment fairs for seniors, because they pay top dollars, and have many jobs available. From a narrow point of view, it is the job of university employment offices to help their students to obtain good jobs that pay high salaries, and make this their dominant concern. But if that is all that matters, then should not U.S. universities be training their economy students to know how to stay on the right side of the law, while helping their future clients to avoid paying U.S. taxes, or to obtain insider information on the prospects of a firm? Yet such saleable skills are not taught in U.S. departments of economics. Nor is there instruction on how U.S. firms can circumvent environmental laws against toxic wastes that cause diseases, yet avoid prosecution.

When students of psychology or journalism sign up to work for tobacco companies, is their future work for those companies not similar to working for waste recycling companies that pollute the environment? Alert local governments shut down and sue such companies, and citizens whose family members have suffered from the pollution bring mass action suits against them – just as there were mass action and state suits against tobacco companies. In that case, should not universities forbid tobacco companies to participate in the employment fairs for their seniors?

Motivated by ethical concerns, some universities do forbid recruitment for the U.S. armed services on their campuses. Again, there is much to be said for and against such a prohibition. On the one hand, if the U.S. is engaged in an unpopular war that many of its citizens feel is unethical and most of the faculty of the university agrees, then prohibition is the likely outcome. On the other hand, the ethical duty of loyal citizens is to defend their own country, and that requires adequately staffed armed services. Therefore, students should be given the right to access military recruitment represented on campus if they so desire, without stigmatizing it by denying it the right of access. Indeed, allowing recruitment the right of access may well augment debate on whether or not service in the military is ethical.

By analogy, allowing tobacco companies to be represented at university employment fairs need not be an ethical blunder, as long as the question of whether accepting such employment is not highly unethical is widely debated. Do seniors understand that in agreeing to work for a tobacco company, their job will be to expand the sales of a highly toxic and addicting product, which is by far the leading preventable cause of death in the U.S.? The more success they have in their work, the more statistical deaths will they have on their consciences. Sooner or later, the full realization, that in order to have well-paying jobs they have sacrificed their personal integrity, is likely to hit them like a thunder bolt. To regain their integrity, they will need the courage to make a difficult change in careers.

But there are signs that University officials are awaking to the dangers of student smoking. After a Harvard University study showed that students who live in nonsmoking dorms are less likely to pick up smoking, college officials have turned to anti-tobacco advocates for help. Time Magazine reported in December 2002 that over the previous two years, the number of state universities with smoke-free dorms had doubled, and now numbered 26.[356]

Has antismoking education for youths been successful? Early in the fight against smoking, each of the three great national societies that focus on the main diseases caused by smoking, namely the American Cancer, Heart, and Lung Associations, developed antismoking programs for schools. During the 1970s, ACS developed a master plan that called for the preparation of smoking education kits. The Greater Boston branch of ACS was asked to design a kit for grade 5, and I was invited to serve on that committee. Meeting every two weeks, it took us two years to finish this kit. Committees in other states designed kits for other grades, and eventually ACS completed kits for grades K through 12, which were available free of charge to all schools. I was far less conversant with the materials developed by the Heart and the Lung Associations, but those that I saw were excellent.

All three of the above societies have continued their educational contributions without pause since the 1970s, and our government agencies also became active in producing antismoking education material for schools. Currently, ACS has available a 1999 brochure, "Resource Guide to Youth Tobacco Cessation Programs," that contains summaries of a large variety of programs for helping teenagers quit smoking. Topics include:[357]

- Arresting smoking starts with interactive multimedia materials.

- A free telephone helpline for teens who wish to quit.

- Kick Ash: helping teens make informed choices about smoking:

- a brief health center intervention for teens who smoke.

- The Mayo Clinic nicotine patch approach to quitting.

- The Lung Association Not on Tobacco (NOT) quitting program.

- Smoke Free Teens: an interactive cessation program for teens, which is a stage-matched cessation self-help program.

- Tobacco Free Schools: a comprehensive 3-part program.

- Several research projects on smoking cessation for teens.

In 1994, the HHS (the United States Department of Health and Human Services) published the Surgeon General's report, "Preventing Tobacco Use among Young People."[358] Its recommendations are presented here in abbreviated form:

1. Most of the American public strongly favors policies intended to prevent teenage smoking, for instance:

    - including tobacco education in schools

    - restricting tobacco advertising and promotions

    - a complete ban of smoking by *anyone* on school grounds

    - prohibiting the sale of tobacco to minors

    - earmarking tax increases on tobacco products for education

2. School-based smoking prevention programs should identify social influences to smoke and teach skills to resist them.

3. The effectiveness of antismoking programs should be enhanced by comprehensive school health education, and community programs that involve parents, community organizations and the mass media.

4. Teenage smokers should be given every encouragement to enter and remain in smoking cessation programs.

5. Actively monitored enforcement of laws against under-age selling of cigarettes is needed to prevent their circumvention.

6. Legislators should act on the knowledge that raising the price of cigarettes decreases their sale.

In 1998, NCI (the National Cancer Institute) issued a plan for research on such topics as the prevention of tobacco use and nicotine addiction. The plan included proposals for basic research on the behavioral, biological and epidemiological factors that underlie the reasons why rational people smoke.[359] The report identified the many different subgroups of school children, for whom special approaches needed to be investigated. Of special interest were questions such as:

• How to identify the children most likely to begin smoking early in childhood. At special risk are those with ADHD (attention deficit hyperactivity disorder), low academic achievement, depression, substance abuse, risk-takers with other behavioral problems, and white females intent on depressing their appetite in order to stay slim.

• How to tailor prevention material appropriately for the very high rate of smoking among Native American children, and also for the high rate of smoking among non-Spanish whites.

- Identifying high-risk sub-groups based on medical conditions such as asthma, diabetes, and pediatric cancer survivors.

- Can family intervention deter youths from taking up smoking?

- How to approach teens who are drop-outs and those who work?

NCI recommended that research on these subjects be based on findings from bio-behavioral research about the factors that influence tobacco use and addiction, and should be conducted in conjunction with state and community research projects. The most important conclusion was, that because tobacco-related cancers exact an enormous toll in the United States and worldwide, NCI should commit funds to research on these issues that are in proportion to the gigantic health burden caused by tobacco use.[359]

School assemblies conducted by physicians or researchers are proved effective if the material presented is appropriate for the age-group targeted, interesting enough to captivate the audience, and asking many questions is encouraged. For cancer research workers such as me, laboratory work gives little evidence of direct (rather than potential long-term) contributions toward cancer prevention and therapy. So when a smoking education film entitled "Getting Through" became available from NIH in 1967, I telephoned the principal of my sons' high school, to ask if he would like to have an assembly at which the film would be shown, and then discussed by me and the students. His response was enthusiastic, and it took just 5 minutes to arrange an assembly for the 10th grade class, over 500 strong, which went over well.

Thus encouraged, I arranged and gave assemblies at other public schools in the Greater Boston area. In time, I developed my own set of projection slides. Some were donated by Dr. Richard Overholt, a thoracic surgeon who had given school assemblies for many years, some were donated by ACS, and some designed by me.

Since I could not give all the assemblies on smoking which schools wanted to have, I founded Volunteers for Health Awareness (VHA), a society whose members presented assemblies on the health effects of smoking and the wiles of the tobacco industry. We soon discovered that the 7th grade was the most effective grade for such assemblies. At the age of 13, most students had not yet started to smoke, and could still see the point of staying clear of the horrendous long-term health risks. Pupils in grade 6 were not quite as mature, and students in grade 8 already included some who had begun to smoke, and were very resistant to information on health risks. Smokers were more interested in hearing about the industry's clever strategies to ensnare them. In higher grades, an increasing number of students were already addicted, and therefore were not responsive to a health approach.

I had my set of color slides copied for the twelve members of VHA, wrote a "potted lecture" for them which most used only until they developed their own, and arranged assemblies for them. We asked principals to use our assemblies as the final episode of their own health education program on smoking. In our best year, we gave a total of 60 assemblies. But by the end of the 1980s, school principals had new and more pressing issues to address in assemblies, and stopped inviting us.

To find out whether such assemblies were useful, I prepared an anonymous questionnaire, which the school administered to the students between 4 and 12 weeks after an assembly. In all, 3,400 questionnaires were completed. Then seven pre-med students from the Tufts Experimental Study Program, who volunteered to work with me for two summers, encoded the responses onto punch cards, which they then sorted on card sorting machines. The most important result was that 29% of current smokers quit after the assembly, and had not started to smoke again when they completed the questionnaire. It was also useful to know that 7th graders evaluated assemblies more positively than 8th graders.[360]

Some health educators believe that the most effective time to educate students about the evils of smoking is before they are coping with peer pressure to smoke.[361] My experience over a 20-year period, during which I averaged about 6 assemblies a year and gave 114 assemblies to a total of around 30,000 students, supports that belief. My very first words at every assembly were that I was a volunteer not paid for my talk to them, and had driven some distance to talk to them, because I thought they were important enough for me to give them a message that could really help them. This introduction tended to forge a bond between the students and someone they had never seen before. Also, assemblies are somewhat special occasions that leave a deeper impression than routine classroom teaching by a familiar teacher. Presenters are listened to intently if they are expert. Best of all, students may become convinced that smoking must be stamped out.

The authors of the 2001 book "Combating Teen Smoking: Research and Policy Strategies" point out that there is a wide variation in the effectiveness of school antismoking programs, and draw a number of important conclusions on strategies that make them successful.[362] They conclude that denying youths an access to tobacco by laws forbidding sales to minors, if actively monitored and enforced, is very effective in reducing teenage smoking, while increasing the price of cigarettes is much less effective. Their strongest recommendation is that we learn from the tobacco industry, and carry out mass-media campaigns based on modern social marketing principles, using strong advertising with a heavy, youth-oriented media blitz. They caution that a successful antismoking campaign is invariably followed by a new tactic devised by the tobacco industry, to ensure that sales stay high. To counter such tactics, antismoking campaigns must evolve continually, and adapt to the changing societal modes, ideals and aspiration of teenagers. Therefore, research is continually needed to identify these changing modes and to use this knowledge optimally to reduce teenage smoking. Also, all new antismoking programs need to be evaluated, and then modified as necessary.

Unfortunately, tobacco is now available to youths on the internet. According to a letter in the April 21, 2004 issue of *JAMA*, 36 minors were recruited to test whether they could buy cigarettes on the internet using a computer without adult help. That 97% succeeded quite rapidly suggests that underage youths can indeed buy tobacco on the internet without any difficulty.

For three decades as of 2006, the American Cancer Society has chosen the Thursday before Thanksgiving for a concerted antismoking campaign, the Great American Smoke-Out. This major event is staged to help smokers kick the habit at least for the day, but ideally for good. In addition, in recent years the National Center for Tobacco-Free Kids, a nonprofit organization in Washington, DC, has organized an annual "Kick Butts Day."[363] A typical program includes extensive preparations prior to the campaign date, such as signing up for an Undercover Cigarette Buying Operation to discover whether under-age buying of cigarettes is really prevented, writing to local media to complain about the industry ads that target young people, discussions that analyze such tobacco industry ads, presentations to classes in grade 7 about the hazards of smoking and deceptive industry advertisements, and asking kids to bring to school items that display tobacco industry logos—or else as many tobacco-associated products as possible for a fun-filled "merchandise dump" on Quit Butts Day. The involvement of printed and electronic media is vital for advertising this day, and for covering its activities. The Campaign for Tobacco-Free Kids provides a fine campaign kit for the Quit Butts Dsy.[363]

Government agencies and the non-profit societies mentioned above also provide excellent free materials for educating children about tobacco. In addition, for-profit organizations sell tobacco prevention products.[364]

Not all states have laws that include a statement on mandatory health education in schools, which includes smoking as one of the subjects which must be covered. In the early 1970's, Chester Kennedy, assistant director of Massachusetts' Department of Public Health, asked me to co-chair a Working Group of Legislators/Health Educators, to pass a law on mandatory health education in Massachusetts schools. On the legislative side, our co-chair was Ralph Parker, Vice-Chair of the Republican Party in the state Senate. Together, we wrote a brief paragraph that identified all the main areas of health education, including smoking. But after two successive years of hard-fought advocacy, our bill still had not passed. Not until the third year did we realize that mention of sex education made it unacceptable. After deleting sex education from our bill, it passed by a landslide. Finally, strong belief in a religion that prohibits all forms of addiction can be highly effective in discouraging kids from smoking. As long ago as 1922, Evangelical Christians such as E. Stanley Jones strongly condemned cigarette smoking.[365] Use of alcohol and tobacco were and still are some of the taboos of many Evangelical Christian sects.[366] Since the carcinogenic effects of smoking are most potent if it is begun early, children from homes where smoking is forbidden have a lower than expected cancer incidence, even if they start to smoke in adulthood.

Mormons and Seventh Day Adventists are asked to abstain from smoking, drinking and extramarital sex, and look askance on drinking coffee and eating hot spices. As a result, their death rate for cancer at sites related to smoking is less than one fourth of that for the United States population, and for cancer of all other sites combined it is only two thirds of the expected rate.[367], [368] These results are very important, for they show that the link between smoking and cancer incidence holds true even for a group of people who smoked *less* than the general public.

The above data show that when religious belief directly pro-hibits unhealthy practices, then the health benefit is direct and can be truly spectacular. Of course, not all Mormons or Seventh Day Adventists were born into families who already belonged to these sects, and indulged in habits that they quit once they joined those sects. This is certainly true for me, for at the age of 19 I also joined a group that frowned on smoking. So I gave up smok-ing a pipe, which then was almost essential for an undergraduate at Cambridge University. While that affiliation lasted only three years, quitting lasted the rest of my life.

The Surgeon General's Report of 1998 reports that 95% of both women and men smokers said that they first tried a cigarette before the age of 18, and over 74% of both sexes began to smoke daily before age 18.[369] So to benefit the majority of people who become smokers, prevention efforts must be aimed at children and adolescents. But now that college students are targeted by the tobacco industry, they also should become a focus of prevention.

As of September, 2005, Big Tobacco was still targeting kids. New brands of cigarettes flavored to appeal to youngsters have recently been marketed by R.J. Reynolds, U.S. Smokeless Tobacco Company and Brown & Williamson. The latter company has also promoted its Kool cigarettes with hip-hop music that appeals to African-American youths. This has prompted the attorneys gen-eral of several states to sue tobacco companies for violating the ban against targeting kids, which is one of the conditions of their settlement of the states' suit against them.[370]

People who become smokers at earlier ages are more likely to continue smoking and to become heavier smokers, than those who started when older. This is yet another reason why the focus of prevention should be on children. They can be prevented from starting by the example of nonsmoking parents, by firmly limit-ing their circle of friends to nonsmokers, and by effective health education from kindergarten through grade 12. But this educa-tion should be targeted especially on grades 5 through 7, when children are first confronted with having to make a decision on smoking. Once they become smokers, quitting is tough, and continuing to smoke can have grave consequences for those children, as well as for society as a whole.

Finally, it should be mentioned that Smoking and Tobacco Control Monograph no. 14, "Changing adolescent smoking prevalence: Where it is and why" published by the National Cancer Institute in 2001, will be helpful for educators and researchers.

TWENTY FOUR

HEALTH WARNINGS, ADVERTISEMENTS, AND LEGISLATION

Writing in the New York Times of July 25, 2003, a reporter questioned the ban of smoking in New York's bars, asking, "If virtue has prevailed in the smoking ban, why are so many people upset?" He found the reason was, that they believe that people have the right to behave as stupidly as they wish, and may prefer not to believe that secondhand smoke can kill. In contrast, the famous whistle-blower of the tobacco company conspiracy, Jeffrey Wigand, is quoted on page 1 of the Boston Globe of July 5, 2003, as saying "You smoke, you die. That's pretty simple."

The Federal Trade Commission (FTC) has a history of reviewing and regulating tobacco products and advertisements that dates back to 1930.[371],[372] In 1962, the FTC's request for technical guidance from the United States Public Health Service was one of the stimuli that resulted in the landmark Surgeon General's Report on Smoking and Health of 1964: America's first official recognition that smoking is a cause of cancer and of other serious diseases. A year after its publication, Congress enacted the Cigarette Labeling and Advertising Act of 1965, that required the following warning to be placed on all cigarette packages in 1966:

—CAUTION: CIGARETTE SMOKING MAY BE HAZARDOUS TO YOUR HEALTH

Then in 1967, John Banzhaf, an attorney acting as a private citizen who later became president of a highly successful antismoking association, ASH (Action on Smoking and Health), petitioned the FTC to apply the Fairness Doctrine to cigarette advertising. Within a few months, the FTC ruled in favor of Banzhaf's petition, and required broadcasters who aired cigarette commercials on television and radio to provide "a significant amount of time" to citizens who wished to point out that smoking "may be hazardous to the smoker's health". In a press interview, the FTC's chief counsel stated that a ratio of one antismoking message to three cigarette commercials seemed adequate to provide "a significant amount of time." Now, radio and TV stations began to air antismoking PSAs (Public Service Announcements) developed by health organizations such as the American Cancer Society and the Heart and Lung Associations, government health agencies, and by professionals already engaged in antismoking activities.[373]

The airing of antismoking messages ended on January 2, 1971, the date on which all cigarette advertising on TV or radio was banned by Federal legislation–the Public Health Smoking Act of 1969. Up until then, the public benefited enormously from the antismoking messages, which served as a very effective foil to the cigarette advertisements. My own activities during this time illustrate what was happening all around the country while the electronic media had to allocate time to rebut tobacco ads.

During this period, I was asked to head the Massachusetts chapter of the National Interagency Council on Smoking and Health, a joint venture of the American Cancer, Heart, and Lung Associations. As a result, members of Volunteers for Health Awareness became familiar crusaders against smoking on radio and TV. WBZ radio of Boston launched the most extensive campaign: a series of eight four-hour talk shows targeted on smoking and the tobacco industry. They were hosted colorful TC star Jerry Williams, who spent the first hour discussing various aspects of the tobacco problem with VHA professionals. Then we spent three hours answering the questions of the people who phoned in.

During this period, VHA members took part in antismoking programs on most of the local radio and TV stations,[374] many of which became enthusiastic crusaders against cigarette smoking. Even after the requirement to air antismoking messages ended in 1971, some stations continued to invite us annually for a session with their talk-show host, and continued to include antismoking messages in fulfilling their federal public service obligations. My own annual half-hour discussions with David McNeil, Boston radio station WCRB's star announcer, continued into the 1980s, and we became good personal friends.

The Act of 1969 required all cigarette packages sold in the United States to display one of the following four health warnings:

- SURGEON GENERAL'S WARNING:
- Smoking Causes Lung Cancer, Heart Disease, Emphysema, and May Complicate Pregnancy

- SURGEON GENERAL'S WARNING:
- Quitting Smoking Now Greatly Reduces Serious Risks to Your Health

- SURGEON GENERAL'S WARNING:
- Smoking by Pregnant Women May Result in Fetal Injury, Premature Birth and Low Birth Weight

- SURGEON GENERAL'S WARNING:
- Cigarette Smoke Contains Carbon Monoxide

Following the passage of this act, the FTC urged Congress to enact legislation that would require similar health warnings on all cigarette advertisements. Cigarette manufacturers first began to include these warnings in 1971 on a voluntary basis. Then in 1972, cigarette manufacturers entered into an agreement with the

FTC, which required the Surgeon General's warnings to appear on all cigarette advertisements in specified sizes and colors.

It is instructive to look at the regulation of tobacco products in other countries, to discover more effective ways in which we could steer potential customers and confirmed smokers away from cigarettes. As to the labeling of cigarette packages in other countries, cigarette manufacturer Brown and Williams say that they comply with the regulations on health warnings in countries where these exist; but in countries where these do not exist, they label cigarette packages with U.S. health warnings.372 Tobacco companies would like the public to see such voluntary labeling as a noble gesture. But more likely, tobacco companies do it merely to protect themselves against lawsuits brought by dying smokers, or after their deaths by their bereaved families.

Canada, which has been particularly concerned about the terrible toll that results from long-term smoking, has passed stringent legislation on labeling that could serve as an ideal model for all countries: it has made "Graphic Cigarette Warnings" mandatory: one-half of the front face of all cigarette packs must carry an officially-designed picture that illustrates one of the following cautionary messages, which must be printed in distinctive, contrasting, large-size print:

- CIGARETTES ARE HIGHLY ADDICTIVE
- (pile of butts pictured)
- CHILDREN SEE- CHILDREN DO
- (smoking parent and child pictured)
- CIGARETTES HURT BABIES
- (pregnant mother pictured)
- DON'T POISON US
- (children pictured)
- TOBACCO USE CAN MAKE YOU IMPOTENT
- CIGARETTES CAUSE STROKES

- CIGARETTES CAUSE MOUTH DISEASES
- CIGARETTES ARE A HEARTBREAKER
- CIGARETTES CAUSE LUNG CANCER
- YOU'RE NOT THE ONLY ONE SMOKING THIS CIGARETTE

The above list is merely a sample of Graphic Warnings. In April, 2002, the Canadian Cancer Society released the results of a survey of over 2,000 Canadians, which showed that three out of four Canadians, including a majority (59%) of smokers, support the picture-based warnings on cigarette packages.[375] The evidence from several reports on the effectiveness of Graphic Warnings has been analyzed by Health Canada. It concluded that size and color contrast are important in insuring that health warnings have a strong impact: the larger the warning, the more effective it is for conveying its message and encouraging smokers to quit.[376]

Tobacco products cause so many ills, that it is difficult to choose which one should be used for antismoking messages. Some messages do include the information that heavy, long-continued smoking can cause infertility. But still unused are the results of a study in the April 20, 2002 issue of *The Lancet*, which reported that smoking more often inactivates sperm carrying the Y chromosome that produces male babies, than sperm carrying two X chromosomes that produces females. As a result, parents who are both heavy smokers produce nearly one-third fewer boys than girls. If only the father is a heavy smoker, then he fathers one-sixth fewer boys than if he were a nonsmoker.

Since cigars also pose serious health hazards (see above), their packages and advertisements must also carry strong warnings in the United States. In a landmark decision of June, 2000, the FTC announced settlements with the seven largest United States cigar companies. Packs of cigars must now carry warnings such as:

- SURGEON GENERAL WARNING:

- Cigar Smoking Can Cause Cancers Of The Mouth And Throat, Even If You Do Not Inhale.
- SURGEON GENERAL WARNING:
- Cigar Smoking Can Cause Lung Cancer And Heart Disease.
- SURGEON GENERAL WARNING:
- Tobacco Use Increases The Risk Of Infertility, Stillbirth And Low Birth Weight.
- SURGEON GENERAL WARNING:
- Cigars Are Not A Safe Alternative To Cigarettes.
- SURGEON GENERAL WARNING:
- Tobacco Smoke Increases The Risk Of Lung Cancer And Heart Disease, Even In Nonsmokers.

Further, an FTC order created a uniform national system of rotating health warnings on cigar products, which preempted state laws that required different health warnings. But the FTC order did not affect any other state or local requirements, such as restrictions on youth access to tobacco products, or restrictions on the placement of advertisements.[377] But United States–mandated warnings are far smaller than their Canadian counterparts.

The National Center for Tobacco-Free Kids has evaluated the evidence from scientific studies conducted in Massachusetts, Canada, and Australia on such factors as the percentage of people who could later recall the health warnings on packages of tobacco products. As a result, the Center recommends the following changes in warnings on advertisements of smokeless tobacco products.[378] Such requirements for warnings would seem to be equally appropriate for all tobacco products:

- *Warnings should be in black on white, or white on black print.*

- *They should have a font size of at least 24 point in ads of 8 x 10 inches, and be proportionately larger or smaller in other ads.*

An insightful comparison of the politics of tobacco control in the United States and in Canada was published in 2002 by Donald Studlar.[379] In view of the need to drive home to current and potential future smokers the impact of the risk that smoking entails, it seems time that our legislators followed Canada's lead: *All warnings should be Graphic, and occupy an area half the size of a cigarette package, and one-quarter of all tobacco advertisements.*

TWENTY FIVE

INDUSTRY DECEPTION, HANDOUTS, REGULATION, AND LAWSUITS

Handouts of cigarettes to potential customers are the most direct way in which tobacco companies can make new addicts. While handouts to minors seem to have stopped in the United States–but not overseas)–handouts to adults continue. Even today, tobacco companies hire young people to give away packages of cigarettes in dance halls, amusement centers, and pubs.[380] When smoking is finally outlawed in all these establishments–and good progress toward that end is being made[381]–tobacco companies undoubtedly will find other ways to accomplish their purpose.

Accepting money from the tobacco industry or its subsidies always has been a temptation–though happily not for the three great national societies that focus on the main diseases caused by smoking, namely the American Cancer Society, and the Heart and Lung Associations. They collaborated to create a joint agency to fight against the aggressive misinformation about the health effects of smoking that were widely disseminated by the Tobacco Industry Council. In my state, this agency was called the Massachusetts Interagency Council on Smoking and Health, which I was asked to chair for the year 1971–1972. As part of our work, we engaged in hot radio debates against speakers provided by the Tobacco Industry Institute, who tried to perpetuate the myth that whether or not smoking caused disease was still an open question.

To prove another myth, that they were concerned about good health, the tobacco industry contributed heavily to all types of health research. I had debated Anne Browder of the Tobacco Institute on a radio show, and later debated its senior member Walker Merryman. A day later, I received a phone call from the Tobacco Institute, asking me if I would serve on one of its panels of scientists, who occasionally visited research laboratories, to judge whether the Tobacco Institute should fund their application for a research grant. It would be lucrative work requiring slim expenditure of my time. But since the hidden purpose was obviously to soften my attacks on their agenda, I did not take the time to enquire what my fee would be. It took me just a few seconds to say, thank you, but I'm much too busy.

In 1973, I felt thunderstruck when Harvard's Finland Institute of Microbiology at Boston City Hospital, which was connected to the Mallory Institute of Pathology where I worked by a short passage, was reported widely in the press to have landed a multi-million dollar grant from a tobacco company. The grant was entitled "Harvard Medical School Study of the Connection Between Smoking and Lung and Heart Disease," and the news release from Harvard Medical School said that "cigarette smoking has been *alleged* to be a cause of these diseases", and "a direct causal relationship... has *not* been established" (the italics are mine).

With such a title and press release, it was quite irrelevant whatever the research might discover eventually. Before research on this grant had even begun, the tobacco industry could harvest millions of dollars in increased sales to smokers, who now felt reassured: nearly a decade after the Surgeon General's report that smoking caused lung cancer, prestigious Harvard Medical School was not sure that it had been proven that smoking caused diseases of the lung and heart, or lung cancer! The industry had scored a terrific publicity scoop in persuading the premier U.S. Medical School to support its fairy-tale.

I lost no time in writing an outspoken letter about this matter to Dean Ebert of Harvard Medical School on my letterhead as Associate Professor of Surgery at Tufts Medical School. But before I mailed it I obtained co-signatures from five like-minded professors at Harvard Medical School. My letter laid out the above facts, and asked that there be no further press releases on this award. The Dean asked the head of the laboratory where the work was to be done, Edward Kass, to respond. He did so in a letter of three single-spaced pages, in which he graciously acknowledged that the point of my letter was well taken, but gently defended the acceptance of the grant. Still, the end result was positive: there were no more press releases, and when the grant ended, Harvard Medical School declined to renew it.

It was not until 2003 that I discovered that this exchange of letters was freely accessible on the web, since it had been used in several lawsuits against the tobacco industry. To access these letters one merely needed to go to www.tobaccodocuments.org, and write my name with middle initial E into the search space. I was delighted to see that my letter to Dean Ebert was used in suing the industry, to prove how much the industry was willing to pay, to have their vital myth confirmed by Harvard. This website also documented the use in lawsuits against the tobacco industry of some of my other forays against tobacco companies, and some of my scientific papers on smoking and cancer. But since word got out that I was writing a book damaging to the tobacco industry, all mention of me on that website has been completely erased.

The temptation for individuals and institutions to accept funds irrespective of their source will always be with us. In 1993, the American Council of Science and Health (ACSH) summarized the American Medical Association's (AMA's) struggle with this issue over the previous 30 years.[382]. After the first Surgeon General's Report on Smoking and Health was published in 1964, the tobacco industry funneled $18 million to AMA for research on tobacco. Until 1978 when the grant ended, it supported the industry's claim that whether or not smoking caused disease was still an open question. Money speaks loudly.

But in the mid 1980's, the AMA's House of Delegates voted to require AMA to divest itself of ownership of tobacco stocks, and told medical schools to stop investing in tobacco stocks. Dr. Alan Blum, founder of "Doctors Ought to Care," led this battle, and also suggested the dropping of stocks of companies which make products used by the tobacco industry–for instance Kodak, which makes cigarette filters, and Kimberly-Clark, which produces cigarette paper. But Blum's plea went unheard.

Even in 1993, AMA confined its divesting of stocks to those companies that directly produce, market, or promote tobacco products. However, at a 1993 AMA meeting, Dr. Joel Dunnington of the University of Texas asked for divestment of the stocks of subsidiaries of tobacco companies, and showed how deeply they are involved in the promotion of tobacco products. For instance, the non-tobacco subsidiary of RJR Nabisco retaliated against an advertising agency that dared to prepare an ad for Northwest Airlines, in which passengers cheered when the pilot announced Northwest's pioneering no-smoking policy. RJR Nabisco had been advertising its Oreos with the help of that advertising agency, and in retaliation for the Northwest Airlines ad, pulled its $84 million in business from the advertising agency. Glen Carter, a medical student delegate from Memphis, said "This is a matter of conscience; the money from these tobacco companies and their subsidiaries is blood money. Let's do the right thing and not let our pocketbooks judge what we want to do." Unfortunately, these testimonies failed to sway the council of AMA: AMA was not willing to lose the funds it was getting from tobacco companies.

Nevertheless, AMA says its "Unshakable stand on tobacco is helping ensure a healthier tomorrow for each of our patients."

AMA did introduce the "Extinguisher" cartoon to school children, and its Student Section started "Docs Against Smoking," which proposed prohibiting smoking on public transportation.

The American Heart Association has never accepted funds from the tobacco industry or its subsidiaries. In 1990, the American Cancer Society (ACS) adopted a policy not to enter into a promotional agreement with any company or any of its subsidiaries, which engaged in producing or wholesale distributing tobacco products. However, the AMA permitted retention of the stocks of tobacco company subsidiaries, and that is the policy that the American Academy of Family Physicians had already adopted in 1987.

While the above information was published by ACSH, it was itself accepting funding from subsidiaries of the tobacco industry, on the premise that if articles published by ACSH were damaging to a company, then it would not contribute to ACSH. ACSH president Elizabeth Whelan said ACSH's key was honesty, commitment to scientific reality, and independence from the wishes of those who funded it.[383] This sounds like a brave statement. But while the articles in ACSH magazine *Priorities* have consistently lambasted tobacco use and marketing, its magazine all too frequently publishes dramatic exposures of what it labels to be witch-hunts of a public over-anxious about contamination of the environment. For instance, ACSH's report of March, 2002, entitled "Cancer Clusters: Findings vs. Feelings" concludes that "Based on the data available today, there is no firm evidence that traces of industrial pollution diffused in the environment are causing cancer clusters."[384] That statement alone is worth many millions of dollars in the courtroom where a chemical company accused of polluting the environment with carcinogens might be defending itself against litigation initiated by cancer patients or their families. But it is patently untrue. For instance, there is a complete consensus on the reliability of the evidence for an increase in cancer incidence in the people who live in the large region affected by the meltdown of the Chernobyl nuclear reactor.

The policy of the many publications that have accepted tobacco advertisements proves all too clearly, that we hate to bite the hand that feeds us. For instance, a study on this question by Kenneth Warner, published in the prestigious NEJM in 1992, found strong statistical evidence that magazines that carry cigarette advertising have a diminished coverage of the hazards of smoking, and that this is particularly true for women's magazines.[385] Not only magazines, but all health-oriented associations such as ACSH should cleanse their image, by refusing advertising and funds from tobacco companies, their subsidiaries, and all organizations sponsored by them.

But tobacco companies did not stop at great generosity (or was it bribery?), to perpetuate their favorite myth. In Britain, they used generosity as bait for a gift that would prove their good will. So in 2001, the editor of the *British Medical Journal*, Richard Smith, threatened to quit his professorship at the University of Nottingham, if it did not return a $5.4 million grant from the British American Tobacco Company, even though the grant was unrelated to health. By accepting it, Smith wrote, Nottingham has "crossed a dangerous line... [The] University looks either grasping, naïve, or foolish."[386]

By his action, Richard Smith had upped the ante on the need to reject tobacco industry money by another notch. His attitude implied that it is not merely health-related institutions that should reject such tainted money, but also if given for projects unrelated to health. Richard Smith's stance made it clear that even by accepting tobacco industry funds that are not related to health, an institution validates the tobacco industry's attempt to project a public-minded spirit. In reality, its actions were probably motivated by the bottom line, and its shareholders cannot accuse it, of having allowed scruples to stand in its way.

During the 1960s and 1970s, it was only to be expected that the tobacco industry would try to bribe researchers to argue in favor of its proposition, that the link between smoking and lung cancer had not been proven. Of course, it is impossible to know which of the several researchers who opposed the link in years past[387] were entirely honest, and who accepted bribes or gifts. But there can be no doubt whatever that the brilliant British statistician Ronald Fisher, who voiced doubts about the link prior to the publication of the first Surgeon General's Report on Smoking and Health in 1964, was entirely honest: at the time, he just did not have the facts needed to draw the right conclusion.

Researchers who accept money from tobacco companies can be expected to justify their decision. But when the objective is to create a less harmful cigarette, then a perfectly legitimate argument in favor of accepting tobacco funds can be made. Even so, the author of the objective report on this topic in Science magazine of 2005 concluded that "institutions will have to decide whether to overlook the source of this funding, or take the moral high road and watch it go up in smoke."[388] In fact, tobacco companies are perfectly capable of funding, equipping and staffing their own Tobacco Research Institute, rather than be allowed to utilize the resources of universities, and to lead them down the slippery moral road of legitimizing the acceptance of money stained with the blood of millions of smokers.

Many years have passed since any credible scientist disputed the link between smoking and the major diseases that it causes. Still, in spring of 2003 I was startled to hear a tobacco industry spokesperson say on the radio "that smoking is known to cause cancer, heart disease, emphysema and chronic bronchitis." Then, in August 2003, spokesman Marc Fritsch of Philip Morris International said that the company is "absolutely in line with whatever the overwhelming majority of the scientific community has to say" on the health effects of smoking. Further, a visit to the web site www.philipmorrisusa.com in 2003 and 2004 revealed that the industry spokespersons whom I had heard on the radio were not kidding: the information given on the website was accurate, concise, and completely in line with the scientific consensus on the health effects of smoking.

Was the tobacco industry "coming clean" to protect the public? Or was this simply an unexpected new line of defense, calculated to protect itself against future suits, to retain present smokers, and to make new addicts who were tough enough to take risks? The one certainty is that this strategy was carefully devised to protect the industry, not the smokers.

But it is easy to understand why executives find the lure of tobacco funds hard to resist. They are in the position to know all too well that additional funds can bring badly needed relief to their companies. It is hard to choose integrity over cash, nor can we expect everyone to believe that integrity is priceless.

Not only Medical Schools, but the American Association for Cancer Research (AACR), the United States society for all basic and most applied cancer research workers, had failed to take an official stance on the link between smoking and lung cancer for many a year, even though the evidence for it continued to accumulate. Meanwhile, the tobacco industry unceasingly advertised its myth that this link remained unproven. But I was convinced that AACR should not restrict its mission purely to the conduct of basic cancer research, but should also concentrate on translating its vital research findings into benefits for the general public– a policy that has been gaining momentum in recent years both within AACR and at the National Cancer Institute, which funds the research of many AACR members. Therefore, at the annual AACR convention of 1982, I asked four of my AACR friends to cosponsor the motion with me, "that current evidence proves that there is a direct link between smoking and lung cancer." Happily, the directors of AACR voted unanimously to affirm that motion, and their action was reported in the national press.[389] That upset the tobacco industry, and an editorial in the Tobacco Observer of

August, 1982 likened the AACR to the authorities who had forbidden Galileo to have freedom of scientific inquiry. It equated Galileo's revolutionary views to the Tobacco Institute's stand that lung cancer remains a medical mystery, which AACR had tried to suppress, and it lambasted me personally for my role in helping to scotch that myth. It was the highest tribute that the industry could have paid me!

The great temptation that a generous offer poses both to individuals and to institutions comes alive in the story of the offer made by George Bernard Shaw to a lady at a party. "Madam," he said, "would you sleep with me tonight if I gave you a million pounds?" To which she replied, "Well... yes." Then Shaw asked her, "But would you sleep with me for one hundred pounds?" To that she replied "That's outrageous. Do you take me to be a whore?" Shaw answered, "Madam, we've already established what you are. We were merely haggling over the price." Institutions should keep this story in mind when tempted to accept money that will sanitize companies that advertise cigarettes to children.

Already in 1988, Richard Daynard of Northeastern University School of Law in Boston had advocated for use of lawsuits against tobacco companies as a useful strategy to reduce smoking.[390] Then in 1990, David Kessler began his six-year tenure as commissioner of the Food and Drug Administration (FDA).[391] Near the end of his tenure, Kessler documented the FDA's attempts to regulate tobacco products.[392] Then in his 2001 book, "A Question of Intent: A Great American Battle with a Deadly Industry," Kessler described the many battles that he had fought as FDA commissioner. Best of all, his fight against the tobacco industry was remarkably successful.

Kessler explained that cigarettes fall between the cracks, because they are not food, drugs, medical devices, or cosmetics. The legacy Kessler inherited was that the FDA should not regulate tobacco, which resulted from the tobacco industry's success in masking its knowledge about the addictive power of nicotine, and its constant effort to addict as many people as possible. In addition, the tobacco crop has a 300-year history of being credited for being a mainstay of the United States economy.[393]

What helped Kessler enormously in his fight were the revelations of Brown & Williamson (B&W) executives such as Jeffrey Wigand, depicted in the movie "The Insider," who leaked inside information to Kessler. Internal memos leaked to The New York Times proved that industry executives had known about the addictive power of nicotine since the early 1960s. A document written by a B&W executive said "We are, then, in the business of selling nicotine, an addictive drug." Further, the industry had programs that had the goal of increasing the nicotine level in cigarettes, thereby increasing their addictive power. Such revelations gave Kessler his case for seeking FDA regulation of the tobacco industry.[393]

Actually, tobacco regulation in the United States has existed for more than a century.[394] For it was then that the Tennessee Supreme Court upheld the conviction of a person for selling cigarettes, holding that these were "wholly noxious and deleterious to health" and that "their use is always harmful..." By 1900, 14 states had outlawed the sale, manufacture, or possession of cigarettes, while 21 other states had considered such a ban but decided against it, and 2 states had passed laws that labeled cigarettes as narcotics.

Until 1995, the Federal Drug Administration (FDA) took the position that it did not have the authority to regulate tobacco products, because it only has the authority that was given to it by Congress in the Food, Drug, and Cosmetics Act of 1938. This was to regulate "articles (other than food) that are intended to affect the structure or any function of the body."[395] Since nicotine could be understood to be a drug, John Banzhaf's Action on Smoking and Health (ASH) petitioned the FDA in 1977 to regulate cigarettes as a drug. FDA denied the petition, and won the lawsuit that ASH brought against it, on the grounds that cigarette manufacturers did not make any health claims for their product. The fact that cigarettes are dangerous or deadly was not held to be sufficient, to permit FDA to control them.

The question of whether FDA should have jurisdiction over tobacco was considered by the United States District Court of North Carolina in 1997. Its verdict was appealed to the United States Supreme Court, which found in 2000 that the FDA does not have the authority to regulate the sale of tobacco products. The decisive reason for this ruling was that FDA had proven conclusively that tobacco products are dangerous, and would have to ban their sale if given jurisdiction. This the Court could not grant, unless and until Congress had approved that radical step. Thus, the Court's decision hinged on whether Congress had approved FDA's control of tobacco – which it had not done.

The creation of a Tobacco Control Agency, a new federal agency to regulate tobacco products, has been suggested by Leonard Glantz and George Annas as a way to protect the public, and to coordinate the various national tobacco control efforts. They thought that the goals of the Agency should be:[394]

1. To reduce smoking, especially by reducing the number of people who start to smoke, and by funding research toward that goal.

2. To increase the number of people who quit.

3. To fund research to make cigarettes "less harmful" (however controversial that quest may seem), and to test the toxicity of cigarettes and set standards for toxicity.

Strengthening the FDA's authority over tobacco is a less radical solution for dealing with the deadlock produced by the Supreme Court's decision. In the February 5, 1997 issue of JAMA, former FDA Commissioner Kessler and coworkers summarized the legal and scientific basis that justifies FDA's jurisdiction over cigarettes and smokeless tobacco. Now, the onus of action is squarely on Congress. Knowing the dangers that tobacco poses, Congress could either create the new agency proposed by Glantz and Annas, or else give the FDA the same kind of limited authority over tobacco products that these experts propose for a new Tobacco Control Agency. FDA already has the breadth of expertise and the regulatory experience that will allow it to carry out these tasks.[396] By such action, Congress would insure that at last, the public would have effective protection that could not be voided by appeals to our courts. Also, FDA should be strengthened by increasing its budget greatly, and by moving its budget appropriation process from agriculture committees to HHS health committees, which are far better fitted to this task.[397]

Testifying before a Congressional committee on June 3, 2003, United States Surgeon General Richard Carmona said that he supported the banning of tobacco products. However, a White House spokesperson commented that this was not the policy of the administration, which was targeted only to crack down on youth smoking. That day, testifying before another congressional committee, the chief executive officer of Philip Morris said that FDA oversight of tobacco would now enable his firm to effectively market two new products that is was developing, that could be less harmful to smokers than existing cigarettes.[398] As of January 2007, Senator Edward Kennedy planned to introduce a bill that would allow FDA to regulate cigarettes.[399]

Regarding how the tobacco industry succeeded in its cover-up, three different books, all dated 1996, reveal the details: *The Cigarette Papers* by Stanton Glantz and coauthors;[400] *Smokescreen. The Truth Behind the Tobacco Industry Cover-Up* by Philip Hilts;[401] and *Ashes to Ashes America's Hundred-Year Cigarette War, the Public Health, and the Unabashed Triumph of Philip Morris* by Richard Kluger.[402] The most exciting of the three books is perhaps *The Cigarette Papers*. In May 1994, Glantz received an anonymous delivery of a big cardboard box full of papers that the tobacco industry would have preferred to keep out of sight: over 10,000 pages of internal papers from B&W. Years earlier, the tobacco industry had sued Glantz not to release the British documentary "Death in the West," which shows real-life cowboys dying of smoking-related diseases contrasted with the tobacco industry's statements. The suit was unsuccessful, and the film proved its worth as powerful rebuttal of Marlboro cowboy ads. Now, Brown and Williams sued Glantz to block his release of their papers, and again, the suit was unsuccessful. Glantz and his team of experts in addiction, law, and health policy spent a year indexing and analyzing the B&W papers, and their book covers the years from 1954 to the late 1960s.400 Glantz and coauthors document that the tobacco industry executives discussed whether to reveal their knowledge of the addictive power of nicotine at the committee meetings prior to publication of the first Surgeon General's Report on Smoking and Health in 1994–and decided against revealing it. The book shows that the industry became expert at public relations: it arranged for its arguments to be published in the popular press, rewarded those with the authority to ensure that movie actors smoked on screen, and paid scientists to go on media tours to argue that the link between smoking and disease remained unproven, and to create the illusion that there was an ongoing "controversy" on this matter.

The book by Hilts uncovers other aspects of the tobacco industry's deceptions. He documents the industry's unrelenting pursuit of youths–for instance it targeted convenience stores near high schools and advertised so heavily in college newspapers in the early 1960s that tobacco ads accounted for 40% of their revenues. He documents the companies' efforts to manipulate the nicotine content of their cigarettes and their knowledge of its addictive effects, which explains why they target youths: unless you hook them young, you may not hook them at all. Hilts notes that at the time of writing (1996), half of all American teenagers owned gifts from the tobacco industry, such as lighters, knives and T-shirts, all with tobacco company logos prominently displayed...[401]

Kluger's book is an encyclopedic history of smoking that substantiates a message similar to that of the other books:[402]

- That for many years, the tobacco industry has known that smoking is dangerous to smokers and nonsmokers alike.

- That cigarettes are essentially a device for delivering a highly addictive drug, nicotine.

- That the industry has willfully and powerfully targeted children.

At a congressional subcommittee meeting in 1994, the top executives of the seven largest United States tobacco companies took an oath and testified that cigarettes are not addictive, and that their dangers were overstated. In contrast, in the June, 2000 trial in Miami, where a class-action suit by half a million Floridians was seeking punitive damages, the president of Philip Morris and the chairman of Brown & Williamson acknowledged that cigarettes make people dreadfully sick. They even said that "Smoking is the cause of lung cancer and other diseases," and when asked, "Is smoking addictive?" replied "Yes."[403]

So it took six years from their denial under oath in 1994, for the heads of leading United States tobacco companies to acknowledge that cigarettes are addictive and harmful. For aiding and abetting the tantalizingly gradual murder of millions of willing but misinformed victims, I believe that those responsible at the highest level should be jailed for life. *But they should be PERMITTED to reduce the length of their sentences by being allowed to smoke as much as they wish.*

The Master Settlement Agreement resulted from the massive evidence that the tobacco companies had steadfastly denied: namely that the hazards of smoking had been proven. Their chief defense, namely that smokers knew the risks, failed to convince. As a result, the suit threatened by 46 states against the tobacco companies *was settled in 1998 by an agreement (the*

"Master Settlement Agreement") to pay them $209 billion, spaced in annual payments over a period of 25 years. These funds were to be split between the states, and could be used by each state as it wished. After that time, payments by the four tobacco companies involved (Brown & Williamson, Lorillard, Philip Morris, and R.J. Reynolds) were to continue indefinitely (essentially, forever), based on the volume of domestic tobacco sales.[404] In addition, the industry agreed to change its marketing methods drastically, and to submit to regulatory control by the FDA.[405] However, as of October of 2003, legislation to grant FDA the authority to regulate tobacco products had hit a major roadblock in the Senate, because several of its provisions fell far short of the standards identified by the American Heart Association and its coalition partners.[406]

The enormity of the damages accepted by the tobacco industry by the above agreement validates the enormity of the damage that smoking inflicts on individual smokers, and on the health-care industry as a whole. That the tobacco industry consented to it indicates that the health effects of smoking described in preceding chapters are all too real, and have such a vast impact, that its extent is hard to grasp. The fact that the settlement provides for payments to continue "for ever" suggests that neither the attorney generals nor the tobacco companies believe that smoking will end very soon. Nor should we worry that tobacco companies will not try to prevent that event from ever occurring. The "Master Settlement Agreement" came after four states had settled their own cases against the industry. When Minnesota won its own lawsuit, settling for $6.5 billion dollars in 1998, it imposed new checks on how cigarettes are marketed in its state, and was the fourth state to win an individual settlement. This was a particularly important victory, for Minnesota insisted that the industry put millions of internal documents on the Internet.

While the plaintiffs in the lawsuit brought by the 46 states were their attorneys general, in the lawsuits that individual states brought, each state contracted with private law firms to represent them at no cost. The law firms would earn nothing if their suits failed, but if they won, they would earn a percentage of the sum their clients were awarded. In fact, they won their suits and earned gigantic fees. The downside to these settlements was that once the suits were settled, this they put a damper on the bad press that the industry had been receiving for decades.

Regarding cases brought by dying smokers or their surviving families, the deep pockets of tobacco companies insured that all cases brought against them are fought tooth and nail. The first smoker to ever receive payment from such a suit was a Florida man who lost a lung to cancer. The award of $750,000 to him for a suit begun in 1995 was appealed to several courts, before it reached the US Supreme Court in 2001. When the Court declined to hear the appeal brought by Brown & Williamson, the smoker collected his award plus interest, a total of almost $1.1 million.

In June 2002, an Oregon appeals court reinstated a $79.5 million punitive-damage verdict against the Philip Morris Company for the death of a school janitor who had smoked Marlboros for four decades. The court said that the link between smoking and lung cancer was so strong that there was "absolutely no basis for a genuine dispute on the issue by the 1970s and 1980s," and that nevertheless, Philip Morris asserted "that smoking had not been proven harmful" to "give smokers a crutch to justify their continuing smoking."

In October 2002, a Los Angeles jury ordered Philip Morris to pay $28 billion in punitive damages to a 64-year old woman with lung cancer, for not warning her of the risks of smoking; but the award was reduced to $28 million on appeal.[407] In June 2001, a Los Angeles jury awarded $3 billion to a smoker who later died, but that award was decreased to $100 million on appeal. In January 2004, a New York jury ordered Brown and Williamson, the Tobacco Institute and the Council for Tobacco Research to pay a total of $20 million dollars to the widow of a Lucky Strikes smoker.[408] In all, as of May 2004, tobacco companies had lost 14 individual cases, and hundreds were pending. But the industry had appealed all awards, and only two smokers had received a money settlement.

In the same month, also pending were appeals on an award of $145 billion in a 1999 class action suit in Florida, and of a $10 billion award in a class action suit in Illinois. Both suits were eventually reversed by the Supreme Courts of those states.

Large awards are intended to punish the industry and compensate the injured smokers or their surviving families.[409] If suits succeed – and few do so–the industry is sure to transfer future damage settlements to smokers, by further increasing the price of cigarettes. Still, this will give smokers yet another motivation to quit, and cause more teenagers to balk at taking up a very expensive habit.

The United States Government has also sued the tobacco industry. Filed in 1999 after five years of preparation, the government's suit asked the industry to disgorge its "ill-gotten gains" of $280 billion, claiming that the industry had marketed its products fraudulently since the mid-1950s. In 2000, a Federal judge dismissed two of the suit's four counts, and ruled that the government could not recover billions of dollars in smoking-related health care costs. But the judge validated the two counts brought under the RICO (Racketeer Influenced Corrupt Organization) statute, and concluded that both the Justice Department and the industry's lawyers estimated the potential liability of the industry to be "in the billions of dollars."[410]

The tobacco industry contributes millions of dollars in political donations before each election, and one of its top priorities has been to terminate this lawsuit, or settle it with weak remedies that permit business as usual. So it was hardly a coincidence, that in 2001 the Bush administration showed its hostility to the government's lawsuit by seeking to deny funding for it and attempt-

ing to settle it prematurely. This caused such an outcry, that nothing came of this effort.[411]

Not until September 2004 did United States District Judge
Gladys Kessler begin to try this crucial case in Washington, D.C.
under the RICO act.[412] The government sought an award of $280
billion to deprive tobacco companies of their illicit profits from
deceiving the public during a "50-year pattern of material mis-
representations, half-truths, deceptions and flat-out lies by the
defendants that continues to this day."[413] Despite destruction of
critical records by the industry,[414] Judge Kessler ruled for the government. But in February 2005 a United States Court of Appeals
struck down this judgment with a 2-to-1 decision.[415]

On resuming the trial under Judge Kessler's jurisdiction, the
government's expert witness on smoking cessation recommended
that the industry pay $130 billion—roughly half the damage origi-
nally sought—to be divided into annual payments of $5.2 billion
over 25 years to help smokers quit.[416], [417] U.S. Surgeon General
Richard Carmona, whose parents died of smoking-connected
diseases,[418] supported the government's case, saying that "If we
do not have a continuing and sustained effort, the smoking rates,
the death rates and the complication rates will rise."[419] Then early
in June 2005, the Justice Department caused consternation by
suddenly reducing its request from $130 billion spread over 25
years to $10 billion over 5 years. Of course, politics were always
a factor in this suit,[420] and soon a Harvard professor who had
acted as a government witness at the trial acknowledged that an
official had urged him to tone down penalties.[421] Further, numerous press reports suggested that political appointees in the Bush
Justice Department may have ordered a reduction of the cessation
remedy, over the strenuous objections of career attorneys within
the department.[422] Within days after the outcry that followed,
the U.S. Justice department increased its request to $14 billion.[423]

But this was 5%—a tiny fraction—of the $280 billion that the
previous administration had requested. In response to this out-

rage, a consortium of six major public health groups filed a motion at the end of June 2005 to become parties to the case, arguing that the government no longer represented them adequately. The group included the American Cancer Society, American Heart Association, American Lung Association, Tobacco-Free Kids Action Fund, Americans for Nonsmokers' Rights, and the National African American Tobacco Prevention Network. Judge Kessler granted this motion in July 2005.417 This vital addition to the suit sought seven provisions that included antismoking education, and required cigarette companies to pay $4.8 billion a year to fund a comprehensive quit smoking program.417

On October 17, 2005, the Supreme Court made public their refusal to hear the Justice Department's appeal against the February 2005 appeals court decision to allow the use of RICO to recoup the tobacco industries' ill-gotten gains, arguing that RICO only permitted "forward-looking orders" that would prevent present and future violations of the law. That day, tobacco stocks rose 6% on the stock market.[424] However, there was still the option to appeal this decision to the Supreme Court.[425]

In August 2006, Judge Kessler issued her 1,742-page ruling in the racketeering suit brought by the Justice Department against the tobacco industry.[426] She found that cigarette makers should be punished for deceiving the public for decades about the dangers of tobacco, which had resulted in "an immeasurable amount of human suffering," and ordered them to make landmark changes in the way tobacco is marketed. She said that the nine-month trial had shown tobacco companies to have "marketed and sold their lethal product with zeal, with deception, with a single-minded focus on their financial success and without regard to the human tragedy or social costs that success exacted." She also said that cigarette makers profit from "selling a highly addictive product which causes diseases that lead to a staggering number of deaths per year, an immeasurable amount of human suffering and economic loss and a profound burden on our national health care system."

Judge Kessler ordered the prohibition of labels such as low tar, light, natural or other "deceptive brand descriptions which implicitly or explicitly convey to the smoker and potential smoker that they are less hazardous than full-flavor cigarettes."

However, she also had good news for the industry. She rejected the proposal that it underwrite a multibillion-dollar program to help smokers quit and to educate young people about the hazards of smoking. Instead, she ordered cigarette companies to begin an advertising campaign in newspapers and on television networks on the adverse health effects of smoking. These remedies applied to Batco; Brown & Williamson; Lorillard; Philip Morris and its parent Altria; and R. J. Reynolds and its parent Reynolds American. Liggett was excluded from this judgment, because the judge held that it was not likely to engage in future violations.

During the trial, cigarette companies said it was unfair for the federal government to seek additional penalties, following the $246 billion settlement with state governments in 1998. After Judge Kessler's ruling was published, spokesmen both for the industry and for the consortium of public health groups expressed their dissatisfaction with parts of the judgment, and this could lead to an appeal.[426] Indeed, former FDA Commissioner David Kessler commented that her ruling laid out the road to an appeal.

It was most disappointing that Judge Kessler's order allowed the industry to run its own antismoking campaign, which is akin to leaving the fox in charge of protecting the chicken coop. Indeed, immediately after the ruling, tobacco stocks rose, illustrating the truth of the saying, "sticks and stones may break my bones, but words can never touch me." The U.S. still had the option of appealing to the Supreme Court a previous ruling that denied payment of many billions of dollars by the tobacco industry, to compensate the U.S. for the health care costs that it paid for people ill from smoking-caused diseases.

Unrelated to the government suit against the tobacco industry was a class-action suit brought by Louisiana smokers duped into smoking by deceptive advertising. On May 21, 2004, a New Orleans jury ordered the tobacco industry to pay $590 million dollars to smokers for cessation aids, which the industry then appealed. But the industry can afford to employ topnotch lawyers who have been scoring notable successes. Thus in December 2005 the Illinois Supreme Court threw out a $10 billion class-action suit against Philip Morris, while in July 2006 the Florida Supreme Court upheld a decision to dismiss a $145 billion judgment in a similar suit against the tobacco companies.[426]

Survival of the tobacco companies is their prime aim, and they seem to be succeeding. They changed one of their long-term strategies in 1999 when they argued before the Supreme Court that the FDA has no right to regulate tobacco products, *because they were too deadly!* That admission won the case, but opened the door for class-action suits brought by and on behalf of dying smokers and their families.

Now the tobacco industry is using three major strategies to ensure its survival. First and foremost, as already mentioned, it is passing all costs on to consumers, and as a result, the price of cigarettes has skyrocketed. Also, new federal and state taxes have been assessed by legislators who do not deny that balancing the budget is their main objective, but claim that such tax hikes are *healthy*, since they put the price of cigarettes out of the reach of children.

The industry's second major strategy is to ensnare new customers among youths and college students, employing psychology and ingenuity to circumvent the law. In March 2004 the New York Times reported strong criticisms of Brown & Williamson by the Campaign for Tobacco-Free Kids and by the Legacy Foundation, for promoting a new version of Kool cigarettes, with high-design packages and different flavors such as Midnight Berry and Mocha Taboo that appeal to teenagers.[427] Such labels have now been prohibited by the ruling of Judge Gladys Kessler of August 2006. However, the industry sponsors advertising in convenience stores where youths shop, and places ads in magazines popular with youths. But most energetic efforts of the industry are targeted on peoples as yet unaware of the effects of smoking: the huge populations of developing nations (see chapter 33).

The third major strategy for survival of the beleaguered tobacco industry is to buy big firms that market healthy consumer goods, and in particular, food products. Such firms bring in large amounts of income independent of the sale of tobacco. Also, they confirm the aura that tobacco companies crave to project–that they sell wholesome products. This is exactly what the industry claimed about tobacco during the decades prior to the 1996 Master Settlement Agreement. In his editorial in the Boston Globe of November 23, 2001, Derrick Jackson published a list of products of the companies now owned by Philip Morris. Jackson suggested that those who believe that buying their products helps to spread death across the planet should leave them out of their shopping cart. A small sample from Jackson's long list includes the following firms and products: Maxwell House (coffees, Sanka); Kraft (Philadelphia cream cheese, Velveeta); Nabisco (Postum, Shake'n Bake, Cream of Wheat); Post Cereals (Wheat Thins, Life Savers); Tobler, and Miller Beer.

Today, every smoker knows what the industry now admits–that smoking is dangerous. But a recent ad for Salem Black Label cigarettes reveals a new wrinkle calculated to retain smokers and attract new ones: "Full Flavor," "Mysteriously Rich. Deliciously Intense." Now the appeal is slanted to confirmed smokers, who know the danger and are tough enough to risk it

Working either individually or in an organized group, ordinary citizens can punish the tobacco industry for lying to the public for so many years, and for continuing to ensnare youths. One way is to lobby for anti-tobacco bills. Another approach is to advocate that pension funds, endowments, and investment funds divest themselves of tobacco stocks. Yet another approach is to check whether local stores are following the 1992 federal law that prohibits sales of tobacco products to minors (anyone under the age of 18)–by sending underage children to buy cigarettes. The law requires states to monitor compliance, and if the law is being broken, letters to the local newspaper and to the state's attorney general can achieve dramatic results.

In many cities, coalitions of citizens have successfully lobbied their local governments to pass smoke-free restaurant ordinances. According to a 1999 study, such laws do not seem to affect tourist business adversely, and may even increase it.[428] It is validated by a study that documented a significant gain in the lung function of bartenders, following the passage of local laws that forbade smoking in bars and taverns.[429] As a result of such laws and of large increases in the tobacco tax, the number of smokers in New York City dropped by 11% between 2002 and 2003.[430] When the city of Helena, Montana passed a law banning indoor smoking in 2002, its only heart hospital recorded a 40% decrease in heart attacks during the next six months; but the number of cases involved in this heartening incident was small.[431]

Because many people suffer from conditions that make them particularly vulnerable to the ill effects of ETS (Environmental Tobacco Smoke) the Americans With Disabilities Act could provide the legal right to a smoke-free environment in the workplace and in public spaces.[432] Since even a whiff of tobacco smoke can cause extreme distress in people acutely allergic to it, as of May 2005, seven states had passed smoke-free workplace legislation, namely California, Delaware, New York, Connecticut, Maine, Massachusetts, and Rhode Island. *Public awareness of the ill effects of ETS is so intense, that a majority of U.S. citizens would be delighted if Congress enacted a federal law to address this problem, as Sweden has done, replacing a patchwork of its local laws.*

Is it ethical to own tobacco stocks? By buying them, one contributes – even if only in a small way–to keeping their price up. In so doing, one supports the tobacco industry, and that is bad. Thus individual people as well as the boards of directors of companies that have thought this matter through will wish to divest themselves of tobacco stocks.

The only time in my life that I made any money for a service that I provided that was connected with smoking, other than royalties from the present book, occurred when the editor of Modern Medicine rang me to ask if I would write an editorial for his magazine, and said I would receive a remuneration of $500. I replied, I would be glad to do so, but would not need any fee. The editor replied, well, this is the standard policy for our editorial writers – and so he trumped any scruples I had.

Regulation of tobacco products remains a vital goal for the future. We have already heard about the health warnings on cigarette and cigar packages, on advertisements of tobacco products, and of the fairness rule on TV ads during the early 1970s, followed by the prohibition of tobacco advertisements on electronic media. But the tobacco industry has found ways to circumvent these regulations and to defeat their intent. One way is to bribe studio personnel to see to it, that some actors smoke on set–but this is virtually impossible to document, since the recipient of a bribe is highly unlikely to admit to accepting it. To prevent this means of popularizing smoking, no film shou9ld be licensed for viewing by children and adolescents unless none of its scenes showed the smoking of tobacco.

Finally, the government started to eliminate its price support program for tobacco growers in May 2001, when the federal quota for tobacco cultivation was cut by approximately 20%. A presidential commission then proposed that tobacco farmers receive an economic incentive to stop growing tobacco and switch to other crops. The commission estimated the cost of the buyout as $16 billion spaced over five years, assuming that three-quarters of tobacco farmers agreed to participate and stopped growing tobacco. A 17-cents increase in the then current 34-cents per pack federal tax would raise $3.4 billion annually. This would be used to pay all current tobacco growing quota holders $8 per pound of tobacco that they were eligible to grow, and farmers who stopped growing tobacco would receive $4 for every pound of estimated production. Commission members (who included tobacco farmers) believed that if the recommendations of the commission were followed, tobacco growing would be reduced, and current tobacco farmers would be compensated handsomely. The Commission recommended that after the end of payments to tobacco farmers, the tax increase should continue and pay for programs on tobacco prevention, smoking cessation, and public health initiatives. But an editorial in the New York Times in September of 2003 warned against making a "going out of business" deal with tobacco farmers–because they have often returned for more and used a pitch that said, this time we mean it. Legislators from tobacco-growing areas asked for unrestricted payouts, since farmers could still grow tobacco–but there was opposition to such a payout.[433]

In June and July 2004, the House and Senate passed differing versions of tobacco buyout legislation,[434] resulting in a $12 billion Tobacco Transition Payment Program (TTPP, the "tobacco buyout").[435] It ended the federal tobacco marketing quota system, which gave tobacco farmers quotas for growing tobacco based on their past growing record, and it ended price support payments. Further, eligible tobacco farmers would be helped to transition to growing tobacco without federal price support, or to grow other crops, by appropriate payments spaced over the next ten years. To receive a payment for 2005, tobacco farmers had to sign up with USDA (U.S. Department of Agriculture) by mid June 2005.[436]

The question of whether FDA should be given authority to regulate tobacco was addressed in some versions of the tobacco buyout legislation. During 2003, AHA (the American Heart Association) supported a bill introduced by Representatives Ganske, Dingell and Waxman, and Senators Kennedy and

DeWine, to provide meaningful FDA authority over the manufacture, sale, distribution, labeling and promotion of tobacco products. But AHA decried bogus FDA legislation sponsored by the tobacco industry introduced in 2003, which would have seemed to permit FDA to regulate tobacco, but in reality would have protected the industry from FDA and other federal agencies.

Finally in June 2005, a bipartisan group of U.S. Senators and Representatives introduced a bill that would allow FDA to regulate tobacco genuinely. It would permit FDA to place tobacco under the same scrutiny as other consumer products, reduce its toxicity, and increase the protection of youths.[437] While America needs a strong FDA,[438] it must not be partly controlled by political influence in the application of its resources and in making its regulatory decisions.[439] As of the end of 2005 legislative session, Congress had not acted on this bill.

We have already seen in chapter 23, that since most vendors have weak age verification procedures or none at all, children can easily buy cigarettes on the internet.[440] But for smokers of any age, there is also the advantage that state sales taxes are not assessed there. In addition, internet sites based in Native American lands where federal taxes do not apply can sell a carton of cigarettes for $10 less than the current price in stores.[441]

In response, anti-tobacco advocates are working to block online sales.[442] But as of May, 2004, only the state of New York had outlawed mail-order purchases of cigarettes, and assessed heavy fines against tobacco distributors who sold cigarettes to anyone in the state except to licensed dealers.[443] Individual states or better yet, Congress should pass laws similar to those in effect in New York state. Alternatively, state taxes could be assessed for all types of online sales, monitored with software developed by the ingenious programmers of the software industry.

Besides the store of documents at www.tobaccodocuments.org that has already been mentioned, the Legacy Tobacco Documents Library at http://legacy.library.ucsf.edu/ contains over 6 million documents related to all aspects of tobacco products and lawsuits against the industry.

Would that all employees of the tobacco industry followed the example of Adrian Thomas, the owner of a drug store in Pennsylvania. For 96 years, his family had sold tobacco in the front of their store and health products in back. One winter day in 1992, sick of realizing how many friends he had lost to cancer and heart disease, Thomas took his entire stock of tobacco products to a parking lot, set a match to his state license to sell tobacco, and used it to burn his entire stock of tobacco.[444]

TWENTY SIX

———

USE, MISUSE, AND EFFECTS OF TOBACCO SETTLEMENT FUNDS

Most of the 46 states that signed the Master Settlement Agreement with the tobacco companies totaling $206 billion began getting their money in December, 1999. Four additional states, Mississippi, Texas, Florida, and Minnesota, reached separate settlements totaling $40 billion. The payments for all settlements were to be spaced over 25 years, reduced if tobacco sales fell, and continued thereafter in amounts linked to tobacco sales. Initially, the tobacco companies financed these payments by increasing the price of a pack by approximately 60-cents. This prompted some states to imposed higher taxes. Of course the cost of all increases, then or later, have been borne by smokers.

As part of the Master Settlement Agreement, between 1999 and 2003 tobacco companies paid $1.45 billion to the American Legacy Foundation. As of November, 2003, this Foundation had spent about $650 million for antismoking ads aimed especially at young people, as well as for programs such as research, polling, and internet campaigns. At that time, the Foundation was urging the Justice Department that if it eventually settled its ongoing lawsuit against the tobacco industry (see chapter 25) then its settlement should include a provision that would renew the industry's contributions to the Foundation.[445]

———

The purpose of the Master Settlement Agreement that the states reached with tobacco companies is stated three times in the first two pages of the final document: it is to stop children from becoming addicted to tobacco. Therefore, the CDC (Centers for Disease Control and Prevention) issued guidelines that asked (but did not mandate) states to spend 20 to 25% of this money on comprehensive antismoking programs. But a year later, only about 8% of this money was being used for that purpose. While some states spent as much as half of the money on a broad range of health-related programs, the majority used it as a substantial new source of revenue, and spent it on whatever else they needed.

There is reliable evidence from California that adequately funded, vigorous antismoking programs, spearheaded by television and print advertisements, could be highly effective. During the five years 1990 to 1995, the California antismoking campaign financed by passage of California's Proposition 99 had been credited with reducing the prevalence of smoking in that state by 28%. But during those years, those who had fought for passage of Proposition 99 had to keep fighting hard, to defeat repeated attempts to divert the antismoking funding.[446]

Two years after the tobacco settlement money began to flow, namely at the end of 2000, some states were spending more on tobacco control than suggested by the CDC's guidelines, while other states were spending little or nothing on it. In Massachusetts, there was a vigorous multifaceted tobacco control program that included highly effective TV and radio advertisement spots. It resulted in a significant drop in adolescent smoking (see chapter 28). But with the downturn in the economy, the tobacco control program was cut by approximately 20% for the year 2000–2001, and by another 20% for the next year, seriously undercutting the state's antismoking efforts.[447] Driven both by decreases in tax revenue (due to the reduction in incomes) and by declining tobacco sales, a similar diversion of antismoking funds occurred in most other states.

During 2002, funds from the Master Settlement Agreement expended per person on antismoking campaigns varied from 10 cents in Pennsylvania, to $15 in Maine. States whose residents smoked most heavily and needed most help provided the least help, and also kept tobacco excise taxes low. In contrast, states with well-funded campaigns succeeded in reducing smoking.[448, 449]

In 2003, states received about $8 billion from the tobacco industry, and deposited 47% of these funds into their general budgets—a sharp increase from 29% for 2002. Seven states even funneled the entire amount of their 2003 tobacco settlement funds into their general budgets. At the time of that settlement, officials of several states pledged to spend much of the settlement money on antismoking initiatives or other health services, but by 2003 many of these pledges had been forgotten.[450]

The smuggling of cigarettes raises additional problems. A world tobacco conference convened by the International Union Against Cancer in August 2000 estimated that nearly one-third of the cigarettes in international commerce are smuggled across national borders, avoiding taxes. Cigarette makers are facing lawsuits for their role in this scenario, but deny that they are responsible, saying they cannot control what happens further down the supply chain.[451] At least, when a tobacco smuggling ring selling counterfeit Marlboro cigarettes manufactured in Asia at $2 per carton was broken up in the United States in January 2004, we can be sure that American tobacco companies were not involved.

Since our states settled with the tobacco industry, the price of cigarettes has increased sharply. According to the Surgeon General's report of 1989, if the cost of cigarettes rises steeply, there is always a decline in tobacco consumption.[452] Accordingly, the 9% drop in cigarette shipments during the previous year reported by a tobacco industry analyst in 2000[453] was followed by a 16% reduction in high school students who had smoked one or more cigarettes during the previous month. But this reduction took place over five years, so the CDC gave most of the credit to education.[454] Nevertheless, the CDC commented that only five states have an excise tax of $1.50 or more per pack of cigarettes, despite how much higher taxes would benefit them, and research that shows that higher taxes reduce smoking by youths.[455]

Despite all the costly consequences of their devious practices, Time magazine reported in July 2001 that the tobacco industry was flourishing, and profits were rising. A pack of Marlboro cigarettes then cost $3.15 and reaped $1.40 in revenues for Philip Morris, 44% of the cost- a huge operating margin.[456]

How do smokers feel about the price increases? Studies both in the United States and in Canada indicate that the higher the taxes, the sadder the smokers. But almost every smoker wants to quit, and price increases nudge smokers closer to quitting. Those surveyed who did quit reported being "significantly happier."[457]

PART III

STRATEGIES FOR QUITTING

If at first you don't succeed, try and try again

TWENTY SEVEN

QUITTING

While quitting safeguards health more effectively the earlier one quits, it is effective at any age. While quitting reduces the risk of developing lung cancer rather slowly, it reduces the risk of heart disease far more rapidly. Regarding the development of a primary cancer in an organ other than the lung, that risk also is greatly decreased by quitting.[458]

Smoking is now a major social handicap, whether one smokes at home, at work, or in any other indoor environment. To a remarkable degree, a smoker's group of friends is restricted to the minority of people who also smoke. Smoking is even a serious barrier to meeting potential lovers. Merely a glance at advertisements for a soul-mate reveals that most mention nonsmoking as a prerequisite for getting acquainted.

There are basically two types of smokers.[459] The first includes people who find it relatively easy to quit, and these are most often adolescents, who are experimenting with new sensations. We can call this group "experimenters," for they have not yet smoked long enough to become addicted–although for many, even occasional smoking can cause addiction. The second type of smokers have become addicted to nicotine and habituated to smoking. They use smoking as a crutch, and self-medicate with nicotine to maintain a positive mood. We can call this group "addicts," and for them quitting is tough. For the Surgeon General's report of 1988 entitled "Nicotine Addiction"[460] concluded that:

- Cigarettes and other forms of tobacco are addicting.
- Nicotine is the drug in tobacco that causes addiction.
- The biologic processes that cause addiction to tobacco are similar to those that cause addiction to heroin and cocaine.

This last conclusion was confirmed by a study published in the journal *Neuron* in 2003 by a team led by Robert Malenka. It concluded that at the molecular level, addictive substances such as alcohol, cocaine, morphine, amphetamines and nicotine, as well as stress, each have their own characteristic mode of action. But all have in common,[231] that they cause brain cells in the part of the brain called the ventral tegmental area (VTA) to become highly sensitive and to produce strong feelings of stimulation.[461]

All tobacco products contain addicting quantities of nicotine. While nicotine addiction has been described in chapter 16, it should be mentioned here, for success in quitting depends on counteracting the pleasure that it provides:[460]

- Stimulation of the brain and pleasurable changes of mood.
- Muscle relaxation.
- Increase in the rate of the heartbeat.

But nicotine also produces the following effects, which lead to addiction, and make it difficult to quit:[460]

- Reinforcing effects: despite physical harm to smokers, nicotine rewards its users sufficiently, so they continue smoking.
- Tolerance develops to nicotine, which requires heavier smoking in order to maintain an adequate blood level of nicotine.

- Physical dependence on nicotine causes withdrawal symptoms in many of those who decide to quit.

- There is a strong temptation to relapse after quitting.

Despite these difficulties, the 2004 Surgeon General's Report estimates that 46 million Americans have quit, which for the first time exceeds the 45.8 million who continue to smoke.[4]

There are many methods of quitting. But the one essential precondition for success is a sincere and strong desire to quit.

Quitting is assisted by the following:

1. Joining a professionally led group to quit together.

2. Using personal counseling by a health professional.

3. Using telephone messages from quit smoking lines maintained by societies, government agencies or health plans.

4. Using "willpower" to quit on one's own is the choice of 9 out of 10 African-American Americans; only 1 in 10 report using formal treatment programs, self-help guides, or nicotine gum.[460]

5. Directly heeding the advice of a physician or health professional, that quitting is essential. This advice is highly effective for those who already have a smoking-related disease.

6. Children can be most valuable advocates, after they learn in school just how deadly smoking can be. They begin to fear that their parent will die, if he or she does not quit.

7. Since peers are vital in people to motivate them to smoke or to abstain, those who wish to quit must divest themselves of their friends who smoke, and make new friends who are nonsmokers.

8. Anti-tobacco programs and advertisements on TV, radio, and in print are very helpful in motivating smokers to quit.

9. Issues for such programs include the deceptive practices of the tobacco industry, progress in the war on smoking, and new developments regarding the many health effects of smoking.

10. President Nixon's War on Cancer may never be 100% won. Since 30% of cancer is caused by smoking, all that is needed to win one-third of the war is to quit, or far better, not to start.

But smokers need to know what strategies for quitting work best.

TWENTY EIGHT

———

SUCCESSFUL ANTISMOKING PROGRAMS AND CAMPAIGNS

There are so many different private and government agencies, societies, and committed individuals who are working to reduce the current death toll from tobacco-caused diseases, that it is not practical to list them all, nor to do justice to their extensive programs. Instead, the most important programs are summarized, and information is given on how to obtain free literature about quitting. While some programs help nonsmokers to avoid starting, most programs focus on helping current smokers to quit.[462, 463] In the next chapter, the best aspects of several programs for quitting are combined into a single guideline.

According to the United States Public Health Service publication *Treating Tobacco Use and Dependence*[464] the success rate of quitting with a quitting aid, compared with the success rate of quitting "cold turkey" without an aid, is as follows:

| THE SUCCESS RATE OF STRATEGIES FOR QUITTING ||
METHOD OF QUITTING	LIKELIHOOD OF SUCCESS
Cold turkey	1.0
Acupuncture	1.1
Nicotine	1.5

Counseling (30 minutes or less)	1.9
Nicotine patch	1.9
Bupropion (non-nicotine drug)	2.1

According to the above report, counseling is highly effective: less than 30 minutes of counseling by an expert in quitting techniques almost doubles the success rate compared to going cold turkey. Further, there is a strong consensus that counseling is very helpful for success in quitting.[465] Pharmacological methods employing nicotine or Bupropion also greatly improve the chance of success.[466] But the best results are obtained by combining sufficiently long counseling with the use of a pharmacological agent.

The Surgeon General's Report of 2000 entitled *Reducing Tobacco Use*[467] refines and strengthens the above conclusions. It reports that programs using advice and counseling have helped a substantial proportion of people to quit smoking. The success rate increases with the intensity of the program, and with more frequent contacts with professionals, and the extension of both over a longer time period. The report also shows that pharmacological treatments can help people to quit. When education is carried out in conjunction with community-based and media-based campaigns, it can postpone or prevent smoking in 20% to 40% of adolescents. Physicians who give their patients who smoke a few words of advice to quit cause 5% to 10% to do so (see chapter 31).

In their report of October 9, 2002 in *JAMA*, Michael Fiore and coworkers wrote that many effective strategies to treat tobacco dependence exist at different levels of our society. They include clinicians, the health care system, society at large, and the community, where school health education can be a major factor. But for the most success in prevention, and in order to help a broad spectrum of people to quit, as many as possible of these levels should be in play simultaneously.

The latest word in the war on smoking is the success of toll-free telephone lines staffed by seasoned counselors who are trained to assess the callers' state of readiness to quit, and then to follow a general script, to motivate smokers to do so. For those who are already ready to quit, the counselors have been taught strategies that help to cope with withdrawal symptoms.[468]

An evaluation of eight different advertising studies designed to prevent people from starting to smoke and persuading them to stop showed that *a focus on industry manipulation and secondhand smoke* are the most effective strategies for convincing people that smoking is not a habit accepted by our society. However, found to be less effective or even ineffective was a focus on reducing youth access and on romantic rejection. The more hard-hitting a campaign was, and the more adequate the funding for prime-time advertising, the better the results.[469]

As already mentioned, even in the short run, a large and aggressive tobacco-control program in California produced a reduction in cigarette consumption and in deaths from heart disease.[470] In January 2003, an issue of the survey "Monitoring the Future" showed a marked decline in teenage smoking for 2001, the latest year for which data were available.[471] In September, 2003, the CDC announced that a newly released study showed that cigarette sales dropped by 43% during the 1990s in four states that had long-running, well-financed anti-tobacco programs.[472] Commenting on a report that lung cancer death rates among adults aged 30 to 39 were falling in most states that have strong anti-tobacco programs, Ahmedin Jemal of the ACS said in December of 2003, "Where you have high tobacco control efforts you have low lung cancer death rates."[473] But recession-driven cuts in tobacco-control programs that occurred in fiscal year 2003–2004[474] may have resulted in an increase in the prevalence of smoking.

The strategy of reducing the ill effects of smoking by switching to cigarettes with low machine-measured yields of tar and nicotine was evaluated thoroughly by the National Cancer Institute in 2001, and resulted in the following conclusions:[475]

A. The scientific evidence shows that public health has not benefited from changes in cigarette design and manufacturing over the last fifty years.

B. People who switch to low-yield cigarettes smoke as intensively as is necessary to compensate completely for less nicotine.

C. By switching to low-yield cigarettes, people believe they are on the way to quitting. This is untrue and counterproductive.

D. Widespread adoption of low-yield cigarettes has not prevented the continuing increase in lung cancer among older smokers.

E. The tar and nicotine yields measured by mechanical cigarette smoking machines are not good guides to the quantities of tar and nicotine that smokers actually absorb when they themselves smoke.

Finally, smokers should be urged to use the most effective quitting methods. The difficulty of quitting is illustrated by a group of patients with COPD who stopped smoking on the same day. Then five months later, those still not smoking again were only 16% for those who received buproprion, and only 9% in the control group without medication.[466]

These low success rates emphasize the vital need to use all available aids to succeed in the difficult challenge of quitting. When multiple strategies are used to reduce smoking, then success is possible. This is illustrated by the 11% decline in smoking prevalence in New York City documented in 2004 and attributed to the combined use of higher taxes on cigarettes to reduce youth smoking, a ban on smoking in the workplace and places with public access, and a vigorous antismoking campaign.[476]

On November, 16, 2006, one week before Thanksgiving, the ACS celebrated its 30th Great American Smoke-Out, in which all smokers in America were encouraged to quit for the day–or for good. This annual ACS ritual, which has already been mentioned briefly in chapter 23, is very helpful in giving smokers a little jolt to remind them that the option to quit is really there. To make it more easily available, ACS provides intense staffing for its usual quit line (1-800-ACS-2345), and a short interactive online quiz, which allows smokers to get a snapshot of their dependence on nicotine, and then helps them to find ideas for building their own personal quit plan.

TWENTY NINE

A COMPOSITE GUIDE TO QUITTING

The goal of this guide is to combine the best features of the many books, pamphlets and programs on quitting smoking listed at the end of this chapter. Even more books on quitting than this are available, to serve the tens of millions of smokers who have wanted to quit. This chapter also includes my suggestions on what can be most useful to help smokers to quit smoking, drawn from my own experience in helping people to quit.

A. REASONS FOR QUITTING

According to the ACS, roughly half of all Americans who ever smoked, 46 million, have quit smoking for good. If so many can succeed, so can all readers who are smokers, for there are excellent reasons for quitting. For instance, people who quit before the age of 35 avoid 90% of the excess health risks that continued smoking causes.[477] But a study in 2002 found that regardless of the age at which one quits, people who stop smoking tend to live much longer than those who continue to smoke. While it is true that younger people benefit the most, even quitting at age 65 can add several years to one's life expectancy: approximately 2 years for men, and 3 years for women.[478, 479]

The message from the United States Surgeon General is that quitting is the single most important step one can take to enhance the quality of one's life. He says that not only you, but the people you live with, especially your children, will be healthier. You will have more energy, breathe easier, and lower your risk of being felled by one of the major killers: heart attack, cancer, emphysema, chronic bronchitis, and stroke.

Perhaps most important, quitting permanently reduces the excess risk of cancer that smoking brings. As noted in chapter 11, smoking causes cancer in many organs other than the lung: the mouth, esophagus, voice box, bladder, kidney, pancreas, cervix, stomach, and many more organs. However, the vast reduction in the excess risk of other smoking-caused diseases is also a very valuable bonus. But besides avoiding some of the long-term risks of smoking, quitting will make former smokers more socially acceptable from the very moment at which they quit. Their families and friends know that when they are forced to breathe ETS (environmental tobacco smoke), they are inhaling poisons that will increase their risk of developing lung cancer. True, the increase in cancer risk from secondhand smoke is far smaller than from the firsthand smoke that smokers themselves incur. But if you love your family, why expose them to *any* unnecessary risk? By quitting, you will delight your family and your nonsmoker friends—and you yourself will be proud of your perseverance and success in reaching a goal that is difficult to reach.

Smoking is expensive. At present, it costs well over $3,000 a year for the average smoker, and cigarette costs keep rising. For a fraction of that cost, smokers could immerse themselves far more extensively in their favorite active or spectator sports. Ex-smokers could also reward themselves by joining a health or athletic club and enjoy the fun and camaraderie available there—and by spending the extra new money on whatever delights them.As mentioned in chapter 28, low-nicotine, low-tar cigarettes do not help. Research has shown that smokers regulate the amount of nicotine that they are absorbing, to reach their accustomed level–simply by smoking more cigarettes. As a result, the exposure to lung carcinogens and tar from smoking low-yield cigarettes can even be larger than from high-yield cigarettes.[480]

B. GETTING READY TO QUIT

First, set a quit date. The best time to choose for quitting is when the pressure is off: the start of a vacation, or of a major holiday. ACS has a splendid free brochure, "How to Stay Quit Over the Holidays." It is full of helpful tips for making quitting enjoyable. But by far the most effective way to quit is with professional help, or in a group led by a professional.

Second, review your past attempts to quit (if any), and think about what worked and what did not.

Third, decide that you will not smoke a single puff–never mind a whole cigarette–once you have stopped smoking. As Alcohol Anonymous says in its motto "It's the first drink that gets you drunk." In the same way "It's the first cigarette that sinks you" – it negates all the effort you have put into quitting up to that point: quitting goes up in smoke.

Fourth, tell your family, friends, and coworkers that you are going to quit and would appreciate their support. Ask them not to smoke near you, or to leave cigarettes out. By "going public" about your plans, you are firmly committing yourself to quitting.

Fifth, the more counseling you have, the better your chances of success. Therefore, call your local or state health department for information about programs in your area. Also, telephone counseling on quitting is available everywhere, and in cities and towns there is also group counseling. It is best to look for a program with a leader trained in smoking cessation. Ideally, each counseling session might be 20–30 minutes long, and there should be 4–7 sessions, spaced over at least 2 or more weeks. Most large hospitals provide such groups, and most medical insurance companies and HMOs (Health Maintenance Organizations) will pay for their moderate cost.

Sixth, medications can help greatly in lessening the urge to smoke. Decide whether or not you plan to use them, and if you decide to use medications, which one or two. The FDA has approved five medications for that purpose. They roughly double the chances of success in quitting. It may be best to draw your physician into your quitting effort and get a prescription for the best medication, for Pierce and Gilpin reported in the September 11, 2002 issue of JAMA that over-the-counter sales reduce the effectiveness of drugs, especially for light smokers.

Over-the-counter medications include:

- Nicotine gum and Nicotine patch

Available only by prescription:

- Nicotine inhaler
- Nicotine nasal spray
- Bupropion SR

All the above agents except Zyban (Bupropion SR) are nicotine substitutes. Zyban is an antidepressant in an extended-release form, and depresses the brain's craving for nicotine. When used together with nicotine replacements, early evidence suggests it is more effective than when used alone.[481]

Nicotine replacements treat the unpleasant withdrawal symptoms and cravings that most smokers experience when they quit. Having one of these substitutes available in case the cravings for nicotine becomes too strong may well spell the difference between success and failure in quitting. Experience shows that the most effective time to start nicotine replacement use is at the very start of the attempt to quit, for one should not wait until difficulties arise.

Nicotine replacements tend to work more slowly and place less nicotine into the bloodstream than smoking. But they are entirely free from the thousands of other poisons in tobacco smoke, and allow a former smoker to focus on the psychological aspects of quitting. Nicotine replacement therapy is not recommended for pregnant women, nor for people with heart or circulatory disease.

Those who decide to use a nicotine replacement should choose the type most convenient and appealing to them. But it is helpful to discuss their choice with their physicians, pharmacists, or support group leaders—for there are certain conditions, such as being after a heart attack, when the use of nicotine replacement or Buprion therapy is not advised.[482] Here is a list of present pharmaceutical options:[483]

Nicotine patches are convenient because they need to be applied only once a day, and many different types are sold over the counter. They are far less obtrusive than nicotine gum, provide a steady blood level of nicotine, and are less likely to result in addiction. If you weigh under 110 pounds or smoke fewer than 10 cigarettes a day, you should use a lower-dose patch. After two months or so, most people are able to switch to lower doses of nicotine, and eventually taper off. The patch can take two to four hours to begin to deliver nicotine, but it can be supplemented by other forms of nicotine replacements, and some studies have shown that combined use is more effective than if a patch is used alone.[487] But one should make certain not to overdose oneself, and be aware that smoking while using a patch can cause a heart attack. Companies that market nicotine patches maintain web sites that provide further information.

Nicotine gum is also sold over the counter, supplies nicotine faster than a patch, and allows one to keep dosing oneself as you wish. It comes in two formulations: 2 milligrams for the average smoker, and 4 milligrams for very dependent smokers. After quitting, most people chew 10 to 15 pieces of nicotine gum a day, then after the first two weeks settle for half that amount. One should chew the gum slowly until it tastes peppery, and then park it between gums and cheek, where it should be held for about half an hour. Its disadvantages are that one may not like to be seen chewing gum. After quitting, one should wean oneself gradually off nicotine gum, but some people find that hard to do. Still, in the long term nicotine gum is less harmful than smoking.

A nicotine inhaler is available by prescription only, and looks like a cigarette–it has a mouthpiece, and a porous plug that contains a nicotine cartridge. This smokeless cigarette helps people, by allowing them to puff and use the same hand motions as when they were smoking. Ex-smokers may need from 6 to 16 cartridges a day. Potential drawbacks are throat and mouth irritation, and coughing.

Nicotine nasal spray also comes by prescription only, and is the fastest nicotine-delivery system. Smokers who quit use about two doses an hour for the first eight weeks, and then gradually reduce the dose and daily frequency during the next six weeks. It has the drawback that some people are embarrassed to use it in public. There is also the possibility that it will cause nose and throat irritation, sneezing, coughing, and watery eyes–although most people develop tolerance to nicotine nasal spray.

Nicotine lollipops pack the punch of 4 or 5 cigarettes. But the FDA advises that they should be avoided, because they pose the risk of accidental use by children. In addition, some contain nicotine salicylate, which the FDA has called "illegal." ACS has asked the government to regulate or make illegal *Aviva*, a mint-flavored candy, and *NicoWater*, water laced with nicotine. Both are intended to get smokers through periods when they cannot smoke, such as a plane flight, and both are unregulated, and thus can be bought by children.[484]

Behavioral therapy is a vital addition to nicotine replacement therapy, since several studies have questioned whether a nicotine patch is effective for long-term success, unless it is supported by counseling. This is especially a problem when patches are purchased over-the-counter.[485, 486] When patches are obtained by prescription, then at least a minimal contact with a health professional is assured.

Long-term use of nicotine products could cause problems, according to a study headed by John P. Cooke and published in Nature Medicine in 2001. It concluded that nicotine stimulates the growth of blood vessels, and while this can be helpful, it can also encourage the growth of tumors and of vessel-clogging plaques. Although Cooke feels that nicotine patches are a very good form of therapy, he advises that they should not be used for long periods. Indeed, one of the best known brands of patches includes on its labels the advice not to use it beyond 10 weeks.

Bupropion SR (Zyban)[487] is an antidepressant that should be combined with counseling to be highly effective. A recent study suggests that it is even more successful than a nicotine patch, but should not be used in patients who are at risk of seizure, because it lowers the threshold for seizures. Still, only 1 in 1,000 users will experience a seizure as a result of its use.[487]

There are several other types of aid to quitting, but I cannot recommend them. *Hypnosis* provides some people with the will to quit that they themselves lack; but experience has shown that the effect of hypnosis usually wears off after four weeks, and at that point most people revert to smoking. *Acupuncture* has also been used to help smokers quit, but the USPHS says that unfortunately, there is little evidence that it is effective. However, researchers are hard at work searching for a drug that will make quitting easier. While new candidates such as "Eighteen-MC" (18-methoxycoronaridine) showed promise in animal tests,[488] they must still pass clinical trials and gain FDA approval before they can be marketed.

Because many smokers are desperate to quit–especially those who have attempted to quit many times before–there is a strong temptation to cash in on their plight. This explains why so many different methods of quitting are advertised. Therefore, it is best to stay with tried and true methods provided by state public health facilities, national societies, and local hospitals.

Seventh, before you sign up for a program, it is best to enquire what its success rate is, six months after the program is finished. The hard fact is that quitting is really tough for most smokers, because they are addicted to nicotine. If no medications are used to help cope with withdrawal symptoms, only about 10% of smokers are able to quit for at least 6 months. But if nicotine replacements are used, then about 30% succeed in quitting for that time. Predictably, the success rate is even higher when both nicotine replacement and Bupropion are used together.

Eighth, it is vital to plan how to deal with withdrawal symptoms prior to quitting. There are both psychological and physical problems to overcome when quitting. But for most people, the psychological challenge is the most difficult.

If one has been smoking for a long time, smoking is part of one's general routine–from getting up in the morning, to going to bed at night. Some people even like to smoke in bed – not aware that this is a major cause of fires (see chapter 15). For many smokers, smoking has become part of eating, drinking coffee, working, walking, reading, and watching TV. It is so closely interwoven into life's activities, that it is hard to untangle this deadly vine that has enveloped one if one is a smoker, so that it no longer poses the danger of eventually choking one. Here are changes that help one to liberate oneself from the weed.

Ninth, The ABC's of Quitting:

- **Avoid situations that remind one of smoking,** be that people, places, or routines. After one has quit for a while, one will be able to handle such challenges more easily.

- **Alter habits.** Instead of coffee, colas or alcohol, one should switch to fruit juices, herbal teas, or water, and take a different route to work or market. Instead of a coffee break, one should take a brisk walk.

- **Alternative aids.** As oral substitutes, one can use sugarless gum, low-calorie raw vegetables such as carrot sticks, bite-sized low-calorie fruits such as grapes, or popcorn.

- **Activities to keep busy.** One should replace bad old habits with new good ones. It helps to join an exercise group to begin a new routine and improve muscle tone, stamina, and energy. Also, sports and games will serve for relaxation. In addition, working at hobbies such as gardening, needlework, woodwork, and home improvement projects, will keep the hands busy and help to distract from smoking.

- **Breathing deeply** briefly when the urge to smoke strikes is very helpful. One should Picture the lungs filling with fresh, clean air. Then every breath is a step on the way to better health.

- **Congratulations** for avoiding the poisons in cigarette smoke, and gaining all the benefits of quitting. It helps to write out a list of what one is avoiding and of what one is gaining.

- **Delay lighting up.** If one feels the urge to smoke is becoming too strong, make oneself wait at least 10 minutes. This simple trick will move one beyond the pressing need to smoke, and will allow one to fill the gap with one of the above remedies.

- **Enjoy rewards** for abstinence. One can choose an instantaneous reward: one of the above oral substitutes: a walk across the work isle to talk to a non-smoking friend, or a trip to the refrigerator or fruit-juice machine. Or else, one might choose a reward one can look forward to, freely earned from the money one saved by not smoking: a new magazine, going out to eat, a long-distance call to a friend, or tickets to a show or sports event. In addition, why not accumulate one's savings to buy a major item one has really craved for a long time, but could not afford.

- **Find help** to tide one over this crisis. Telephone one of the resource contacts: friends or support group members, or one of the volunteer or state or government resource lines, where one can get a caring expert- or helpful recorded messages to tide one over this difficult moment.

- **Get more sleep** and more rest: one should try to go to sleep earlier. Exercising during the day will tire one out and help one to sleep.

- **Hot baths** or showers will help to reduce stress, as will reading a really enjoyable book.

- One should **integrate spiritual practices** into the armament against stress. Prayer and meditation have been used very successfully by AA (Alcoholics Anonymous) in conquering addiction to alcohol, and are an integral part of many recovery programs. Both are helpful in reducing the stress of stopping to smoke.

- **Joyful, supportive reading matter** full of helpful tips should help one to quit. Hopefully, this book will serve in this way, as will some of the other material mentioned here.

Tenth, well before one's Quit Date, one should have all the necessary decisions made and all needs for support in place, ready to use when needed. One should familiarize oneself with the items chosen from the above lists. Before one quits smoking, it helps to practice actually using these support items. Quitting is a very important event, and to succeed one needs all the determination and help that one can marshal.

On the day before the quit date, one should plan an easy day for the quit day, and aim to avoid stress. One should stock up on low-calorie snack foods, and buy whatever pharmacological aids to quitting—such as nicotine patches—one plans to use to help in quitting. One should remind family and friends, that their help and encouragement is vital during the next week or two. If another smoker can be persuaded also to quit—be it a family member or a friend—this will make quitting more of a game. In any case, it helps to line up someone who will listen sympathetically while one is in process of quitting.

Most important, a celebration should be planned for the quit day – am event one will really enjoy as a reward for quitting. Other rewards for each day one remains smoke-free should also be planned, as well as for each smoke-free week.

Just before going to bed, one should smoke as rapidly as possible just three cigarettes—no more, and only if one is still in excellent health. This strategy should make one feel sick of cigarettes. Then at once, one should set about hunting down all stores of cigarettes, looking in coat pockets and in the car: one should wet them, then flush them to oblivion. Also, one should throw all ashtrays and lighters into the trash. One must be absolutely thorough in expurgating anything that reminds one of smoking. For a happy future, one should remember that cigarettes are the most deceptive of friends, and in realty one's worst enemies. Now is the time to take a long bath and get a good night's sleep, to be well rested for the big day ahead.

C. WHAT A FORMER SMOKER SHOULD DO ON THE QUIT DATE

Start by congratulating yourself: you are now an ex-smoker, and this is start of the rest of your life as a non-smoker. This is the time to use the aids to quitting set out under *"Ninth"* above. For easier access, here they are *in a nutshell*:

Brief ABC's of Quitting for a smoker

- **Avoid situations** that remind you of smoking.

- **Avoid stress:** plan an easy day for yourself.
- **Alter your habits:** instead of coffee, drink tea, take walks.
- **Additional aids:** use sugarless gum, carrot sticks, popcorn.
- **Activities to keep busy:** exercise, enjoy one of your hobbies.
- **Breathing deeply** a few times to relax yourself.
- **Congratulate yourself** for inhaling health instead of poison.
- **Delay lighting up:** delaying 10 minutes will reduce the urge.
- **Enjoy rewards:** low-calorie food, drink, or talk to a friend.
- **Find help:** telephone your resource contact or a help line.
- **Get more rest**–and to sleep well, exercise more than usual.
- **Hot baths** or showers help, as does reading an enjoyable book.
- **Integrate spiritual practices** such as prayer or meditation.
- **Juices and water** help to flush nicotine out of your system.

The Lung Association's book listed at this chapter's end contains the following suggestion for doing a *"Relaxercise"* (a meditation exercise) at least once a day, until you feel secure that you are done with cigarettes:

- Sit down anywhere and close your eyes.
- Think about something that makes you feel good.
- Relax your shoulders.
- Close your mouth. Inhale slowly and as deeply as you can.
- Hold your breath while you count to four.
- Exhale slowly, letting out all the air from your lungs.
- Slowly repeat these breathing exercises five times.

For instructions on using the highly rated "relaxation response" technique developed by Dr. Herbert Benson of Harvard Medical School, please visit www.health.harvard.edu/womenextra.

If you are having trouble quitting, using a nicotine replacement is a vital aid for most people. Your body has become accustomed to nicotine, and will now be recovering from that addiction. *Think of your withdrawal symptoms as being really recovery symptoms*–your body is now returning to its normal non-addicted state. Therefore, using a nicotine replacement of your choice (see *"sixth"* above) will lesson your symptoms greatly.

Tobacco companies are aware how helpful nicotine replacement is in quitting. For an article in the August, 2002 issue of *JAMA* documents three instances in which tobacco companies–which had well-hidden ties with pharmaceutical companies–pressured them to reduce both their marketing and their quit educational material for products such as Nicorette, nicotine patches, and nicotine-release gum.[489] The tobacco companies would never have risked the bad publicity from the discovery of this very nasty trick, unless they thought that *nicotine replacements greatly eased the problems of recovery symptoms.* These may include:[502]

- *Irritability:* to be fought with the stress management tools set out above.

- *Fatigue:* fought by taking naps, avoiding caffeine.

- *Insomnia:* eased by exercise and *relaxercise.* Be sure to avoid caffeine, caffeinated drinks and cocoa after 8 pm.

- *Cough: dry throat, nasal drip:* combated by drinking plenty of fluids and eating cough drops.

- *Dizziness:* requires extra caution when driving, operating machines, climbing stairs. Change positions slowly.

- *Poor concentration:* makes it wise to plan a light work load and avoiding demanding assignments for the first week.

- *Constipation, gas:* counteracted by drinking plenty of fluids and adding roughage (fruits, vegetables) to diet.

- *Hunger:* requires you to be prepared with low-calorie snacks and to drink water or low-calorie liquids.

- *Craving for a cigarette:* reduced by *Relaxercise*, exercise, waiting out the urge, distracting yourself, taking a walk.

Most important, remember that these symptoms indicate that your body is fighting off its dependence on nicotine, and before long, all these symptoms will tail off, then vanish.[490]

D. WHAT TO DO TO STAY CLEAN

As you need them, use all the aids set out under *B* above. Several of these aides will always be available to you. Also, review your reasons for quitting in the first place, some of which are set out under *A* above. In addition, there are great benefits from quitting that vary over time:[491]

20 minutes after quitting, your blood pressure will drop to the level it was at *before* you smoked your last cigarette.

2 hours after quitting, the carbon monoxide level in your blood will have dropped back to normal.

1 day after quitting your chance of a heart attack has already decreased a little.

Between 1 and 9 months after quitting, your circulation and lung function are improved. Also, you will have achieved a decrease in coughing, fatigue, shortness of breath, sinus congestion, and the risk of lung infection.

1 year after quitting, you will have cut in half your excess risk of heart disease, and have access to a considerably lower cost for life insurance.

15 years after quitting, when compared to a nonsmoker, your large excess risks of heart disease and of stroke have now vanished. Your excess risk of lung cancer has decreased dramatically, and your risks of cancer of the mouth, throat, food-pipe, bladder, kidney and pancreas have also decreased.

25 years after quitting, the risk of lung cancer is about one-tenth that of an active smoker. If you have smoked for many years, the risk will never be quite as low as for a life-long nonsmoker,[492] and the health effects of smoking will never vanish completely.[493] But the risk of those effects will have decreased enormously.

Additional aids include:[494]

- Think of yourself as a nonsmoker, helping to keep air fresh.
- Change your habits to avoid smokers, until sure of yourself.
- Recognize that a cigarette will not help in a tough situation.
- Avoid use of alcohol since it is a common stimulant of relapse.
- Continue to exercise.

E. HOW TO AVOID WEIGHT GAIN AFTER QUITTING

Nicotine speeds up your heart beat and with it the rate at which your body is working–your rate of metabolism. In essence, your body's life expectancy is fully wound at birth, and unwinds throughout life like the spring of a clock. When nicotine makes your clock run faster than the speed intended for it by nature, the spring also runs down faster, and with it your life-span.

Because nicotine increases your metabolism, your body burns about 200 to 300 more calories per day than if you did not smoke. But when you quit, you will quickly return to your natural rate of metabolism. Therefore, if you do not wish to gain weight, you should reduce your food intake by 200 to 300 calories.

But there is also a second reason why smokers tend to gain weight after they stop smoking. Smoking is a habit that accustoms you to bring your hand up to the mouth to deliver an oral stimulant–tobacco smoke. Eating snacks provides the same sort of hand motion and also has rewards, hence there is a tendency to compensate for the former with the latter–and thus gain weight.

As a result of those two factors, many smokers do gain some weight when they quit. Even without a special emphasis on diet and increasing exercise, the gain is usually under 10 pounds. For some people, the fear of weight gain is sufficient reason to decide against quitting. But according to a study conducted by the CDC and the National Center for Health Statistics, smokers who quit smoking only gain an average of 4 to 7 lbs within the first 10 years after quitting, and "this in no way counteracts the substantial health benefits of quitting smoking."[495] So, since the weight gain is usually small, it is far more dangerous to continue smoking than to gain a little weight.

But it is another matter entirely to become obese, which for people of average height means being overweight by about 30 pounds for a woman, and about 38 pounds for a man. According to CDC statistics for 2000 reported in the New York Times of March 10, 2004, obesity caused by poor diet and physical inactivity was the underlying cause of death of only 10% fewer Americans than were killed by smoking. It seems that obesity is fast catching up with the present leading cause of death–smoking.[496]

ACS advises that the best way to handle weight gain is to quit smoking first, then, once you have that monkey off your back, take steps to reduce your weight. While quitting, focus on ways to stay healthy rather than on your weight. Eat plenty of fruits and vegetables, but limit fatty foods. Drink plenty of water, get enough sleep, and try to increase regular exercise–though if you do not already exercise, you should check first with your doctor before starting to exercise.

One way to increase an exercise that is available to almost everyone is to walk more. Walking is a good form of exercise and helps to increase your chance of quitting permanently. It helps to reduce stress, burn calories, tone muscles, and requires no special equipment, clothing or expenditure. Walking with a friend, for instance for half an hour after lunch, can be even more enjoyable than walking alone.

F. HOW TO MANAGE STRESS AFTER YOU QUIT

One of the reasons you used to smoke was to manage stress. That is why your choice of a Quit Date should be one on which you expect that stress will be minimal—for instance when you arrive at the destination for the start of your vacation. Then when you return to work after your vacation and stress begins to build again you will benefit from using the stress managing techniques.

Among the best stress-reduction techniques are exercise, sports, and games that specially appeal to you. Also, reward yourself by going to events that you have long craved to attend, which you can now afford with money saved by not smoking. Stress Management Programs are very helpful, and most towns and all cities have several listed under that title in the yellow pages of the telephone directory. Libraries and bookshops stock many books on stress-reduction and on how to relax. A typical paperback, anything but modest, is *"The Healthy Mind, Healthy Body Handbook. How to Use your Mind to Relieve Stress, Boost Immunity, Stay Well, Improve Mood, Manage Illness, Reduce Costs,"* by David Sobel and Robert Ornstein. But such books cover many different topics, while the American Lung Association's "7 Steps to a Smoke-Free Life" focuses only on quitting smoking, and lists many ways to reduce this partic9ular type of stress.[502]

An important study published in the American Psychologist in 1999 concluded that while smokers are right in believing that smoking relieves stress, the startling fact is that *it merely relieves the stress of wanting to smoke.* Once a smoker has quit smoking, both stress and mood fluctuations are reduced.[497]

G. HOW TO REMAIN FREE OF THE WEED

On analogy with an alcoholic who is on the wagon but continues to stave off drink by remembering that alcohol will always remain enticing, so an ex-smoker is wise to remember that while the lure of tobacco will diminish, the enemy is never completely vanquished, and one must remain ever on guard. Experience has shown that at least for the first year after quitting, it is best to renew one's acquaintance every month with whatever methodology was used to achieve quitting–be that quit groups, counseling, books, pamphlets, telephone messages, or the vast amount of helpful material available on the internet.

A single slip is a dangerous sign of a potential relapse, and all ex-smokers should be conscious of–and try to avoid–tempting situations. Even in the most ordered of lives, there are times when stress builds up. Then ex-smokers need to return to the stress-reducing techniques that they used initially to quit.

Lack of time is often quoted as a reason for neglecting such effective relaxing techniques as exercise, sports, and games. But by taking the time to engage in a thoroughly enjoyable activity in a different setting, the batteries of body and mind are recharged, and the time spent is doubly repaid by time gained through renewed physical and mental vigor. Thinking becomes clearer, and difficult decisions become easier to make correctly.

Perhaps because Mark Twain said, "Quitting is easy. I've done it a thousand times," some psychologists ease the conscience of relapsed ex-smokers by telling them that the best baseball hitters succeed only one of three times at bat. But I cannot give defeatist advice. When you want to reach for that first cigarette that will spell doom, ask yourself- am I going to sacrifice all that hard-won success for one miserable little weed? Say, "Away with you- I'm through with coffin nails," and flush your tempter down you-know-where. As Shakespeare said in *Macbeth*, Aroimt thee witch. As for young people who might be tempted to start, this chapter shows how difficult it is to quit, once one is addicted -so it is much wiser not to start in the first place.

H. IS THERE INSURANCE REIMBURSEMENT FOR QUITTING TREATMENT?

Research has shown that the cost effectiveness of smoking cessation it is extremely high.[498] For that reason, clinicians have recommended that all forms of drug dependence should be insured, treated, and evaluated like other chronic illnesses.[499] As a result, an increasing number of HMOs are willing to pay for part or all of pharmacological quitting aids, such as nicotine patches, and for the counseling that is so helpful for success.

Further, in 1999 the Internal Revenue Service decided that cessation programs, doctor's bills, and prescription drugs for quitting are valid medical deductions, just like efforts to treat other types of drug addictions or alcoholism. But nonprescription items such as nicotine patches or gums are not deductible, and the total of all one's medical bills presently must exceed 7.5% of the adjusted gross income to qualify as an itemized deduction.[500] In April 2006 ABC announced that for the first time, there were more ex-smokers than smokers in America. They hoped that their "Quit to Live" campaign, which they started after famed anchor Peter Jennings' death from a smoking-caused disease, would save many people from his fate.

I. HELP ON ISSUES CONNECTED WITH SMOKING AND QUITTING[501]

The books on quitting that are listed below can be purchased from most bookstores. There are also many free publications on quitting available from the societies and agencies that are listed below. Also, a great deal of information can be found on the internet by searching for "smoking" or "quitting smoking."

AMERICAN CANCER SOCIETY

800-ACS-2345 (800-227-2345), or website www.cancer.org

Quitting Smoking. An excellent 40-page explanation of the trials, tribulations and benefits of quitting can be downloaded, as can *Tips After Quitting,* a 2-page outline. Brief pamphlets include *When Smokers* Quit, *Smart move! A Stop Smoking Guide.* Also, *The Decision is Yours.* Available for a fee: *Kicking Butts. Quit Smoking and Take Charge of Your Health* (2002).

AMERICAN LUNG ASSOCIATION:

212-315-8700, website www.stateoftheair.org

"7 Steps To A Smoke-Free Life" (John Wiley & Sons) is an excellent 226-page book available at book stores.[502] Also, the Association has eleven separate 2–4 pages long information capsules for downloading under the tab *Quit Smoking,* found under "Consumer and Patients."

UNITED STATES PUBLIC HEALTH SERVICE:

- Agency for Healthcare Research and Quality: 800-358-9295 www.ahcpr.gov/clinic. A 5-page outline, *You Can Quit Smoking,* can be downloaded from its internet site.

- The Public Health Service has a 12-page guide in outline form, *You Can Quit Smoking.*[503]

- Centers for Disease Control and Prevention (CDC), Office on Smoking and Health, (800-232-1311), (404-488-5705), or (770-488-5705), www.cdc.gov/tobacco.htm, or www.cdc.gov/health/tobacco.htm

- National Cancer Institute, Cancer Information Service, 800-4-CANCER (800-422-6237), http://cancer.gov or www.nci.nih.gov

- Surgeon General's website on tobacco www.surgeongeneral.gov/tobacco

- National Library of Medicine, 800-272-4787 www.nlm.nih.gov

EXCELLENT OLDER BOOKS RECOMMENDED FOR SMOKERS WHO WISH TO QUIT:

- John W. Farquhar and Gene A. Spiller, *The Last Puff: Ex-Smokers Share the Secrets of their Success* (W. W. Norton, 1990).
- Tom Ferguson, *The No-Nag, No-Guilt, Do-It-Your-Own-Way Guide to Quitting Smoking* (Ballantine, 1987).

THIRTY

ARE GENETICS INVOLVED IN THE SUSCEPTIBILITY TO ADDICTIONS?

O ur genetics and our environmental history determine almost everything about us. The Communist creed in Stalin's Russia required that the old dispute between the importance of nature (inheritance, *i.e.* genetics) as contrasted with nurture (environment) in determining such matters as the likelihood that one would take up smoking would be determined by nurture, not by nature. This Stalinist view led to a disastrous failure when seed crops were chosen on the basis that only the environment mattered rather than the genetics of the seed. Similarly, the likelihood that we will fall prey to addiction to smoking is influenced not only by our environment but also by our inheritance.

Probably the best way to obtain reliable information on the effect of genetics is to study twins. There are two types of twins: identical ("monozygotic") twins that developed from a single fertilized ovum that produces two persons of identical genetic constitution and sex; and non-identical ("dizygotic") twins that develop from two separate ova that produce two individuals who *differ* in their genetic constitution, and who may or may not differ in sex. Comparing the behavior of identical and non-identical twins is very revealing, because the environment in which a given set of twins develop is often the same for each of a pair of twins. Generally, whether or not they are identical or non-identical twins, not only the environment to which a given pair of twins is exposed is the same, but also the home and the family. When the environment is the same for both twins, then it is eliminated as a factor, and the effect of having an identical as contrasted to a non-identical inheritance is revealed.

In reality, the situation regarding identical twins is not quite as simple as sketched out above. Their position in the uterus is not identical, so subtle differences in development can arise by the time of birth. Nor can the environmental experiences that they encountered during their childhood be exactly identical. Nevertheless, the difference between true the identity and the real identity of genetically identical twins is very small, compared to the vast difference between genetically non-identical twins.

A study of male twins of both types, led by Dorit Carmelli, pinpointed the effect of genetics both on the tendency to start smoking and on the likelihood of quitting. The behaviors that were studied included having never smoked, being a former or a current smoker, smoking a pipe or cigar, and quitting. For all of these smoking-related behaviors, the rate of concordance (meaning that both twins were alike in their behavior) was between 18% and 60% higher for genetically identical twins than for non-identical twins. The authors concluded that their study proved that there were moderate genetic influences on lifetime smoking habits, and cited many other studies that supported their conclusion.[504]

But it will be a comfort to smokers, that the authors found only "moderate" genetic influences that could be invoked to explain smoking, or the likelihood of quitting. That means that most of the likelihood that one should choose to smoke is environmentally conditioned, and is thus under the control of the smoker. Therefore, the decision to start smoking, to continue to smoke, or to quit smoking is far more strongly under control of each individual person, than preordained by inheritance.

Therefore, it need not disturb any present or former smoker to know, that Kenneth Blum and coauthors have suggested that all addictive behaviors have a common genetic connection. Their theory- and it is merely that- is that addictive, impulsive, and compulsive behavior, such as smoking, alcoholism, substance abuse, food bingeing, and pathological gambling, as well as personality disorders, are all part of what they term the "reward deficiency syndrome." They believe that all are based on a common genetic deficiency in the "dopamine D_2 receptor" of the brain. This deficiency makes it difficult for dopamine, a vital signaling molecule, to bind to its receptor (binding site) in the brain in sufficient quantity. As a result, key reward areas of the brain are deprived of sufficient stimulation. This produces a craving for more stimulation, and hence, addiction to habits that at least initially can satisfy that craving.[505]

A further piece of evidence that supports the dopamine D_2 receptor theory is that about 80% of patients in mental institutions are smokers.[506] If this theory is correct, then the exceptionally high percentage of smokers among these patients suggests that they are attempting to compensate for their very low levels of reward stimulation. This explanation is supported by the fact that it is even more difficult for these patients to quit smoking, than for the general public.

A report in the journal *Science* in 2001 on 'behavioral addictions' used sensitive scan techniques to investigate the brain's reward system. The brain seems to recognize a reward stimulus as a reward, irrespective of whether it comes from a normal brain signaling molecule, an externally supplied chemical, or an experience. When a reward is involved, there is the risk that our vulnerable brains become trapped in a compulsion. Thus, gamblers get high, show tolerance, and experience withdrawal symptoms- just like drug addicts. Even some so-called 'sex addicts' qualify as addicts, because they obsess about their favorite practice, never get enough, feel out of control, and as a result experience serious disruptions in their lives. The report concludes that the evidence points to a common basis for all addictions.[507]

THIRTY ONE

ROLE OF PHYSICIANS, HEALTH CARE AND PUBLIC HEALTH EXPERTS

Richard Overholt, a surgeon who founded the Overholt Thoracic Clinic in Boston and campaigned vigorously against smoking, told me of one situation in which the advice to quit is highly effective: when a physician tells patients that their very lives depended on quitting. This is the advice that physicians commonly give to elderly patients if they are smokers who have just survived their first heart attack, or else are at high risk of it, or are developing emphysema or chronic bronchitis.

The success of those few words illustrates the importance that patients attach to the advice of their physicians. There are at least five reasons why patients give them special attention. First, studies have shown that even if physicians place a minimal emphasis on quitting, it produces positive results.[508] Second, physicians are among the most trusted of professionals. Third, smokers pay an average of four visits a year to their physicians. Fourth, when visiting physicians one is fully aware that one's good health depends on their judgment and advice. Fifth, access to physicians can be difficult to arrange, and one usually has to wait- so appointments with physicians are seen as special events.

Researchers led by Virginia Quinn, reporting in the *American Journal of Preventive Medicine* (vol. 29, pp. 77-84, 2005) suggest that physicians should use the "5A's" of tobacco cessation treatment that the U.S. Public Health Service promotes:

- *Asking* patients about tobacco use
- *Advising* smokers to quit
- *Assessing* smokers' willingness to try quitting
- *Assisting* smokers with cessation treatment
- *Arranging* follow-up contacts

Quinn said that smokers expect doctors to address smoking and are more satisfied with their health plans when they do that.

A book published in 2003, "The Smoking Puzzle," asks the question why older smokers, who are close to suffering the consequences of their long-term habit, do not stop smoking. The answer given in the book is, to give these smokers an educational intervention equivalent to the shock of developing a smoking-caused disease.[509] In the light of Richard Overholt's experience, it is personal physicians who are most likely to succeed in administering this shock therapy, for the admonition of a physician is taken seriously. Also, physicians tend to be highly inventive and are able to craft their own shock therapy that will not violate the vital place of truth in the physician-patient relationship. Since it is never too late to quit (see chapter 29) this strategy is even appropriate for smokers who are old.

The United States Public Health Service has available two free guides to help orient physicians who wish to protect their smokers by asking them to quit. One is entitled *Quick Reference Guide for Smoking Cessation Specialists*,[464] and is based on an earlier thorough review entitled *Smoking Cessation*,[510] that is authored by the same group. It concludes with the statement, "There is no clinical intervention available today that can reduce illness, prevent death, and increase the quality of life more than effective tobacco treatment intervention." The guide provides physicians with the tools for treating smokers both willing and unwilling to quit, and to help smokers who have quit to avoid a relapse. The major findings of *Smoking Cessation*[464] (which is available free of charge from 800-358-9295) are:

- It is vital that physicians determine and document the smoking status of their patients at every visit.

- Effective quit smoking treatments are available, and every patient who smokes should be offered one or more of them.

- At least, a brief cessation treatment should be provided to every smoker, since even these have some effectiveness.

- In general, the more intense and long-continued the cessation treatment, the greater its effectiveness.

- One or more of the most effective treatment modes should be included in quit smoking treatments, and these are

- Nicotine replacement therapy (nicotine patches or gum)

- Social support (professional encouragement and assistance)

- Training in skills to achieve and maintain abstinence

Most medical schools have been slow to incorporate training on smoking prevention and cessation into the curricula for their medical students, thereby missing a vastly important opportunity.[511] But at the University of California–San Francisco, for many years each first year medical student has been given a copy of "How to Help Patients Stop Smoking" published by the American Medical Association in 1994. This describes the National Cancer Institute protocol "Ask-Advise-Assist-Arrange" for smoking intervention in the physician's office, and includes advice on nicotine replacement therapy.[512]

As late as 1999, the majority of United States medical school graduates were not adequately trained to treat nicotine dependence, nor had a model core tobacco curriculum been created.[513] But in 2000, the United States Department of Health and Human Services updated its "Quick Reference Guide for Clinicians" referred to above,[464] and the American Cancer Society published an article on "New Treatments for Smoking Cessation" by John Hughes in the ACS journal *CA*.[514] This was followed in the March/April 2003 issue of *CA* by an excellent article on tobacco control for clinicians who treat adolescents.[515] Together, these articles are suitable for use in medical school curricula, and by physicians in their offices.

Although the above guides are available, a survey conducted by Spangler and coauthors in the September 4, 2002 issue of JAMA concluded that there are still many gaps in integrating tobacco intervention training throughout the curricula of all four years of medical school. Then the April 28, 2004 issue of *JAMA* reported that a new report from the Institute of Medicine calls for changes in the medical school curriculum, and asks that students should be given a better understanding of harmful behaviors such as smoking. The committee of experts that who authored this report urged that basic behavioral and social science content be included in all four years of medical school training, and in the United States Medical Licensing Examination. Hopefully, this book is sufficiently wide in its coverage that it can serve as a text.

But it is not only physicians, but all types of health professionals, especially public health professionals, who have a vital role to play in the two-pronged attack on smoking: first, discouraging youths and young people from taking up smoking, and second, helping smokers to quit. Preventing people from starting a new habit–which initially makes one sick–is much easier than coaxing a long-term nicotine addict to quit. Pediatricians and family physicians urgently need to start talking with their youthful patients about the reasons for not taking up smoking.

Since smoking is by far the worst preventable health menace, the challenge for all health-related professionals is to find their own way to fight it effectively. I was reminded of this by my dental hygienist, Anne Jensen, who related to me how she has managed to persuade several of her patients to quit smoking. She tells them, they can see (and feel) what great difficulty she has in removing the yellowish-brown tobacco stain that sticks tenaciously to their teeth–despite constant tooth brushing. Then she asks them to visualize how their lungs must look–since unlike their teeth they can't benefit from twice a day brushing!

In order to fight smoking, one does not have to be a health professional: every nonsmoker can invent his or her own novel attack. If one wraps up a reproving message inside a compliment, then it becomes more thought provoking. For instance, when I see a woman taking her smoking break on the sidewalk, I smile at her as I pass and comment, "if you wish to be as lovely inside as you are outside, you might think about quitting." Depending on the woman, I might exchange lovely for handsome or stylish.

Health professionals, educators, legislators, and nonsmokers whatever their station in life, have a unique opportunity to play a key role in curbing the global menace of smoking. Even though the AIDS epidemic is on the upswing, by 2002, the total number of people worldwide who had ever died of AIDS was 'only' 20 million people, although 40 million people are now infected,[516] nearly 95% of whom live in developing countries. Because HIV infection is spreading rapidly in Africa, parts of China, Eastern Europe, and central Asia,[517] we can expect the number of worldwide deaths from AIDS to increase rapidly. A United Nations AIDS report of July, 2002 projected 70 million deaths from AIDS within the next 20 years. In contrast, WHO estimated that the number of people who died worldwide from tobacco-related diseases in just one year, 2000, was 4.2 million,[518] and this number is estimated to grow to 10 million by 2025.[519] Hopefully, an effective vaccine against HIV will be discovered long before deaths from AIDS could grow to challenge tobacco's unenviable record as the most potent worldwide threat to human health.

Finally, if we widen our perspective to think decades ahead, then Richard Overholt's advice to his smoking patients, that their very lives depended on quitting, might well be true for all smokers, irrespective of age, even without any sign of disease. Unfortunately, most smokers who feel well would not believe that their lives may depend on quitting, even though eventually this could prove to be true. But lacking present evidence of disease, and not looking ahead into the future—and sometimes just trying desperately to survive that very day—they see no need to quit.

PART IV

SOCIETAL AND GLOBAL PROBLEMS

Children are the future – and we're all Adam's children

THIRTY TWO

———

SOCIETAL PROBLEMS AND SOLUTIONS: HEAD START AND BEYOND

There is a surprisingly strong link between smoking and little education, as well as between smoking and an upbringing in poverty. As of 1998, of the people who had only 9 to 11 years of education (high school dropouts) 37% were smokers, while of those with 16 or more years of education and graduation from college only 11% were smokers.[520] So there is an *inverse* relationship between the level of education and smoking: the less education, the higher the likelihood of smoking. There is also the same inverse relationship between poverty and smoking–the poorer people are, the higher the likelihood that they are smokers.

The eye-opening truth is that there is an equally strong link between little education and a shortened life-span, and between poverty and a shortened life-span. For this relation to be true there must also be a relation between little education and a shortened life-span, and that is true. Thus, U.S. citizens without a high school education have a life expectancy 9 years shorter than that of people with a high school education![521] While smoking is responsible for part of this differential, other factors also play a major role in poverty-stricken neighborhoods: danger, stress, drug use, poor housing, poor nutrition, and diseases that often progress to a critical stage because of lack of access to preventive health care.[522]

Race is only a minor factor in these death statistics, for U.S. citizens with the lowest economic status are deprived of 8 years of life if they are white, 10 years if non-white.[523] In contrast, the *racial gap in education is enormous.* African-American and Hispanic youths with low incomes only made up 1% of those in the top 10% of the high school graduates in 1992.[524] Indeed, Abigail and Stephan Thernstrom have called the racial gap the major civil rights issue of our time. In their recent book "No Excuses: Closing the Racial Gap in Learning," they use data from NAER (National Assessment of Educational Progress) to report that the average African-American or Hispanic student leaves high school performing at a level roughly four years behind his white and Asian peers. A majority of African-American twelfth graders have scores "below basic" in five of the seven subjects tested by NAEP. Further, the racial gap in education has recently been growing. But in this case, the link between education and smoking is invalid: smoking among African-American high school students has decreased substantially. Between 1997 and 2001, the percentage of current African-American cigarette smokers dropped from 28% to 16% for males, and from 17% to 13% for females[525] = so smoking is not a factor in racial educational differences.

Surprisingly, the Thernstroms dismiss most of the usual explanations, namely poverty, differences in family income, public spending on schools, and heredity. They believe that *what is relevant is the view which the children bring to learning from their culture.* White and Asian children tend to approach school thinking that learning is important, and expect to succeed. In the past, too many African-Americans and Hispanics children have not been convinced that learning is important, or that if they learn, they can expect to succeed. Even as long ago as 1966, James Coleman concluded in his book "Equality of Educational Opportunity" that this is a basic cultural problem.

To modify these deeply ingrained cultural patterns, the Thernstroms suggest that schools could do far more to instill students with *"a culture of success."* Charter schools are already closing the racial gap in educational achievement, since they are freed from many bureaucratic rules and regulations, and are chosen by the parents whose children attend them. The model that the Thernstroms favor is the KIPP (Knowledge is Power Program), which has succeeded in many urban settings.[526] Leaders of the African-American and Hispanic communities are working hard to instill into their children a love of learning, and a belief that it can open up rich opportunities for their futures.

Still, ingraining children with a culture of success is a challenge when all around them they see poverty and failure. A poor attitude to education is tied not only to smoking, but to a whole host of other ills, such as the prevalence of drugs, gangs and crime. To concentrate merely on upgrading schools is by no means sufficient. The whole underpinnings of society in poverty-stricken neighborhoods must be upgraded, by providing adequate recreation facilities and most important, viable employment opportunities for disadvantaged youths and adults. By fighting against poverty, poor education, lack of health insurance, and underemployment, *all* societal evils are confronted and reduced. Smoking is merely one of the many evils that shackle the poor.

The daily disciplinary problems facing educators in schools are intimately connected with success in learning. *Without sufficient discipline, all learning stops, and with it, all hope of success.* It is not only the trouble makers who fail to learn, they also prevent the other children in the class from learning. Thus, it is the most critical problem facing inner city schools. Perhaps my experiences in just two of the 60 different schools in which I gave assemblies on smoking (see chapter 23) will illustrate the destructive power of loss of discipline. I made the mistake of arriving an hour too early for my assembly to 8th graders at the school of the Catholic Cathedral in Boston. To while away the time, a teacher invited me into his 8th-grade classroom. I forget what he was teaching to the 30-odd boys and girls in his class. But that was irrelevant, for more than 90% his time was spent in trying to keep order. Constant heckling by a few boys made teaching all but impossible. After my assembly, this young and highly competent Catholic layman told me that during the current school year, the stress of disciplinary problems had caused three of his fellow teachers to have nervous breakdowns.

After an assembly for 8th graders at another middle school in Boston, the assistant principal took me to see what went on in three different classrooms. The teacher in the first class that we visited had arranged the children in study groups of four at separate tables, an arrangement favored by the then latest teaching plans. When we came in close tor the end of a period, the students were chatting away. At a table we stopped at, no one had yet opened the book they were supposed to read...

In the classroom next door there was chaos. The teacher and a few children were standing by the blackboard, but most others were walking about, laughing and having fun. The teacher had lost all control, and moved haltingly, seemingly in a daze. I began to understand that losing control of a class devastates the self-image of a teacher, for learning becomes impossible.

Let me insert a word to the reader, who is unlikely ever to have experienced a situation in a classroom faintly similar to the one I describe above. I certainly had not dreamed it could exist. It is utterly foreign to the discipline in typical American suburban classrooms, which the great majority of readers will have experienced. But to return to the inner city school in which I was scheduled to give an assembly on smoking:

Finally, the assistant principal took me into the best classroom in the school. As we walked in and sat down at desks in the back, the students paid not the slightest attention to us. Every student was totally absorbed in solving an apparently fascinating problem in arithmetic fractions. The teacher, a short, spare male, was giving a rapid-fire performance that had the students mesmerized. They alternately watched the teacher, then scribbled away in their notebooks, solving the problem in a step-by-step fashion. After the class I asked him for the secret of his success. His enigmatic reply was "My strong right arm", and he cocked his arm. I assumed his success was due to his minute planning, which ensured that his students succeeded at each step of each task. He seemed to be challenging them within the bounds of their abilities and building up their confidence. This was probably all true. But his ability to subdue his troublemakers was what he himself thought was vital to success.

In contrast to the tribulations in inner-city schools, students in the suburbs were highly disciplined. The schools were modern, the classrooms spacious and well-lighted, and the students really interested. Seventh graders were the ideal audience for my assemblies, and I noticed that they were just as quick to pick up new information as adults, if the playing field was level–if the subject matter was equally new for both students and adults. Consequently, I treated all students as intelligent young adults. Talking to attentive audiences was a delight, and their many questions suggested that my message had been heard.

I no longer give school assemblies, but hear from teachers that the disciplinary troubles remain unchanged, and that even some suburban high schools have problems. If a teacher loses control of a classroom, it is a devastating experience that causes intense suffering and can lead to depression. All too many inner city teachers feel locked into having no choice but to teach in schools where discipline is a problem. In contrast, teachers who succeed in their profession love it, and delight in success and in the esteem which their students give them.

Am I overstating the disciplinary problems? Had I not seen them, I would have found them unbelievable. Unfortunately, there is ample support for what I saw. Public Agenda, a research and policy organization in New York City, issued a report in April 2003, that concluded that many high schools have ill-mannered pupils, demoralized teachers, uninvolved parents, and are bureaucratically run. According to 40% of high school students surveyed, there was at least one serious fight a month in their school, and only 15% of teachers said that teacher morale was good. Shirley Igo, president of the National Parent Teacher Association, commented that this was "a true reflection of how the public feels."[527]

Further, there is evidence that school discipline is deteriorating rather than improving in some areas. In Houston's Schools, the number of assaults rose steadily each year between 1999 and 2003.[528] As of January, 2004, an overhaul of New York City's school system revealed "glaring problems with the disciplinary system" and severe overcrowding in some schools.[529] Nationally, even kids in kindergarten and first grade are reported to be acting out in outrageous ways.[530,531]

Unfortunately, some teachers are not blameless. According to a New York Times editorial of 2003 about failing teachers in New York City schools, "the true extent of school violence, the utter chaos in some of the classrooms, the fraudulent grading and promotion practices, the widespread contempt heaped upon the students, and the scandalous lack of parental involvement–have not yet been fully and honestly revealed.[532] New York City's teacher's union has urged faster evaluation and removal of incompetent teachers.[533] Or are they just not tough enough?

Before I explain why I gave up giving assemblies to inner city students I need to give evidence that I am not a scared cat. For the Albuquerque 5-man team in the Rocky Mountain Ski Association, I raced downhill and slalom for each of the four years I lived there, and skied Tuckerman Ravine on Mount Washington for twenty successive years. I also spent thirty years white water canoeing and kayaking with AMC (Appalachian

Mountain Club) groups in the roiling rivers of New England, and loved to surf in the ocean on Cape Cod, and in a standing wave that forms before high tide at Cohasset harbor in Massachusetts.

But to succeed in tough environments n schools, the replacement teachers need to be thoroughly trained to handle disciplinary problems, fully dedicated, creative enough to make stepwise lessons and fun homework assignments, and backed up by an administration that is equally dedicated, and is able to give teachers full support, especially where discipline is involved. Parent involvement in and support of schools is also crucial. Happily, there are several programs that are designed to achieve some of these goals. Unfortunately, all are underfunded.

Teach for America (TFA) was one of the five federal AmeriCorps education and literacy programs that Laura Bush vowed to support during the presidential campaign of 2000. Then in his State of the Union address of 2002, George Bush said "I hope young Americans all across the country think about joining Teach for America." For the 2003–2004 school-year, over 3,000 of the brightest and best motivated among 25,000 applicants had been chosen to teach in the nation's toughest schools for a two year period, and to receive almost $5,000 per year in college scholarship money. TFA has another sterling virtue: it gives its prospective teachers a five week training course that prepares them for teaching at a school in a low income district. Further information about TFA is available at www.teachforamerica.org.[534]

As of 2003, New York City had taken a novel approach to dealing with its disciplinary problem: it was devoting $43 million to hire a parent coordinator paid $30,000 to $39,000 a year, to encourage parents to participate in their children's education. Another solution is to build small high schools with specialized curriculums. While their cost per pupil is higher, they have much lower dropout rates, so that their cost per graduate is much lower—and the goal should be graduation.[535]

"Head Start" is one of the most valuable solutions to the above problems. The goal of this program is to prepare children from poor families for school, by stimulating their willingness and ability to learn. Also vital, it accustoms children to an orderly classroom setting, and to view learning as a challenging game. Education is vital if children are to grow up into adults who can hold down good jobs, earn good salaries, and escape the host of destructive social ills that are allied to poverty.

Head Start built on the feedback beginning to surface from studies such as The High/Scope Perry Preschool Study, which divided 123 poor, African-American children 3 and 4 year olds living in Ypsilanti, Michigan into two groups. One was sent to an excellent preschool, the other was not. Then, beginning in the 1960s, the children in the two groups were interviewed and followed for many years. It was found that children who had gone to the preschool lived much more happily. They were more likely to graduate from high school, earn good money, and own their homes. Girls who went to preschool were five times as likely to be married at age 27, as those who did not go to preschool.[536]

When Sargent Shriver became director of the Office of Economic Opportunity, he invited Julius Richmond–who later became a United States Surgeon General–to found and direct Head Start, which began in 1965 as a national program.[537] Its goal was to help children who grew up in poverty to acquire learning patterns and emotional maturity that would help them to succeed. At first, Head Start targeted 4- and 5-year olds, and innovated the funding of high staffing: one qualified teacher and two aides per fifteen children.

Applications for the funding of Head Start programs were solicited from United States counties, and asked to follow these guidelines:

- They were to be comprehensive child development centers.

- When needed, medical, dental, and psychological evaluation was to be available for every child.

- At least one hot meal was to be served each school day.

- Families who needed social services were to be informed of their availability elsewhere in their community.

- A structured curriculum was favored over "free play."

- Active parent participation was to be strongly encouraged.

- Volunteers were welcome, and over 100,000 quickly appeared.

- Programs were to be governed by the local community's citizens.

- Staff had career ladders, and was released to attend schooling.

- The evaluation of each program was not to focus merely on IQ.

- A special effort was made to encourage the 300 poorest counties in the United States to submit applications for a Head Start Project.

Thanks to its energetic and innovative director, the Head Start program developed extraordinarily quickly. Happily, its early-intervention efforts have resulted in long-term gains by participating children.[538] By 2003, each Head Start Program had to meet high performance standards, and the private agencies that had contracts were closely monitored.[539] As of July 2003, Head Start served 900,000 children. But of eligible children, this included only 60% of 3- to 5-year olds, and only about 3% of those 6 months to 3-year old.[540] Although there is an urgent need to increase Head Start funding to include the children from poor families who are presently excluded, reauthorization of Head Start for 2005 will only increase its funds by about 2% to 5%.

When Head Start began in 1965, there were no states that funded early childhood programs that were administered separately as was Head Start. By 1998, 39 states had such programs, and spent about $1.4 billion of their own funds to serve 700,000 children. Currently, Georgia and New York offer a universal program for 4-year old children, regardless of family income.[541]

But Head Start faces a problem. In 2003, the House of Representatives passed a bill by one vote, which would authorize an experiment to give eight states block grants that would allow their governors to control Head Start funding. In contrast, direct federal funding insures that Head Start is not used as a political football, by permitting governors to select Head Start providers. It also insures that Head Start funds are not used to substitute for similar programs presently funded by the states themselves. The bill does have one bright spot: it would require that at least half of Head Start's teachers have four-year college degrees by 2008. But unless Congress funds the additional $2 billion that this would cost, this provision is meaningless.[542]

The Early Head Start Program began in 1995 as a response to the "quiet crisis" which the Carnegie Corporation of New York said was facing American infants, toddlers, and their mothers in 1994. The goal of the program is to improve the development of 2- and 3-year old children. It helps mothers to teach their infants to talk, learn and become disciplined. It teaches mothers to give their children love and emotional security, and councils them to contact other agencies that can aid them and their children.[543]

By 2002, the Early Head Start Program had expanded to serve 55,000 children and their families in over 660 communities across the United States, and consumed around 10% of the Head Start budget. A short-term evaluation of the program in 2002 saw "a consistent pattern of statistically significant but modest favorable impacts across a range of outcomes, with larger impacts in several subgroups.[543] Long-term results were not yet available.

While few definitive data substantiate the benefits of small class size for 3 to 5-year olds, a study of Tennessee schools in the late 1980s produced strong evidence that lowering class size raises the academic performance of young students. After a school aid program in California excluded state contributions for an entire grade level if any single classroom in that grade had more than 20 students, student achievement tests showed a modest jump. Initially, it was not clear whether this resulted from smaller class sizes or the upgrading of teacher competence. But the president of the California Teachers Association, faced with elimination of state assistance for 2003–2004 due to the budget crisis, said "It's the only major reform in California enacted in the past 20 years that has worked."[544] Parents strongly support smaller class sizes, while teachers say that miracles of small class size unfold each day, because discipline is far easier to maintain, and teachers give students more individual attention.[545]

No Child Left Behind (NCLB) was the education program that President Bush announced three days after he took office in January of 2001, and the NCLB Act was passed just a year later.

Its goal was to improve the performance of America's elementary and secondary schools, and to insure that no child was trapped in a failing school. It also held states, school districts and schools to greater accountability, gave students attending low-performing schools a greater choice of schools, provided more flexibility in the use of federal education funds, and placed a strong emphasis on reading, especially in early grades.

The NCLB program would be ideal, if it extended Head Start's benefits to elementary and secondary schools. But the two programs differ radically. While Head Start supplies all funding for its programs, NCLB asks states for big improvements but provides only about $1 billion a year, which is very far short of the money needed to pay for them.[546] It penalizes financially schools that do not measure up to its standards, and this can overwhelm school districts that lack the funds to improve their schools. Although the Department of Education fared better in the President's 2005 year budget request than all departments other than NASA, the increase over 2004 was a mere 5.6%.[547] Further, some other valuable programs, such as the NSF's {National Science Foundation's) largest program to improve student achievement in science and math were to be phased out, and its responsibility shifted to the Department of Education.[548] As for the use of NCLB provisions by students during the 2002–2003 school year, 46% of students eligible for special tutoring opted to receive it. But only 2% of eligible students took advantage of the opportunity to transfer to better schools.[549]

Time magazine of March 2004 evaluated the accomplishments and shortcomings of NCLB by focusing on a single school in Iowa, which made the program's list of "Schools in Need of Improvement" (translation, failed schools). Without improvement, the school faced consequences such as allowing its students to transfer elsewhere, having to offer free tutoring, and bringing in outside experts. After that, the state could have taken it over and fired the entire staff. By focusing hard on NCLB's tests, the school greatly improved its pupils' scores. Of course, many teachers resented that time previously spent on social studies, history, geography, and creative writing had to be sacrificed.[550] Also, many schools could no longer afford classes for gifted students.

But learning to read, write and do simple mathematics in the early grades is an essential foundation for all later learning. When high schools were graduating some students who could not read, then it was time to end that situation–even if it required a drastic and imperfect solutions such as NCLB. But in time, the present severe regulations of NCLB will undoubtedly be improved. One slight improvement has been, that NCLB now permits 1% of a district's learning-disabled children to take alternative tests with special accommodations such as extra time, instead of requiring them to achieve at the same rate as other students.[550] Hopefully, social promotions will end, and failing students will be kept back to repeat their grade–a policy that succeeds.[551]

A lack of jobs for disadvantaged adolescents turns them loose onto the streets. There, some befriend street-wise peers, who introduce them, first of all, to cigarettes. But a 1985 study showed that youths who smoke are 3 times more likely to drink alcohol, 8 times more likely to smoke marijuana, and 22 times more likely to use cocaine, as youths who do not smoke.[552] Several other studies also link smoking to use of alcohol and illegal drugs, and disruptive classroom behavior–and *vice versa*.[553] Thus, each stage in the progression from lack of jobs to smoking, to drugs and to crime is a gateway to the next stage–not in the sense of cause and effect, but as a marker. Once one stage is reached, the risk for progressing to the next stage is higher than for youths for whom society has provided money for jobs.

Only 5% of the teens awarded summer jobs in Boston in 2003 were labeled as "at-risk youths" by the Police Department.[554] It seems that for youths with police records, crime pays better. At least, most of the other 95% of youths given jobs were protected from following that path. The need for jobs is underlined by the report "L.A.'s Streets of Death" in the New York Times of June, 2003. It estimates that during the last 20 years, 10,000 youths were killed in Los Angeles in gang-related homicides.[555]

As of October, 2003, the high school drop-out rate in Chicago was at an all-time high, and 22% of Chicagoans aged 16 – 24 were both out of school and out of work. According to Neeta Fogg at Chicago's Northeastern University, failure to complete high school and then to find work is close to economic suicide, for it makes it hard to find work for the rest of one's life. By dropping out of high school, a large number of healthy young men and women sacrifice their potential to live rich, satisfying and constructive lives.[556] When the income of families is raised, the attitude and behavior of children in school is improved.[557]

To raise incomes for people in poor neighborhoods, far more job training, job finding assistance, and jobs are urgently needed.

Children are our most precious resource, and those nurtured by Early Head Start and Head Start should be given equal support in adolescence, which is a critical time for their future. This has been long recognized, and is addressed by programs funded by a variety of sources: federal, state, local (city or school district), businesses, private foundations, public benefactors and from Head Start. But the sum total is far below the need.

Programs for disadvantaged adolescents should be as diverse as they are themselves. They have multiple needs, each of which deserves appropriate solutions tailored to particular age-groups and societal subgroups. For children from kindergarten to grade 6, elementary schools provide sports programs that keep those who are athletic occupied at least during some of their spare time. For children who prefer indoor recreation, some schools provide it in after-school hours. While most of these programs are available at schools in districts where the average income is ample, present funding extends these benefits only to a minority of school districts at or below the poverty level. It is there that they are most urgently needed and have the most impact.

For middle school children below the age at which their state permits legal employment, the same strategy as mentioned above is used to keep the children off the street. It is important that programs for these older children extend into vacations, and especially the summer vacations. Most middle schools offer a variety of after-school programs and community clubs, such as Boys and Girls clubs, and scouting. Also, Big Brother and Big Sister programs are common in inner city areas.

The need is especially great for middle school children whose parents work. Sixteen percent of 10 to 14 year olds in Massachusetts take care of themselves after school on at least 3 days a week.[558] Nationwide, on a regular basis, more than 3 million children under age 13 (some as young as 5) are left to care for themselves for at least a few hours a week.[559]

While some after-school programs are held at schools, others use libraries, existing neighborhood recreation facilities and YMCAs. Monitoring is provided by teachers, social workers, librarians, parents, ministers, and volunteers. Federal grants to states are far too low, to help states to fund enjoyable after-school programs in more than a few impoverished areas. It is there that funds are needed for summer camps, which allow inner city youths to experience the beauty of nature, to enjoy new, unfamiliar kinds of recreation, and to breathe clean, fresh air.

Work Start programs are vital to accustom youths to the routine and benefits of a working life. Beginning at the legal age for youth employment, they provide funds for after-school work, during vacations–especially the long summer vacation. But here also, the need for funds far outstrips their availability.

Schools need to become multiservice centers, by staying open for more after-school programs, summer programs, and services provided through community partnerships for counseling, job training, health monitoring, and other helpful activities. [560]

Scholarships for disadvantaged youths who wish to go on to college are available from the colleges themselves, from private foundations, from local and state sources, and from the federal Department of Education. But since these depend upon SAT test scores, special coaching classes for college admission should be provided to help students to raise their SAT grades. As for college costs, many universities admit students on merit and then give them scholarships dependent upon their financial needs. For instance, in October, 2003, the University of North Carolina at Chapel Hill announced that it would cover the full costs of an education for students from families of the working poor.[561]

Regarding federal support, three United States agencies have programs that support some of the above programs for disadvantaged youths: the Department of Labor (DOL, at www.dol.gov)

the Department of Education (DE, at www.my.ED.gov), and the Department of Health and Human Services (HHS, at www.hhs. gov). All states, and through them towns and school districts, receive federal funds. Also, states provide their own funding for such programs, as do most cities, towns, and local school districts.

For the fiscal year 2003–2004, DOL was seeking $1 billion for Youth Grants and over $1.5 billion for Job Corps, which now includes programs previously called Youth Activities. But in July, 2003, the Department of Education changed the formula of "Pell grants," by which students from low-income families receive federal aid for college tuition. For the year 2004–2005, this will trim $270 million in funds, barring 84,000 college students from receiving any award at all![562]

Federal funds are allocated according to a formula that favors areas with high unemployment rates and areas with low income. But unfortunately, the funding does not consider local living costs, which short-changes the youths of some states. Also a recession has reduced business support for youth programs.

Boston serves as an example of the current status of work-related assistance. The funds available for Boston's youth programs in 2001 totaled $10.1 million, which funded 11,500 jobs. Only 8% of this total came from federal funds, only 6% from state funds, while 86% came from the city of Boston. In 2003, the total available was $3.9 million, which funded only 6,800 jobs. This reflects a cut of more than 50% in federal and city funding, and a cut close to 50% in state funding. As a result, only 22% of Boston's youths aged 14 to 18 were helped in 2003.[563]- By May 2004, funding had shrunk even further.[560]

There are at least three major questions that impact the funding of work programs. First, do these programs really work? Second, what goals might be set to help underprivileged children succeed? Third, is there the will to fund these programs fully so that no youth is neglected, even in a time of economic downturn?

First, past experience suggests that the introduction of smaller class sizes and new programs will produce measurable benefits only slowly. One cannot hope to change the entire setting in which children from poor families live, merely by extending educational benefits and by providing after-school and holiday employment for the children. Such changes have a strong beneficial effect, but in addition, affordable housing and more job opportunities are crucial for raising the standard of living above the poverty level. While the expansion of existing funding during periods of depression and shrinking revenues seems impractical, real merit lies only in doing what seems impossible.

Second, regarding the problems of schools in poverty-stricken areas, where student achievements are low and the drop-out rate is high, more funding is needed for items such as:

- Smaller class sizes, which greatly help in keeping discipline.

- Attracting dedicated and able teachers to inner city schools. Their salaries should be *higher* than those in suburban schools.

- In schools with problems, new teachers and appropriate present staff should be trained in strategies for keeping discipline.

- Chronic troublemakers should be rehabilitated either in special classes or in schools set up to accomplish that purpose.

- Schools with disciplinary problems should teach their students non-aggressive behavior. One such program for early grades is LIFT (Linking the Interests of Families and Teachers). It rewards good behavior with armbands, toys, and team points.[564]

- Research into violence prevention needs strong support.[565, 566]

Third, regarding the full funding of the broad array of programs that are essential for the neediest in our society, our priorities need to be reorganized. During the last century, we developed vaccines and antibiotics that increased our average lifespan by 50%, and put men on the moon and brought them back alive. Compared to such miracles, raising the educational level of disadvantaged children and assisting their parents to advance beyond poverty seems to be entirely within America's capability. Failing to do so will be vastly more costly than achieving it.

There already exists a consensus of parents, teachers, religious leaders, social workers and all concerned with the welfare of children, that *no child should be left behind*. But whenever there is an economic downturn, both federal and state funds fail to accomplish this goal. To secure the necessary funds will require concerted lobbying at all levels of our society.

While children are championed by parents, teachers and sociologists, they are handicapped because they cannot organize, lobby for themselves, and have no vote. In contrast, the American Association of Retired Persons (AARP) that includes vast numbers of people aged 50 and over, lobbies powerfully, and has massive voting prowess. As a result, Social Security and Medicare are strongly championed by legislators. Yet funding for children's programs can change their lives and benefit them throughout their entire lifespan. While programs for oldsters should not be cut, the funding of programs for needy children is far more pressing.

But the above programs are all officially sponsored and funded. Is there nothing that the individual citizen can do to make the disadvantaged and immigrants feel accepted into society, treated well, and given their fair share of job opportunities and the chance for advancement? Of course there is: there is a great deal each and every one of us can do. We can make a real effort to go out of our way to accept them, and treat them in every way exactly as we treat those of our own group. Most important of all, we can give them job opportunities, and help them to succeed in their new jobs. Once they find the promise of a good life is open to them, once they feel truly accepted and have a good job, they will overcome their disaffection and become useful citizens.

One national objective was to reduce cigarette smoking among adults to 12% or less by 2010.[567] But there will always be smokers, because nicotine is just another potent addicting drug. A minority of people–hopefully a small one–will always succumb to the temptation of drugs and then become addicted. But to achieve a major reduction in smoking in our society will require generous funding of antismoking education and advertising, a major increase in the funding of educational and job programs for the neediest, and a generous investment in families living in poverty. For these, vastly more funds are needed to improve childcare, education, health, and work opportunities. This is a far more humane and worthy goal than putting a man on Mars.[568]

When Bill Gates was an undergraduate in the Department of Computer Science at Harvard, my son John was a graduate student in that department, but he had no idea that this bright-eyed, highly motivated lad would become the richest man in the world. According to the *New York Times* of July 13, 2003, Gates aims to spend billions to attack illnesses in the neediest countries in the world- which is wonderful. But it would be equally wonderful, if Gates and other United States benefactors devoted an equal amount of money and effort to reduce poverty in the desperately needy neighborhoods of their own country, by providing services, jobs and support for good education. An in-depth look at that problem is provided by the book *Poverty in America* by John Iceland (University of California, 2003).

A search for "Head Start" on the internet produces a vast amount of information about Head Start and its various programs. There, the Administration for Children & Families of Health and Human Services (HHS), the United States Department of Education, and many local Head Start programs currently post their missions and activities. The national Performance Standards for Head Start programs include recommendations for maintaining discipline, but this is such a severe problem in public schools that it needs special emphasis. The program of Sabine Parish School Board Head Start (betsy@sabine.k12.la.us) highlights this vital issue. The Head Start Bureau is at 330 C Street, S.W., Washington, D.C. 20447, and has an Information and Publication Center at 1200 N. Henry Street, Suite E, Alexandria, VA 22314-0417 (703-683-5767). The National Head Start Association, which advocates for Head Start in Congress, is at 1651 Prince Street, Alexandria, VA 22314 (703-739-0875) www.nhsa.org. No Child Left Behind (NCLB) can be accessed on the web at www.ed.gov/nclb or at www.isbe.state.il.us/nclb.

THIRTY THREE

SMOKING AS A WORLDWIDE PROBLEM

Tobacco companies are rapidly losing cigarette sales in the United States. Profits at the nation's largest cigarette maker, Philip Morris USA, fell by 13% in 2002,[569] and fell further in 2003 and 2004.[570] In America, the public has seen the CEO's of all major tobacco companies testifying under oath that nicotine is not addictive- when their own research, which they suppressed from the public, had proven the opposite long ago. Their honesty matches that of their advertisements, which depict smokers as beautiful, stylish–and bursting with health!

Today, the public knows that secondhand smoke is poisonous. As a result, smoking is prohibited in many public places and offices, and not tolerated in most homes. In the United States, the nonsmoking majority tends to take a dim view of smoking.

Faced with these realities and harassed by lawsuits, how can tobacco companies increase their sale of cigarettes? Their answer has been to create multinational tobacco companies, which are expanding rapidly throughout the world. According to The Boston Globe of May 6, 2002, even as long ago as 1998 Philip Morris was making five times as much sales profit overseas, as it did in the United States. According to the New York Times of July 30, 2003, the same strategy was being pursued by the world's second largest tobacco company, British American Tobacco, which is based in England. It is a well calculated plan, for as of 2002, 80% of the world's 1.3 billion smokers lived in developing countries[571] and in Asia smoking was growing at 8% a year – an explosive rate.

By using the same slick advertising campaigns and devious tactics used in Western nations before laws were passed to ban them, tobacco companies are succeeding in addicting children and adults in developing nations. Wherever in the world there are no explicit laws that forbid it, tobacco companies now sponsor popular sports events and concerts, give away logo-emblazoned gear on proof of purchase, and advertise cigarettes with thinly veiled appeals to teenagers and women. One of the many slogans used the world over is LSMFT–Lucky Strike Means Free Thinking. The inference is that smoking an American brand allows one to take part in America's freedom, independence, and prosperity.

As in the United States, tobacco companies are expert at circumventing the local laws against smoking in foreign countries. In Malaysia, for instance, where tobacco advertising is banned, the Salem Cool Planet campaign sponsored a concert in the stadium of the nation's capital in 2001. The concert was preceded by weeks of heavy advertising–for the Salem concert, not for cigarettes!

For the world as a whole, smoking is an enormous problem in terms of human cost, and its economic burden is equally gigantic. A book by Frank Sloan and coauthors entitled "The Price of Smoking" (2004) analyses the economic impact of smoking in an innovative way, combining the internal costs of smoking – those paid by the smoker – with its external costs – those imposed on their families, their health care system, and society as a whole. The authors are the first to estimate the lifetime costs of all aspects of smoking. They cite convincing evidence that large tax increases are justified by its financial and social costs. In addition, higher taxes serve to reduce smoking.[572] The economic impact of smoking was also cited in 2004, in an excellent book edited by Eric Feldman and Ronald Bayer, entitled "Unfiltered: Conflicts over Tobacco Policy and Public Health." Tax revenues and other economic factors figure prominently in determining the attitude that various nations take toward smoking.[573]

The two books mentioned above, both published in 2004, and previous books in this area agree, that there are three vital economic supports for tobacco. First, it is an important cash crop for farmers in many countries, including the United States and European countries. Second, it is a highly lucrative commercial commodity that enriches tobacco companies. Third, it brings in substantial revenues not only for nations but also for individual states in the United States. Not surprisingly, both farmers and tobacco companies lobby extensively for tobacco. But also it is surprising and sad, that some nations are swayed more by the benefits that the tax revenues on tobacco provide, than by the need to safeguard their citizens' health and wellbeing.[573]

Fortunately, WHO (the World Health Organization) has been working to reign in the worldwide addiction to nicotine. Unfortunately, the United States is the world's largest exporter of tobacco. During the first years of President George Bush's administration, it acted in step with its economic interests—even though some of its citizens and organizations are leaders in the antismoking movement. Still, individual Americans whose hearts are in the right place can work wonders, by supporting the organizations that lead the fight against smoking (see Appendix), and by lobbying local, state and federal legislators to pass antismoking legislation.

North American countries are presently in the midst of a major epidemic of smoking-related diseases, even though the consumption of cigarettes is declining. This incongruity exists, because many of the health-related effects of smoking are cumulative and surface only decades after smoking is begun. Thus, global data indicate that developed nations presently have a higher incidence of lung cancer than many developing nations.

But as this chapter demonstrates, it will only be a matter of time before the latter catch up with the former.

INCIDENCE OF LUNG CANCER PER 100,000 PEOPLE[90]*		
AREA	MALES	FEMALES
Eastern Europe	65.7	8.7
Northern America	61.2	35.6
Southern Europe	56.9	9.2
Western Europe	50.9	12.0
Northern Europe	44.3	21.3
China	42.4	19.0
Australia/New Zealand	39.1	17.4
Japan	38.1	12.3
Western Asia	33.1	5.5
Caribbean	27.1	9.9
South-Eastern Asia	27.1	8.9
South America	23.7	7.6
Southern Africa	23.1	6.9
Central America	16.1	6.5
Northern Africa	12.0	2.2
South Central Asia	11.9	2.4
Middle Africa	4.7	0.7
*Based on 2002 data		

As for the future situation in the United States, there is strong evidence that lung cancer rates could be reduced, if the effectiveness of antismoking campaigns were increased.[574]

The public distaste with environmental smoke is revealed by the passage of Smokefree Workplace Laws.[575] By December 2005, the U.S. states of California, Delaware, New York, Connecticut, Maine, Massachusetts, Rhode Island, and Vermont had passed such laws, and Washington State was planning a vote on this issue. In addition, five other states had passed similar laws that only exempted bars from compliance.[576]

In Canada, anti-tobacco legislation worked spectacularly well for a few years. The book by Rob Cunningham, *Smoke and Mirrors: The Canadian Tobacco War*, tells the whole story.[577] It traces the rise and fall of Canadian tobacco taxes, which were among the highest in the world, until smuggling from the United States forced a rollback. Taxes for a carton of cigarettes rose by $2 in 1985, by another $4 in 1989, and by an additional $6 in 1991–and local and provincial taxes boosted the retail prices even higher. While in 1982 Canada had the highest per capita consumption of cigarettes in the world, once these high taxes kicked in, cigarette use decreased by 40% in 7 years. By 1992, Canada's cigarette consumption had dropped from 1st to 13th place in the world.

Unfortunately, this story has an unhappy ending–as do many stories about legislation on tobacco. Although Canadian lawmakers banned tobacco advertising, that did not include the sponsorship of sporting events. The tobacco industry managed to incorporate this loophole into the Canadian Tobacco Products Control Act of 1988, and then exploited it to the full. Another loophole was opened by failure to set into law the requirement that health warnings on cigarette packages had to have contrast. So tobacco companies set the warnings in gold lettering and used a yellow background to make them invisible. A former Minister of Defense quipped, if the Canadian army knew as much about camouflage as the tobacco companies did, "nobody'd ever find our fellows."

Because cigarettes cost much less in the United States, the smuggling of cigarettes was inevitable. Cunningham's book presents strong evidence that it was promoted by tobacco companies, who had the gall to lament publicly the breakdown of law and order.[577] When in 1994 the government caved in to calls to roll back taxes, the retail prices of cigarettes dropped by 50% almost overnight. The final blow came a year later: by one vote, Canada's Supreme Court struck down the advertising ban as a violation of its Charter of Rights.

But while the deep pockets of Big Tobacco changed the mind of legislators, the Canadian people are as much against pollution with environmental smoke as are Americans. In November 2005, Nova Scotia became Canada's 9th Smokefree Province/Territory, and its Smoke-free Places Act even included outdoor areas of bars and restaurants. Canada's remaining four provinces/territories have only weaker laws in place.[578]

In Caribbean countries and Latin America, cigarette smoking is increasing, especially among the young. If concerted efforts are not made to decrease tobacco use, these countries are sure to be swept by an even worse epidemic of smoking-related diseases than North America is now experiencing. In 1992, the United States Surgeon General, together with the Pan American Health Organization, published *Smoking and Health in the Americas*, which summarized the situation on the entire American continent.[579] The sections of this publication that focused on the Caribbean and Latin America reveal that when tobacco companies lost sales in North America after the Surgeon General's Report of 1964, they formed subsidiary multinational companies that then mounted multi-faceted advertising campaigns similar to those originally used in America. These campaigns steered consumer preferences away from the local brands to American brands, and this ruse resulted in a rapid increase in the sale of American cigarettes.

A major break in this escalation came during the economic downturn that hit most countries in the Caribbean and in Latin America during the 1980s, proving once again that as the price of cigarettes relative to earnings soars, the consumption of cigarettes drops.[579]

Still, most South American countries have passed some laws that have proved effective in decreasing cigarette consumption By mandating the following:

- High taxes on tobacco products.

- Restrictions on advertising, with loopholes carefully plugged.

- Prominent, contrasting health warnings on tobacco packages.

- Strictly enforcing age limits on access to tobacco products.

- Strictly enforcing fines for smoking in indoor public places.

- A continuing public information campaign against smoking.

- School education on the health effects of smoking.

- Help from the press and media in the fight against tobacco.

- Class-action, state and personal law suits against Big Tobacco.

But legislative approaches vary widely. In many countries, anti-tobacco programs have gaps, and since enforcement depends on funding, it tends to be spotty. Some countries have developed national antismoking coalitions, promoted education and media-based campaigns, and are working to tighten up surveillance of tobacco companies. But unfortunately, few countries have adopted a truly unified program, such as Canada developed during the years when its tobacco control program was on the upswing.

Still, there are a number of good omens. Regional and international plans for tobacco control are being implemented, and the peoples of the Caribbean and Latin America are becoming aware of the costs and hazards of smoking. In 2006, Uruguay became the first country in South America to go smoke-free, and to prohibit smoking in workplaces, restaurants and bars.[580] But only adequate funding of appropriate programs and constant vigilance against the artfully disguised and ever-changing wiles of Big Tobacco can ensure progress in the fight against tobacco.

In many European countries, a higher percentage of people smoke than in the United States.[581] In 2001, a summary of ten studies carried out in six European countries found that compared to nonsmokers, male smokers had a twenty-fourfold higher risk of lung cancer, and over 90% of lung cancer was attributable to smoking. For female smokers, the equivalent values were ninefold and 60%.[582]

France is a good example of a European country where smoking is not taken very seriously: even President Jaques Chirac is a cigarette smoker. A spokesperson for the National Antismoking Committee in France said that as of 2004, about 35% of French citizens over 18 were smokers, but that this might be an underestimate. On paper, France has tough antismoking laws, with high taxes on cigarettes that are frequently increased. In France, tobacco companies may not sponsor public events, and since 1992, smoking has been banned in all enclosed public places except in specially designated areas. But for many years the law had no teeth, was ignored with impunity, and few nonsmokers asserted their rights. In 2005, an official of France's cancer society said that Parisians just ignore the voluntary smoking ban in their restaurants and cafes.[583] But in October 2006, a parliamentary committee approved a proposal for mandatory banning of smoking in public areas – but this had not yet been approved by parliament.[584] Unlike other European countries, France has not run public service campaigns on the health hazard of smoking, nor do French physicians warn their patients of its dangers–and one-third of them smoke themselves.

While the percentage of smokers in France is only 5% to 10% higher than in America, there is a striking difference in how smokers are perceived in the two countries. In America, smokers are often seen as losers, and only 10% of those with college and graduate degrees smoke. In direct contrast to the situation in America, in France nearly one-third of high income earners smoke – slightly more than lower wage earners.

As for Europe as a whole, according to the *New York Times* of August 11, 2003, about one-third of Europeans smoke, compared to a little over one-quarter of Americans. The fraction of smokers is somewhat lower in Britain and Sweden, but higher in Greece, Spain and Hungary. Still, the anti-tobacco trend has reached Europe. In 2006, England put into effect a smoke-free workplace law,[585] while Spain restricted smoking in bars.[586] But in general, state and private organizations in Europe still lag far behind the United States in campaigning to stop the young from starting to smoke, and in persuading existing smokers to quit.

Still, European governments are becoming more aggressive in publicizing the hazards and costs of smoking. As of November 2005, the Irish Republic, Northern Ireland, Italy, Sweden, and Norway had passed Smoke-free Workplace Laws. In addition, Scotland and England passed similar legislation that went into effect in 2006.[587] For Europe as a whole, this represents a good start – the tide is beginning to turn.

The Wall Street Journal of July 2001 reported that Philip Morris had reacted in a most "creative" way to charges from Czech health officials, that smoking creates a huge burden of health care costs. *Philip Morris said that the premature demise of smokers saved the Czech government $24 to $30 million in health care, housing, and pensions!* To Philip Morris, the only thing that matters is the bottom line.[588] *The callousness of this classic response merits a place in The Guinness Book of Records.*

To counteract the public's understanding of its true nature, Philip Morris has tried to disguise itself by changing its name to Altria. It is hard to conceive of *Altria* as not being a takeoff on *altrix* – only the change of a single letter separates Altria from the Latin name for foster-mother or nurse: a benign and nurturing person, as in *altruistic*, that is defined as "unselfishly concerned for the welfare of others". To be more accurate we should call Philip Morris "Altria the *lethal* Altrix!"

In Hungary, the per person cigarette consumption is among the highest in the world. In 1999, the percentage of smokers among youths was 37% at age 15, and 46% at age 17. A number of legislative failures contributed to this high rate of smoking: no regulations against selling cigarettes to minors; few advertising restrictions and low fines for their violation; free distribution of cigarette samples; weak health warnings; availability of contraband cigarettes; and lack of enforcement of existing regulations. Hopefully, a 2001 survey of smoking in Hungary by WHO, and Hungary's development of a tobacco control plan as part of WHO's Framework Convention on Tobacco Control,[589] will provide substantial improvements with time.[590]

The potent effect of smoking in Middle Europe is illustrated by the lung cancer death rate of Austrian men in 2002. It was 81% higher than the death rate from colorectal cancer, the next most deadly scourge. For women, the trend in deaths from lung cancer suggested they would soon overtake deaths from breast cancer.[591]

The EU (European Union) outlawed tobacco advertisements in newspapers and magazines in 2002, on the internet beginning in 2005, and at international sporting events as of 2006. The EU Health Commissioner called this ban "another nail in the coffin of the tobacco industry." But a previous ban was struck down in court, and a future legal challenge by the tobacco industry seems likely.[592] In 2003, the European Union sued RJ Reynolds, alleging that it allowed cigarettes to be smuggled tax-free into Iraq.[593]

In Eastern Europe's Russia and Poland, smoking rates have long been very high. But in 1995, Russian president Boris Yeltsin banned the Russian media from advertising alcohol and tobacco, saying they were a threat to public health. In 2004, Moscow schools launched a major campaign against smoking.[594] In 1995,

Poland also banned tobacco advertising on radio and television, and in youth publications. At long last, Russia and Poland are being serious about discouraging smoking.

In Asian countries such as China and Indonesia, a high percentage of men are smokers. Every year between 1996 and 1999, JAMA (the Journal of the American Medical Association) published major articles, editorials and letters about the growing epidemic of tobacco-related diseases in China. As of 1999, the 1.2 billion Chinese, who comprise 20% of all humanity, smoked 30% of the world's cigarettes; 63% of Chinese males but only 4% women were current smokers. Amazingly, more than 1,000 brands of cigarettes were available, and the average price per pack ranged from 25 cents in rural areas to 63 cents in urban locations, while Western brands were a little more expensive. *JAMA* reported that on average, Chinese smokers expend about 25% of their very low income on cigarettes.[595] However, smoking cessation is only one of a number of several measures that Chinese physicians advocate.[596]

Writing in the *British Medical Journal* of 2001, an editorial commented that the mainland Chinese are about 40 years behind Western nations, in which smoking-related deaths peaked in the mid-1970s. But in more modernized Hong Kong, smoking is the eventual cause of death for almost one-third of male smokers aged 35 to 69. It was predicted that if cigarette smoking in China continues its present upward spiral, then the "Chinese who smoke like Westerners will die from tobacco like Westerners."[597]

As one might expect, there are differences in the way that people of different races smoke, and in the way they process the chemicals in tobacco smoke. For instance, African Americans smoke fewer cigarettes than Caucasians, but inhale more deeply; they have a higher incidence of lung cancer, but a lower incidence of COPD (chronic obstructive pulmonary disease).[598] Other than race, social and cultural factors play a major role in the decision of whether or not to smoke.[599]

In Japan, about 54% of men and 14% of women were smokers in 1998, when the most common type of cancer changed from stomach cancer to lung cancer. Unfortunately, Japanese physicians were ineffective in helping smokers quit, because an estimated 27% of male physicians and 7% of women physicians smoked. Nicotine gum and patches for nicotine replacement to aid quitting were not approved until about a decade later than in the United States.[600] Vietnam has the highest percentage of male smokers in the world, 73%–higher even than Indonesia, where 53% of men smoke. Vietnam is a Communist country of 72 million people who were living in extreme poverty, on an annual income of $200 per person. As in China, smokers spend up to 25% of their income on cigarettes.[601] Only 4% of Vietnamese women smoke, perhaps because males are in control. For the economy as a whole, the cost of the diseases that cigarettes cause poses staggering burdens.[602, 603]

Although Vietnam has banned cigarette advertising in its media, the multinational tobacco corporations are allowed to advertise at tobacco stores, to sponsor sports and cultural events, and to give away baseball caps, T-shirts, umbrellas, and other goodies in exchange for empty cigarette packs. Attractive young women are hired to hand out free samples, subliminally linking sex to smoking. While domestic tobacco companies garner most of the market share by selling cheap cigarettes, they have had to intensify their marketing practices to stay competitive.

Still, Vietnamese men also have some advantages. Youths only start to smoke at around age 19–approximately four years later than in most other parts of the world. Also, men have a mean life expectancy of only 60 years, so they die before the full impact of smoking-caused diseases can hit them. In North Vietnam, many men smoke water pipes, and drawing tobacco smoke through water may well lessen its toxicity.[601]

While health education has convinced the majority of the Vietnamese population that smoking is dangerous, this has not reduced smoking. Forceful steps are needed to outlaw the many loopholes that enable tobacco corporations to advertise cigarettes. Vietnam needs to institute high taxes on cigarettes, insist on prominent health warnings on cigarette packs, and ban sales to minors. As elsewhere in the developing world, the key is the adoption of a comprehensive national tobacco control campaign as well as international regulations as outlined by WHO.

In some rural parts of India, cancer of the mouth is the most common type of cancer, because betel nut chewing is more popular than smoking. But in the great majority of Indian states, cigarette smoking predominates.[604] Roughly 65% of Indian men either chew or smoke tobacco, and tobacco kills about 800,000 people a year. To fight this deadly problem, India implemented a Tobacco Control Act in 2004. This act outlaws smoking in public places, prohibits the advertisement of tobacco, and sets a fine of 200 Rupees (about $5) for sales to minors.[605] Well done, India.

In Africa, New York Times journalist Marc Lacey reported in 2003 that tobacco companies were very powerful. For instance in Uganda where jobs are scarce, British American Tobacco employs half a million people. Lacey concluded that the more destitute a country, the more likely that tobacco companies would run amok in marketing their deadly produce. The goal of antismoking advocates in Africa is to regulate tobacco, not to outlaw it. Despite strong opposition from tobacco companies, no-smoking signs are slowly surfacing throughout Africa.

The multi-author book *Tobacco Control in Developing Countries* edited by Jha and Chaloupka gives a detailed account of that situation as of the year 2000. The book focuses mainly on economic factors, for instance the link between smoking and poverty, the costs of smoking for society, reliance on tax revenues derived from tobacco sales, and issues due to the worldwide smuggling of cigarettes. The book also covers the topics discussed in chapter 25 of this book, such as the advertisement of tobacco and the laws on smoking, as well as questions such as whether increasing the cost of cigarettes decreases smoking.[606]

The United States is involved in ongoing international efforts to curb smoking. The Office of Smoking and Health of CDC (the Centers for Disease Control and Prevention) promotes international surveillance cooperation as part of its Global Youth Tobacco Survey, which involves about 100 different countries. The National Institutes of Health have a worldwide tobacco control research and training program, co-sponsored by WHO, which includes research to identify the best strategies for reducing the number of people who start to smoke.[607]

California's vigorous antismoking campaign (see chapter 23) proves that such programs can achieve success.[608] But these United States initiatives are mere pin pricks in the war against the escalating worldwide smoking epidemic. The current United States administration must turn its back on the lobbyists of Big Tobacco, and decisively reverse its pro-tobacco stance![609]

In 2005, the Interagency on Smoking and Health, a national collaborative venture between the American Cancer Society, the American Heart Association, and the American Lung Association, was revived again. It had existed briefly during the late 1960s, with branches in most states.[610] In that era, I was the chairman of its Massachusetts branch. Now that we have a far deeper knowledge of the many different aspects of the tobacco problem, as documented in this book, the Interagency promises to become a vital weapon in the worldwide fight against smoking.

Crafting a strong Global Tobacco Treaty has been vital,[611] because the tobacco business is indeed a global enterprise. National borders are crossed in cigarette advertising, and in smuggling cigarettes to evade taxes. The WHO article "Tobacco or health. A global status report" says that the worldwide battle against smoking must be fought much harder if it is to be won.[612]

Work on an international treaty on tobacco control began at the World Health Assembly of WHO, which authorized the start of negotiations in 1999.[613] Representatives from countries that eventually numbered 168 have met several times since then to negotiate the FCTC (Framework Convention on Tobacco Control). Its principal goals were to regulate tobacco, make manufacturers liable, control cigarette smuggling, and monitor nations to ensure that they were using effective means to control smoking.[613]

Meanwhile, Europeans were working on tobacco control. In February, 2002, 51 European countries joined to adopt the *Warsaw Declaration for a Tobacco-Free Europe*. It served as a model for the FCTC treaty, for its measures included higher taxation of cigarettes; bans on tobacco advertising, sponsorship, and promotion; restrictions on smoking in the workplace and in public spaces; legislation requiring larger health warnings on cigarette packages; and improved access to therapy for quitting to smoke.[614]

In May 2003 the FCTC treaty was signed by 168 participating countries, including the United States. By November 2004, the forty individual nations needed to ratify the treaty had signed it, and made its provisions binding as of March 2005. But the other 128 countries which signed the treaty in 2003 had not yet ratified it, leaving them free to ignore its provisions.[615]

United States participation in the FCTC treaty began at its first meeting in 1999 while Donna Shalala was president Clinton's Secretary of Health and Human Services: the United States took the lead in creating an effective treaty that would reduce global tobacco use. However at the second session, in May 2001, the Bush administration's newly appointed United States delegation supported the deletion of 10 of the 11 items that Philip Morris wanted to expunge, even though this clashed with the general consensus. At the third session in November 2001, after having experienced strong criticism for their stance, the new United States negotiators retreated from several of their previous positions. But on many key issues, they continued to oppose vital public health measures.[613]

In his book, *Ashes to Ashes*, Richard Kluger has amply documented that Big Tobacco digs "into its deep pockets to resist
the social tide through the purchase and manipulation of the
political process." For instance as of 2004, the tobacco industry
had paid the American Medical Association $14 million over
14 years.[616] In this instance, the industry had tried to impose its
will on the Administration's policy by contributing $7.0 mil-
lion to the Republican campaign of 2000, and $1.4 million to
the Democratic campaign. At any rate, in May 2001 the United
States delegation's position was expressed in language that must
have pleased the tobacco industry. Shakespeare might well have
described it as "full of sound and fury, signifying nothing."

Until the last moment before the final vote on the FCTC
treaty in May 2003, it seemed that those well-placed millions
would leave the treaty with holes large enough to allow through
thousands of trucks loaded with cigarettes and logo-marked
gifts for kids in developing countries. Then Tommy Thompson,
Secretary of HHS, finding that only one country–the Dominican
Republic–supported the United States stance against the
treaty,[617] announced a complete turn-around: the United States
would support the treaty as written, without requesting changes.
Perhaps the administration was tired of the bad publicity that
followed each of its previous anti-environmental votes on global
issues. Still, this vote seemed to be merely a momentary bow to
expediency and public opinion, rather than to signal a reversal
of policy. But as of October 2006, President Bush had not yet
asked the Senate to ratify the treaty,[618] nor did he indicate that he
would do so. This deprived the United States from voting on such
important treaty issues such as tobacco smuggling. Even without
U.S. leadership, as of October 2006, 168 nations had signed the
FCTC treaty, and 140 had ratified it. But the treaty already had
been in effect since 40 countries ratified it in February 2005.[619]
At that time, the nations which had ratified it met in Switzerland
with representatives of Western nations experienced in fighting

against Big Tobacco, and counseled developing nations on how to put in place effective measures to safeguard their people.

The provisions of this treaty are as follows: ratifying nations must eliminate all tobacco advertising and sponsorship–except for nations such as the United States, where the constitution would not permit a complete ban; warning labels must occupy at least 30% of the front and back of every pack of cigarettes; non-smokers must be protected from tobacco smoke in indoor work areas; the content of tobacco products must be strictly regulated; tobacco taxes should be increased; nations should work together, to fight tobacco smuggling, and to promote tobacco prevention, cessation and research programs.[620, 621]

The strongest pressure for adopting WHO's global anti-tobacco FCTC treaty came from developing countries, for it is there that tobacco clouds the future most severely.[622] While developed nations have ample experience with the methods used by the tobacco industry to sell their wares, developing nations are still very vulnerable to the tactics of Big Tobacco. Only water-tight, legally binding global regulations against tobacco companies provided by a strong FCTC treaty can protect them.[623]

Perhaps in response to intensive campaigning by the media, the current administration asks Congress annually for many billions to control the AIDS epidemic, and roughly 10% of this money is allocated to international programs to fight AIDS.[624] Is the goodwill stemming from this noble effort worth squandering for the few millions of dollars that the tobacco industry channels to politicians? The death toll from the epidemic caused by smoking greatly exceeds the death toll from AIDS. But because a powerful industry opposes the fight against smoking, it will require a major concerted effort to ensure that knowledge about the consequences of smoking, not payoffs from the industry, will guide United States policy. Those who should coordinate such an effort are the three major American societies – Cancer, Heart and Lung – working together and with the National Institutes of Health, to mobilize a groundswell of popular support for a fully integrated attack on smoking. But the fight against smoking should not be long-term but permanent, for a pack of cigarettes is the cheapest drug one can buy for a temporary kick. For this reason, smoking is here to stay, so the fight against smoking can never be won, and to save lives must ever be fought vigorously.

PART V

OTHER AIRBORNE HAZARDS

Clean air and sunshine and plenty of grace
slam the door in the doctor's face

Part V deals with airborne hazards that cause lung cancer and are especially dangerous for smokers, because several, namely asbestos, radon and certain other radioactive substances, have been shown to be synergistic with smoking in causing lung cancer.[110] Synergism implies that the joint action of two substances produces a significantly greater effect than would be expected if their effects were merely additive. But while other airborne substances that cause lung cancer have not been investigated as thoroughly in smokers and nonsmokers, the available evidence indicates that they are more dangerous for smokers, whether or not they are synergistic with smoking.

The formal proof that two substances are synergistic requires a knowledge of their dose-response curves.[625] For if the dose-response curve of a carcinogen curves upward, then if dose A produced X numbers of cancer cases, then dose 2A would produce *more* than 2X numbers of cases. In that case, if the dose B of another carcinogen that exactly mimics the action of carcinogen A were added to its dose A, then the number of cancer cases produced would be the same as that of 2A, or *more* than

2X. Hence, the excess number of cases above 2X would be the result of an upward curving dose-response curve, and not because of synergism.

But even if the second carcinogen is not synergistic with the carcinogens in tobacco smoke, those carcinogens that smokers have inhaled have already placed them up on the dose-response curve. When they now inspire yet another type of lung carcinogen, this carcinogen will produce a larger number of cancers than in nonsmokers. Because some of the common respiratory carcinogens discussed in the next three chapters have been proven to be synergistic with tobacco smoke[110] they are much more dangerous for smokers, since they have already inhaled one set of carcinogens.

THIRTY FOUR

AIR POLLUTION

My involvement with smoke abatement dates back to 1948, when I wrote "Pittsburgh Fights Smoke" for the British journal *Smokeless Air,* while in graduate school at Carnegie-Mellon University. The Smoky City, as Pittsburgh then was aptly named, had just passed a smoke abatement ordinance which increased the amount of sunshine it received during the next winter by 39%. I said that air pollution is a weed grown on industrial soil, and because a single weeding still leaves the roots in the earth, it must be constantly weeded, and never given a chance to regrow. The long-term impact of Pittsburgh's smoke abatement ordinance is documented in the 2003 book edited by Joel Tarr, "Devastation and Renewal. An Environmental History of Pittsburgh and its Region." Further improvements have been achieved in Pittsburgh by burning natural gas and using diesel-electric locomotives.

In the Briton of 1960, before the time when the heavy air pollution in its cities was fought vigorously and brought under control, the incidence of lung cancer in nonsmokers was twice as high in urban as in rural areas.[626] But in the United States of 1979, nonsmokers who lived in urban rather than rural areas had only a slightly higher percentage of deaths from lung cancer. However for smokers, this differential was much higher.[627]

Based on evidence of respiratory illnesses and early deaths, EPA (the Environmental Pollution Agency) established new air quality standards in 1997 under the federal Clean Air Act. It based these standards on fine particles (PM2.5–particles that measure less than 2.5 microns [millionth of a meter] in diameter). For only such tiny particles–less than one-thirtieth the thickness of a human hair–can penetrate into the minute airways of the lung that lead to the air-sacks, which are vital for lung function. The act specified that averaged over a year, the concentration of PM2.5 particles should not exceed 15 micrograms per cubic meter, nor 65 micrograms per cubic meter on any one day.

Motivated by public awareness of the dangers of air pollution and by the EPA limits, the density of fine airborne particles as measured in 51 major U.S. metropolitan centers decreased by roughly one-third between 1980 and 2000, and the reduction was highest in the cities with the most air pollution. By year 2000, fine particles averaged approximately 13 micrograms per cubic meter of air in United States cities, with a range from 6 to 19 micrograms. After challenges by industry groups and three states, the Supreme Court upheld the EPA standards in 2001.[628]

In 2002, the American Cancer Society published the results of a carefully controlled long-term study of the effects of air pollution on half a million people. It concluded that for each increase of 10 micrograms of fine particles per cubic meter of air, as measured in representative samples, deaths from lung cancer increased by 8%, and deaths from cardiopulmonary diseases increased by 6%. On the average, living in an urban environment in the United States increased the risk of death from lung cancer and from cardiopulmonary diseases by roughly 11% and 8% respectively.[629] These risks are similar to those for nonsmokers who live with one or more smokers for many years, and thus are long exposed to secondhand cigarette smoke (see next chapter).

In December 2003, a federal appeals court denied the administration's proposal to permit thousands of aging power plants to upgrade their plants without installing modern pollution controls.[630] This weakening of the Clean Air Act would have substantially increased air pollution and with it, its contribution to the causation of cancer and cardiopulmonary diseases. Further, the main pollutant emitted by power plants is soot, and according to NASA scientists, soot is responsible for causing as much as one quarter of all observed global warming.[631]

As of February, 2004, the American Lung Association called for strengthening EPA's Clean Air Act of 1997, so as to prevent an estimated 15,000 premature deaths each year. The proposal was to tighten all the EPA standards in a way that would protect those most sensitive to air pollution – who include infants and children, people with asthma, the elderly, and people with heart disease, lung disease, and diabetes. Finally, it is very disconcerting to hear from Bruce Barcott, writing in the New York Times Magazine of April 4, 2004, that the current administration has "quietly–and radically–transformed the nation's clean-air policy" to the great detriment of this policy.

The two types of lung cancer from which heavy smokers are most likely to die are *squamous cell* and *small cell (oat cell)* carcinoma of the lung. It is worrying that a third type of lung cancer, *adenocarcinoma*, which is far less common in heavy smokers, has been rising from about 12% in 1965 to about three times this percentage thirty years later. But it is possible that this increase has been due largely to improvements pathologists have made in classifying lung cancers, rather than to increased exposure to environmental carcinogens other than tobacco smoke.[632]

THIRTY FIVE

———

ASBESTOS, SILICA, DUSTS, AND VOLATILE CHEMICALS

Asbestos was mentioned by a student of Aristotle around 300 BCE as a substance that when doused with oil and set on fire, burned without being harmed. Its name "*asbestinon*" (unquenchable) was mentioned around 50 CE in Pliny's book, *Natural History*. Its fire-resisting properties eventually led to its widespread use.[633]

We have long known that the inhalation of asbestos fibers is the main cause of mesothelioma, an otherwise rare cancer that originates in the lining cells of the pleura. This is the membrane that envelops the lung and lines the cavity in which the lung lies; it also lines the abdominal cavity, and covers many of its contents. About 80% of mesotheliomas arise in people exposed to asbestos in the workplace, and occasionally in their family members = due to asbestos fibers that still cling to the clothes of workers when they return home—and in people who live near asbestos mines. To a lesser extent, asbestos also causes other types of lung cancer, cancers of the gastrointestinal tract and larynx, asbestosis (a type of lung congestion), and benign lung disorders. When asbestos is the cause of mesothelioma, both normal lung and mesothelioma tissue can contain 100 times as many asbestos fibers as unexposed lung tissue.[634]

Asbestos fibers are composed of long chains of silicon and oxygen atoms. They are fireproof, stronger than steel, and quite

———

325

resilient. As a result, asbestos was used for a wide variety of purposes: fire insulation, brake linings, spray on coatings to protect steel structures against buckling during fires, and for thousands of other uses. By 1973, the annual production of asbestos in the United States stood close to one million tons.[633]

But by the mid-1960s, it had become known that the extremely fine size of asbestos fibers made them dangerous to inhale. Soon, it was found asbestos fibers can cause cancer. By 1979, when Irving Selikoff and the ACS' Cuyler Hammond chaired a conference on asbestos at the New York Academy of Sciences, it was known that its carcinogenicity depends on its particular type and size when suspended in air. If the diameter of particles is more than 3 micra (millionths of a meter) in size, about half do not penetrate into the lung, but instead are swallowed. As the diameter of the particles increases above 3 micra, their penetration deep into the lung diminishes rapidly.[635]

Of the two main types of asbestos, amphiboles and chrysotile asbestos, the former is more dangerous, because the fibers are straighter and thus can penetrate deeper into the lung. Chrysotile fibers are less dangerous, because they tend to occur in bundles, and are also more soluble. However, processing can vastly increase their danger, because it breaks up the bundles of fibers into shorter and thinner fibers that are readily inhaled deep into the lung. This explains why asbestos for manufacturing textiles or insulation is tenfold to fiftyfold more dangerous than asbestos that is mined or milled. The risk of lung cancer in asbestos workers is directly proportional to their cumulative exposure to asbestos fibers: twice the exposure, twice the risk.[110]

Once the danger that asbestos poses became understood, the EPA banned its use. Although that ban was lifted in 1991, the use of asbestos is now restricted to a few specialty applications, such as protection of the steel casing of space rockets. A vast program of removing or at least encasing all asbestos in public and private buildings and schools has been very nearly completed.

There is now a consensus that asbestos acts in synergism with tobacco smoke to cause lung cancer. An example will illustrate what a threat synergism poses. Suppose a nonsmoker who is a long-term asbestos worker had fivefold the risk of lung cancer compared to a nonsmoker in the general population. Suppose also that the average long-term smoker who is not an asbestos worker had a twentyfold higher risk of lung cancer than a nonsmoker. Since the dose-response curves for lung cancer that results from asbestos working and from smoking are linear, then if an asbestos worker (with a fivefold risk) was also a smoker (with a twentyfold risk), then if these two risks were merely *additive*, an asbestos worker who smoked would have a twenty-fivefold risk of lung cancer. But in reality, the risk is not twenty-fivefold but 5 x 20 or hundredfold higher, compared to someone who was neither an asbestos worker nor a smoker! Thus, synergism can have a very potent deleterious effect.[625]

The finding of synergism between smoking and asbestos was used by asbestos workers in 2000 to sue tobacco companies, which had long been aware of the special risk that smoking poses for asbestos workers, but had failed to warn them against smoking. In December, 2002, Halliburton company, an industrial giant, agreed to pay about $4 billion to settle a class action suit by hundreds of thousands of people exposed to asbestos while working at plants that produced asbestos, or at other places such as steel mills, where asbestos was used.[636] In the same month, Hartford Financial Services, a large insurance company, paid $1.5 billion to settle asbestos claims.[637] As a result of such lawsuits, more than 70 companies went out of business. In July, 2003, the Senate Judiciary Committee approved a bill that would end all asbestos lawsuits by creating an industry-financed trust fund to compensate people with asbestos-related illnesses.[638] But on April 22, 2004 the New York Times reported scant hope that legislators could reach agreement on the problem of what constitutes fair compensation for the 200,000 or more asbestos lawsuits pending in state and federal courts. According to the New York Times of May 18, 2004, some estimates claim that companies had already paid $70 billion in asbestos claims, with insurance companies paying about 40% of this amount.

Silica has only tangentially been blamed for causing cancer. Its real hazard is the causation of silicosis, a chronic lung disease characterized by scarring of the lung and shortness of breath, which can exacerbate with time and eventually lead to death. It is caused by the inhalation of fine airborne crystalline silica or quartz dust. For at least 70 years, silicosis has been recognized as a hazard for coal miners, since they must drill through rock to reach coal seams, and inhale the fine rock dust that their drills aerosolize (suspend in the air).

But it is only within the last few years that lawsuits have escalated against companies that exposed workers to silica or quartz. As of 2003, one large insurer faced over 30,000 silica-related claims. Most of these claims were for the causation of silicosis, not of cancer.[639]

Other respiratory carcinogens. A 1999 report by Chatzis and coworkers from Greece shows that the occupational inhalation of other substances can add to the risk of lung cancer produced by smoking. These "cocarcinogens" (additive carcinogens) include wood dusts (inhaled in carpentry and construction work), benzidine (from textile and dye industries), shale and mineral oils (from petroleum and oil industries), and coal tar and soot (from coke ovens and metal casting furnaces). After pooling data for all cases of occupational exposures due to these carcinogens (which included asbestos) and removing the effects of smoking by compensating for it, it was found that occupational exposure to the above substances trebled the risk of lung cancer.[640]

Finally, there is a consensus that benzene inhalation causes leukemia. But there is controversy on the risk posed by benzene at low levels of exposure (Hayes *et al.*, J. Toxicology and Environmental Health, 2000).

THIRTY SIX

RADON, NUCLEAR REACTORS, DIRTY BOMBS, AND ATOM BOMBS

Radon is an invisible and odorless radioactive gas that emanates naturally from the earth and from rocks. It is of concern, because it can seep into a house through cracks in the foundation and joints. We now believe that it is the second leading cause of lung cancer, about 9% of lung cancer deaths – vastly fewer than smoking, but still not negligible.[641]

Radon derives from the element uranium-238, which is very widely distributed in the earth's crust and rocks. Uranium-238 is unstable and decays (decomposes) very slowly in a stepwise fashion into 13 different elements, one of which is radon. Radon emits alpha rays that can mutate cells and cause cancer, but radon is also unstable and decays into other radioactive elements. These include the radioisotope (an element with an unstable nucleus that emits radiation as it decays to another nuclear state) polonium-218, which is not a gas but a solid that also produces alpha rays, and proves to be the main cause of injury to the lung.[642] For polonium-218–and other solid radioisotopes produced in the decay chain that starts with uranium-238 and ends with inert lead–sticks to dust particles that are inhaled and are deposited in the bronchial tree, where it causes damage.[643]

Radon became of concern in the 1950s, when the high incidence of lung cancer in uranium miners was traced to the high levels of radon in uranium mines, which supplied this ore for nuclear reactors and atomic bombs. Several studies have shown that the incidence of lung cancer in uranium miners rises in direct proportion to the radon concentration in their mines, and the time-period for which the miners were exposed to it. This even holds true for miners with cumulative radon exposures only three to six times higher than the lifetime exposure to radon in an average house.[110] Further, four sets of experts have reviewed the data on radon inhalation: ICRP (International Commission on Radiological Protection); the National Academy of Sciences committees BEIR IV, and BEIR VI; and the Office of Radiation Programs of the U.S. EPA (Environmental Protection Agency). The reports from all these sources concluded that the percentage of exposed people who developed lung cancer was directly proportional to the concentration of radon that they had inhaled, multiplied by the time period for which inhalation had occurred.

As for the magnitude of the risk from radon, the above reports varied in their estimates of how many deaths from lung cancer were caused by radon in the U.S. The EPA estimate of 20,000 deaths per year was criticized for being too high. The estimate of 13,000 deaths per year made by the NRC was then reevaluated by a panel headed by Jonathan Samet (the chairperson of BEIR VI), and the NRC estimate was found to be three times too high for adults and five times too high for children.[644] But more recent studies have reinforced the previous data on the danger posed by radon as being higher than the latter estimate.[641]

The Indoor Radon Act of 1988 was sparked by the data on cancer causation by radon. This act set a national, long-term goal of achieving indoor radon levels similar to outdoor levels, and it allowed EPA to set the level of tolerable radon concentration in a building at 150 Becquerel (Bq, a unit of radioactivity per cubic meter). This level has not been changed since 1991. At that time, testing a house for radon cost between \$10 and \$30, and the cost of reducing elevated radon levels below 150 Bq/m^3 ranged from \$500 to \$1500 for most houses. EPA has estimated that there may be several million homes with radon levels above 150 Bq/m^3, and more than 100,000 homes with levels above 750 Bq/m^3.[645]

The extrapolation of data obtained for miners exposed to high dose levels of radon to the relatively low levels that people experience while living for many decades in their homes has been criticized as yielding too high a risk estimate. But this criticism was refuted by Richard Guimond's article in *Science*, which reported that the risk from long-term exposures to low radon levels was greater than the risk from short-term exposures to high radon levels.[645] Further, Pershagen and coworkers found that the low levels of radon inhalation that are incurred in homes, whether alone or in synergism with smoking, increased the risk of lung cancer,[646] and this was confirmed by Darby and coworkers in 1998.

The risk of lung cancer from radon exposure in English homes was consistent with the risks mentioned above, according to a 1998 report in 1998 by famed British epidemiologist Richard Doll and his team. They concluded that radon in homes causes about one in twenty lung cancers in the United Kingdom, most of which occur in combination with smoking. The risk of lung cancer from radon was "about the size that has been postulated on the basis of studies of miners exposed to radon."[647] More work is needed to estimate the risk of lung cancer from radon to *nonsmokers*.[648] Since the causation of lung cancer from inhaling radon is in synergism with smoking, smokers should test the concentration of radon in their houses if they are directly built on rocks.

UNDERSTANDING ABBREVIATIONS FOR RADIATION UNITS			
pico-	(p)	one quadrillionth	(10^{-12})
nano-	(n)	one trillionth	(10^{-9})
micro-	(μ)	one millionth	(10^{-6})

milli-	(m)	one thousandth	(10^{-3})
centi-	(c)	one hundredth	(10^{-2})
kilo-	(k)	one thousand times	1,000
mega-	(M)	one million times	1,000,000
giga-	(G)	one trillion times	1,000,000,000

WHAT RADIATION UNITS MEASURE[649]

WHAT IS MEASURED OLDER UNIT NEWER UNIT INTERRELATIONSHIP

Radiation emanating from a radioactive source: curie (Ci) Becquerel (Bq) 1 Ci=37billion Bq (The Chernobyl meltdown released 81 MCi radioactive cesium)

Radiation absorbed rad (dose of radiation absorbed by body) *by body tissues* gray (Gy) 1 rad=1/100 Gy Radiation from nature [cosmic rays, rocks] is 0.12 rad per year

Personal risk from radiation: rem (radiation absorbed by body) 1 rem = 1/100 Sievert (Sv)

Relationship between radiation absorbed by the body and risk is: rad x Q = rem, and gray x Q = Sievert. Q is a Quality Factor that depends on the radiation's ability to transfer energy to the body. The Q value for natural radiation is 2.5.

If a house is built directly on shattered rock without an intervening air space, homeowners should test their homes for radon. A simple and inexpensive do-it-yourself test kit is sold at most hardware stores. If the radon level is above 150 Bq/m³, appropriate action should be taken to reduce it below this level. At or near this level of radon, this is easily done by installing an exhaust fan in the basement. At higher radon levels, cracks in the foundation and joints should be sealed.

Radon is also absorbed by and released from water. So in 1999, EPA asked states to limit the concentration of radon in water to

11 Becquerel per liter. But for homes where ventilation had been installed to reduce the concentration of radon, FDA suggested that a radon level of 150 Becquerel per liter of water was tolerable.

In 2003, Norway decided to protect its citizens by measuring radon levels in all houses and ground floor apartments over the next decade. If it was over 200 Bq/m^3 it was to be reduced below this level by installing ventilation and repairing cracks in the foundation. Norwegian scientists estimated that saving one life by this policy would cost roughly $1 million.[650] Norwegians are to be congratulated for setting the example of valuing life highly enough, to be willing to pay a steep price for saving it. More information is available on www.epa.gov/radon, and a 15-page "Citizen's Guide to Radon" is available by calling 800-SOS-Radon.

Nuclear reactors are regulated by the NRC. As of 2005, there were 104 plants licensed to produce nuclear power in the United States. There were 69 plants that operated Pressurized Water Reactors, and 35 Boiling Water Reactors. In addition, there were 52 research and test reactors under the guidance of NRC.

Partial meltdown of the Three Mile Island nuclear reactor at Middletown, Pennsylvania in March 1979 galvanized the public. Although it led to no deaths or proven injuries to plant workers or members of nearby communities, it resulted in halting construction of new nuclear power plants. On the positive side, it led to sweeping changes in emergency response planning and reactor operator training, and caused NRC to tighten its oversight over nuclear power plants.[651]

Even the partial meltdown of a nuclear reactor releases many radioactive elements into the atmosphere, of which iodine-131 is by far of most immediate concern in a large area downwind of the reactor. During the initial catastrophe, it is in this area that iodine-131 will be inhaled by people located there. Unless there are unusual weather conditions, exposure will diminish with distance from the reactor. Iodine-131 localizes in the thyroid, where it can cause dysfunction and/or cancer. The effects of iodine-131 inhalation are vastly reduced by swallowing non-radioactive iodine tablets, which are available over the counter, and contain many times the quantities of iodine as that in the radioactive iodine which are likely to have been inhaled. Since the thyroid gland absorbs radioactive and non-radioactive iodine with equal avidity, a large intake of non-radioactive iodine ensures that only a tiny fraction of radioactive iodine is taken up by the thyroid.

The major intake into the body of iodine-131, and of many other radioactive materials, occurs through the food chain. The radio-active material falls out onto grass, is eaten by cows, and contaminates their milk. The risk that iodine-131 poses for thyroid cancer is highest for a newborn child and falls off progressively with age. The risk for a newborn child is one hundred times as large as for a 50-year old person. As a result of the partial meltdown of the reactor at Three Mile Island, NRC estimated that the dose averaged over 2 million people in the area was only 1 millirem, compared to the natural radioactive background dose of 125 millirem per year for that area![651]

Since the half-life of iodine-131–the time in which it loses 50% of its radioactivity–is only 8 days, it is a significant hazard only for about three months after a meltdown, and taking iodine tablets during this period provides highly effective protection. While a meltdown releases far smaller amounts of other radioactive atoms than iodine-131, some decay much more slowly. They are also of concern, because they can be absorbed in the same way as iodine-131, and might increase the likelihood of cancer of organs other than the thyroid.

The future of nuclear power was projected in detail in the splendid September 2006 issue of the Scientific American. Nuclear power plants are only one of the many technologies needed to keep the emission of carbon dioxide from spiraling out of control and hastening global warming. To displace coal, Socolow and Pacala suggested that the 2006 output of nuclear power be tripled.[652] Further, Deutch and Moniz argued that nuclear power could stave off more than a billion tons of carbon emissions annually.[653]

Critical for expanding construction of nuclear power plants are first – location; second – design to minimize the possibility of a meltdown; third – processing fuel to use it economically, so as to guard against its use for atom bomb production, and to facilitate its disposal; fourth – long-term storage of spent fuel; fifth – security: guarding nuclear power plants against attack by terrorists; and sixth – economics.

First, as regard location, after previous meltdown incidents a nuclear power plant should be built far removed from population centers. Even though NRC has greatly improved its oversight of nuclear power plants, the public deserves plans for their total safety–for promises can fail for a great variety of causes.

Second, as regards reactor design, the dominant design is the light-water reactor that uses ordinary water rather than heavy water which contains the hydrogen isotope deuterium. After a cessation of reactor building in the U.S. since the meltdown incidents, generation III+ light-water reactors are now planned. These are reactors that incorporate better fuel technology, with advanced features beyond those in generation III reactors, which already possess "passive safety" – the ability to shut down automatically in case of an accident. Globally since the year 2000, 20,000 megawatts of nuclear capacity have come online. At this point in time, the generation III+ design is most likely to be built in the U.S. for at least a decade or two.[653]

Generation IV reactors are still in the experimental stage. They include pebble-bed nuclear power reactors, a new design claimed to be meltdown-proof (MIT Technology Review, March, 2004). If this claim proves to be true, then pebble bed reactors would compete with generation III+ light-water reactors. They have the advantage that instead of building a massive 1,000 megawatt plant, modules each producing only 100 megawatts could be built, later supplemented by additional modules as required.[653]

Third, processing of nuclear fuel to use it economically, to guard against its use for atom bomb production, and to dispose of spent fuel still remain major problems. In an "open fuel cycle," also called a "once-through" cycle, the uranium fuel is burned once in a reactor and then stored. In contrast, France currently uses a "closed fuel cycle," in which plutonium is separated from spent fuel and then burned in a reactor. It is even possible to burn virtually all very long-lived radioactive elements in a "fast reactor," of which there are several types.[654] But all reprocessing is expensive and highly dangerous, and plutonium can be diverted to make nuclear weapons. For these reasons, U.S. experts prefer the once-through cycle.[653]

Fourth, the long-term storage of spent fuel has proved to be a major problem, since long-lived radioisotopes such as plutonium remain radioactive for millennia (thousands of years). Most U.S. nuclear power plants store their spent fuel rods temporarily in water tanks on their plant site – a highly unsatisfactory situation. As of 2009, the Department of Energy (DOE) had created a large facility where the radioactive spent fuel is handled robotically. First it is made into glass cylinders by mixing it with special silica sand and heating it to a high temperature. Then the vitrified cylinders are encased in stainless steel cylinders and closed by a plug that is welded in place. The cylinders are then transported to a temporary storage facility.

For the next few decades, these highly radioactive cylinders could be stored in a few high-security lots in remote areas.[655]

DEO has spent years preparing a permanent site for nuclear waste in a deep salt depository within Yucca Mountain in Nevada. But it is feared that in thousands of years even the stainless steel canisters encasing the vitrified nuclear waste might leak, contaminating underground water with radioactivity and carrying it into the local water supply.[656] Further, the site has more water than was anticipated, so it remains uncertain whether NRC will license it. Even if it licensed, it may not be ready to accept waste before 2015. In contrast, Finland is moving forward with its plans to complete a storage facility 500 meters underground by 2020, with spent fuel encased in iron canisters sealed within a copper shell intended to resist corrosion.[657]

DOE is currently funding research on two different methods for disintegrating the long-lived atoms of radioactive waste. The goal is to recycle much of the 2,000 tons of highly radioactive spent fuel that U.S. atomic power plants produce each year, and to burn the recycled fuel again in atomic power plants.[658] One method entails firing protons produced in a synchrotron into the heart of a nuclear reactor,[659] but it still seems far from being able to handle large amounts of high-level nuclear waste.

Fifth, there is the problem of guarding nuclear power plants against attacks by terrorists. The terrorists might try to cause a meltdown, or steal fuel rods. A meltdown would be catastrophic, and even a single spent fuel rod could be subdivided into many parts, to provide the radioactive material needed to make several "dirty bombs." In this age of terrorism, the adequate guarding of nuclear power plants is therefore essential. But in addition, modern society uses a very large number of radioactive sources which could be used to make a dirty bomb (see below).

Sixth, money is the root of all evil, and thus economics plays a large role in whether or not more nuclear power plants will be built in the U.S. In 2003, a study at MIT estimated the cost of electricity produced by a new light-water reactor at 6.7 cents per kilowatt-hour, compared to 5.8 cents for a new gas-powered plant and 4.2 cents for a new coal plant. But to overcome the hurdle of restarting nuclear power plant manufacture after a long Sabbath, the Energy Policy Act of 2005 included a powerful incentive: a tax credit of 1.8 cents per kilowatt-hour for the first 6,000 megawatts of new plants that go into operation.[653]

"Dirty bombs" and atom bombs are totally different weapons. A dirty bomb (also called a Radiological Dispersal Device or RDD) is a primitive weapon that incorporates one or more radioactive materials and a high explosive such as dynamite. It is vastly easier to assemble than an atomic bomb, which is described in the next section. In contrast to an atomic bomb, the explosive force of a dirty bomb is merely that of its conventional explosive. Unlike an atomic bomb, a dirty bomb does not produce a hurricane-force blast of air, a heat wave, an intense blast of radiation, or contamination of the stratosphere. Also, the immediate lethal effects of a dirty bomb depend entirely on its conventional explosive, not on its content of radioactive material.

The degree to which the radioactive content of a dirty bomb contaminates its surroundings depends on three factors: first, on the quantity and type of radioactive material and of conventional high explosive that it contains; second, on the wind and weather conditions; and third, on its location when detonated.[660] All of these variables are critical, but most important is the amount and type of the radioactive material dispersed by the bomb, its half-life, its biological effects when inhaled or ingested, and how long it is allowed to remain on streets and buildings and thereby cause whole body irradiation to the people exposed to it, before decontamination is completed. Unlike an atomic bomb, a dirty bomb is very unlikely to release radioactive iodine.[651]

Regarding the disruption caused by a dirty bomb, the NRC says that it could contaminate up to several city blocks.[660] A spokesperson for the Federation of American Scientists—which tends to be alarmist – testified on this question before the Senate in March, 2002. He said that tens of city blocks could be contaminated at a level that would require evacuation;[661] but this is merely a guesstimate.

The most serious effect of the explosion of a dirty bomb would be to create panic. The fear and disruption of civic life generated will be far greater than justified by the degree of exposure to radiation. Unfortunately, rationality does not always remove fear. Since pictures of the victims of the two atomic bomb explosions in Japan were widely displayed in the printed and electronic media, people throughout the world are apt to link radiation exposure with terrible consequences. Further, because our senses cannot detect radiation, it is commonly viewed as sinister. Nor is it unreasonable to believe that even small amounts of radiation may not be entirely safe. Therefore, after a dirty bomb is exploded, the public's perception of its danger may be much higher than its assessment by radiation experts, who may find it difficult to convince the public that they are right.[662]

The public will be more likely to believe official bulletins on the dangers to which they have been exposed by the explosion of a dirty bomb, if people have already been educated regarding what levels of radiation exposure are harmless, and what levels are dangerous. To accomplish this, a national campaign is needed to educate the public on the sources of radiation to which they are already exposed, namely natural background radiation, and radiation given for medical purposes. In addition, the public needs to know what levels of radiation exposure experienced over a stated period of time have been certified by appropriate government agencies as permissible for the public at large. The public also needs to know that higher exposure levels are permitted for radiation workers—people whose work is with radiation, such as nuclear power plant personnel. People should know that if they are contaminated by the explosion of a dirty bomb, they can be safeguarded by prompt decontamination. They should have clear directions on what to do if a dirty bomb is exploded: where to go to be decontaminated, and to be taught how they can do it themselves. While government agencies have published excellent reports that cover practically all aspects of dirty bombs, an information campaign for the general public has yet to be implemented.

Regarding terrorist activity in the United States, in 2002 Jose Padilla was arrested in the United States for involvement with al-Qa'ida in planning a dirty bomb attack. In 2003, the British Broadcasting Corporation (BBC) reported that British agents who had infiltrated al-Qa'ida training camps in Afghanistan discovered radioactive materials, and training manuals that described how best to use dirty bombs.[663] In January 2005, the FBI launched a massive manhunt for six illegal immigrants suspected of planning to explode a dirty bomb.[664]

In October 2005, President Bush declared that ten terrorist attacks of various types had been foiled within the United States.[665] But *in the entire world*, there were 175 cases of incidents involving the smuggling or attempted procurement of radioactive material during the decade preceding 2002. In addition, radioactive material disappeared after the chaotic fragmentation of the Soviet Union. Further, IAEA (the International Atomic Energy Agency) has reported that the "materials needed to build a 'dirty bomb' can be found in almost any country in the world, and more than 100 countries may have inadequate control and monitoring programs necessary to prevent or even detect the theft of these materials."[666] In 2002, a member of Harvard University's Belfer Center for Science and International Affairs was quoted in *Science* magazine as saying that there are literally millions of radiological sources in the world that could be used in a dirty bomb.[667]

In the United States, businesses and research facilities have lost track of 1,500 pieces of equipment with radioactive parts. The NRC calls these and other sources outside official control "orphaned" radioactive sources. But it is even of more concern that radioactive materials could be stolen from many facilities: hospitals that use radioactive sources such as cobalt-60 for therapy of cancer patients, food irradiation plants that use powerful radioactive sources, academic and industrial research laboratories that use radioactive materials, nuclear power plants, high-level radioactive waste that is presently stored within the grounds of 70 U.S. nuclear power plants,[668] as well as at commercial and army sites, and in trucks that transport radioactive sources.[669] Nevertheless, NRC (the Nuclear Regulatory Commission) claimed in 2004, that only a single high-risk radioactive source had been stolen and not recovered in the United States.[660]

The best responses to the threat of dirty bombs include the detection, infiltration and dismantling of terrorist cells both in the United States and worldwide. Also, potential terrorists should be denied access to the United States. These measures are currently being pursued by the Homeland Security Secretariat, and by foreign governments endangered by terrorist organizations.

Regarding the importation of radioactive materials or bombs, illicit nuclear materials that could be used to make dirty bombs must be found and confiscated. To this end, Homeland Security has been installing radiation monitoring equipment at seaports, airfields and borders both in the United States and overseas. The U.S. is also monitoring the buildings of suspected organizations and the homes of individual suspects. Homeland Security said that since the 9/11 attack in 2001, by the end of 2006 the U.S. had invested $9 billion in port security. As of October 2000, almost 200 radiation monitors had been installed at ports, and about 70% of incoming cargo was being screened. But only about 5% of all shipping containers were being inspected visually before leaving a foreign port. Members of Congress wanted to have radiation screening of all shipping containers, and improvement in the system used to decide which containers are opened and inspected with hand-held radiation monitors.[670]

The most likely place that terrorists may choose to explode a dirty bomb might be the center of a large U.S. city such as New York, Washington, Los Angeles, or Chicago. However, many other cities might be on the terrorists' list. Judging from 9/11, a terrorist group might well aim to achieve maximum disruption by setting off dirty bombs simultaneously in several U.S. cities.

As to the effectiveness of radiation monitoring, some of the radiation monitors tested by the Department of Homeland Security fail to identify certain radioactive materials. These detectors range from the size of a steam iron to the size of a small car. Hopefully, the next generation of detectors will have sufficient discrimination to identify radiation sources without the need to open shipping containers.[671] But there are serious obstacles to overcome, such as the ability to use lead to shield nuclear materials from detection.[672] Unfortunately, the materials in atom bombs – highly enriched uranium or weapons-grade plutonium – are much less radioactive than the radioactive elements or isotopes that could be used in a dirty bomb, and are therefore difficult to discover except with neutron detectors.[673]

The success of radiation detection equipment at custom stations and ports will also hinge on effective intelligence that will warn authorities that certain cargos requires careful scrutiny. But terrorists might exploit the lengthy U.S. borders and the long distances that exist between legal points of entry to smuggle radioactive contraband into the United States. Also, the nation's ports were designed to speed commerce, not to provide security, and their staff is often overwhelmed by the huge quantity of imports.[673]

Internally absorbed radioisotopes can remain in the body for extensive periods of time and thus pose long-term hazards. Thus, the personnel of monitoring teams should wear protective masks when entering contaminated areas, and trucks carrying filtering masks should drive to those areas, to give them to exposed people and protect them from inhaling radioactive particles, while they flee from contaminated areas as rapidly as possible. In contrast, external radiation is absorbed by the whole body only during the brief period during which civilians or radiation monitoring staff remain in contaminated areas before their decontamination.

In terms of preparedness, it is insufficient to be prepared at the federal level, since several cities could be hit at once. Therefore, every city in the U.S. should stock monitoring equipment for identifying the different radioactive materials that a dirty bomb could disseminate. It is equally essential to train sufficient personnel in the use of monitoring equipment, including techniques for monitoring and decontaminating people, streets and buildings. It is crucial that long before the need arises, a national consensus be established on the radiation level at which a single building or even a whole area should be evacuated after explosion of a dirty bomb. The monitoring personnel should also be trained for action should the unthinkable happen – the explosion of an atomic bomb.

But training against radiological terror weapons is not sufficient. The radiological monitoring personnel should also be trained for use of the very different detection equipment and decontamination protocol that would be needed after the explosion of bombs that contain chemical or biological toxins or infectious agents such as smallpox. Radically different protective clothing and breathing masks[674] will be required to safeguard against bioterrorism than against radiological agents.

Preparedness requires creation of a disaster command center that will coordinate the team-work between the several disparate entities involved in response to any disaster, whatever its nature – whether caused by war, terrorists, or natural causes such as floods, tidal waves, hurricanes, tornadoes, earthquakes, volcanic eruptions, or even a comet. The capabilities, entities and personnel involved would include:

1. Direct communications to local, state and national government.

2. Specialists trained in monitoring, removing and disposing of radiologic, chemical, biological and infectious agents, whatever their nature or source. Different strategies would need to be worked out, to combat pollution with different agents.

3. Specialists in crowd communication and control are needed.

4. Direct links should be in place to:

    •   the local police, fire departments and hospitals

- local power, fuel, and phone companies
- local and national printed and electronic media
- local, regional and national disaster command centers
- a network of cyberlinks staffed by volunteers

Many drills would be necessary to familiarize participants with their detection equipment, and to practice concerted, swift action by such a disparate group of people in order to respond to a disaster. Such a drill was run in San Diego in August 2006, but it involved only a few of the resources listed above. A unique feature of this exercise was the use of Microsoft's "Simple Sharing Extensions" system by several large software companies. This allowed them to share a single set of digital satellite maps, which were continually updated for event data relayed in by emergency workers throughout the San Diego area.[675]

Injury from the radiation dispersed by an explosion will be minor, if the response teams act swiftly, which will be critical for minimizing the consequences. To do so, team members need to know the highest level of radiation exposure that they can tolerate without unacceptable risks to their future health, or they will hesitate to act. Since the radiation exposure is the product of the rate at which radiation is emitted and the time for which it is absorbed, team members should adjust the time they stay in the contaminated area to ensure that it does not exceed their tolerable level of radiation exposure. They should also measure radiation levels in the buildings surrounding the blast, to decide if the people who live or work there may continue to do so, or will have to be evacuated for a period of time calculated from the intensity of the radiation, its half-life, and the effectiveness of the decontamination performed.

For response team personnel, the highest tolerable limit of radiation exposure specified by EPA in consultation with NRC is 5 rem per year. A rem stands for radiation equivalent man, and is the biologically effective radiation dose that results from absorbing a physical radiation dose of one rad. One rad is the radiation dose human beings absorb on average from natural radiation sources in a time span of approximately 8 years.

For the civilian population, the present EPA guidelines specify that evacuation is mandatory if the projected external radiation dose is greater than 5 rem per year, and evacuation should be considered if the external dose is 1–5 rem per year.[676] Whole body irradiation from external sources such as radioactive dust lying on a street or deposited on buildings will only penetrate into the body beyond the skin if the radioactivity emitted by it is sufficiently energetic. But the risks of total body irradiation are much smaller than if the same material is inhaled or ingested when risks depend on the quantity of the material absorbed internally and on the type and half-life of radiation that it emits. After these risks are assessed, people at danger should be treated by whatever appropriate means are available. To block the internal uptake of a radioactive element, a much larger quantity of the non-radioactive form of the same element should be swallowed or injected. This is how the uptake of the radioactive isotope iodine-131 is effectively blocked.

What should be done immediately after a dirty bomb attack?[677] Response team personnel should assemble rapidly at their headquarters, don protective clothing and masks, and use vans equipped with the necessary radiological measuring instruments to drive as close to the site of the explosion as their radiation instruments suggested would not overexpose them during the short time required to make their vital initial assessment of the nature of the radioactive substances disseminated, and the dose distribution at various distances from the epicenter.

Next, they would monitor people to determine who should be sent to decontamination centers, and who had been exposed highly enough to be sent to a medical facility. It would be vital to have previously selected, prepared and adequately equipped decontamination centers where a vast number of minimally exposed or unexposed "worried well" could be separated from those in need of urgent decontamination. To ease their mind, the worried well might be advised to discard their outer clothing and wash all exposed skin, while those seriously contaminated should be allowed to shower, given uncontaminated clothing, and if not experiencing acute radiation symptoms – nausea, vomiting, weakness, abdominal distress, dizziness (which are unfortunately also the symptoms of half of the victims of epidemic hysteria) – sent home with instructions to come back later for a thorough radiological and medical examination.[674]

Other means by which terrorists could contaminate civilians with radioactive materials include the targeting of atomic power plants, which U.S. Representative Edward Markey has alleged that al-Qa'ida is planning to do. Presumably, the intention would be to cause a meltdown. The nuclear industry contends that the nation's nuclear plants are adequately protected by double-fenced perimeters, concertina wire, sensors inside the fences, and thick concrete walls and reinforced steel walls inside the buildings. But critics who include lawmakers say that 37 of the 81 federal exercises run between 1991 and 2001 have turned up significant weaknesses in security. Unfortunately, nuclear facilities fought against federalizing the security guards, which would have improved and standardized their training.[678] Further, if a plane were crashed into a nuclear plant, a meltdown might occur.

The table below lists the properties of radioisotopes that might be used to make a dirty bomb. All emit radiation. Their main risk from internal or external irradiation is cancer.

RADIOACTIVE ISOTOPES OF POSSIBLE USE IN A DIRTY BOMB*			
ISOTOPE	HALF-LIFE (YEARS)	BIOLOGIC EFFECT IN BODY	EMISSIONS**
Cesium-139 (Cs-139)	30.2	Localizes in many organs	Beta particles, Gamma rays

Cobalt-60 (Co-60)	5.3	Localizes in liver, kidney, bones	Gamma rays
Plutonium-239 (Pu-239)	24,000	High risk	Alpha particles, neutrons
Strontium-90 (Sr-90)	29.1	Localizes in bones, teeth	Gamma rays
Uranium-235 (U-235)	700 Million	Most of U-235 and U-238 excreted	Alpha particles and neutrons
Uranium-238 (U-238)	4.7 billion	**Small deposition** in bones, liver	Alpha particles and neutrons

*These isotopes can cause cancer after a time that depends on their quantity, time present within the body, presence of other carcinogens, and susceptibility of the exposed person to cancer. ** While gamma rays are highly penetrating, alpha and beta particles are not, but still carcinogenic when highly energetic.

The biological effect of total body irradiation has been evaluated for several decades since the explosion of the atomic bombs at Hiroshima and Nagasaki. Those who received whole body radiation exposure from these bombs but survived have been monitored with utmost care. Their study has produced invaluable data on the excess cancer incidence in various body organs that can eventually results from exposure to whole body radiation. The increase in the risk of cancer in any given body organ from exposure to whole body irradiation for people in contaminated areas is cumulative over the time spent in those areas, and is directly proportional to the dose of radiation absorbed, and there is no a threshold below which radiation has no effect.[679]

Regarding the effect of inhaled radioactive matter or gas, the data on radon inhalation discussed under its own heading are of great value for estimating the excess cancer risk following the inhalation of radioactive aerosols produced by the explosion of a dirty bomb. But other causes of radiation carcinogenesis have also been studied, for instance the inhalation of plutonium-239 in a nuclear facility at Mayak in Russia, that caused lung cancer in workers exposed to high doses. While the data for radon inhalation in uranium miners revealed a linear relationship between radiation dose and lung cancer, at Mayak the excess risk of lung cancer at low doses of plutonium-239 were higher than expected for a linear relationship.[680] As in the case of asbestos and of radon, lung cancer incidence from inhalation of plutonium-239 was synergistic with smoking, and most of the men who developed lung cancer were smokers. This strongly suggests that it is smokers who will be at most risk of lung cancer, should they inhale a highly radioactive aerosol produced by the explosion of a dirty bomb.

The explosion of a dirty bomb will contaminate with radioactivity the ground and the exterior of buildings in the area surrounding the blast and downwind from it. The following estimate of the excess relative risk of cancer in various body organs (the increase in risk relative to a person who has not received the stated radiation dose) was made in 2000 by the United Nations Scientific Committee on the Effects of Atomic Radiation.[681]

ESTIMATED TEN-YEAR RISK OF CANCER INCIDENCE FROM WHOLE-BODY IRRADIATION FOR AN AGE OF 30 YEARS AT THE TIME OF EXPOSURE[681]		
% EXCESS RELATIVE		
RISK PER REM		SEX RATIO
CANCER TYPE	MALE	FEMALE	FEMALE/MALE
Esophagus	0.91	1.88	2.1
Stomach	0.26	0.54	2.1
Colon	0.46	0.95	2.1
Liver	0.61	1.66	2.7
Lung	0.30	0.99	3.3
Breast	0.00	1.34	-

Bladder	0.46	0.94	2.1
Other cancer	0.38	0.77	2.1
All solid cancer	0.38	0.77	2.1
Leukemia	1.24	0.94	0.8

Except in the case of leukemia, the latent period (the time interval between irradiation and the appearance of cancer) is very long, and depends on the type of radiation emitted by the radioisotope and the radiation dose absorbed cumulatively over time. If the public is to understand the degree of danger from the explosion of a dirty bomb, the dose of radiation received from it should be compared with the average dose we receive from natural sources:

(a) We are all continually exposed to ionizing radiation,[682] although we are unaware of it:

- We breathe in tiny amounts of radioactive radon.

- The ground we walk on and the buildings we live and work in are very slightly radioactive.

- Our bodies contain traces of radioactivity from food and drink.

- Cosmic rays from space fall on us throughout our entire lives.

The natural background radiation that a human being in the U.S. absorbs from all the above sources on the average adds up to a physical dose of 0.12 rad per year,[649] and a biologically effective dose of 0.15 rem per year.[683]

(b) The biologically effective radiation dose from medical sources averages approximately 0.12 rem per year in cities where there is more than one physician for every 1,000 people. However, in cities where there is less than one physician for every 10,000 people, the dose may be as low as 0.02 rem.[684] Easy access to a physician results in extensive use of diagnostic X-rays. But modern X-ray machines and CT scanners deliver reduced dosages.

(c) Cosmic rays that hit us in the thin air at 35,000 feet during a long-distance airplane flight deliver approximately 0.005 rem.[683] Since this exposure to radiation is cumulative, this dose is not negligible for airplane personnel and frequent flyers.

For terrorists to explode a dirty bomb among civilians would show an utterly despicable disregard for humane considerations. For babies and young children would be at highest risk of injury from inhaling the radioactive aerosol that a bomb would produce, and from whole body exposure to radioactive particles deposited on the ground and on buildings. As of mid-2014, even the most ruthless terrorists have never exploded a dirty bomb anywhere.

A number of publications deal with dirty bombs.[685] In addition, a search for "dirty bombs" on the internet produces over 100,000 "hits," so this subject is not irrelevant, and there is much information on this subject. In order to understand the nature of dirty bombs, it is helpful to know essential facts about nuclear bombs, which are outlined below. But it would take a long book to do justice to their catastrophic effects.

SOURCES FOR RADIOACTIVE MATERIALS:

- Unmanned Russian lighthouses that have nuclear batteries
- Batteries from decommissioned Russian submarines in storage

The explosion of a dirty bomb produces a dust-cloud that can extend several miles downwind. Inhaling or swallowing the radioactive dust particles can produce cancer after a latent period of many years. It is disturbing to know that the critical mass of an atom bomb can be as small as a softball.

The monitoring of shipping containers is done first by X-raying their contents, then with a large radiation monitor past which containers can be driven at up to 8 mph. If any problem is detected, then a hand-held radiation detector is used to locate it more closely. As of April 2007, there were 300,000 alarms, but not a single discovery of a potential dirty bomb or of atomic bomb material.

Atomic bombs have an interesting history. By the year 1942, both the Allies and the Third Reich were far enough advanced in nuclear physics to know that a fission bomb was practical, but would require at least two years to produce. Hitler felt that if the war had not been won by that time, it would be lost–so he decided against making an atom bomb. U.S. generals thought that the war would continue for at least two more years, and the risk was too great to take, that Germany – which had Nobel Laureate Heisenberg directing its nuclear effort–would be first to produce an atom bomb. So in cooperation with Britain, the U.S. launched the Manhattan Project, a massive industrial effort that was even more extensive than the U.S. auto industry of that era.

The explosion of U.S. atomic bombs at Hiroshima and Nagasaki ended the war with Japan in 1945. As of 2007, there were roughly 30,000 nuclear bombs in the world. All but 200 of these bombs were stored in Russian and U.S. arsenals. The U.S. has enough of these monstrous weapons to kill most of the earth's inhabitants.

Atomic bombs are of two very different types: fission bombs, and fusion bombs. Fission means "splitting apart." Thus, fission bombs utilize the splitting of an atom with high atomic weight into two atoms with lower atomic weights, which together add up to a slightly smaller mass than that of the original atom. Still, the atomic destruction of this tiny mass of matter produces a vast amount of energy, which gives rise to a huge explosion.

In contrast to fission, fusion means merging together. Thus, fusion bombs such as the hydrogen bomb utilize the ability of two atoms of low atomic weight, such as deuterium–an isotope of hydrogen with an atomic weight of 2 = to fuse together to form a single atom, namely helium, with an atomic weight of close to 4. But the atomic weight of helium formed by this fusion is slightly smaller than the sum of the atomic weights of two hydrogen atoms. The difference in the mass of the helium formed by fusion of two hydrogen atoms and their mass is converted into energy, and the destruction of this small amount of mass still produces a huge amount of energy and results in a vast explosion. Happily, fusion bombs are much harder to construct than fission bombs, because they require a fission explosion that surrounds an inner core of deuterium to blast the deuterium atoms together and fuse them together to create helium. In the process, they release gigantic amounts of energy, resulting in a devastating explosion.

In contrast, construction of an atomic bomb requires highly refined fissile materials such as uranium-235 or plutonium-239. To produce these, a nation must mount a vast, expensive and sophisticated industrial effort. Further, the bomb must contain a fission trigger that fires the separate fissile components together, to produce the critical mass required for an atomic explosion. Happily, highly radioactive materials such as uranium-235 of plutonium-239 are deadly dangerous and require personnel carefully trained in radiation physics to handle them safely.

The blast effects of an atomic bomb are measured in terms of *kilotons* (thousands of tons), and for *hydrogen bombs*, even in *megatons (millions of tons)* of conventional explosives, for these bombs are thousands or millions of times more powerful than a ton of a conventional high explosive. Further, the runaway nuclear reaction in an exploding atom bomb releases a hurricane-force wind blast that blows down buildings, a searing heat wave that incinerates its surroundings, and an intense blast of radiation. The last two effects diminish in intensity in parallel with the square of the distance from the epicenter of the explosion. Depending on the energy of the explosion and the distance from the epicenter, the heat wave may kill instantly those exposed to it, while the radiation that strikes victims who are sufficiently close may kill them within hours, weeks, or months. For those further from the epicenter, radiation exposure eventually causes cancer, depending on the radiation dose absorbed. Compared to unexposed people, excess cases of leukemia begin to appear a year or two after total body irradiation, while an excess incidence of solid cancers begins about a decade after irradiation, and continues to the end of the life-span of those exposed.

A nuclear explosion releases a cloud of radioactive particles into the atmosphere, from which they fall out to contaminate areas downwind from ground zero. The most dangerous contaminant is iodine-131, which is absorbed by the thyroid and can eventually cause thyroid cancer. But its absorption is readily blocked by swallowing pills of non-radioactive sodium iodide. In addition, a nuclear explosion is powerful enough to propel tiny radioactive particles into the stratosphere. From there, they fall out over the entire surface of the earth over the next two or three years. Strontium-90 is the most dangerous isotope that reaches the stratosphere. It has a half-life of 28 years, and is incorporated into the food chain once it falls out onto the ground. Strontium-90 is distributed so widely, that its fallout near the epicenter is only three times higher than at the most distant parts of the globe. When absorbed in high enough concentration, strontium-90 causes osteogenic sarcoma (bone tumors). Happily, it would require a major nuclear war in which hundreds of atom bombs were exploded, to present a significant hazard to human beings. However, in the case of a meltdown of an atomic reactor, the initial danger to large areas downwind of an atomic explosion is iodine-131. But atomic bombs also disperse strontium-90, which is a dangerous isotope because it has a long half-life – almost 29 years–and is blasted aloft into the global stratosphere. Then over the next two to three years it falls out onto the earth's surface, where it is incorporated into the food chain and consumed by animals and human beings. It is dispersed so effectively, that the strontium-90 fallout onto the area where the bomb exploded is only about three times higher than over the rest of the world. Because strontium-90 causes osteogenic sarcoma (bone cancer) in experimental animals,[686] even small amounts ingested in foods could reinforce a person's genetic and environmentally acquired susceptibility for developing osteogenic sarcoma. But in order for the world's population to be exposed to sufficient strontium-90 to experience serious consequences from its fallout, a full-scale nuclear war would have to be fought, in which 1,000 or more atom bombs were exploded. The immediate carnage and destruction that such a war would wreak is incomparably worse than the long-term effects of strontium-90 fallout. Only madmen would actuate the nuclear option, for it would guarantee mutual destruction, and risk ending civilization as we now know it.

As regards preparedness by the U.S. military to respond to a nuclear weapons attack, a report released by the Commission of the National Guard and Reserves in 2008 found a lack of troops, equipment and training, and concluded that the military was unprepared for an attack. Because much of the military was deployed in Afghanistan and Iraq, the country would have to rely on the Reserves. During 2009, it was planned to train and equip National Guard and Reserve units to form a three-tiered military response team. A few hundred first responders would be followed by about 1,200 troops which would include medical and logistics forces. A third wave of about 2,500 support forces would be composed of aircraft units and engineers. Although fully equipping and training the Guard would require billions of dollars, [687] this could deal only with a single nuclear explosion—but crazed terrorists might set off multiple explosions.

Finally, the need to consider defenses against dirty and nuclear bombs would not exist, if terrorists realized that murdering women, children and other noncombatants, which would inevitably result from the explosion of such weapons, would dishonors the very God whom they mean to glorify by their actions. Would not a God who is loving and merciful abhor murderers, and condemn terrorists to hell? If clerics of all faiths would strive with all their might to impress this message on their followers, then our world would be a safer and more humane place in which to live. In fact, the New York Times of October 7, 2005 did report a warning from one senior al-Qa'ida leader to another: that attacks on civilians could jeopardize their broader cause.[688] This message needs to be repeated again and again, until its truth is accepted universally. The world needs to guard itself well from inhumane sociopaths, of which Stalin, Hitler and Mao are prime examples, famous only for their inhumanity.

AFTERWORD

_____

A t the World Economic Forum in Davos, Switzerland in 2003, Bill Gates announced a $200 million medical research initiative entitled "Grand Challenges in Global Health." It is disappointing that the seven Goals and Grand Challenges later chosen by medical researchers included only items such as infectious diseases, which would yield quick results, and not tobacco use.[689] Still, tobacco _was_ included in the call _JAMA_ issued for papers for a June 2004 issue devoted to Grand Challenges.[690] Would that "The Road Ahead" not only for Bill Gates,[691] but for all foundations and individuals focused on helping people worldwide, will include tobacco, as well as the many humane causes noted in chapter 32.

Lately, the United States has been reluctant to assume its ethically mandatory role to be a leader, rather than a hesitant follower, in the global battle against tobacco. Unfortunately, this is a reluctance mirrored by the United States stance on many vital global issues. Some of these issues are environmental while others are humane in nature. However, today the United States is acting ethically in response to HIV, malaria, and many other deadly diseases. But a similar response and action in concert with other United Nations resolutions is needed to base United States leadership a foundation of sound ethical principles. The United States should participate enthusiastically in U.N. actions on environmental issues such as pollution of air, soil and water, greenhouse gases and global warming, maintenance of clean water supplies, preservation of flora and fauna, sustainable agriculture, and renewable energy. The administration has allowed industry to win the battle of pollution control at EPA–a very bad omen.[692, 693]

Also, the United States should participate in actions called for by U.N. resolutions on issues only some of which it supports presently: crop failure and starvation; population control; help for natural disasters; poverty and lack of education; rights abuse against minority groups; international courts to adjudicate between opponents; exploitive multinational corporations; and addictive drugs such as tobacco. Such issues should all be part of a humane, fully integrated U.S. global ethical strategy, not disparate entities. The aim should be to benefit all of humanity, especially developing nations–not merely the United States. Pursued wholeheartedly, humanity would benefit, the United States would gain respect, and causes for disliking it would lessen.

But I cannot end this book without returning to its first theme, which motivated me to write it- the suffering I saw graphically displayed when I sat at my father's bedside during the final four days of his doomed fight against an implacable foe: cancer caused by his smoking addiction. As famed cancer researcher Irving Selikoff said, "Statistics are merely aggregations of numbers with the tears wiped away," and Dileep Bal wrote in a memorable editorial in the American Cancer Society's journal *CA* in 2001, "the human dimension of our subject- the suffering and sorrowful loss- should never be forgotten."[694] Indeed, this is the most potent source of motivation for the fight against smoking, not cold statistics.

One of my father's favorite sayings was, *dum spiro, spero*- while I breathe, I hope. It is an appropriate wish for the son of a cigarette victim. Nor should it be hard for readers to guess what I hope this book will challenge them to think about, and then set about doing.

Here, then, is a final challenge to readers: to engage their emotions in the fight- not only against tobacco, but also against poverty and poor education, for success in these goals is crucial for reducing smoking, as well as the many other social ills cataloged in chapter 32. But why stop there? Our challenge is to fight against all forms of illness, be it physical, emotional, or economic. Everyone is capable of producing an impact, be that through expertise, or else through infectious empathy that translates into active commitment to a chosen cause. As the great and wise Mahatma Gandhi once said:[694] *"If you want to change the world, be that change."*

SUMMARY

Where there is smoke, there is fire

There is no substitute for reading the material in individual chapters. For topics that are of special interest to readers, the chapters cover their subjects in far greater depth than this Summary. Still, busy readers may find it useful to have an overview of all the topics and major conclusions.

1: OVERVIEW OF HEALTH EFFECTS

Smoking is the most important preventable cause of death of the major diseases that kill human beings: heart disease and stroke, cancer, and chronic obstructive pulmonary disease. In the United States, it is the primary cause of death for one fifth of all deaths, and directly responsible for nearly one-third of all deaths from heart disease and cancer. Each year, smoking kills more than 440,000 people, wastes 5 million years of potential life, and costs more than $75 billion in health care.

2: HOW CHEMICALS CAUSE CANCER

A normal cell becomes a cancer cell when it acquires a heritable change that renders it at least partly unresponsive to control of its growth beyond the bounds set by the body's genetic blueprint. Chemicals can cause cancer directly, by binding to the DNA of a cell in a way that mutates (changes) the DNA to allow the cell to multiply without restraint. But chemicals can also produce this change indirectly, by binding to cell proteins or to RNA, which then interact with DNA. Alternatively, chemicals can damage the mechanism by which damage to DNA is repaired. Cancer can also be caused by radiation and by certain types of viruses. The cumulative dose of a carcinogen absorbed is most important in determining whether or not cancer ensues.

3: HISTORY

In 1492, Christopher Columbus' crew discovered that American Indians were smoking tobacco. Still, tobacco was not introduced into Europe until 1585. Cigarette smoking began in the late nineteenth century, and received a big boost during World War I. Roughly two decades later, women started to smoke in large numbers. A publicity campaign against smoking was first launched in Nazi Germany, then in Britain in 1962, and finally in the United States in 1964 with the publication of the first Surgeon General's Report on Smoking and Health. Because of the long time-lag between smoking and disease, cigarette smoking peaked in the United States in 1963, but the lung cancer death rate did not peak until 30 years later; by that time, the number of smokers had dropped by almost one-half. Smoking is closely tied to lack of advanced education. In 1998, a national survey found that 37% of adults with 11 or fewer years of education were smokers, while only 11% of adults with 16 or more years of education smoked.

4: TOBACCO SMOKE CONSTITUENTS

Tobacco smoke contains literally dozens of carcinogens. Some are present in the gaseous phase of smoke, others are attached to the tiny smoke particles. The carcinogens in the gaseous phase include dimethylnitrosamine, hydrazine, and vinyl chloride. But the most potent carcinogens are attached to smoke particles. They include benzopyrene, polonium-210, arsenic, and also beta-naphthylamine that causes bladder cancer.

5: HEART DISEASE AND NICOTINE

Perhaps people underestimate the life-robbing potency of coronary heart disease (CHD) acquired from smoking, because cancer seems a much greater threat. In fact, over three times as many smokers die prematurely from heart disease than from cancer.

The cause of heart disease is nicotine. It causes a rapid increase in blood pressure and in heart rate, and by making the heart work harder, nicotine wears it out faster. But nicotine also promotes formation of atherosclerotic plaques in blood vessels, and these are a main cause of heart attacks and strokes. Tobacco smoke also contains carbon monoxide, which decreases the oxygen-carrying capacity of blood red cells, forcing the body to produce more red cells, thereby thickening the blood and increasing the risk of clot formation.

Smoking merely 1 to 4 cigarettes a day can double or treble a woman's risk of fatal heart disease. For both men and women, quitting rapidly reduces the excess risk of a heart attack caused by smoking. Quitting permanently is especially important for smokers who already have CHD, for it reduces their risk of death from CHD by one-third. It is also vital for women on oral contraceptives, since smoking greatly increases their risk of a heart attack.

6: STROKE

Smoking causes vascular disease throughout the body. Thus, the damage is not limited to the blood vessels of the heart, but also affects the blood vessels of the brain. This explains why cigarette smoking causes more than 50% of the deaths from cerebrovascular (brain blood vessel) disease in people under 65 years in age.

Overall, compared to nonsmokers, male smokers have a 72% higher risk of stroke, while female smokers have a 43% higher risk. Since women used to smoke fewer cigarettes, their risk is smaller than that for men but it is still a major hazard.

7: LUNG CANCER

The most common sites at which lung cancer begins are the points where the air vessels divide, for it is there that smoke particles impinge and form the heaviest deposit of tar. Lung cancer comprises roughly two-thirds of all the different types of cancer caused by smoking. According to the Surgeon General's Report of 2001 entitled "Women and Smoking," lung cancer accounts for 29% of all cancer deaths in the United States. A few decades ago, deaths from lung cancer were far higher for men than for women. But now, lung cancer is the most common cause of cancer deaths in women, and 90% of these deaths are caused by smoking. For women who smoke two or more packs a day, the risk is twentyfold higher than for nonsmokers. Women who stop smoking greatly reduce their risk of dying prematurely. Very similar statistics apply to men, and for both men and women, quitting helps at any age.

8: SCREENING FOR LUNG CANCER

The screening of long-term smokers to detect early lung cancer is a worthwhile goal, because the five-year survival rate is 50% if it is discovered early, while it is only 15% for all lung cancer cases. Besides older methods such as conventional X-rays and sputum cytology (microscopic screening for cancer cells), there are several promising new techniques. These include Low-radiation dose Computed Tomography (LCT, also called spiral CT), fluorescence bronchoscopy, and other novel methodologies.

As yet, none of the above techniques for early detection of lung cancer have been validated to produce a decrease in death rate. While the American Cancer Society does not recommend lung cancer screening, nor does it discourage it: it leaves that decision up to those at risk and to their physicians. Since research into new and more sensitive methods for diagnosis of lung cancer is proceeding rapidly, people at risk are encouraged to inquire at institutions with state-of-the-art capabilities, as to the benefits, risks, and limitations of testing for early detection of lung cancer. Although the development of sensitive new diagnostic procedures will help, smokers will benefit far more from quitting, and this will reduce their need to be tested.

9: HEREDITY AND SUSCEPTIBILITY TO LUNG CANCER

Two different genes that increase the risk of lung cancer were discovered in 1990. As to the first of these two genes, the 10% of Americans who lack it are exceptional: they have a *low* susceptibility for developing lung cancer, and thus a relatively *low* risk of lung cancer even if they smoke. But they have no protection for the many other serious diseases that smoking causes. But the other 90% of Americans who do not have this gene are at grave risk of developing lung cancer if they smoke.

The second gene has the opposite effect: it *increases* the risk of lung cancer in the roughly 10% of people who have inherited a single copy of it. But for the 1 person in 300 in the U.S. population who inherited two copies of this gene, the risk of lung cancer is much higher, and the people in this tiny minority develop 10% of all lung cancers. Hopefully, in future all smokers will be tested for possession of this gene, for even having a single copy of this gene makes smoking extremely risky. But only to a somewhat lesser degree, this holds true for the 90% of people who do *not* possess this gene, but persist in smoking.

10: THERAPY OF LUNG CANCER

Once lung cancer has been diagnosed, it must be "staged" to determine its size, and whether metastases are present. Non-small-cell lung cancer is the type of lung cancer found in 75% of all cases. For about 30% of patients with this type, it is discovered at a sufficiently early stage that they can have surgery; of these patients, 42% survive five years after diagnosis. But for those whose cancer is already too advanced for surgical treatment, only 5% are alive at that time. Of the remaining 70% of patients, 30% have inoperable cancer that is confined to their lung. The other 40% of patients have metastases, and the majority of these do not survive one year. However, chemotherapy with multiple types of drugs has allowed one-third of these patients to survive over one year. But since chemotherapy is toxic and thus hard to bear and has only marginal benefits, the decision on whether to use it is best left to each patient, after being informed of its risks and benefits.

But in 2004, researchers found that about 10% of patients with non-small-cell lung cancer have a genetic mutation that often permits the drug *gefitinib* to shrink their cancer dramatically. This is a wonderful success story for researchers.

11: OTHER TYPES OF CANCER

The carcinogens in tar particles and gaseous tobacco smoke cause cancer wherever they impinge, or are absorbed:–the mouth, larynx, bronchi, and lung. But some of the tar is swallowed, and therefore can deposit carcinogens in the esophagus, stomach, and intestines, increasing their risk of cancer. Also, wherever tar or gaseous smoke contacts cells, carcinogens can be absorbed into the blood stream and then transported throughout the body. This is the cause for the excess risk of cancer development in the kidneys, bladder, pancreas, marrow, breast, skin, liver, cervix, uterus, and prostate. Smoking causes approximately 90% of cancers of the larynx, 70% of cancers of the mouth and esophagus, and increases the risk for cancers of the bladder or kidneys fourfold.

Some carcinogens pass from the bloodstream through the kidneys to the bladder, where accumulate in urine and cause bladder cancer.

12: MALE/FEMALE DIFFERENCES IN CANCERS LINKED TO SMOKING

Women who smoke have an elevated risk of cancers that arise in female sex organs, namely the breast, cervix, and uterus. Perhaps because their body mass is smaller, the risk of bladder cancer is higher for women than for men who smoke the same number of cigarettes. The risk of bladder cancer is higher for women than for men who smoke the same number of cigarettes. In addition, a group of women possess only small amounts of an enzyme that detoxifies lung carcinogens, and for them, smoking increases the risk of lung cancer fourfold.Unique to women are the effects of smoking on the developing fetus. Smoking during pregnancy depresses the baby's birth weight, doubles the risk of spontaneous abortion, increases the risk of malformations and still births, and doubles a child's risk of attention deficit disorder (ADD). As for men who smoke, that almost doubles their risk of developing prostate cancer.

13: CHRONIC OBSTRUCTIVE PULMONARY DISEASE (COPD)

COPD includes three separate diseases which together constitute it: emphysema, chronic bronchitis, and chronic obstructive bronchitis—and smoking is the major cause of all three diseases. Most patients with COPD suffer from all three diseases, but the relative severity of these diseases varies for different patients. In all three diseases, tar from cigarette smoke physically obstructs small air passages. The Surgeon General's Report on Smoking and Health of 1989 concluded that cigarette smoking is overwhelmingly important in causing COPD, and would be uncommon if no one smoked. But because of smoking, it is the fourth most common cause of death in the U.S.

Although people dread lung cancer far more than COPD, it is a fearsome disease from which approximately as many people die as from lung cancer. Eventually, many of its sufferers have to fight for every breath that they take. Therapies can ease the symptoms of COPD, but cannot reverse it. The most beneficial treatment is to quit smoking, for this can have a favorable effect on COPD.

14: OTHER HEALTH EFFECTS

In sufficiently high concentrations, nicotine is poisonous, and can cause green tobacco sickness in tobacco harvesters. Since tobacco smoke damages the lung's ability to defend itself against bacteria, smokers have a fourfold higher risk of contracting pneumonia than nonsmokers. This causes around 500,000 hospitalizations and 40,000 deaths a year in the United States. As a result, smokers are more frequently absent from work. Tobacco tar deposits on the teeth and gums, and produces gum disease. Compared to nonsmokers, smokers have about a threefold higher risk of losing all their teeth.

Compared to nonsmokers, smokers also assume a higher risk of losing their most vital senses. Loss of hearing is 70% higher, and age-related macular degeneration—progressive damage to the retina of the eye—is more than 100% higher. Moreover, smoking advances by about 5 years the rate at which old age deteriorates physical functions such as agility and strength. Also advanced are other age-related physical changes that include wrinkling of skin, graying and loss of hair, and loss of male sex performance. Smoking also produces a higher risk of events that threaten life itself or its quality: fatal rupturing of the abdominal aorta, inflammatory bowel disease, a delay in wound healing, impairment of cognitive ability, and perhaps also, development of Alzheimer's disease. Nicotine reduces appetite by shifting the body's craving from food to nicotine, so promotes weight loss.

15: ACCIDENTAL DEATHS AND INJURIES

Cigarette smoking is a major cause of fires and of certain other types of accidents. Each year, roughly 1,000 Americans die from fires ignited by cigarettes, many caused by people who fall asleep in bed while smoking, or else from smoking and drinking. Although cigarettes can be made to extinguish if not drawn upon, what is needed is the passage of a federal law that mandates that all brands of cigarettes incorporate this safety feature. Also, because it is distracting to light a cigarette while driving, car accidents are 50% more likely for smokers than for nonsmokers.

16: NICOTINE ADDICTION

In 1988, Surgeon General Everett Koop published a report on the health consequences of smoking entitled "Nicotine Addiction." He warned smokers that tobacco products are as addictive as cocaine or heroin, and that it is the nicotine content that causes addiction. All these three drugs cause addiction by a similar mechanism: they hijack the brain's pathways to pleasure, memory, and motivation. Even two months after quitting one of these drugs, the chemistry of the brain has not yet returned to normal. Hopefully, these insights into drug addiction will help in the design of more effective ways to quit (see Part III).

17: MENTAL DIFFICULTIES AND SMOKING

Twice as many mentally ill smoke as people in the general population, and they consume nearly half of all cigarettes sold in the United States. To some extent, the likelihood of taking up smoking and of developing a major depression is inherited, and there is evidence for some degree of linkage between smoking and depression: smokers have an increased risk that depression, panic attacks, or else schizophrenia may develop later on in life.

18: CIGARS, PIPES AND SNUFF

Depending on their size and kind, cigars contain roughly 3 to 20 times the amount of nicotine as a cigarette, and may take up to two hours to smoke. Nearly three-quarters of those who smoke cigars smoke only occasionally, and the majority do not inhale. Still, drawing on lighted tobacco causes smoke to be sucked into the mouth, throat, larynx, and to a lesser extent into the upper reaches of the lung. As a result that is surprising, cigar smokers have overall risks of cancer that are higher than for nonsmokers by factors of fourfold for the mouth, tenfold for the larynx, five-fold for the lung, and approximately threefold for both pancreas and bladder. My great-granduncle Berthold, with whom I lived in England for two years until he died at the early age of 70, was a habitual cigar smoker – but he was also overweight, despite often quoting the proverb, enough is as good as a feast – and that is a significant additional health risk. Further, habitual cigar smokers like my uncle Berthold have risks of developing chronic obstructive pulmonary disease (COPD) or heart disease that are similar to those of cigarette smokers.

Pipe smoking was popular during the 20th century, but by its end, only 1% of the population still smoked pipes. Since the risks of this dying habit are only slightly smaller than those of cigar smoking, its demise will not be mourned.

Nowadays some adolescents smoke bidis (mini-cigarettes) and kreteks (clove cigarettes). Smoking bidis is far more dangerous than smoking ordinary cigarettes, while smoking kreteks is at least as dangerous as cigarettes. Chewing tobacco and using snuff are also a menace if used long-term. Both these forms of "smoke-less tobacco" increase the risks of developing cancer of the mouth, throat, larynx and esophagus.

19: ENVIRONMENTAL TOBACCO SMOKE

The United States Surgeon General's report of 2001 concluded that ETS (Environmental Tobacco Smoke) causes lung cancer, heart disease, and exacerbates allergy. Even the tobacco industry no longer disputes this conclusion. Still, as of 1998, one-third of review articles on the effects of ETS had failed to find evidence that it causes disease. But the authors of 74% of these negative reviews had a gainful connection to the tobacco industry, and if that was the case, the odds were 88:1 that they would *fail* to find harmful effects for ETS. So much for intellectual honesty.

Regarding the effect of ETS on the risk of lung cancer, the risk for nonsmoking women married to smokers is approximately 30% higher than if their husbands did not smoke; but if their husbands are chain smokers, the risk is 80% higher. The excess risk for long-continued exposure to ETS in the work place is also 30%. But children continually exposed to ETS are at highest excess risk for later development of lung cancer. These results are backed by laboratory studies, which show that people exposed to ETS absorb a potent tobacco-specific lung carcinogen, NNAL.

As regards coronary heart disease, long-term exposure to ETS by nonsmokers increases their risk of heart disease by 30%. While it has been proven that smoking during pregnancy harms the fetus, that ETS harms the fetus is still unproven.

Tobacco smoke acerbates asthma, from which roughly 2 million children suffer in the United States. Neither they nor adults allergic to tobacco smoke should be exposed to ETS. Happily, recent laws that forbid smoking in public places have vastly reduced the serious plight of those allergic to tobacco smoke.

Smokers are being exiled from their places of work onto the street, and then asked to move away from entrances. Nor are smokers welcome in most homes, for most homes are smoke free. The American Medical Association says that nonsmokers should not permit smoking in their homes, cars, or workplaces, and that people should minimize the time spent inhaling ETS.

20: SEARCH FOR A SAFER CIGARETTE

Smoking tobacco can never be safe. It is impossible to eliminate the dozens of carcinogens that are in tobacco smoke, nor all the tar that causes COPD, nor all the nicotine that makes smoking addictive but causes heart disease. During the second half of the last century, the average tar yield of American cigarettes declined by nearly one-third, and the nicotine yield by about one-half. But this increased sales, for as the industry well knew, smokers compensated for low-nicotine content by smoking more cigarettes.

While low-yield cigarettes do slightly reduce the symptoms of developing COPD, quitting is incomparably more beneficial. Unfortunately, tobacco is not federally regulated, so the public has no unbiased information it can use to evaluate the inflated claims of cigarette makers. For decades, the industry has lobbied against federal legislation that would reduce the fire hazard of cigarettes by making cigarettes self-extinguishing. But New York State passed a statue that required all cigarettes sold after June, 2004 to meet a rigorous self-extinguishing standard. A like nationwide law in Canada become effective at the end of 2004.

21: CAN DIET HELP?

Smokers who eat a diet low in fat and very high in fruit and vegetables may well reduce their risk of lung cancer by 50%. But in comparison, quitting sufficiently early can eventually reduce that risk by 1,000%. There is no definitive evidence that dietary supplements can reduce the risk of lung cancer in smokers; indeed, supplements of beta-carotene slightly increase that risk.

22: MARIJUANA—A VERY DIFFERENT TYPE OF CIGARETTE

In Europe, almost 40% of those aged 15 to 34 have tried pot (marijuana), and different countries vary greatly in their control of its use. In the United States, marijuana was the most widely used illicit drug in 2002. As of early 2004, the United States prohibited the possession of marijuana. Because for each proposed medical use of marijuana there are many conventional therapies, the Supreme Court has upheld a federal ban on the medical use of marijuana. Most "medipot" cases fall under local jurisdiction, but some police officers refuse to prosecute them.In 2003, Canada permitted the medical use of marijuana grown under government contract- despite objections from Canadian medical organizations, that clinical trials to test marijuana had not yet been done. Also, Canada's Supreme Court endorsed criminal penalties for smoking marijuana, but left open the possibility that the Canadian parliament could decriminalize its casual use.

The smuggling of powerful Canadian marijuana into the United States is already a $4 billion a year underground industry. In addition, large amounts of marijuana are smuggled into the United States from clandestine growers in Columbia and Mexico.

People differ widely in their immediate reaction to smoking marijuana, which may range from none, to feeling relaxed, high, or else even anxious and paranoic. Other problems include trouble with memory, thinking, and learning; distortion of sights, sounds, time, and touch; loss of coordination; increase in heart rate; and not bothering to use safeguards against venereal infections such as AIDS when having sex. About 40% of long-term marijuana users experience some of the following serious deleterious effects: loss of short-term memory; slowness of learning; damage to lung functions similar to that of cigarette smokers; developmental problems in adolescents; the amotivational syndrome–loss of energy and behavioral disruptions; decreased sperm viability, and interference with ovulation and pre-natal development. The amount of carcinogens absorbed from smoking five joints (cigarettes) of marijuana a week is equivalent to smoking a pack of cigarettes a day. But the occasional use of marijuana is less harmful than the habitual use of alcohol and/or tobacco.

A serious charge against smoking pot is that it acts as a gateway drug to use of strongly addicting drugs: the risk of using heroin is seventeenfold greater for those who have smoked marijuana than for those who have not. A study of twins has shown that marijuana use is a potent "marker" for a later switch to dependence on more potent drugs or alcohol. The younger the age at which marijuana smoking is begun, the higher that risk. For 20-30% of its users, marijuana is addicting. In 1997, about 47% of United States high school students said they had smoked marijuana at least once. To counteract marijuana smoking, schools only should use proven anti-drug programs. Most important, parents should advise their children not to experiment with marijuana–nor with tobacco, inhalants, LSD, heroin, or cocaine.

23: PREVENTION: CHILDREN, ADOLESCENTS, AND YOUNG PEOPLE

Every day another 3,000 children at an average age of 13½ years begin to smoke cigarettes. Indeed, approximately 80% of eventual smokers start before the age of 18. Social factors that motivate youths to smoke include poverty and little education, bad childhood experiences, adoption of a sedentary lifestyle, and most important, having parents or friends who smoke.

Tobacco companies use many tricks to lure youths to start smoking, such as ads showing attractive, cool youngsters who smoke. The ads are heaviest in magazines read by youths and young adults. Also, a major avenue for tobacco promotion is through paying the producers of films and videos to include sequences of smoking in them. The success of this campaign is suggested by the frequency of smoking in films rated G, PG and PG-13, which are intended for viewing by children. Fighting against the industry's efforts are state departments of public health, government agencies, foundations, and health educators in schools. All are handicapped by having much smaller funds than tobacco companies.

When in 1992 the United States Supreme Court allowed states to sue the tobacco companies, it took another six years before the following settlement was reached: the industry will pay $10 billion per year forever to the 50 states and some territories. As part of the previous (1998) settlement between tobacco companies and the states that sued them, the companies undertook to warn youths not to smoke. But the industry spikes its antismoking ads with psychologically crafted subliminal messages that turn them into powerful ads to start smoking. What else could be expected from turning the fox loose in the chicken koop?

Experts from ACS, FDA, and CDC say that there is an urgent need to pass legislation that will accomplish the following three goals: strong regulation of tobacco by the FDA; effective clean indoor air laws; and a Smoking Cessation Act, that will expand Medicare and Medicaid coverage for smoking-cessation expenses.

Previously, physicians and medical scientists used to volunteer in the Greater Boston area to give school assemblies on the health effects of smoking. This is no longer the case. However presently, free antismoking brochures for schools are available from ACS, and from the Lung and the Heart Associations, the U.S. Department of HHS, the National Cancer Institute, and from Tobacco-Free Kids. Still, the most successful strategies for discouraging youths from smoking are laws that forbid sales to minors and also are monitored for compliance, the raising of taxes on tobacco, and advertising against smoking using a strong, youth-oriented media blitz based on modern social marketing principles. To counter the inevitable industry lobbying to reverse antismoking legislation, antismoking advocates must respond with even stronger lobbying. Unfortunately, states are using few of the funds from the tobacco settlement for antismoking messages.

24: HEALTH WARNINGS, ADVERTISEMENTS, AND LEGISLATION

A year after the first Surgeon General's Report on Smoking and Health of 1964, Congress enacted the Cigarette Labeling and Advertising Act. From then on, cigarette packages had to carry the warning, "CAUTION: CIGARETTE SMOKING MAY BE HAZARDOUS TO YOUR HEALTH." Then in 1967, a suit by crusading attorney John Banzhaf forced the FDC to apply the Fairness Doctrine to cigarette advertising. From then on, television and radio stations had to air antismoking messages. These ended in 1971, when all cigarette advertising on TV and radio was banned. But for years afterwards, public-spirited stations provided time for free antismoking messages. In 1969, a law was passed requiring all cigarette packages sold in the U.S. to display one of four potent health warnings. Then in 1972, the requirement for warnings was extended to all cigarette ads.

In Canada, Graphic Cigarette Warnings were mandated to show memorable pictures that illustrated powerful antismoking messages printed in large type and strong color contrast, taking up half the space of the front of a pack. These Canadian warnings are wonderful models for what future legislation in the United States should mandate.

25: INDUSTRY DECEPTION, HANDOUTS, REGULATION, AND LAWSUITS

Accepting money directly or indirectly from the tobacco industry or its subsidies has been a great temptation for individuals, institutions, businesses, and the media. The sums dispensed by this immensely wealthy industry to achieve its goals are large enough to overcome ethical scruples–unless the best interests of the public are held to be more important.In fact, many organizations have been unswervingly committed to the public will. These include societies concerned with the diseases caused by smoking: ACS, and the American Heart and Lung Associations.In 1972, the tobacco industry was still telling the public that the link between smoking and disease was unproven. It paid scientists to say so, and funded research focused on that link. Even the Harvard Medical School accepted a multi-million dollar grant, and sent out a news release that said that a direct causal relationship between smoking and disease was still under study.In Britain in 2001, the tobacco industry gave a multi-million dollar grant to Nottingham University for research *not* related to health. Now the objective was merely to prove that the industry had the public's good at heart. But the editor of the *British Medical Journal* threatened to quit his professorship at that university, if it failed to return the industry's money. Bravo.

Organizations that have failed their ethics test include the American Medical Association (AMA), the American Academy of Family Physicians (AAFP), and the American Council on Science and Health (ACSH). For AMA and AAFP, the issues involved failure to divest of the stocks of tobacco companies and of their whole or part-owned subsidiaries; for ACSH, the issue was acceptance of grants. Nor are magazines guiltless: those that carry cigarette advertisements cover the hazards of smoking less extensively.

David Kessler began his six-year tenure as commissioner of FDA in 1990. His battle to establish FDA control over tobacco ended with the Supreme Court decision of 1999. It held that FDA cannot regulate tobacco products since they are so deadly that the FDA would have to prohibit their sale—a radical step only Congress should take. Kessler was helped enormously by insiders of tobacco companies, who testified that their executives had known for decades the facts they were protesting: that smoking is dangerous to smokers and nonsmokers, that tobacco delivers highly addictive nicotine, and that children were the most important targets.

These revelations resulted in a spate of lawsuits against tobacco companies. After four states settled their cases against the industry, the other 46 states combined to threaten a huge lawsuit against the industry. This resulted in a settlement in 1997, in which tobacco companies agreed—depending on tobacco sales being high enough—to pay approximately $10 billion per year forever, to be split between the 50 states and federal territories.

But these settlements placed "caps" on the damages that tobacco companies would have to pay to settle lawsuits brought by smokers, and allowed the companies to make the price increases needed to ensure a healthy profit. As of May 2004, there were 14 successful individual suits, but only two litigants had received money. A class-action suit by Florida smokers that was awarded $145 billion in 2000 was still under appeal, as was a suit for $280 billion by the United States government, for damages sought from the industry for marketing its products fraudulently.

To ensure survival, the tobacco industry employs three major strategies. First, it passes all costs on to consumers; Secondly, it targets youths, college students, undereducated people and people in underdeveloped nations. Third, it buys firms that sell healthy consumer goods, both for profitability and to acquire a better image.

Nonsmokers can help to fight smoking by advocating for divestment of tobacco stocks, checking observance of the federal law that forbids tobacco sales to minors, and lobbying for smoke-free laws in their states. As of May 2004, ten states had passed smoke-free workplace laws. Congress should pass legislation that applies such laws nation-wide, and creates a new federal Tobacco Control Agency—or else strengthen the FDA's authority over tobacco, increase its budget, and move it from agriculture to health care committees.

Two loop-holes still exist in the sale of cigarettes. State taxes are not collected on internet sales. This could be remedied by software that monitoring all internet sales and required the paying of state taxes. In addition, out-of-state mail-order sales need to be assessed state taxes. Remedial legislation, modeled on that of New York State, would bring in welcome new revenues.

26: USE, MISUSE, AND EFFECTS OF TOBACCO SETTLEMENT FUNDS

The settlement for $246 billion that 46 states reached with tobacco companies stated that its purpose was to stop children from becoming addicted to tobacco. But while the CDC suggested that states spend 20 to 25% of this money on comprehensive antismoking programs, the majority of states used it as a new source of revenue. Even in states that adequately funded vigorous antismoking programs which initially were very effective in reducing smoking, a gradual diversion of antismoking funds occurred—driven by declining tax revenues due to reduced business incomes, and declining tobacco sales due to tax-free internet sales. As a result, the price of cigarettes has increased greatly since 1999, as smokers must pay for the damages assessed against the tobacco companies, and also as state taxes increased. A sudden rise in the cost of cigarettes always causes a decline in their consumption. So in May 2002, CDC reported that 16% fewer high school students had smoked during the previous month, than 5 years previously.

27: QUITTING

A vital precondition for success in quitting is a strong desire to quit. While a large choice of different strategies is available for quitting, to succeed it is vital to really believe *that the most effective way we have to reduce our risk of heart disease, stroke, cancer, and respiratory disease is not to smoke.*

But fires are much easier to prevent than to extinguish—and addiction to nicotine is as difficult to reverse as addiction to heroin or cocaine. All three drugs act on the same area of the brain, and produce strong feelings of stimulation. To withdraw from addiction to any of these drugs takes a major effort.

28: SUCCESSFUL ANTISMOKING PROGRAMS AND CAMPAIGNS

Education from community-based and media-based campaigns have prevented or postponed smoking in 20% to 40% of adolescents. According to the United States Public Health Service, it is least effective to quit "cold turkey" on one's own, or to use acupuncture. Compared to these two methods, people who use nicotine gum are 50% more successful. But smokers who use the nicotine patch, the drug bupropion, or brief counseling are twice as successful in quitting as people who use no aids. Using a nicotine inhaler, or more than 8 hours of counseling, are even more effective. Physicians who take the time to advise their patients not to smoke cause 5% to 10% of smokers to quit. They are even more effective, if they warn their patients that unless they stopped smoking, their life would be at risk. But switching to low-tar cigarettes does not lower the health effects of smoking and is no substitute for quitting.

29: A COMPOSITE GUIDE TO QUITTING

Reasons for quitting include immediate benefits to health and to social acceptability. But quitting permanently succeeds in producing huge reductions in the risks for heart attack, stroke, cancer, and chronic obstructive pulmonary disease. In addition, the average smoker spends well over $3,000 a year on cigarettes, so quitting frees up lots of money for fulfilling unfulfilled desires.

If you are a smoker who is getting ready to quit, you should first set a quit date, at a time when the pressure is off. Second, review your past attempts to quit, and discover what worked for you. Third, decide that once you have stopped, you will never again take a single puff. Fourth, alert your caring friends and family that you plan to quit and need their support. Fifth, telephone for information about quit smoking programs, and if time permits, choose a first rate help program and attend it – that will ensure that you get valuable peer support. Sixth, since medications can help greatly, decide whether you will use them, and if so, choose one or two of the five approved by the FDA. They are very helpful to tide you over, should your craving for nicotine become strong, especially at the very start of quitting. But they are not recommended for people with heart or circulatory disease, nor for pregnant women. Helpful over-the-counter medications include the nicotine patch and the nicotine gum.

The FDA advises against use of nicotine lollipops, because children can use them accidentally. Prescriptions are required for nicotine inhalers that look like cigarettes, for nicotine nasal sprays that deliver nicotine quickly, and for bupropion (Zyban), an antidepressant that aids quitting, and is even more effective when nicotine replacement is used as well. The addition of counseling on quitting, especially if it is extended over several sessions, greatly increases the chances for success, whether or not nicotine replacements or bupropion also are used. Seventh, it is vital to plan how to deal with psychological and physical withdrawal symptoms prior to quitting. For many smokers, smoking has become part of eating, drinking coffee, working, walking, reading, and watching TV. To untangle yourself from this deadly vine that will slowly choke you, use the "ABCs of quitting." These help you to replace situations that remind you of smoking–be that people, places, or routines–with more healthful ones. To succeed in quitting, it helps to change your usual kind of drink to a different one; to take a brisk walk instead of smoking and to choose a new route; to use low-calorie food substitutes such as carrot sticks or grapes; to replace smoking with good new habits such as exercising more, playing your favorite game or sport more often. This will tire you out, and thus insure that you will sleep better. Also, spend longer at your most enjoyable hobbies. When you feel a strong urge to smoke, take a few deep breaths and congratulate yourself for avoiding the many poisons in cigarette smoke. Wait at least ten minutes, fill the gap with one of the above remedies, and reward yourself for your abstinence by taking an oral substitute, by chatting with a non-smoker friend, or by spending money saved by not smoking for something you really crave. To tide you over a crisis, telephone one of your resource contacts, or read the helpful hints of your favorite quit guide. To reduce stress, take a hot shower or bath, or read an enjoyable book; for help, use meditation, or if religious, pray for strength to succeed.

To succeed in quitting, make all your decisions in advance, and have your support options ready to use before you quit. For your quit date, plan an easy day for yourself–such as the start of a long weekend or a vacation. Also, plan the events of the quit date, prepare and purchase all physical aids you have decided to use, such as low-calorie foods and nicotine replacements. As your last act on the night before your quit day, permanently dispose of anything associated with smoking. The proper fate for it is to be flushed down a toilet, not smoked. Detailed directions for the day prior to quitting, for the quit day, and for subsequent days are given in chapter 31, as are also other helpful aids such as use of "Relaxercise."

Some smokers who quit develop detoxification symptoms, for instance fatigue, irritability, insomnia, cough, dizziness, difficulty concentrating, constipation, increased appetite, and cravings for nicotine. All will fade in a very few weeks if one or more of the many appropriate antidotes are used. But never give in to the wish for just one cigarette, or else all the effort expended will have been wasted–for just one cigarette!

It helps to recount the health benefits gained by quitting: between 1 and 9 months after quitting, the function of the circulation and lung are improved, as is coughing, fatigue, and shortness of breath. One year after quitting, the excess risk of heart disease is cut by half. Fifteen years after quitting, the huge excess risks of heart disease and of stroke have vanished. In addition, the large excess risks for cancer of the lung, mouth, throat, esophagus, bladder, kidney and pancreas have decreased dramatically. Twenty five years after quitting, the risk of lung cancer is down to 10% of that for a smoker.

Nicotine increases the body's metabolism, so a smoker burns about 200 to 300 more calories per day than a nonsmoker. But when one quits, the metabolism quickly returns to normal, and appetite improves. So first, one should concentrate on quitting; later, one should reduce food intake, or else exercise more, to burn up the unused calories. Try to keep any weight gain under 10 pounds.

Smoking relieves the stress of needing to smoke, and once one has quit, that stress wanes. To be successful, one needs to practice other stress-reduction techniques. By engaging in an enjoyable activity in a different setting, the batteries of body and mind are recharged. The time spent is repaid by renewal of physical wellbeing, and of mental clarity and vigor.

Stress management programs, and books on stress-reduction and relaxing are helpful. Also, meditation and prayer are proven mainstays of many programs for recovery from addictions. By all means, reward yourself with the money saved by quitting by buying longed-for items, going to enjoyable events, and eating out.

While the lure of tobacco will diminish within a few weeks, one must remain ever on guard to remain a nonsmoker. To avoid slips, tempting situations should be avoided. When stress builds, one needs to reuse the stress-reducing techniques used to quit.

As for reimbursement of costs associated with professional advice on quitting, health maintenance organizations are becoming willing to pay for them. Finally, many excellent publications on how to quit are available free of charge from public and private agencies. The present Appendix contains a long list of organizations that give help on quitting and extol its benefits.

30: ARE GENETICS INVOLVED IN ATTRACTION TO ADDICTIONS?

Nature (genetics) and nurture (environment) both determine almost everything about us—including whether we are susceptible to addictions. The best way to separate the effect of these two factors is to study twins. Such studies have shown that there is a moderate genetic influence on whether one smokes—but this can be overridden by one's will. The decision to smoke or to quit is far more under individual control than preordained by genetics.

Research suggests that all addictive behaviors—smoking, drinking to excess, substance abuse, gambling, food bingeing, and various other behavioral problems – all are based on a common genetic deficiency: the brain cannot bind a sufficient quantity of the signaling molecule dopamine, which conveys the sensation of "enjoyable stimulation." In that case, the brain craves more stimulation, and habits that can satisfy that craving can lead to addiction. The brain recognizes a reward stimulus as a reward, irrespective of its source—whether it comes from a brain signaling molecule, a chemical supplied externally, or an experience such as sex; this points to a common basis for addictions. Since about

80% of patients in mental hospitals are smokers, they seem to share a low level of reward stimulation, and by smoking attempt to compensate for it. This thought helps to foster empathy for those confined to mental health hospitals.

31: PHYSICIANS' ROLE IN QUITTING AND PREVENTION OF SMOKING

Most people esteem their physicians highly. As a result, people are more likely to follow their advice than that of anyone else. When physicians tell their patients, "You really must stop smoking" and explain why that is so essential, patients are more likely to respond positively than to any other warning.

United States medical schools were slow to teach medical students how to advocate against nicotine dependence, how to treat it, and how to instruct their future patients on smoking cessation. But now, medical schools use a 4-year tobacco curriculum. So at last, physicians are well trained to play a key role in preventing their patients from starting to smoke, or else helping them to quit smoking. Excellent materials on how to quit are available free of charge for use by physicians in their offices, and for use in medical schools (see p.).

32: SOCIETAL PROBLEMS AND SOLUTIONS: HEAD START AND BEYOND

There are many notable exceptions to the rule that poor people tend to be poorly educated. But on average, poverty and scant education run together in being inversely related to smoking: the poorer or the less educated one is, the more likely one is to smoke. If poverty and poor education are reduced, so also is smoking, and along with these social evils also others such as drugs, gangs, and crime.

Long ago in my youth, I learned that the following saying was attributed to the Jesuits: "Give me your child until it is seven, and you can have it ever after" – meaning, once schooled in Catholicism early in life, the child will remain a good Catholic ever after. Sociological research agrees that the Jesuits had it right. Early experience is vital in determining a child's future. With this thought in mind, the Head Start Program began in the United States in 1965 as a major national program, under the direction of former Surgeon General Julius Richmond. It has proved valuable in preparing children aged 3 to 5 from poor districts for school, by accustoming them to an orderly classroom, and by teaching them that learning at school can be an enjoyable and challenging game. This prepares them to accept the future schooling that is vital if they are to grow up into adults who can hold down good jobs and earn good salaries.

The Head Start program succeeds by demanding high staffing: one qualified teacher and two aides per fifteen children. Still, after three decades, it became obvious that starting with 3 year olds was too late. So beginning in 1995, a new program, Early Head Start was added. It targets 1 to 3-year old children from disadvantaged homes, and provides assistance to their mothers. I would like to be able to report that this program also insists on teaching children only in English, for this is a vital skill for the children of immigrants. Sadly, I have been unable to confirm that a stress on teaching only in the state's official language is a firm requirement for either Head Start or Early Head Start.

Indeed in 2006, Jack Shonkoff, head of Harvard's Center on the Developing Child, said that early education should start at birth. So should efforts to protect the child against abuse, neglect, deep poverty, and maternal depression, all of which harm the child. Shonkoff believes that investing in babies and toddlers means spending much less later on crime and healthcare.[695] This makes good sense.

As of 2003, the U.S. budget for Head Start exceeded $6 billion per year, and it served 900,000 children from families at or below the Federal poverty line. Still, only about 40% of eligible 3- and 4-year olds could be accommodated. So 39 states supplemented Head Start by funding another 700,000 children. Early Head Start was funded at a level of approximately 10% of the funding of Head Start. There was opposition to the proposal that these programs should be administered by states rather than federally, since this would mean loss of federal supervision of the high standards of Head Start.

NCLB (No Child Left Behind) was the program that President Bush announced right after he took office in 2001, and Congress passed NCLB a year later. Its goal was to improve elementary and secondary schools, and to insure that no child is trapped in a failing school. Also, a major goal was to teach children to read in early grades. NCLB would be ideal if it extended Head Start's benefits to elementary and secondary schools, and were generously funded. But unlike Head Start, it curtails its outreach by requiring school districts to do much of the funding, and also penalizes schools that fail to meet its standards.

There is sound evidence that lowering class size raises the academic performance of younger students. Teachers can maintain discipline more easily, and give students more individual attention. Adequate funding for children's programs can benefit students for a lifetime. But to turn "No Child Left Behind" into reality by making the necessary funds available will take concerted and persistent lobbying at every level of government.

The disciplinary problems facing teachers in inner city schools in America can be enormous. Unruly students can wear down the teachers' spirits, and make it difficult to recruit new and competent ones. One way to ensure competent teachers are available is to contract them to receive their entire college tuition, if they will contract to teach in inner city schools for five years after they graduate – or else repay the financial aid for the years short of the contractual five years. In addition, teachers for inner city schools need to be trained in strategies for keeping discipline, and school administrators and parents must make every effort to give them full support in this quest, for students in inner city schools see drug lords riding around town in black Cadillac's and are not convinced that book learning will be helpful to them. In contrast, suburban schools have far fewer disciplinary problems.

A large infusion of funds is needed to improve the woes of schools in poverty-stricken areas. Such funds will allow additional training for teachers, a reduction in class size, and an increase in after-school and vacation programs. To relieve teachers of stress, persistent troublemakers should be placed in special classes or in special schools with hardened teachers.

Suburban elementary schools in America presently provide a large variety of indoor and outdoor recreational programs, which keep the children occupied after school and during vacations, especially during the long summer vacation. But schools in poverty-stricken areas, where such programs are most needed, lack the necessary funding. Indeed presently, federal and state funds for after-school programs and summer camps benefit only a fraction of impoverished youths in America.

For older youths, Work Start programs, funded from federal, state or local sources, help to finance work after school hours and during vacations. They keep youths off the streets and accustom them to the benefits of a working life–but the need for funds far outstrips their availability. This also holds for college-bound students who come from disadvantaged neighborhoods and need special coaching if they are to be accepted. But when an economic downturn occurs, all sources of funding are reduced. Then a lack of jobs for disadvantaged adolescents turns them loose on the streets. There, street-wise peers may introduce them first to cigarettes, then to marijuana, then to addictive hard drugs and alcohol, and show them that crime can pay. This we must not permit, for children are our most precious resource. Those nurtured by Head Start also should be nurtured in adolescence.

Black academics such as Henry Gates, Jr. believe that the youths of their community need to realign their self-perception. He says blacks slander themselves when they say that a black youth with a book is acting white. The black comic Bill Cosby insists that black teenagers should do their homework, stay in school, master English, and stop having babies. Why are he and Gates pilloried for "blaming the victim?" Dr. James Cromer, a black child psychiatrist at Yale, says that blacks are worse off than before the Brown vs. Board decision of 1954[696] that outlawed segregation in public schools, because blacks "have abandoned our own black traditional core values that sustained us through slavery and Jim Crow segregation." But despite the desegregation decision, fifty years later, Boston public schools were still largely segregated.[697]

Black youths believe that the easiest way to get ahead is to become an athlete, but the facts are that there 31,000 black physicians and 33,000 black lawyers, but only a total of 1,400 blacks in football, basketball and baseball. Dena Wallerson, a black academic, says that "we talk about leaving no child behind but the reality is that we are allowing our own children to be left behind." It not only be might be the fault of society, but also of blacks, that nearly one-third of black children are born into poverty.[698] One major detrimental factor is the large hole in the heart of too many black families: the father has moved out, in part to court a younger woman than his wife, and also because then the family can collect assistance funds from the state.[699] It is sad indeed that in black districts of Providence, R.I. and many other U.S. cities, 40% of black men had a criminal record and had lost their right to vote.[700]

It would be encouraging if I could conclude that the federal, state and city programs have helped to reduce the large divide between the living conditions, income, education, and degree of patriotism of the disadvantaged inner city dwellers as compared to suburban middle-class Americans, but that divide still exists.[701] The most positive conclusion I can draw is that lacking the above programs, the divide would be even greater, and disaffection of the disadvantaged from society would be even more worrisome.

Still, the above programs are all officially sponsored and funded. Is there nothing that the individual citizen can do to make the disadvantaged and immigrants feel accepted into society, treated well, and given their fair share of job opportunities and the chance for advancement? There certainly is. We should make a real effort to go out of our way to accept such people and treat them as well as those of our own group. Once people feel truly accepted and have a good job, they will overcome any disaffection, and become valuable, satisfied citizens.

Another national goal should be to reduce adult smoking. To achieve it, Congress and the states should generously fund antismoking education and media advertisements. It is even more vital to address the root of the problem, by greatly increasing the funding for educational and job programs for needy children over the entire age range from preschool to grade 12.

33: SMOKING AS A WORLDWIDE PROBLEM

To compensate for lower cigarette sales in the United States and other Western countries, and harassed by lawsuits, tobacco companies have formed multinational tobacco companies, which are rapidly expanding worldwide. By 1998 Philip Morris was profiting five times as much from overseas sales than from domestic ones. For of the world's 1.3 billion smokers, 80% live in areas other than North America and Western Europe. There, multinational tobacco companies use strategies that are now outlawed in most Western countries: advertising campaigns, sponsorships of sports events, and circumvention of laws that threaten tobacco sales, which the industry achieves by giving generous rewards to those who do its bidding6. As a result, the number of smokers in developing countries is exploding.

Because many health effects of smoking only surface decades after habitual smoking is begun, North America is experiencing an epidemic of smoking-related diseases, even though cigarette consumption is declining. Because the countries of the Caribbean and Latin America have a rising cigarette consumption, they are certain to experience similar epidemics in future decades. Still, most of these countries have instituted some beneficial reforms:

high taxes on tobacco products, restrictions on advertising, the plugging of loopholes in legislation, requirements for large health warnings in contrasting print on cigarette packs, strictly enforced age limits on access to tobacco products, school education on the health effects of smoking, fines for smoking in indoor public places, a public information campaign against smoking, class-action suits against tobacco companies, and the adoption of a unified program that includes the above features.

But by 2004, only Canada had used a unified anti-tobacco program, and employed it only until tobacco industry lobbying halted it.In most European countries, the percentage of smokers is higher than in the United States. Smoking is popular in the Czech Republic, where Philip Morris argued that the premature death of smokers is beneficial, since it saves its government between $24 million and $30 million on health care, housing, and pensions a year! In countries where smoking is common, many of the laws needed to decrease smoking have not been passed, or else are not enforced. But as of November 2005, the Irish Republic, Northern Ireland, Italy, Sweden, and Norway had passed Smokefree Workplace Laws. In Scotland and England, similar legislation was to go into force in 2006.

Smoking rates are especially high in Russia, China and Indonesia. China accounts for 20% of our globe's humanity, but the Chinese smoke 30% of the world's cigarettes. There, 63% percent of males and 4% of women are current smokers, and smokers expend on the average roughly 25% of their income on cigarettes. In Japan, the most common type of cancer in Japanese men changed from stomach cancer to lung cancer in 1998, and approximately 54% of men and 14% of women are smokers. In Vietnam 73% of men smoke, and they spend almost 25% of their annual income on cigarettes. But only 4% of Vietnamese women smoke.

Multinational corporations have made the sale of tobacco a global enterprise in which national borders are crossed and tobacco is smuggled to evade taxes. To reduce tobacco use worldwide, in 1999 the World Health Assembly of WHO began to negotiate FCTC–the Framework Convention on Tobacco Control. During the Clinton administration, the United States supported strong provisions for FCTC. But during the Bush administration the United States opposed the inclusion of vital public health provisions up until just days before the final vote on the FCTC treaty in May, 2003, when the U.S. reversed its stance.

The provisions of the treaty mirror those of the Warsaw Declaration for a Tobacco-Free Europe, adopted by 51 European countries in 2002. They bind participating countries to restrict advertising, raise tobacco taxes, require larger warnings on cigarette packages, and reduce secondhand smoke. To become effective, the treaty must be ratified by at least 40 nations. As of May 2004, only 27 nations had ratified it. If the United States were to do so, many other nations would follow.

34: AIR POLLUTION

My involvement with smoke abatement dates back to 1948, when I wrote "Pittsburgh Fights Smoke" for a British journal, *Smokeless Air* while in graduate school at Carnegie-Mellon University. The Smoky City, as Pittsburgh was aptly named, had just passed a smoke abatement ordinance that increased the amount of sunshine received during the next winter by 39%. I said that air pollution is a weed grown on industrial soil, and because a single weeding still leaves the roots in the earth, it must be constantly weeded out, and never given a chance to regrow. The long-term impact of Pittsburgh's smoke abatement ordinance is documented in the 2003 book edited by Joel Tarr, "Devastation and Renewal. An Environmental History of Pittsburgh and its Region." Further improvements have been achieved by burning natural gas and using diesel-electric rather than coal locomotives.

In the Briton of 1960, before the time when the heavy air pollution in its cities was fought vigorously and brought under control, the incidence of lung cancer in nonsmokers was twice as high in urban as in rural areas.[702] In the United States of 1979, nonsmokers who lived in urban rather than rural areas had only a slightly higher percentage of deaths from lung cancer. But for smokers, this differential was much higher.[703]

Based on evidence of respiratory illness and early death, EPA (Environmental Pollution Agency) established new air quality standards in 1997 under the federal Clean Air Act. It based these standards on fine particles (PM2.5- particles that measure under 2.5 microns [millionth of a meter] in diameter). For only such tiny particles (less than one-thirtieth the thickness of a human hair) can penetrate into the minute airways of the lung that lead to the air-sacks, in which expired air is exchanged for fresh inspired air. The Act specified that averaged over a year, the concentration of PM2.5 particles may not exceed 15 micrograms per cubic meter, nor 65 micrograms per cubic meter on any one day.

Motivated by public awareness of the dangers of air pollution and by the EPA limits, the density of fine airborne particles as measured in 51 major United States metropolitan centers decreased by roughly one-third between 1980 and 2000; and the reduction was highest in the cities that had the most air pollution. By year 2000, fine particles averaged approximately 13 micrograms per cubic meter of air in United States cities, with a range from 6 to 19 micrograms. Although challenged by industry groups and three states, the Supreme Court upheld the EPA standards in 2001.[704]

In 2002, the American Cancer Society published the results of a carefully controlled long-term study of the effects of air pollution on half a million people. It concluded that for each increase of 10 micrograms of fine particles per cubic meter of air as measured in representative samples, deaths from lung cancer increased by 8%, and deaths from cardiopulmonary diseases increased by 6%. On the average, living in an urban environment in the United States increases the risk of death from lung cancer and from cardiopulmonary diseases by roughly 11% and 8%, respectively.[705] These risks are similar to those for nonsmokers who live with one or more smokers for many years, and thus are constantly exposed to secondhand cigarette smoke (see next chapter).

In December 2003, a federal appeals court denied the administration's proposal to permit thousands of aging power plants to upgrade their plants without installing modern pollution controls.[706] This weakening of the Clean Air Act would have substantially increased air pollution and with it, its contribution to the causation of cancer and cardiopulmonary diseases. Further, the main pollutant emitted by power plants is soot, and according to NASA scientists, soot is responsible for causing as much as one quarter of all observed global warming.[707]

As of February, 2004, the American Lung Association called for strengthening EPA's Clean Air Act of 1997, so as to prevent an estimated 15,000 premature deaths each year. The standards proposed would tighten the EPA standards in a way that would protect those most sensitive to air pollution. These include infants and children, especially those with asthma, the elderly, and people heart disease, lung disease, and diabetes. Finally, it was disconcerting to hear from Bruce Barcott, writing in the New York Times Magazine of April 4, 2004, that the current administration has "quietly–and radically–transformed the nation's clean-air policy" to its great detriment.

The two types of lung cancer from which heavy smokers are most likely to die are *squamous cell* and *small cell (oat cell)* carcinoma of the lung. It is worrying that a third type of lung cancer, *adenocarcinoma,* which is far less common in heavy smokers, has been rising from about 12% in 1965 to about three times this percentage thirty years later. But it is possible that this increase has been due largely to improvements pathologists have made in classifying lung cancers, rather than to increased exposure to environmental carcinogens other than tobacco smoke.[708]

35: ASBESTOS, SILICA, DUSTS, AND VOLATILE CHEMICALS

Asbestos was mentioned by a student of Aristotle around 300 BCE as a substance that when doused with oil and set on fire, burned without being harmed. Its name "*asbestinon*" (unquenchable) was mentioned around 50 CE in Pliny's book, *Natural History*. Its fire-resisting properties eventually led to its widespread use.[709]

We have long known that the inhalation of asbestos fibers is the main cause of mesothelioma, an otherwise rare cancer that originates in the lining cells of the pleura. This is the membrane that envelops the lung and lines the cavity in which the lung lies; it also lines the abdominal cavity, and covers many of its contents. About 80% of mesotheliomas arise in people exposed to asbestos either because they live close to an asbestos mine, or because they live in a home into which asbestos fibers are brought in, clinging to the work clothes of kin or partner who are exposed to asbestos at their place of work.

To a lesser extent, asbestos also causes other types of lung cancer, and cancers of the gastrointestinal tract and larynx. Further, exposure to asbestos causes asbestosis (a type of lung congestion specifically caused by asbestos), and various benign lung disorders. When asbestos is the cause of mesothelioma, both normal lung tissue and mesothelioma tissue can contain 100 times as many asbestos fibers as present in unexposed lung tissue.[710]

Asbestos fibers are composed of long chains of silicon and oxygen atoms. They are fireproof, stronger than steel, and resilient. As a result, asbestos was used for a wide variety of purposes: fire insulation, brake linings, spray on coatings to protect steel structures against buckling during fires, and for thousands of other uses. By 1973, the annual production of asbestos in the United States stood close to one million tons.[633]

But by the mid-1960s, it had become known that the extremely fine size of asbestos fibers made them dangerous to inhale, and soon it was found asbestos fibers can cause cancer. By 1979, when Irving Selikoff and the ACS' Cuyler Hammond chaired a conference on asbestos at the New York Academy of Sciences, it was known that its carcinogenicity depends on its particular type and size when suspended in air. If the diameter of particles is more than 3 micra (millionths of a meter) in size, about half of the asbestos fibers do not penetrate into the lung, but instead are swallowed. As the diameter of the particles increases above 3 micra, their penetration deep into the lung diminishes rapidly.[711]

Of the two main types of asbestos, amphiboles and chrysotile asbestos, the former is more dangerous, because the fibers are straighter and thus can penetrate deeper into the lung. Chrysotile fibers are less dangerous, because they tend to occur in bundles, and are also more soluble. However, processing can vastly increase their danger, because it breaks up the bundles of fibers into shorter and thinner fibers that can penetrate deeper into the lung. This explains why asbestos used to manufacture textiles or insulation is tenfold to fiftyfold more dangerous than asbestos that is mined or milled. The risk of lung cancer in asbestos workers is directly proportional to the cumulative length of the exposure to asbestos fibers.[110]

Once the danger that asbestos poses became understood, the EPA banned its use. Although that ban was lifted in 1991, the use of asbestos is now restricted to a few specialty applications, such as protection of the steel casing of space rockets. A vast program of removing or at least encasing all asbestos in public and private buildings and schools has been very nearly completed.

There is now a consensus that asbestos acts in synergism with tobacco smoke to cause lung cancer. An example will illustrate the threat that synergism poses. Suppose a nonsmoker who is long-term asbestos worker has fivefold the risk of lung cancer compared to a nonsmoker in the general population. Suppose also that the average long-term smoker who is not an asbestos worker has a twentyfold higher risk of lung cancer than a nonsmoker. Since the dose-response curves for lung cancer that results from asbestos working and from smoking are linear, then if an asbestos worker (with a fivefold risk) was also a smoker (with a twentyfold risk), then if these two risks were merely *additive*, an asbestos worker who smoked would have a twenty-fivefold risk of lung cancer. Then because of synergism, the risk is not twenty-fivefold but 5 x 20 or hundredfold higher, compared to someone who is neither an asbestos worker nor a smoker! Thus, synergism has a very potent effect.[625]

The knowledge that smoking and asbestos acted in synergism was used by asbestos workers in December 2000 to sue tobacco companies, which had long been aware of the special risk that smoking poses for asbestos workers, but had failed to warn them against smoking. Beginning in December, 2002, Halliburton Company, an industrial giant, agreed to pay about $4 billion to settle a class action suit by hundreds of thousands of people exposed to asbestos while working at plants that produced asbestos, or at places such as steel mills, where asbestos was used.[712] In the same month, Hartford Financial Services, a large insurance company, paid $1.5 billion to settle asbestos claims.[713] As a result of such lawsuits, considerable more than 70 companies went out of business. In July, 2003, the Senate Judiciary Committee approved a bill that would end all asbestos lawsuits by creating an industry-financed trust fund to compensate people with asbestos-related illnesses.[714] But on April 22, 2004 the New York Times reported scant hope that legislators could reach agreement on the problem of what constitutes fair compensation for the 200,000 or more asbestos lawsuits pending in state and federal courts. According to the New Work Times of May 18, 2004, some estimates claimed that companies had already paid $70 billion in asbestos claims, with insurance companies paying about 40% of this amount.

Silica has only tangentially been blamed for causing cancer. Its most serious hazard is the causation of silicosis, a chronic lung disease characterized by scarring of the lung and shortness of breath, which can exacerbate and eventually lead to death. It is caused by the inhalation of fine airborne crystalline silica or quartz dust. For at least 70 years, silicosis has been recognized as a hazard for coal miners, since they must often drill through rock to reach the coal seams, and inhale the fine rock dust that their drills aerosolize (suspend in the air). But it is only within the last few years that lawsuits against companies that exposed workers to silica or quartz dust have escalated. As of 2003, one large insurer faced over 30,000 silica-related claims. Most of these claims were for the causation of silicosis, not of cancer.[715]

Other respiratory carcinogens. A 1999 report by Chatzis and coworkers from Greece showed that the occupational inhalation of other substances can add to the risk of lung cancer produced by smoking. These "cocarcinogens" (additive carcinogens) include wood dusts (inhaled in carpentry and construction work), benzidine (from textile and dye industries), shale and mineral oils (from petroleum and oil industries), and coal tar and soot (from coke ovens and metal casting furnaces). After pooling data for all cases of occupational exposures due to these substances (that included asbestos) and removing the effects of smoking by compensating for it, the above occupational exposures trebled the risk of lung cancer.[716]

Finally, there is a consensus that benzene inhalation causes leukemia, even though there is controversy on whether low levels of benzene pose a risk (Hayes *et al.*, J. Toxicology and Environmental Health, 2000).

36: RADON AND NUCLEAR REACTORS

Radon is an invisible and odorless radioactive gas that emanates naturally from earth and rocks the world over. It is of concern, because it can seep into a house through cracks in the foundation and joints. We now believe that it is the second leading cause of lung cancer, which causes about 9% of lung cancer deaths – vastly fewer than smoking.[717]

Radon derives from the element uranium-238, which is very widely distributed in the earth's crust and rocks. Uranium-238 is unstable and decays (decomposes) slowly in a stepwise fashion into 13 different elements, one of which is radon. Radon emits alpha rays that have a short range but are powerful, so they can mutate cells and cause cancer. But radon is also unstable and decays into other radioactive elements. These include the radio-isotope (an element with an unstable nucleus that emits radiation as it decays to another nuclear state) polonium-218, which is not a gas but a solid that also produces alpha rays, and proves to be main cause of injury to the lung.[718] For polonium-218–together with other solid radioisotopes produced in the decay chain that starts with uranium-238 and ends with inert lead–sticks to dust particles that are then inhaled and deposited in the bronchial tree, where they can cause serious damage.[719]

Radon became of concern in the 1950s, when the high incidence of lung cancer in uranium miners first was traced to the high levels of radon in uranium mines that supplied this ore for nuclear reactors and atomic bombs. Several studies have shown that the incidence of lung cancer in uranium miners rises in direct proportion to the radon concentration in their mines, and to the time-period for which the miners were exposed to it. Studies have shown that this holds true even for miners with relatively low cumulative radon exposures, such as exposures only three to six times higher than the lifetime exposure to radon in an average U.S. house.[110] Further, four sets of experts have reviewed the data on radon inhalation: ICRP (the International Commission on Radiological Protection), the National Academy of Sciences committees BEIR IV and BEIR VI, and the Office of Radiation Programs of the U.S. EPA (Environmental Protection Agency). The reports from all four of these sources concluded that the percentage of exposed people who developed lung cancer was directly proportional to the concentration of radon inhaled, multiplied by the time period for which inhalation occurred. As for the magnitude of the risk from radon, the above reports all varied in their estimates of how many deaths from lung cancer were really caused by radon in the United States. The EPA estimate of 20,000 deaths per year was criticized for being too high. The estimate of 13,000 deaths per year made by NRC was then reevaluated by a panel headed by Jonathan Samet (the chairperson of BEIR VI), and the NRC estimate was found to be three times too high for adults and five times too high for children.[720] But more recent studies have reinforced the previous conclusions.[641]

The data on cancer causation by radon sparked the Indoor Radon Act of 1988 that set a national long-term goal of achieving indoor radon levels similar to outdoor levels. It allowed EPA to set the level of tolerable radon concentration in a building at 150 Becquerel (a unit of radioactivity) per cubic meter, a level that has not been changed since 1991. At that time, testing a house for radon cost between $10 and $30, and the cost of reducing elevated radon levels below 150 Bq/m³ ranged from $500 to $1500 for most houses. EPA has estimated that there may be several million homes in the U.S. with radon levels above 150 Bq/m³, and more than 100,000 homes with levels above 750 Bq/m³.[721]

The extrapolation of data obtained for miners exposed to high dose levels of radon to the low levels that exist in homes has been sharply criticized. But this was justified by Richard Guimond, who reported that the risk from long-term exposures to low radon levels was greater than the risk from short exposures to high radon levels.[645] Further, Pershagen and coworkers showed that the low levels of radon inhalation incurred in homes, whether alone or in addition to smoking, increased the risk of lung cancer. [722] This was confirmed by Darby *et al.* in 1998. In 1998, Richard Doll reported that the risk of lung cancer from radon exposure in English homes agreed with the above risks.

UNDERSTANDING ABBREVIATIONS FOR RADIATION UNITS			
pico-	(p)	one quadrillionth	(10^{-12})
nano-	(n)	one trillionth	(10^{-9})
micro-	(μ)	one millionth	(10^{-6})
milli-	(m)	one thousandth	(10^{-3})
centi-	(c)	one hundredth	(10^{-2})
kilo-	(k)	one thousand times	1,000
mega-	(M)	one million times	1,000,000
giga-	(G)	one trillion times	1,000,000,000

WHAT RADIATION UNITS MEASURE[723]

WHAT IS MEASURED UNITS INTERRELATIONSHIP

Radiation emanating from a radioactive source <u>curie</u> (<u>Ci</u>) <u>Becquerel</u> (<u>Bq</u>) 1 Ci=37billion Bq (The Chernobyl meltdown released 81 MCi of radioactive cesium).

Radiation absorbed <u>rad</u> (radiation *by body tissues* absorbed dose) <u>gray</u> (<u>Gy</u>) 1 Gy = 100 rad (Radiation from nature [*e.g.* cosmic rays] is 0.12 rad per year).

Personal risk from <u>rem</u> (radiation equivalent man) *absorbed radiation* <u>Sievert</u> (<u>Sv</u>) 1 Sv = 100 rem (Radiation from nature–*e.g.* cosmic rays–is 0.3 rem per year).

Relationship between radiation absorbed by the body and risk is: rad x Q = rem, and gray x Q = Sievert. Q is a Quality Factor that depends on the radiation's ability to transfer energy to the body. The Q value for natural radiation is roughly 0.3/0.12=2.5

According to Doll *et al.*, radon in homes in the United Kingdom causes about one in twenty lung cancers, most of which occur in combination with smoking. The risk of lung cancer from radon was "about the size that has been postulated on the basis of studies of miners exposed to radon."[724] Regarding the risk to *nonsmokers*, a review in 2002 concluded that the available data are limited, and further study was needed.[725]

In summary, it is now firmly established that radon inhalation can cause lung cancer, and that its effect is greatly increased by its synergism with smoking. Owners should test their houses for radon, as should potential buyers–especially if their house is built directly on rock or shattered rock without an intervening air space. A simple, inexpensive do-it-yourself test kit is available at most hardware stores. If the radon level is above 150 Bq/m^3, appropriate action should be taken to reduce it. At fairly low levels of radon, this is can easily be done by installing an exhaust fan in the basement. At higher levels, cracks in the foundation and joints should be sealed.

Radon is also absorbed by and released from water. So in 1999, EPA asked states to limit the concentration of radon in water to 11 Becquerel per liter. But for homes where ventilation had been installed, RPA suggested that a radon level of 150 Becquerel per liter of water was tolerable.

In 2003, Norway decided to protect its citizens by measuring radon levels in all houses and ground floor apartments over the next decade. If the radon level was over 200 Bq/m^3, it would be reduced below it by installing ventilation and repairing cracks in the foundation. Norwegian scientists estimated that saving one life by this policy would cost roughly $1 million. Norwegians are to be congratulated for setting the example of valuing life high, and be willing to pay enough to save it.[726] More information on radon is available at www.epa.gov/radon, and a 15-page "Citizen's Guide to Radon" is available by calling 800-SOS-Radon.

Nuclear reactors are regulated by the NRC. As of 2005, there were 104 plants licensed to produce nuclear power in the United States. There were 69 plants that operated Pressurized Water Reactors, 35 Boiling Water Reactors, as well as 52 research and test reactors that were under the guidance of NRC.

The meltdown of a nuclear reactor releases many radioactive elements into the atmosphere, of which iodine-131 is by far of most immediate concern in a large area downwind of the reactor. During the initial catastrophe, iodine-131 will be inhaled by people located immediately downwind from the reactor. Unless there are unusual weather conditions, exposure will diminish with distance from the reactor. Iodine-131 localizes in the thyroid, where it can cause dysfunction and/or cancer. The effects of iodine-131 inhalation are vastly reduced by taking non-radioactive iodine tablets, which contain many times the quantities of the radioactive iodine that are inhaled. Because the thyroid gland absorbs radioactive and non-radioactive iodine with identical avidity, a large intake of non-radioactive iodine ensures that only a tiny fraction of radioactive iodine is taken up by the thyroid. However, the major intake of iodine-131 (and of the many other radioactive materials) occurs through the food chain. The radioactive material falls out onto grass, is eaten by cows, and contaminates their milk. The risk that iodine-131 poses for thyroid cancer is highest for a newborn child and falls off progressively with age: the risk for a newborn child is one hundred times larger than for a 50-year old person.

Since the half-life (the time required to lose 50% of its radioactivity) of iodine-131 is only 8 days, it is a significant hazard only for about three months after a meltdown, and taking iodine tablets during this period provides highly effective protection. While a meltdown releases far smaller amounts of other radioactive atoms, some of these decay much more slowly than iodine-131. They are also of concern, because they might increase the natural susceptibility to cancer of certain human organs.

The future of nuclear power was projected in detail in the splendid September 2006 issue of the Scientific American. Nuclear power plants are only one of the many technologies needed to keep the emission of carbon dioxide from spiraling out of control and hastening global warming. To displace coal, Socolow and Pacala suggested that the 2006 output of nuclear power be tripled.[727] Further, Deutch and Moniz argued that nuclear power could stave off more than a billion tons of carbon emissions annually.[728]

The critical issues in expanding the construction of nuclear power plants are first – a location far from population; second – a design to minimize the possibility of a meltdown; third – the processing of fuel to use it economically, to guard against its use for atomic bomb production and to facilitate its disposal; fourth – a plan for long-term storage of spent fuel; fifth – the guarding of nuclear power plants against attack by terrorists; and sixth – economics that justify their construction and operation.

First, as regard location, after previous meltdown incidents a nuclear power plant should be built far removed from population centers. Second, as regards reactor design, the dominant design is the light-water reactor that uses ordinary water rather than heavy water, which contains the hydrogen isotope deuterium. After a cessation of reactor building in the U.S. since the meltdown incidents, generation III+ light-water reactors are planned. These are reactors that incorporate better fuel technology, with advanced features beyond those in generation III reactors that already possess "passive safety" – the ability to shut down automatically in case of an accident. Globally since the year 2000, 20,000 megawatts of nuclear capacity have come online. At this point in time, it seems that the generation III+ design is most likely to be built in the U.S.[653]

As of 2006, generation IV reactors were still in the experimental stage. They included pebble-bed nuclear power reactors, a new design claimed to be meltdown-proof (MIT Technology Review, March, 2004). If this claim proves to be true, then pebble bed reactors would compete with generation III+ light-water reactors. Pebble bed reactors have the advantage that instead of building a massive 1,000 megawatt plant, modules each producing only 100 megawatts could be built, later supplemented by additional modules as required.[653]

Third, the processing of fuel remains a major problem. It must be used economically, it must be guarded against use for atom bomb production, and the disposal of spent nuclear fuel still remains a major problem. In an "open fuel cycle" also called a "once-through" cycle, the uranium fuel is burned once in a reactor and then stored. In contrast, France currently uses a "closed fuel cycle" in which plutonium is separated from spent fuel and then burned in a reactor. It is even possible to burn virtually all very long-lived radioactive elements in a "fast reactor" of a suitable type.[729] But all reprocessing is expensive and highly dangerous to personnel, and the plutonium produced must be guarded against its diversion to make nuclear weapons. For this reason, U.S. experts prefer the once-through cycle.[653]

Fourth, the long-term storage of spent fuel has proven to be a major problem, since long-lived radioisotopes such as plutonium remain highly radioactive for thousands of years. Most U.S. nuclear power plants currently store their spent fuel rods temporarily in water tanks on their plant site. DOE (Department of Energy) has spent years preparing to bury nuclear waste in a deep salt depository at Yucca Mountain in Nevada. But there is fear that the planned containers might leak, and thereby contaminating underground water with radioactivity and carrying it into the local water supply.[730] Also, Yucca Mountain has more water running within it than was anticipated, so it remains uncertain whether NRC will license it. Even if licensed, it may not be ready to accept waste for several years.

In contrast, Finland is planning to complete a storage facility 500 meters underground by 2020, with spent fuel encased in iron canisters sealed within a copper shell that is intended to resist corrosion.[653] One strategy that is advocated to deal with high-level radioactive waste in the US for the next few decades is to store it in huge casks in a few high-security lots in remote areas.[731]

There is also ongoing research on disintegrating the long-lived atoms of radioactive waste. As of 2006, DOE was funding research on two different methods for recycling much of the 2,000 tons of highly radioactive spent fuel that U.S. atomic power plants produce each year. Success in this area would reduce the heat buildup in stored spent fuel, and permit it to be burned again in atomic power plants.[732] A previous attempt to do this task by firing protons produced by a synchrotron into the heart of a nuclear reactor[733] is effective to deal with small amounts of spent fuel, but is probably unsuitable to be scaled up to degrade large amounts of high-level nuclear waste.

Fifth, there is the problem of guarding nuclear power plants against attack by terrorists. Terrorists might try to cause a meltdown, or to steal fuel rods. A meltdown would be catastrophic, and even a single spent fuel rod could be divided into sufficiently many parts, to provide the radioactive material needed to make many "dirty bombs." In this age of terrorism, the adequate guarding of nuclear power plants is therefore essential. But as mentioned below, modern society also deploys a very large number of radioactive sources that could be used in a dirty bomb.

Sixth, since money is the root of all evil, economics are likely to determine, whether more nuclear power plants will be built in the U.S. In 2003, an MIT study estimated the cost of electricity produced by a new light-water reactor at 6.7 cents per kilowatt-hour. This compares with 4.2 cents for a new coal plant and 5.8 cents for a new gas-powered plant. To overcome the hurdle of restarting nuclear power plant manufacture after a long Sabbath, the Energy Policy Act of 2005 included a powerful incentive: a tax credit of 1.8 cents per kilowatt-hour for the first 6,000 mega-watts of new plants that go into operation.[653]

37: DIRTY BOMBS

Dirty bombs and atomic bombs are totally different weapons. A dirty bomb (also called a Radiological Dispersal Device or RDD) is a primitive weapon that incorporates one or more radioactive materials with a high explosive such as dynamite, and is vastly easier to assemble than an atomic bomb. In contrast, the construction of an atomic bomb requires highly refined fissile materials such as uranium-235 or plutonium-239. To produce these, a nation must mount a vast expensive and sophisticated industrial effort. The bomb must contain an explosive trigger that fires the separate fissile components together, to produce the critical mass required for an atomic explosion. On the other hand, little expertise is needed to explode an assembled atomic bomb.

The blast effects of an atomic bomb are measured in terms of *kilotons* (and for *hydrogen bombs*, even in *megatons*) of conventional explosives. Thus, these bombs are thousands or even millions of times more powerful than a ton of a conventional high explosive. The runaway nuclear reaction in an exploding atomic bomb releases a wind blast of hurricane-force that can blow down buildings, as well as a searing heat wave that incinerates its surroundings, and an intense blast of radiation. The intensity of the last two of these effects decreases in step with the square of the distance from the epicenter of the explosion. Depending on that distance, the heat wave may kill victims instantly or else slowly, while the radiation may kill within hours or weeks. For those further from the epicenter, radiation causes an excess risk of cancer that depends on the dose absorbed by the victims. The incidence of leukemia in excess of that in unirradiated people begins to appear a year or two after irradiation and then continues to the end of the lifespan, while an excess incidence of solid cancers begins about a decade after irradiation, and continues to the end of life. A nuclear explosion releases a cloud of radioactive particles into the atmosphere where they contaminate areas downwind from ground zero, and is powerful enough to propel tiny radioactive particles into the stratosphere from which they fall out over the entire surface of the earth over the next two or three years. Additional facts about nuclear bombs are given following the present discussion of dirty bombs.

In contrast, the explosive force of a *dirty bomb* is equal to that of a conventional bomb that contains the same amount of the same explosive. Thus, a dirty bomb does not produce either a hurricane-force blast of air, a heat wave, an intense blast of radiation, or contamination of the stratosphere. Its (immediate) lethal effects depend only on its conventional explosive, not on its content of radioactive material.

The degree to which the radioactive material contained in a dirty bomb contaminates its surroundings depends first of all on the quantity and type of radioactive material, and of conventional high explosive that it contains, secondly on the wind and weather conditions, and thirdly on its location when detonated.[734] All these variables are critical, but most important is the amount and type of radioactive material dispersed by the bomb, its half-life, its biological effects when inhaled or ingested, and how long it is allowed to remain on streets and buildings before they are decontaminated, and thereby cause whole body irradiation to people exposed to it.

Regarding the disruption caused by a dirty bomb, The NRC says that a single bomb could contaminate several city blocks.[660] A spokesperson for the Federation of American Scientists–which tends to be alarmist – testified on this question before the Senate in March, 2002. He said that tens of city blocks could be contaminated at a level that would require evacuation.[735] But it must be emphasized that this is merely a guesstimate.

For terrorists to explode such a weapon among civilians would show an utterly despicable disregard for humane considerations. For the youngest of children would suffer by far the greatest harm from inhaling the radioactive aerosol that it would produce, and from the exposure to radioactive particles deposited on the ground and buildings. At the time of writing (2014), terrorists have not yet exploded such an inhumane device.

The most harmful effect of the explosion of a dirty bomb would be to create panic. The fear and disruption of civic life generated would be far greater than justified by the severity of injuries from exposure to radiation. Unfortunately, rationality does not always remove fear. Since pictures of the victims of the two atomic bomb explosions in Japan were widely displayed in U.S. media, in the popular mind radiation exposure is linked to horrific injuries. Because our senses cannot detect radiation, it is common to view it as sinister, and to believe that no amount of radiation is safe. For this reason, after a dirty bomb is exploded, the challenge for radiation experts will be to convince the public that their assessment of the radiation danger is credible, for it may be far smaller than generally supposed.[736]

The public will be more likely to believe official bulletins on the dangers estimated to have been incurred after the explosion of a dirty bomb, if the public is already educated on what levels of radiation exposure are almost harmless, and what levels are dangerous. In any case, a national campaign is needed to convince the public that prompt decontamination is necessary for people who have been exposed downwind from the explosion of a dirty bomb, and if necessary, to justify the closing of streets and the evacuation of buildings in the vicinity of the explosion. Also, the public needs to be given accurate data on what does and what does not constitute a tolerable level of radiation exposure over a stated period of time, and needs to be given clear directions on what to do if a dirty bomb is exploded. Government agencies have published excellent reports that cover practically all aspects of dirty bombs, but as of 2014, such an information campaign has not been implemented, perhaps because the threat level is not severe.

Still, terrorists have been active in the U.S. In 2002, Jose Padilla was arrested in for involvement with al-Qa'ida in planning a dirty bomb attack. In 2003, the BBC (British Broadcasting Corporation) reported that British agents who had infiltrated al-Qa'ida training camps in Afghanistan discovered radioactive materials, and training manuals that described how best to use dirty bombs.[737] In January 2005, the FBI launched a massive manhunt for six illegal immigrants suspected of planning to explode a dirty bomb.[738] In October 2005, President Bush declared that ten terrorist attacks of various types had been foiled within the U.S.[739]

In the entire world, there were 175 cases of incidents involving the smuggling or attempted procurement of radioactive material during the decade preceding 2002. In addition, radioactive material disappeared after the chaotic fragmentation of the Soviet Union. Further, the IAEA (International Atomic Energy Agency) has reported that the "materials needed to build a 'dirty bomb' can be found in almost any country in the world, and more than 100 countries may have inadequate control and monitoring programs necessary to prevent or even detect the theft of these materials."[740] Finally, a member of Harvard University's Belfer Center for Science and International Affairs was quoted in 2002 in the journal *Science* as saying that there are literally millions of radiological sources in the world that could be used in a dirty bomb.[741]

In the U.S., businesses and research facilities have lost track of 1,500 pieces of equipment with radioactive parts. The NRC calls these and other sources outside official control "orphaned" radioactive sources. But it is even of more concern that radioactive materials could be stolen from many facilities: hospitals that use radioactive sources such as cobalt-60 for therapy of cancer patients, food irradiation plants, academic and industrial research laboratories that use radioactive materials, nuclear power plants, high-level radioactive waste presently stored within the sites of 70 nuclear power plants as well as at commercial and army sites,[742] and in trucks that transport radioactive sources.[743] Still, in 2004 NRC (Nuclear Regulatory Commission) claimed that only a single high-risk radioactive source had been stolen and not recovered in the U.S.[660]

The best responses to the threat of dirty bombs include the detection, infiltration and dismantling of terrorist cells both in the U.S. and worldwide. Certainly, potential terrorists should be denied entrance to the U.S. These measures are currently being pursued in the U.S. by Homeland Security, and by foreign governments endangered by terrorist organizations.

Regarding the importation of radioactive material, it is essential to detect and confiscate illicit materials that could be used to make dirty bombs. This can be done by installing radiation monitoring equipment both in the U.S. and overseas at seaports, airfields and borders, as well as by monitoring the buildings of suspected organizations and the homes of individual suspects. In April 2006, Homeland Secretary Chertoff said that since the 9/11 attack of 2001, by the end of 2006 the U.S. would have invested $9 billion in port security. By 2006, about 200 radiation monitors had been installed at ports and were screening about 70% of incoming cargo. But only about 5% of all shipping containers were being inspected visually before leaving a foreign port. Still, members of Congress wanted to have radiation screening of all shipping containers, and improvement in the system used to decide which containers were to be opened and inspected with hand-held radiation monitors.[744]

The most likely place that terrorists might choose to explode a dirty bomb might be the center of a large U.S. city such as New York, Washington, Los Angeles, or Chicago. However, many other cities might be on the terrorists' list. Judging from 9/11/01, a terrorist group might well aim to achieve maximum disruption by setting off dirty bombs simultaneously in several U.S. cities.

As to the effectiveness of radiation monitoring, some of the radiation monitors tested by the Department of Homeland Security failed to identify certain radioactive materials. These detectors ranged from the size of a steam iron to the size of a two-door Jeep. Hopefully, the next generation of detectors will have sufficient discrimination to identify radiation sources without the need to open shipping containers.[745] But there are serious obstacles to overcome. For instance, a lead shield could be used to hide nuclear materials from detection.[746] Further, the materials in atom bombs – highly enriched uranium or weapons-grade plutonium – are much less radioactive than the radioactive elements or isotopes that could be used in a dirty bomb, and thus are difficult to discover except with neutron detectors.[747]

The success of radiation detection equipment at custom stations and ports will also hinge on effective intelligence that will warn authorities that certain cargos require careful scrutiny. But a terrorist also might exploit the long distances between various legal points of entry. Also, the nation's ports were designed to speed commerce, not to provide security, and their staff is often overwhelmed by the quantity of imports.[673]

Internally absorbed radioisotopes can remain in the body for long periods of time and pose long-term hazards. Thus, the personnel of monitoring teams should wear protective masks when entering contaminated areas, and trucks carrying filtering masks should drive to those areas, to distribute t5hem to those exposed and protect them from inhaling radioactive particles while they flee from contaminated areas as rapidly as possible. In contrast, external radiation is absorbed by the whole body only during the brief period during which civilians or radiation monitors stay in the contaminated areas that have not yet been decontaminated.

In terms of preparedness, it is not sufficient that there is federal preparedness, for bombs could be exploded simultaneously in several cities. Thus, every city in the United States should have monitoring equipment for identifying the radioisotopes and radioactive elements that a dirty bomb could disseminate, and personnel should be trained in its use, and also in monitoring and decontaminating people, streets and buildings, for this would be essential after the explosion of a dirty bomb. The same personnel should also be trained for action should the unthinkable happen – the explosion of an atomic bomb. In addition, they should be trained for the very different detection equipment and decontamination protocol that would be needed after the explosion of bombs that contain chemical or biological toxins, or else infectious biologic agents such as smallpox. Quite different types of protective clothing and breathing masks should be available to safeguard against bioterrorism employing toxins or infectious agents.[748] *Preparedness requires creation of a disaster command center* that will coordinate the team-work between the several disparate entities involved in any disaster, whatever its nature – be it caused by terrorists, war, or natural disasters such as earthquakes, volcanic eruptions, floods, tornadoes, hurricanes, tidal waves, or even the landing of a comet. The entities and capabilities involved would include:

1. Equipment to permit direct communication to local, state and national governments.

2. Specialists trained and practiced in monitoring, removing and disposing of radiologic, chemical, biological and infectious agents. Depending on the agent, very different strategies and equipment will be required to decontaminate people, streets, and buildings.

3. Specialists in communication to crowds, and control of crowds.

4. Direct links to local police and firefighters.

5. Direct links to local power, gas, and phone companies.

6. Direct links to local and national radio and TV stations.

7. A national network of links to other disaster command centers, so that outside help could be summoned quickly.

8. A network of cyberlinks provided by volunteers.

9. Training of volunteers to form a corps similar to the Home Guard that was formed in Britain during the second World War.

Annual drills would be necessary to familiarize participants with their detection equipment, and practice concerted and swift action to respond to a disaster. Such a drill was run in San Diego in August 2006, but involved only a few of the resources listed above. However, a unique feature of this exercise was the use of Microsoft's "Simple Sharing Extensions" system by several large software companies. It enabled them to share a single set of digital satellite maps, which were continually updated for event data relayed by emergency workers throughout the San Diego area.[749]

Injury from the radiation dispersed by an explosion of a radioactive device will be minor, if the response teams act swiftly. This will be critical for minimizing its consequences. To do so, team members need to know the highest level of radiation exposure that they can tolerate without unacceptable risks to their future health, or they will hesitate to act. Since the radiation exposure is the product of the rate at which radiation is emitted and the time for which it is absorbed, team members can adjust the time they stay in the contaminated area, so that they will not exceed receiving the permissible level of radiation exposure. The radiation levels in the buildings near the blast should be monitored, to decide if the people who live or work there should be evacuated for a period of time depending on the intensity of the radiation and on its half-life.

For response team personnel, the highest tolerable limit of radiation exposure specified by EPA in consultation with NRC is 5 rem per year. A rem stands for radiation equivalent man. It is the biologically effective radiation dose that results from absorbing a physical radiation dose of one rad (a unit of radiation dose).

For the civilian population, the present EPA guidelines specify that evacuation is mandatory if the projected external radiation dose is greater than 5 rem per year, and evacuation should be considered if the external dose is 1–5 rem.[750] The depth of penetration into the body of radiation absorbed by the body from external sources such as radioactive dust lying on a street or deposited on buildings will depend on the nature of the radioactive material. But the risks it poses will probably be greater if it is inhaled or ingested. These risks depend on the quantity of the material deposited internally and on the type and halflife of radiation it emits. These risks must be assessed, and people in danger treated by appropriate means.

What should be done immediately after a dirty bomb attack?[751] Response team personnel should assemble rapidly at their headquarters, don protective clothing and masks, and use vans equipped with the necessary radiological measuring instruments to drive close to the site of the explosion. There, they should rapidly assess the nature of the radioactive substances disseminated, and the dose distribution at various distances from the epicenter. Next, they should direct people who thought they had been contaminated to a medical facility that had been previously selected, prepared and adequately equipped to triage (sort apart) the vast number of minimally exposed or unexposed "worried well" from those in need of urgent care. To ease their mind, the worried well might be advised to discard their outer clothing and wash all exposed skin, while those shown by radiation monitors to be seriously contaminated should shower, be given uncontaminated clothing, and if not experiencing acute radiation symptoms – nausea, vomiting, weakness, abdominal distress, dizziness (unfortunately also the symptoms of half the victims of epidemic hysteria) – sent home with instructions to come back later for a thorough radiological and medical exam.[674]

Other means by which terrorists could contaminate civilians with radioactive materials include the targeting of atomic power plants, which U.S. Representative Edward Markey has alleged that al-Qa'ida is planning to do. Presumably, the intention would be to cause a meltdown. The nuclear industry contends that the nation's nuclear plants are adequately protected by double-fenced perimeters, concertina wire, sensors inside the fences, and thick concrete walls. Inside the buildings are reinforced steel walls. But critics who include lawmakers say that 37 of the 81 federal exercises run between 1991 and 2001 have turned up significant weaknesses in security. Unfortunately, nuclear facilities fought against federalizing the security guards, which would have improved and standardized their training.[752]

The discussion of the radiation science that underlies the response to dirty bombs has been left to the last, for it may not interest all readers. The table below lists the properties of several of the radioisotopes that might be used to make a dirty bomb. All of them emit radiation, and the main risk of exposure, whether from internal or external irradiation, is cancer.

RADIOACTIVE ISOTOPES OF POSSIBLE USE IN A DIRTY BOMB*			
ISOTOPE	HALF-LIFE (YEARS)	INTERNAL BIOLOGIC EFFECT	EMISSIONS**
Cesium-139 (Cs-139)	30.2	Disseminates widely in the body	Beta particles, Gamma rays
Cobalt-60 (Co-60)	5.3	Lodges in liver, kidney, bones rays	Gamma rays

Plutonium-239 (Pu-239)	24,000	Extreme risk if internalized	Alpha particles, neutrons
Strontium-90 (Sr-90)	29.1	Like Ca localizes in bones and teeth	Gamma rays
Uranium-235 (U-235)	700 M	Most of U-235 and U-238 is excreted	Alpha particles and neutrons
Uranium-238 (U-238)	4.7 B	A little stays in bone and liver	Alpha particles and neutrons

*Within the body, all the above isotopes can cause cancer at the sites of deposition. But this may take decades, and depends on the isotope, its quantity, time at that site, presence of other carcinogens, and susceptibility of the person to cancer.

** While gamma rays are highly penetrating, alpha and beta particles have short ranges. Sr-90 decays to Y-90 that emits gamma rays.

#M stands for Millions, B stands for Billions.

The biologic effect of total body irradiation has been evaluated for many decades since the explosion of the atomic bombs at Hiroshima and Nagasaki. Those who received whole body radiation exposure but survived have been monitored with utmost care, and has produced invaluable data on the excess cancer incidence in various body organs that eventually results from exposure to whole body radiation. The increase in the risk of cancer in any given body organ from exposure to whole body irradiation for people in contaminated areas is cumulative over the time spent in those areas, and is directly proportional to the dose of radiation absorbed. There is no threshold below which radiation has no effect.[679,753]

Regarding the effect of inhaled radioactive matter or gas, the data on radon inhalation (see above) are of great value for estimating the excess cancer risk following the inhalation of radioactive aerosols produced by the explosion of a dirty bomb. But other causes of radiation carcinogenesis have also been studied, for instance the inhalation of plutonium-239 in a nuclear facility at Mayak in Russia, which caused lung cancer in workers exposed to high doses of radiation. In contrast to data for radon inhalation in uranium miners, where there was a linear relationship between radiation dose and lung cancer, at Mayak the excess risk of lung cancer at low doses of plutonium were unexpectedly *higher* than expected for a linear relationship.[754] As in case of asbestos and of radon, lung cancer incidence from inhalation of plutonium-239 was synergistic with smoking, and most of the men who developed lung cancer were smokers. This strongly suggests that it is smokers who will be most at risk of lung cancer, should they inhale a highly radioactive aerosol produced by the explosion of a dirty bomb.

The radioactivity from explosion of a dirty bomb will contaminate the ground and the exterior of buildings in the area surrounding the blast and downwind from it. The following estimate of the excess relative risk of cancer (increase in risk relative to a person who has not received the radiation) in various body organs was made in 2000 by the United Nations Scientific Committee on the Effects of Atomic Radiation.[755]

ESTIMATED CANCER INCIDENCE FROM WHOLE-BODY IRRADIATION FOR AN ESTIMATED AGE OF 30 YEARS AT THE TIME OF EXPOSURE.[681]		
	RISK PER REM		SEX RATIO
CANCER TYPE	MALE	FEMALE	FEMALE/MALE
Esophagus	0.91	1.88	2.1
Colon	0.46	0.95	2.1
Liver	0.61	1.66	2.7
Lung	0.30	0.99	3.3
Other cancer	0.38	0.77	2.1
Leukemia	1.24	0.94	0.8

Except in the case of leukemia, the latent period (the time interval between irradiation and the appearance of cancer) is very long, and depends on the type of radiation emitted by the radioisotope and the radiation dose absorbed cumulatively over time. If the public is to understand the degree of danger from the explosion of a dirty bomb, the dose of radiation received from it should be compared with the average dose we receive continually from natural sources, which are as follows:

(a) We are all continually exposed to ionizing radiation, although we are unaware of it. We breathe in tiny amounts of radioactive radon, the ground we walk on and the buildings in which we live and work are very slightly radioactive, our bodies contain traces of radioactivity that is contained in our food and drink, and cosmic rays fall on us continually.[756] The natural background radiation that human beings absorb in the U.S. from all these sources adds up to a physical dose of 0.12 rad per year,[649] and a biologically effective dose of 0.15 rem per year.[757]

(b) The biologically effective radiation dose from medical sources averages approximately 0.12 rem per year in cities where there is more than one physician for every 1,000 people. However, in cities where there is less than one physician for every 10,000 people, the dose may be as low as 0.02 rem.[758] Easy access to physicians results in extensive use of X-rays. Still, modern X-ray machines and CT scanners are engineered to deliver reduced dosages of radiation.

(c) Cosmic rays that hit us in the thin air at 35,000 feet during an intercontinental airplane flight deliver approximately 0.005 rem.[683] Although this is a small dose, this exposure to radiation is not negligible for airplane personnel and frequent flyers.

A number of good books are devoted solely to the subject of dirty bombs. In addition, a search for "dirty bombs" on the internet produces over 100,000 "hits," so there is a vast amount of information on this subject. But in order to understand the nature of dirty bombs, it is helpful to know essential facts about nuclear bombs. Only these are covered below, because it would take a long book even to begin to do justice to their horrendous biological effects.

Atomic bombs have an interesting history. By the year 1942, both the Allies and the Third Reich were far enough advanced in nuclear physics to know that a fission bomb was practical, but would require at least two years to produce. Hitler felt that if the war had not been won by that time, it would be lost–so he decided against making an atomic bomb. U.S. generals thought that the war would continue for at least two more years, and that the risk was too great to take, that Germany – which had Nobel Laureate Heisenberg directing its nuclear effort–would be first to produce an atomic bomb. So in cooperation with Britain, the U.S. launched the Manhattan Project, a massive industrial effort that was more extensive than the US auto industry of that era.

Atomic bombs are of two very different types: fission bombs, and fusion bombs. Fission means "splitting apart," and the fundamental process that fission bombs utilize is the splitting apart of an atom with high atomic weight into two atoms with lower atomic weights, which together add up to a slightly smaller mass than that of the original atom. Remarkably, the tiny difference in mass between the mass of the original atom and the combined masses of the two atoms into which it has been split is converted into a vast quantity of energy, which produces a huge explosion.

In contrast, fusion means "merging together." A fusion bomb such as the hydrogen bomb utilizes the ability of two atoms of low atomic weight to fuse together to form a single atom with an atomic weight that is smaller than the sum of the atomic weights of the two atoms. But the difference in mass between the mass of the original two atoms and the mass resulting from their fusion is about 1,000 times greater than that released by atomic fission. Thus, fusion bombs are approximately 1,000 times more powerful than fission bombs, at least in the particular situation when two atoms of the hydrogen isotope deuterium with atomic weight 2 are fused together, to form an atom of helium with atomic weight 4. Happily, deuterium fusion bombs are much harder to construct than fission bombs, because they require a fission explosion surrounding the deuterium, to blast the deuterium atoms together in order to set off a fusion reaction. Then the sudden release of vast amounts of energy results in a massive explosion.

As in the case of a meltdown, the initial danger to large areas downwind of an atomic explosion is iodine-131. But atomic bombs also disperse strontium-90. This is a dangerous isotope because it has the long half-life of nearly 29 years, and is blasted aloft into the global stratosphere. Then over the next two to three years it falls out the entire surface of the earth, where it is incorporated into the food chain and consumed by human beings. It is dispersed so effectively, that the strontium-90 fallout onto the area where the bomb exploded is only about three times higher than the fallout over the rest of the world. Because strontium-90 causes bone cancer in experimental animals, as I verified experimentally,[759] even small amounts ingested in foods reinforce the genetic and environmentally acquired susceptibility that people have for developing osteogenic sarcoma. But in order for the peoples of the world to experience really serious consequences from strontium-90 fallout, a full-scale nuclear war would have to be fought, and 1,000 or more atomic bombs would have to be exploded. This is highly unlikely.

The immediate physical carnage and destruction that such a war would wreak is incomparably greater than the long-term damage caused by the fallout of strontium-90. But only madmen would actuate the nuclear option that would risk ending civilization.

Finally, the need to consider defenses against dirty bombs would not exist, if terrorists motivated by religious convictions realized that indiscriminate murdering that does not spare women, children and noncombatants dishonors the very God whom they mean to glorify: for God is loving and merciful, and abhors murderers. If only terrorist leaders could impress this message on their troops! Indeed, the New York Times of October 7, 2005 reported a warning from one senior al-Qa'ida leader to another, saying that attacks on civilians could jeopardize their broader cause.[760]

AFTERWORD

Under the Bush administration, the United States was hesitant to assume its ethically mandatory role to lead the global battle against tobacco—a reluctance mirrored by its stance on global environmental pollution and warming. The United States would benefit greatly from a consistent global ethical strategy that was not selective for high profile issues such as AIDS, but included all aspects relevant for worldwide health.

Vital global environmental issues on which the United States should be a leading participant in United Nations actions include pollution of air, soil and water; global warming; ample supply of clean water; preservation of flora and fauna; sustainable agriculture; and renewable sources of energy. The U.N. also undertakes many humane endeavors that the U.S. should support more generously. These include elimination of poverty and starvation; helping the survivors of natural disasters; providing first-rate universal education; guarding against rights abuse of minority groups; supporting international courts that adjudicate between opponents; guarding against abuse by multinational corporations; and fighting against addictive drugs like tobacco. According to Time magazine of January 13, 2014, even smoking e-cigarettes on state-owned property was forbidden my Oklahoma Governor Mary Fallin, as being a stepping stone on the way to smoking tobacco.

Adoption of a strong humanitarian strategy by the United States would banish some of the reasons for its dislike. The U.S.

should also stress foresight and prevention of health tragedies—which is much better than cure, and much less costly.

As discussed by Kathy Brayo in the Boston Sunday Globe of February 23, 2014, a debate has emerged about whether e-cigarettes foster the use of tobacco. While some experts predict that e-cigarettes will end smoking, others disagree. But there is no disagreement that smokers of e-cigarettes eventually smoke tobacco more frequently than nonsmokers. The article therefore concluded that the smoking of e-cigarettes should be discouraged. This article was followed by an editorial on March 21, that asked, Do e-cigarettes help smokers quit? The editorial claimed that this question was hotly debated, and that in March, 2014, a study of 59 websites selling e-cigarettes found that 95% made health-related claims. But a public health expert commented that the science to support these claims was not yet available.

Finally, I should not leave the impression that I despise smokers, for my beloved father was thoroughly addicted to the weed. Although I don't remember being aware that I was exposed by him to thick secondhand smoke, that was undoubtedly the case. But this exposure did not addict me to nicotine, nor harm me. Perhaps my great love for and immersion in outdoor sports helped to clear my lungs from vestiges of soot deposited by that smoke. Nor should I avoid mentioning a sensitive matter for people who work with tobacco products or advertise them. Since the end result of tobacco use can be serious illness and premature death, anyone who promotes the sale of tobacco or profits by it is contributing to human suffering. Is this not unethical?

Readers may be amused to read one of the first words spoken to put tobacco in its place, which here shall be my last. James I, who became King of England in 1604 and is known best for authorizing the King James Bible, had a surprisingly cogent comment about tobacco use that I quote from Alister McGrath's book, "*In the Beginning. The story of the King James Bible and how it changed a nation, a language and a culture* (2001):"

ARNOLD E. REIF

"Have you not reason then to be ashamed and to forbear this filthy novelty? In your abuse thereof sinning against God, harming yourselves both in person and goods, and making yourselves to be wondered at, and to be scorned and held in contempt; a custom loathsome to the eye, hateful to the nose, harmful to the brain, dangerous to the lungs..."

APPENDIX

---

1. RESOURCES ON ANTISMOKING, DISEASES, AND SERVICES

UNITED STATES PUBLIC HEALTH SERVICE:

- Office on Smoking and Health, Mail Stop K-50, 4770 Buford Highway, NE, Atlanta, GA 30341-3717, 770-488-5706, press 3, www.cdc.gov/tobacco.htm

- Agency for Healthcare Research and Quality, 800-358-9295 www.ahcpr.gov/clinic

- Centers for Disease Control and Prevention (CDC), Office on Smoking and Health, 800-232-1311, 404-488-5705 or 770-488-5705 www.cdc.gov/health/tobacco.htm, or www.cdc.gov/voacca

- National Cancer Institute, Cancer Information Service, 800-4-CANCER: 800-422-6237; http://cancer.gov, or www.nci.nih.gov.

- For a trained counselor: 877-44U-QUIT, visit www.smokefree.gov–Surgeon General's site on tobacco: www.surgeongeneral.gov/tobacco

- National Library of Medicine, 800-272-4787 www.nlm. nih.gov

AMERICAN CANCER SOCIETY:
800-ACS-2345; 800-227-2345, or website
www.cancer.org

AMERICAN LUNG ASSOCIATION:
212-315-8700, or website
www.lungusa.org

AMERICAN HEART ASSOCIATION:
800-AHA-USA1; 800-242-8721, or website
www.americanheart.org

AMERICAN STROKE ASSOCIATION (ASSOCIATED WITH AM. HEART ASSN.):
888-4-STROKE; 888-478-7653, or website
www.StrokeAssociation.org

2. RESOURCES FOR ANTISMOKING EFFORTS

- National Center for Tobacco-Free Kids, 1400 I Street, NW, Suite 1200, Washington, DC 20005, 202-296-5469 www.tobaccofreekids.org
- Action on Smoking and Health (ASH), John F. Banzhaf, III, 2013 H Street, N.W., Washington, DC 20006, 202-659-4310 www.ash.org
- Tobacco Control Resource Center, and Tobacco Products Liability Project, Richard A. Daynard, Northeastern University School of Law, 102 The Fenway, 117 Cushing Hall, Boston, MA 02115-5000 617-373-2026 www.tobacco.neu.edu For the Tobacco Products Liability Reporter (TPLR), visit www.tplr.com

- Smoke Free, Joe Cherner, Joe@smokefree.org

3. SOCIETIES SPECIALIZING IN CERTAIN CANCERS OR SERVICES

American Brain Tumor Association, 800-886-ABTA
Cancer Patients Action Alliance (CAN ACT) 718-522-4607
Cancer Care, Inc., and National Cancer Care Foundation 212-302-2400
Candlelighters Childhood Cancer Foundation 800-366-2223
CANSURMOUNT, American Cancer Society group that tries to match a volunteer who has had cancer with a patient for hospital visits 800-ACS-2345: 800-227-2345
Clinical Center of the National Institutes of Health, Patient Referral Service, 301-496-5583
Food and Drug Administration, MedWatch Program 800-332-1088
Heredity Cancer Institute 402-422-6237
Hereditary Colon Cancer Registry: enquiries to 402-422-6237
Hospice Link, Hospice Education Institute 800-331-1620
Intestinal Multiple Polyposis and Colorectal Cancer 301-791-7526
International Myeloma Foundation 800-452-CURE
Leukemia Society of America 800-955-4LSA
National Brain Tumor Foundation 415-296-0404
National Breast Cancer Coalition 202-296-7477
National Coalition for Cancer Survivorship 301-650-8868
National Kidney Cancer Association 708-332-1051
National Oral Health Information Clearinghouse 301-402-7364
National Women's Health Network 202-347-1140
The Skin Cancer Foundation 212-725-5176
United Ostomy Association 800-826-0826
Y-ME Hotline counseling for breast cancer patients, family and friends 312-986-2141

ENDNOTES

——————

1. World Health Organization. Updated status of the WHO Framework Convention on Tobacco Control, Jan. 29 (2008), www.who.int/tobacco/framework/countrylist/en/index.html.

2. Reif, A. E., and Heeren, T., Consensus on synergism between cigarette smoke and other environmental carcinogens in the causation of lung cancer. *Advances in Cancer Research*, vol. 65, pp. 161-186 (1999).

3. American Cancer Society. Cancer Statistics, 2007. *CA. Cancer J. Clin.*, vol. 58, pp. 1-30 (2008). (NOTE TO AER: MUST CHECK this endnote for accuracy)

4. U.S. Department of Health and Human Services. *The Health Consequences of Smoking. A Report of the Surgeon General* (Bethesda: U.S. Department of Health and Human Services, Centers for Disease Control and Prevention, Office on Smoking and Health, 2004).

5. Kolata, Gina, Focus in cancer on 'prevention' divides experts. *The New York Times*, pp. A1-15, Jan. 11 (2004).

6. Reif, Arnold E., The causes of cancer. *American Scientist*, vol. 69, pp. 437-447 (1981).

7. Weinberg, Robert A., *The Biology of Cancer* (New York: Garland Science, 2007).

8. Knudson, A. G., Jr., Mutation and cancer: statistical study of retinoblastoma. *Proc. Natl. Acad. Sci. USA*, vol 68, pp. 820-823 (1971).

9. Knudsen, Erik S., and Knudsen, Karen E., Retinoblastoma tumor suppressor: where cancer meets the cell cycle. *Experimental Biology and Medicine*, vol. 231, pp. 1271-1281 (2006).

10. Van Dyke, Terry, p53 and tumor suppression. *New Engl. J. Medicine*, vol. 356, pp. 79-81 (2007).

11. Mooi, W. J., and Peeper, D. S., Oncogene-induced cell senescence–halting on the road to cancer. *New Engl. J. Medicine*, vol. 355, pp. 1037-1046 (20068).

12. Loberg, Robert D., Bradley, Deborah A., Tomlin, Scott A., *et al.*, The lethal phenotype of cancer: the molecular basis of death due to malignancy. *CA. Cancer J. Clin.*, vol. 57, pp. 225-241 (2007).

13. Burstein, Harold J., and Schwartz, Robert S., Molecular origins of cancer. *New Engl. J. Medicine*, vol. 358, p. 527 (2008).

14. Croce, Carlo M., Oncogenes and cancer. *New Engl. J. Medicine*, vol. 358, pp. 502-511 (2008).

15. Karr, Paul, Pocahontas' revenge. *Massachusetts Audubon Society's Sanctuary*, vol. 32, no. 1, p. 11 (1992).

16. Centers for Disease Control and Prevention, Tobacco use- United States, 1900-1999. *JAMA*, vol. 282, pp. 2202-2204 (1999).

17. Micozzi, Marc S., The Nazi War on Cancer. *New Engl. J. Medicine*, vol. 341, pp. 380-381 (1999). Also see Proctor, Robert N., *The Nazi War on Cancer* (Princeton: Princeton University, 1999).

18. Doll, Richard, and Hill, Bradford A., Smoking and carcinoma of the lung. *British Medical Journal*, vol. 221, pp. 739-48 (1950).

19. Wynder, E. L., and Graham, E. A., Tobacco smoking as a possible etiologic factor in bronchogenic carcinoma. *JAMA*, vol. 143, pp. 329-336 (1950).

20. Doll, R., and Hill, A. B., The mortality of doctors in relation to their smoking habits. A preliminary report. *British Medical Journal*, vol. 1, pp. 1451-1455 (1954). A final report followed in the same journal two years later, in vol. 2, pp. 1071-1081 (1956).

21. Hammond, E. C., and Horn, D. Smoking and death rates- Report on forty-four months of follow-up on 187,783 men. I. Total mortality. *JAMA*, vol. 166, pp. 1159-1172 (1958). Part II of this report, on "Death rates by cause," was published in *JAMA*, vol. 166, 1294-1308 (1959).

22. Reif, Arnold E., International Cancer Congress. *Science*, vol. 128, pp. 1512-1522 (1958).

23. Royal College of Physicians, Smking and Health. *Summary and Report of the Royal College of Physicians of London on Smoking in Relation to Cancer of the Lung and Other Diseases.* (New York: Pitman, 1962).

24. U.S. Department of Health and Human Services. *The Health Consequences of Smoking. A Report of the Surgeon General.* (U.S. Department of Health and Human Services, Centers for Disease Control and Prevention, Office on Smoking and Health, 1964).

25. U.S. Department of Health and Human Services. *Reducing the Health Consequences of Smoking. 25 Years of Progress. A report of the Surgeon General.* (U.S. Department of Health and Human Services, Centers for Disease Control and Prevention, Office on Smoking and Health, 1989).

26. U.S. Department of Health and Human Services. *The Health Consequences of Smoking. Cancer. A report of the Surgeon General.* (U.S. Department of Health and Human Services, Centers for Disease Control and Prevention, Office on Smoking and Health, 1982).

27. U.S. Department of Health and Human Services. *The Health Consequences of Involuntary Smoking. A Report of the Surgeon General.* Centers for Disease Control and Prevention, Office on Smoking and Health, 1986).

28. U.S. Department of Health and Human Services. *The Health Consequences of Smoking. Nicotine Addiction. A Report of the Surgeon General.* Centers for Disease Control and Prevention, Office on Smoking and Health, 1988).

29. University of Wisconsin Family Medicine, Doctors Ought to Care (DOC), www.fammed.wisc.edu/education/doc/index.html.

30. For portions of this resume I am much indebted to Michael Cummings, Professor of Social and Preventive Medicine, SUNY Buffalo, and Chairman, Department of Health Behavior, Roswell Park Cancer Institute.

31. Centers for Disease Control and Prevention, State-specific prevalence of current cigarette smoking among adults and the proportion of adults who work in a smoke-free environment- United States, 1999. *JAMA*, vol. 284, pp. 2865-2866 (2000).

32. Office on Smoking and Health, Trends in cigarette smoking among high school students- United States, 1991-1999. *JAMA*, vol. 284, pp. 1507-1508 (2000).

33. American Cancer Society, *Cancer Prevention & Early Detection Facts & Figures* (Atlanta: American Cancer Society, 2006).

34. Centers for Disease Control and Prevention, Cigarette smoking among adults- United States, 1998. *JAMA*, vol. 284, pp. 2180-2181 (2000).

35. Gilman, Sander L., and Xun, Zhou, *Smoke: A Global History of Smoking* (London, Reaction Books, 2005).

36. Wynder, Ernst L., and Hoffman, Dietrich, Tobacco and health: a societal challenge. *New Engl. J. Med.*, vol. 300, pp. 894-903 (1979).

37. Koh, Howard K., Kannler, Christine, and Geller, Alan C., Cancer prevention: preventing tobacco-related cancers. In: *Cancer. Principles & Practice of Oncology*, 6th edn., DeVita, Vincent T., Jr., Hellman, Samuel, and Rosenberg, Steven A., eds. (2001), pp.549-560.

38. Fowles, Jefferson, and Bates, Michael, *The Chemical Constituents of Cigarettes and Cigarette Smoke. Priorities for Harm Reduction,* www.ndp.govt.nz/tobacco/tobaccochem.pdf (2000).

39. International Agency for Research on Cancer (IARC), *Overall Evaluations of Carcinogenicity to Humans,* http://www-cie.iarc.fr/monoeval/crthall.html

40. National Cancer Institute, *Cigarette Smoking and Cancer: Questions and Answers,* http://cis.nci.nih.gov/fact/10_14.htm (2004).

41. Kelley, Thomas F., Polonium-210 content of mainstream cigarette smoke. *Science,* vol. 149, pp. 537-538 (1965).

42. Hecht, S. S., Approaches to chemoprevention of lung cancer based on carcinogens in tobacco smoke. *Environ. Health Persp.*, vol. 105, Suppl. 4, pp. 955- 963 (1997).

43. Luthi, Teres, Another smoking gun: Nicotine, too, may promote cancer. *The Sciences,* vol. 34, no. 1, pp. 11-12 (1994).

44. Hoffmann, D., and Hoffmann, I., The changing cigarette, 1950-1995. *J. Toxicol. Environ. Health*, vol. 50, pp. 307-364 (1997).

45. Hecht, S. S., Ornaf, R. M., and Hoffmann, D. Chemical studies on tobacco smoke. XXXIII. N'-nitrosonornicotine in tobacco: analysis of possible contributing factors and biological implications. *J. Natl. Cancer Inst.*, vol. 54, pp. 1237-1244 (1975).

46. Denissenko, Mikhail F., Pao, Annie, Tang, Moon-shong, and Pfeifer, Gerd P., Preferential formation of benzo[a]pyrene adducts at lung cancer mutational hot spots in *p53. Science*, vol. 274, pps. 430-432 (1996).

47. Brennan, Joseph A., Boyle, Jay O., Koch, Wayne M., *et al.*, Association between smoking and mutation of the p53 gene in squamous-cell carcinoma of the head and neck. *New Engl. J. Med.*, vol. 332, pp. 712-717 (1995).

48. Office of Environmental Health Hazard Assessment (OEHHA), Methanol. CAS Registry No. 67-56-1, downloaded at www.oehha.ca.gov/ on May 12 (2005).

49. Beauchamp, R. O., Jr., Irons, R. D., Rickert, D. E., *et al.*, A critical review of the literature on nitrobenzene toxicity. *Crit. Rev. Toxicol.*, vol. 11, pp. 33-84 (1982).

50. American Lung Association, Search LungUSA for carbon monoxide toxicity, at www.lungusa.org/ last updated May (2004).

51. Office of Environmental Health Hazard Assessment (OEHHA), Hydrogen cyanide. CAS Registry No. 74-90-8, downloaded at www.oehha.ca.gov/ on May 12 (2005).

52. Office of Environmental Health Hazard Assessment (OEHHA), Hydrogen sulfide. CAS Registry No 7783-06-4, downloaded at www.oehha.ca.gov/ on May 12 (2005).

53. Mayo Clinic staff, Sperm smarts: optimizing fertility. Web site www.mayoclinc.com/ updated June 3 (2004).

54. University of Wisconsin-Stevens Point staff, Smoking and your reproductive health. Web site www.wellness.uwsp.edu/MedInfo/ updated July (2001).

55. U.S. Department of Health, Education, and Welfare. *The Health Consequences of Smoking. Cardiovascular Disease. A Report of the Surgeon General.* Centers for Disease Control and Prevention, Office on Smoking and Health, 1983).

56. Ayanian, John Z., and Cleary, Paul D., Perceived risks of heart disease and cancer among cigarette smokers. *JAMA,* vol. 281, pp. 1019-1021 (1999).

57. U.S. Department of Health and Human Services. *The Health Consequences of Smoking. A Report of the Surgeon General* (2004).

58. *Nicotine Addiction. A Report of the Surgeon General* (1988).

59. Krupski, W. C., The peripheral vascular consequences of smoking. *Annals of Vascular Surgery,* vol. 5, pp. 291-304 (1991).

60. Levy, Daniel, and Brink, Susan, *A Change of Heart: How the Framingham Heart Study Helped Unravel the Mysteries of Cardiovascular Disease* (New York: Alfred A. Knopf, 2005).

61. D'Agostino, Ralph B., Grundy, Scott, Sullivan, Lisa M., *et al.,* Validation of the Framingham coronary heart disease prediction scores, *JAMA,* vol. 286, pp. 180-187 (2001).

62. Rosenberg, Lynn, Miller, Donald R., Kaufman, David W., *et al.,* Myocardial infarction in women under 50 years of age. *JAMA,* vol. 250, pp. 2801-2806 (1983).

63. Ridker, Paul M., Rifal, Nader, Rose, Lynda, *et al.,* Comparison of C-reactive protein and low-density lipoprotein cholesterol levels in the prediction of first cardiovascular events. *New Engl. J. Med.,* vol. 347, pp. 1557-1565 (2002).

64. Jee, Sun Ha, Suh, Il, Kim, Il Soon, *et al.,* Smoking and atherosclerotic cardiovascular disease in men with low levels of

serum cholesterol. The Korea Medical Insurance Corporation study. *JAMA*, vol. 282, pp. 2149-2155 (1999).

65. Williams, Redford B., Barefoot, John C., and Schneiderman, Neil, Psychological risk factors for cardiovascular disease. More than one culprit at work. *JAMA*, vol. 290, pp. 2190-2192 (2003).

66. Willett, Walter C., Green, Adele, Stampfer, Meir J., *et al.*, Relative and absolute excess risk of coronary heart disease among women who smoke cigarettes. *New Engl. J. Med.*, vol. 317, pp. 1303-1309 (1987).

67. Critchley, Julia A., and Capewell, Simon, Mortality risk reduction associated with smoking cessation in patients with coronary heart disease. A systematic review. *JAMA*, vol. 290, pp. 86-97 (2003).

68. U.S. Preventive Services Task Force. Screening: Abdominal aortic aneurysm. www.ahrq.gov/clinic/uspstf/uspsaneu.htm (2005).

69. Parmet, Sharon, Lynm, Cassio, and Glass, Richard M., Smoking and the heart. *JAMA*, vol. 290, p. 146 (2003).

70. Colcombe, Stanley J., Erickson, Kirk I., Raz, Naftali, *et al.*, *Aerobic fitness reduces brain tissue loss in aging humans. The J. Gerontology, Series A: Biolog. Sci. and Med. Sci.*, Vol. 58, pp. M176-M180 (2003).

71. Menec, Verena H., The relation between everyday activities and successful aging: a 6-year longitudinal study. *The J. Gerontology, Series B: Psychological Sci. and Social Sci.*, Vol. 58, pp. 574-582 (2003).

72. Marenberg, Marjorie E., Risch, Neil, Berkman, Lisa F., *et al.*, *New Engl. J. Med.*, vol. 330, pp. 1041-1046 (1994).

73. Weintraub, William S., and Diamond, George A., Predicting cardiovascular events with coronary calcium scoring. *New Engl. J. Med.*, vol. 358, pp. 1394-1396 (2008).

74. Wilson, P. W., D'Agostino, R. B., Levy, D., *et al.*, Prediction of coronary heart disease using risk factor categories. *Circulation*, vol. 97, pp. 1837-1847 (1998).

75. *The Health Consequences of Smoking. Cardiovascular Disease. A Report of the Surgeon General.* (1983), p. 171.

76. Wilson, E., Enhancing smoke-free behaviour: prevention of stroke. *Health Reports,* vol. 6, no. 1, pp. 100-105 (1994).

77. Editorial, Preventing strokes: understanding stroke and evaluating your risk. The first of two parts. *Harvard Men's Health Watch*, pp. 4-7, Oct. (2003).

78. Vermeer, S. E., Prins, N. D., den Heijer, T., *et al.*, Silent brain infarcts and the risk of dementia and cognitive decline. *New Engl. J. Med.*, vol. 348, pp. 1215-1222 (2003).

79. Straus, Sharon E., Majumdar, Sumit R., and McAlister, Finlay A., New evidence for stroke prevention. Scientific review. *New Engl. J. Med.*, vol. 288, pp. 1388-1395 (2002).

80. Straus, Sharon E., Majumdar, Sumit R., and McAlister, Finlay A., New evidence for stroke prevention. Clinical applications. *New Engl. J. Med.*, vol. 288, pp. 1396-1398 (2002).

81. Gillyat, Peta, and Huston, Larry, *Stroke, A Special Report* (Boston: Harvard Medical School Health Publications Group, 1998).

82. Lerner, Barron H., In unforgettable final act, a King got revenge on his killers. *New York Time*, p. D5, Jan. 25 (2005).

83. Doll, Richard, Peto, Richard, Boreham, Jillian, *et al.*, Mortality in relation to smoking: 50 years' observation on male British doctors. *Brit. Med. J.*, vol. 328, pp. 1519-1533 (2004).

84. Stampfer, Meir, Editorial. New insights from the British doctor study. *Brit. Med. J.*, vol. 328, pp. 1507 (2004).

85. Reif, Arnold E., Public information on smoking: An urgent responsibility for cancer research workers. *J. Natl. Cancer Inst.*, vol 57, pp. 1207-1210 1976).

86. Quotation of American Cancer Society data by Kathy Vesha, www.thelantern.com/media/paper333/news/2005/11/18/ Campus/.

87. U.S. Department of Health, Education, and Welfare. *The Health Consequences of Smoking. Women and Smoking. A Report of the Surgeon General.* Centers for Disease Control and Prevention, Office on Smoking and Health, 2001), available online at www.cdc.gov/tobacco/sgr/sgr_forwomen/ataglance. htm.

88. North American Association of Cancer Registries, CDC, NCHS, ACS, and NCI, Annual report shows overall decline in U.S. cancer incidence and death rates; feature focuses on cancers with increasing trends. *News from the NCI (National Cancer Institute)*, June 5, pp. 1-5 (2001). <newscenter.cancer. gov/pressreleases/reportnation.html>

89. Poswillo, David, and Alberman, Eva, *Effects of Smoking on the Fetus, Neonate, and Child* (Oxford: Oxford University, 1992).

90. Parkin, Max, Bray, Freddie, Ferlay, J., *et al.*, *CA. A Cancer J. for Clinicians*, vol. 55, no. 2, pp. 74- 108 (2005). Data derived from Figure 5. Although these data were published by the American Cancer Society in 2005, they refer to the latest year for which statistics are available, 2002.

91. Reif, Arnold E., and Baker, Helen S., Inhalation studies with toluidine blue aerosol in rats *Arch. Ind. Health*, vol. 14, pp. 560-568 (1956).

92. Reif, Arnold E., Aerosols: Physical properties, instrumentation and technique. In *Aviation Medicine- Selected Reviews*, ed. by White, C. S. (New York: Pergamon, 1958).

93. Parmet, Sharon, Lynm, Cassio, Glass, Richard M., Lung cancer. *JAMA*, vol. 289, p. 380 (2003).

94. Polsky, Isabel, The Uncertain Benefits of CT Scanning for lung cancer. *Focus on Healthy Aging, Mount Sinai School of Medicine*, vol. 4, no. 8 (2001).

95. mith, Robert A., von Eschenbach, Andrew C., Wender, Richard, *et al.*, American Cancer Society Guidelines for the Early Detection of Cancer: Update of Early Detection Guidelines for prostate, colorectal, and endometrial cancers. Also: Update 2001- Testing for early lung cancer detection. *CA A Cancer J. for Clinicians*, vol. 51, no. 1, pp. 38-75 (2001).

96. National Cancer Institute, Screening for lung cancer. Screening/Detection- Health Professionals. CancerNet http://cancernet.nci.nih.gov/cgi-bin/ (2001).

97. Pamela Marcus, Pamela, *et. al.*, *J. Nat. Cancer Inst.*, vol. 92, pp. 1308-1316 (2000).

98. Mahadevia, Parthiv J., Fleisher, Lee A., Frick, Kevin D., *et al.*, Lung cancer screening with helical computed tomography. A decision and cost-effectiveness analysis. *JAMA*, vol. 289, pp. 313-322 (2003).

99. Mahadevia, Parthiv J, and Powe, Neil R., Cost-effectiveness of screening for lung cancer: Reply. *JAMA*, vol. 289, pp. 2358-2359 (2003).

100. National Cancer Institute, National Cancer Institute launches lung screening study. National Cancer Institute web site http://newscenter.cancer.gov/pressreleases/ (2000).

101. Lardinois, Didier, Weder, Walter, Hany, Thomas F., Staging of non-small-cell lung cancer with Integrated Positron-Emission Tomography and Computed Tomography. *New Engl. J. Med.*, vol. 348, pp. 2500-2507 (2003).

102. Harris, Curtis A., Cover legend, p53 mutational spectrum and frequency of G – T transversions in lung cancers from

cigarette smokers and never smokers. *Cancer Research*, vol. 55, no. 11, June (1995).

103. Granat, Pepi, Lung cancer screening. *JAMA*, vol. 285, p. 163 (2001).

104. Patz, Edward F., Jr., Goodman, Philip C., and Bepler, Gerold, Screening fir kung cancer. *New Engl. J. Med.*, vol. 434, pp. 1627-1632 (2000).

105. Petty, Thomas L., Screening strategies for early detection of lung cancer. *JAMA*, vol. 284, pp. 1977-1980 (2000).

106. Scriver, C. R., and Childs, B., *Garrod's Inborn Factors in Disease* (New York: Oxford University, (1989), p. 170.

107. Fisher, R. A., *Smoking. The Cancer Controversy* (Edinburgh: Oliver & Boyd, 1959).

108. Reif, Arnold E., Effect of cigarette smoking on susceptibility to lung cancer. *Oncology*, vol. 38, pp. 76-85 (1981).

109. Burch, P. R. J., Smoking and lung cancer. The problem of inferring cause. *J. R. statis. Soc.*, vol. 141 A, 437-477 (1968).

110. Reif, Arnold E., and Heeren, Timothy, Consensus on synergism between cigarette smoke and othe environmental carcinogens in the causation of lung cancer. *Adv. Cancer Res.*, vol. 65, pps. 161-186 (1999).

111. Reif, Arnold E., Smoked out. *The Sciences*, vol. 21, no. 9, pps. 2-3 (1981).

112. Caporaso, N. E., Tucker, M. A., Hoover, R. N., *et al.*, Lung cancer and the debrisoquine metabolic phenotype. *Journal of the National Cancer Institute*, vol. 82, pps. 1264-1272 (1990).

113. Sellers, T. A., Bailey-Wilson, J. E., Elston, R. C., *et al.*, Evidence for mendelian inheritance in the pathogenesis of lung cancer. *Journal of the National Cancer Institute*, vol. 82, pps. 1272-1279 (1990).

114. Bonney, G. E., Interaction of genes, environment, and lifestyle in lung cancer development. *Journal of the National Cancer Institute*, vol. 82, pps. 1236-1237 (1990).

115. Reif, Arnold E., Heredity as a determining factor in which smokers die of lung cancer. *J. Natl. Cancer Inst.*, vol. 83, pp. 64-66 (1991).

116. Carney, Desmond N., and Hansen, Heine H., Non-small cell lung cancer- Stalemate or progression? *New Engl. J. Med.*, vol. 343, pp. 1261-1262 (2000).

117. Pieterman, Remge, van Putten, John W. G., Meuzelaar, Jacobus J., *et al.*, Preoperative staging of non-small-cell lung cancer with positron-emission tomography. *New Engl. J. Med.*, vol. 343, pp. 254-261 (2000).

118. Martini, Nael, Operable lung cancer. *CA—A Cancer Journal for Clinicians*, vol. 50, no. 3, p. q79 (2000).

119. Bach, Peter B., Cramer, Laura D., Warren, Joan L., *et al.*, Racial differences in the treatment of early-stage lung cancer. *New Engl. J. Med.*, vol. 341, 1198-1205 (1999).

120. Schiller, Joan H., Harrington, David, Belani, Chandra P., *et al*, Comparison of four chemotherapy regimens for advanced non-small-cell lung cancer. *New Engl. J. Med.*, vol. 346, pp. 92-98 (2002).

121. Bushinsky, David A., Lung cancer- Time to move on from chemotherapy. *New Engl. J. Med.*, vol. 346, pp. 126-127 (2002).

122. Dillman, Robert, *et al.*, *J. Natl. Cancer Inst.*, Sept. 4 (1996).

123. Editorial, Lung cancer: 10-year survey. *CA—A Cancer Journal for Clinicians*, vol. 50, p.179 (2000).

124. Goldman, Erik, Gene predicted lung cancer outcomes. *Chest Physician*, vol. 2, no. 11, pp. 1-3, Nov. (2007).

125. Hurria, Arti, and Kris, Mark G., Management of lung cancer in older adults. *CA A Cancer J. for Clinicians,* vol. 53, no. 6, pp. 325-341 (2003).

126. Arcasoy, Selim B., Kotloff, Robert M., Lung Transplantation. *New Engl. J. Med.,* vol. 340, pp. 1081-1090 (1999).

127. Detterbeck, Frank C., Socinski, Mark A., Rivera, M. Patricia, and Rosenman, Julian G., *Diagnosis and Treatment of Lung Cancer. An Evidence-Based Guide for the Practicing Clinician* (Philadelphia: W.B. Saunders, 2001).

128. Silverman, D. T., Dunn, J. A., Hoover, R. N., *et al.,* Cigarette smoking and pancreas cancer: a case-control study based on direct interviews. *J. Natl. Cancer Inst.,* vol. 86, pp. 1510-1516 (1994).

129. Ross, Ronald K., Paganini-Hill, Annlia, Landolph, Joseph, *et al.,* Analgesics, cigarette smoking, and other risk factors for cancer of the renal pelvis and ureter. *Cancer Res.,* vol. 49, pp. 1045-1048 (1989).

130. Kono, S., Ikeda, M., Tokudome, S., *et al.,* Cigarette smoking, alcohol, and cancer mortality: a cohort study of male Japanese physicians. *Jap. J. of Cancer Res.,* vol. 78, pp. 1323-1328 (1987).

131. Hansson, L. E., Baron, J., Nyren, O., *et al.,* Tobacco, alcohol, and the risk of gastric cancer. A population-based case-control study in Sweden. *Internat. J. Cancer,* vol. 57, pp. 26-31 (1994).

132. Sherman, C. B., Health effects of cigarette smoking. *Clinics in Chest Med.,* vol. 12, pp. 643-658 (1991).

133. Newcomb, P. A., and Carbone, P. P., The health consequences of smoking. Cancer. *Medical Clinics of N. America,* vol. 76, pp. 305-331 (1992).

134. Sandler, Robert S., Sandler, Dale P., Comstock, George W., *et al.,* Cigarette smoking and the risk of colorectal cancer in women. *J. Natl. Cancer Inst.,* vol 80, pp. 1329-1333 (1988).

135. Editorial, Smoking linked to increased colorectal cancer risk. *CA A Cancer J. for Clinincians*, vol. 51, no. 1, p. 9 (2000). This report refers to a study in *J. Natl. Cancer Inst.*, vol. 92, pp. 1888-1896 (2000).

136. Kinlen, L. J., and Rogot, E., Leukaemia and smoking habits among United States veterans. *Brit. Med. J.*, vol. 297, pp.657-659 (1988).

137. Wyshak, Grace, Frisch, Rose, Albright, Nile L., *et al.*, Cigarette smoking and benign breast disease. *New Engl. J. Med.*, vol. 319, pp. 1736-1737 (1988).

138. Ambrosone, C. B., Freudenheim, J. L., Graham, S., *et al.*, Cigarette smoking, *N*-acetyltransferase 2 genetic polymorphism, and breast cancer risk. *JAMA*, vol. 276, pp. 1494-1501 (1996).

139. Adami, H. O., Lund, E., Bergstrom, R., *et al.*, Cigarette smoking, alcohol consumption and risk of breast cancer in young women. *Brit. J. Cancer*, vol. 58, pp. 832-837 (1988).

140. Vatten, L. J., and Kvinnsland, S., Cigarette smoking and breast cancer: a prospective study of 24,329 Norwegian women. *Eur. J. Cancer*, vol. 26, pp. 830-833 (1990).

141. Reynolds, P., Hurley, D. E., Goldberg, H., *et al.*, Active smoking, household passive smoking, and breast cancer: Evidence from the California Teachers Study. *J. Natl. Cancer Inst.*, vol. 96, pp. 29-37 (2004).

142. Hampton, Tracy, Smoke gets in your organs. *JAMA*, vol. 290, p. 2117 (2003).

143. Castelao, J. Esteban, Yuan, Jian-Min, Skipper, Paul L., *et al.*, Gender- and smoking-related bladder cancer risk. *J. Natl. Cancer Inst.*, vol. 93, pp. 538-545 (2001).

144. D'Avanzo, B., Negri, E., La Vecchia, C., *et al.*, Cigarette smoking and bladder cancer. *European J. Cancer*, vol. 26, pp. 714-718 (1990).

145. Phillips, A. N., and Smith, G. D., Cigarette smoking as a potential cause of cervical cancer: has confounding been controlled? *Internat. J. Epidem.*, vol. 23, pp. 42-49 (1994).

146. Herrero, Rolando, Brinton, Louise A., Reeves, William C., *et al.*, Invasive cervical cancer and smoking in Latin America. *J. Natl. Cancer Inst.*, vol. 81, pp. 205-211 (1989).

147. Cramer, D. W., Harlow, B. L., Xu, H., *et al.*, Cross-sectional and case-controlled analyses of the association between smoking and early menopause. *Maturitas*, vol. 22, pp. 79-87 (1995).

148. Brodish, Paul H., The "smoking" unborn. *Priorities for Health*, vol. 11, no. 1, pps 12-14 (1999).

149. Ebrahim, Shahul H., Floyd, R. Louise, Merritt, Robert K., *et al.*, Trends in pregnancy-related smoking rates in the United States, 1987-1996. *JAMA*, vol. 283, pp. 361-366 (2000).

150. Voelker, Rebecca, Environmental tobacco smoke affects birth weight. *JAMA*, vol. 279, p. 739 (1998).

151. Wang, Xiaobin, Zuckerman, Barry, Pearson, Colleen, *et al.*, Maternal cigarette smoking, metabolic gene polymorphism, and infant birth weight. *JAMA*, vol. 287, pp. 195-202 (2002).

152. Vorji, S. K., and Cottington, Eric M., Smoking and low birth weight. *New Engl. J. Med.*, vol. 318, p. 785 (1988).

153. Walsh, R. A., Effect of maternal smoking on adverse pregnancy outcomes: examination of the criteria of causation. *Human Biology*, vol. 66, pp. 1059-1092 (1994).

154. Ness, Roberta B., Grisso, Jeane Ann, Hirschinger, Nancy, *et al.*, Cocaine and tobacco use and the risk of spontaneous abortion. *New Engl. J. Med.*, vol. 340, pp. 333-339 (1999).

155. Arya, S. N., Rajiv, K., and Arya, S., Hazards of smoking. *J. Indian Med. Assoc.*, vol. 89, 98-100 (1991).

156. United States Pharmacopeial Convention, *Drug Information for the Health Professional*. United States Pharmacopeial Convention (1995).

157. Milberger, Sharon, Biederman, Joseph, Faraone, Stephen V., *et al.*, Is maternal smoking during pregnancy a risk factor for attention hyperactivity disorder in children? *Am. J. Psychiatry*, vol. 153, 1138-1142 (1996).

158. Benowitz, N. I., Nicotine replacement therapy during pregnancy. *JAMA*, vol. 266, pp. 3174-3177 (1991).

159. Mills, James L., Cocaine, smoking, and spontaneous abortion. *New Engl. J. Med.*, vol. 340, pp. 380-381 (1999).

160. Mennella, Julie A., and Beauchamp, Gary K., Smoking and the flavor of breast milk. *New Engl. J. Med.*, vol. 339, pp. 1559-1560 (1998).

161. Honda, G. D., Vasectomy, cigarette smoking, and other risk factors for prostate cancer in young men: a case-control study. *Dissertation Abstracts Int. [B]*, vol. 47, no. 9, p. 3725 (1987).

162. Barnes, Peter J., Chronic obstructive pulmonary disease. *New Engl. J. Med.*, vol. 343, pp. 269-280 (2000).

163. Barnes, Peter J., Small airways in COPD. *New Engl. J. Med.*, vol. 350, pp. 2635-2637 (2004).

164. Editorial, Emphysema and chronic bronchitis. They take your breath away. *Harvard Men's Health Watch*, vol 7, no. 11, pp. 1-5 (2003).

165. American Lung Association, Chronic Obstructive Pulmonary Disease (COPD) Fact Sheet. Web site www.lungusa.org, last updated November (2004).

166. Shaw, Jonathan, Clearing the air. How epidemiology, engineering, and experiment fingered fine particles as airborne killers. *Harvard Magazine*, vol. 107, no. 5, pp. 28-35 (2005).

167. Tashkin, D. P., Detels, R., Simmons, M., *et al.*, The UCLA population study of chronic obstructive respiratory disease: XI. Impact of air pollution and smoking on annual change in forced expiratory volume in one second. *Am. J. Respir. Crit. Care Med.*, vol. 149, pp. 1209-1217 (1994).

168. Hansel, Trevor T., Tennant, Rachel C., Erin, Edward M., *et al.*, New drugs for COPD based on advances in pathophysiology. *In* Hansel, T. T., and Barnes, P. J., eds., *Recent Advances in the Pathophysiology of COPD* (Basel: Birkhäuser, 2004). pp. 189-226.

169. Gilchrist, Frances, Kon, Onn Minn, and Polkey, Michael I., Lung function in COPD. *In* Hansel, T. T., and Barnes, P. J., eds., *Recent Advances in the Pathophysiology of COPD* (Basel: Birkhäuser, 2004), pp. 31-46.

170. Fletcher, Charles, and Peto, Richard, The natural history of chronic airflow obstruction. *Brit. Med. J.*, vol. 1, pp. 1645-1648 (1977).

171. Ito, Kazuhiro, Ito, Masuko, Elliott, W. Mark, *et al.*, Decreased histone deacetylase activity in chronic obstructive pulmonary disease. *New Engl. J. Med.*, vol. 352, pp. 1967-1976 (2005).

172. Barnes, Peter J., Oxidative stress in COPD. *In* Hansel, T. T., and Barnes, P. J., eds., *Recent Advances in the Pathophysiology of COPD* (Basel: Birkhäuser, 2004). pp. 61-74.

173. Shapiro, Steven D., COPD unwound. *New Engl. J. Med.*, vol. 352, pp. 2016-2019 (2005).

174. Rogers, Duncan F., Mucus hypersecretion in COPD. *In* Hansel, T. T., and Barnes, P. J., eds., *Recent Advances in the Pathophysiology of COPD* (Basel: Birkhäuser, 2004). pp. 101-120.

175. Hogg, James C., Chu, Fanny, Utokaparch, Soraya, *et al.*, The nature of small-airway obstruction in chronic obstructive pul-

monary disease. *New Engl. J. Med.*, vol. 350, pp. 2645-2653 (2004).

176. Shapiro, Steven D., COPD unwound. *New Engl. J. Med.*, vol. 352, pp. 2016-2019 (2005).

177. Stoller, James K., Acute exacerbation of chronic obstructive pulmonary disease. *New Engl. J. Med.*, vol. 346, pp. 988-994 (2002).

178. Editorial, How to cope with COPD. *Harvard Women's Health Watch*, vol. 9, no. 8, pp. 3-4 (2002).

179. Foreman, Judy, Not breathing easier. *The Boston Globe*, pp. C11-12, May 20 (2003).

180. Gross, Thomas J., Hunninghake, Gary W., Idiopathic pulmonary fibrosis. *New Engl. J. Med.*, vol. 345, pp. 517-525 (2001).

181. Pouwels, Romain A., Lofdahl, Claes-Goran, Laitinen, Lauri, *et al.*, Long-term treatment with inhaled Budesonide in persons with mild chronic obstructive pulmonary disease who continue smoking. *New Engl. J. Med.*, vol. 340, pp. 1948-1953 (1999).

182. Cole, Cynthia, Colton, Theodore, Shah, Bhavesh L., *et al.*, Early inhaled glucocorticoid therapy to prevent bronchopulmonary dysplasia. *New Engl. J. Med.*, vol. 340, pp. 1005-1010 (1999).

183. Martin, Richard J., and Walsh-Shukys, Michele C., Bronchopulmonary dysplasia- no simple solution. *New Engl. J. Med.*, vol. 340, pp. 1037-1038 (1999).

184. Niewoehner, Dennis E., Erbland, Marcia L., Deupree, Robert H., *et al.*, Effect of systemic glucocorticoids on exacerbations of chronic obstructive pulmonary disease. *New Engl. J. Med.*, vol. 340, pp. 1941-1947 (1999).

185. Mao, Jenny T., Goldin, Jonathan G., Dermand, John, *et. al.*, A pilot study of all-*trans*-retinoic acid for the treatment of

human emphysema. *Am. J. Respir. Crit. Care Med.*, vol. 165, pp. 718-723 (2002).

186. Drazen, Jeffrey, and Epstein, Arnold M., Guidance concerning surgery for emphysema. *New England J. Med.*, vol. 348, pp. 2134-2135 (2003).

187. Geddes, Duncan, Davies, Michael, Koyama, Hiroshi, *et al.*, *New Engl. J. Med.*, vol. 343, pp. 239-245 (2000).

188. Drazen, Jeffrey M., Surgery for emphysema- not for everyone. *New Engl. J. Med.*, vol. 345, pp. 1129-1130 (2001).

189. Piantadosi, Steven, and members of the National Emphysema Trial Research Group, A randomized trial comparing lung-volume-reduction surgery and medical therapy for severe emphysema. *New England J. Med.*, vol. 348, pp. 2059-2073 (2003).

190. Fessler, Henry E., Reilly. John J., Jr., and Sugarbaker, David J., *Lung Volume Reduction Surgery and Emphysema* (New York: Marcel Dekker, 2004).

191. Sin, Don D., McAlister, Finlay A., Man, S. F. Paul, *et al.*, Contemporary Management of Chronic Obstructive Pulmonary Disease. Scientific Review. *JAMA*, vol. 290, pp. 2301-2312 (2003).

192. Man, S. F. Paul, McAlister, Finlay A., Anthonisen, Nick R., *et al.*, Contemporary Management of Chronic Obstructive Pulmonary Disease. Clinical Applications. *JAMA*, vol. 290, pp. 2313-2316.

193. Anthonisen, N. R., *et al.*, Effects of smoking intervention and the use of an inhaled anticholinergic bronchodilator on the rate of decline of FEV1; the Lung Health Study. *JAMA*, vol. 272, pp. 1497-1505 (1994).

194. Parmet, Pamela, Lynm, Cassio, and Glass, Richard M., JAMA patient page. Chronic obstructive pulmonary disease. *JAMA*, vol. 290, p. 2362 (2003).

195. Baraldo, Simonetta, Zuin, Renzo, and Saetta, Marina, The pathology of COPD. *In* Hansel, T. T., and Barnes, P. J., eds., *Recent Advances in the Pathophysiology of COPD* (Basel: Birkhäuser, 2004). pp. 21-30.

196. Sherman, C. B., The health consequences of cigarette smoking. Pulmonary diseases. *Med. Clinics of N. America*, vol. 76, pp. 355-375 (1992).

197. Gajalakshmi, Vendhan, Peto, Richard, Kanaka, Thanjavur Santhanakrishna, *et al.*, Smoking and mortality from tuberculosis and other diseases in India: retrospective study of 43,000 adult male deaths and 35,000 controls. *Lancet*, vol. 362, pp. 507-515 (2003).

198. Voelker, Rebecca, Risk of tobacco sickness. *JAMA*, vol. 283, p. 1557 (2000).

199. Lloyd, Marion, Tobacco's perils visit a Mexican village. Pesticides stake a claim on farmers. The Boston Globe, p. A15, April 27 (2003).

200. Nuorti, J., Pekka, Butler, Jay C., Farley, Monica M., *et al.*, Cigarette smoking and invasive pneumococcal disease. *New Engl. J. Med.*, vol. 342, pp. 681-689 (2000).

201. Sheffield, John V. L., and Root, Richard K., Smoking and pneumococcal infection. *New Engl. J. Med.*, vol. 342, pp. 732-734 (2000).

202. Altman, Lawrence K., Smoking tied to pneumonia cases in war zone. *N.Y. Times*, p. A9, Sept. 10 (2003).

203. Aligne, C. Andrew, Moss, Mark E., Auinger, Peggy, *et al.*, Association of pediatric dental caries with passive smoking. *JAMA*, vol. 289, pp. 1258-1264 (2003).

204. Cruickshanks, Karen J., Klein, Ronald, Klein, Barbara E. K., *et al.*, Cigarette smoking and hearing loss. The Epidemiology of Hearing Loss Study. *JAMA*, vol. 279, pp. 1715-1719 (1998).

205. Seddon, Johanna M., Willett, Walter C., Speizer, Frank E., *et al.* A prospective study of cigarette smoking and age-related macular degeneration in women. *JAMA*, vol. 276., pp. 1141-1146 (1996).

206. Christen, William G., Glynn, Robert J., Manson, JoAnn E., *et al., JAMA*, vol. 276, pp. 1147-1151 (1996).

207. Klein, Ronald, and Klein, Barbara E. K., *et al.*, Smoke gets in your eyes too. *JAMA*, vol. 276, pp. 1178-1179 (1996).

208. Slade, John; Spilich, George; Nelson, Heidi D., Nevitt, Michael C., Stone, Katie L., *et al.*, Smoking, alcohol, and neuromuscular function in older women. *JAMA*, vol. 273, pp. 1333-1334 (1995).

209. U.S. Department of Health and Human Services. *Reducing the Health Consequences of Smoking. 25 Years of Progress. A Report of the Surgeon General.* (U.D. Department of Health and Human Services. Centers for Disease Control and Prevention, Office on Smoking and Health, 1989), Fig. 9, p.146.

210. Boyd, Alan S., *et al.*, Cigarette smoking-associated elastic changes in the skin. *J. Amer. Acad. Dermatology*, vol. 41, pp. 23-26 (1999).

211. See *Am. J. Epidemiol.*, vol. 135, pp. 839-842 (1992).

212. Editorial, Erectile dysfunction: Can it be prevented? *Harvard Men's Health Watch*, vol. 7, no. 10, pp. 4-8 (2003).

213. Whelan, Elizabeth M., Are some risks of smoking more potent than others? *Priorities for Health*, vol. 11, no. 3, p. 16 (1999).

214. Osborne, M. J., and Stansby, G. P., Cigarette smoking and its relationship to inflammatory bowel disease: a review. *J. Royal Soc. Med.*, vol. 85, pp. 214-216 (1992).

215. Silverstein, P., Smoking and wound healing. *Am. J. Med.*, vol. 93, pp. 22S-24S (1992).

216. Perkins, K. A., Epstein, L. H., Stiller, R. H., *et al.*, Acute effects of nicotine on hunger and caloric intake in smokers and non-smokers. *Psychopharmacology*, vol. 103, pp. 103-109 (1991).

217. Perkins, K. A., Weight gain following smoking cessation. *J. Consulting & Clinical Psychol.*, vol. 61, pp. 768-777 (1993).

218. Editorial, Smoking, drinking, and thinking. *Harvard Men's Health Watch*, vol. 5, no. 11, p. 7 (2001).

219. Atkinson, Holly G., *Living Fit* (1998).

220. Mullin, Rachel. Fire attributed to a cigarette. *The Boston Globe*, p. B5, Nov. 9 (1999).

221. Editorial, Tobacco torches. *The Boston Globe*, p. A22, March 2 (2001).

222. Istre, Gregory R., McCoy, Mary A., Osborn, Linda, *et al.*, Deaths and injuries from house fires. *New Engl. J. Med.*, vol. 344, pp. 1911-1916 (2001).

223. Marshall, Stephen W., Runyan, Carol W., Bangdiwala, Shrikant I., *et al.*, Fatal residential fires. Who dies and who survives? *JAMA*, vol. 279, pp. 1633-1637 (1998).

224. Mallonee, Sue, Istre, Gregory R., Rosenberg, Mark, *et al.*, Surveillance and prevention of residential fires. *New Engl. J. Med.*, vol. 335, pp. 27-31 (1996).

225. Sacks, J. J., and Nelson, D. E., Smoking and injuries: an overview. *Preventive Med.*, vol. 23, pp. 515-520 (1994).

226. Byrne, Gregory, Nicotine likened to cocaine, heroin. *Science*, vol. 240, p. 1143 (1988).

227. Henningfield, J. E., Cohen, C., and Slade, J. D., Is nicotine more addictive than cocaine? *Brit. J. Addiction*, vol. 86, pp. 565-569 (1991).

228. Pich, Emilio Merlo, Pagliusi, Sonia R., Tessari, Michela, *et al.*, Common neural substrates for the addictive properties of nicotine and cocaine. *Science*, vol. 275, pp. 83-86 (1997).

229. Editorial, Smoke screen. *Science,* vol. 274, p. 20 (1996).

230. Helmuth, Laura, Beyond the pleasure principle. *Science,* vol. 294, pp. 983-984 (2001).

231. Nestler, Eric J., and Malenka, Robert C., Addicted Brain. *Sci. Amer.,* vol. 290, no. 3, pp. 78-85 (2004).

232. Lasser, Karen, Boyd, J. Wesley, Woodhandler, Steffie, *et al.,* Smoking and mental illness. A population-based prevalence study. *JAMA,* vol. 284, pp. 2602-2610 (2000).

233. Johnson, Jeffrey G., Cohen, Patricia, Pine, Daniel S., *et al.,* Association between cigarette smoking and anxiety disorders during adolescence and early adulthood. *JAMA,* vol. 284, pp. 2348-2351 (2000).

234. Wu, L., and Anthony, J. C., Tobacco smoking and depressed mood in late childhood and early adolescence. *Am. J. Public Health,* vol. 89, pp. 1837-1840 (1999).

235. Breslau, N., and Klein, D. F., Smoking and panic attacks: an epidemiologic investigation. *Arch. Gen. Psychiatry,* vol. 56, pp. 1141-1147 (1999).

236. Kelly, C., and McCreadie, R. G., Smoking habits, current symptoms, and premorbid characteristics of schizophrenic patients in Nithsdale, Scotland. *Am. J. Psychiatry,* vol. 156, pp. 1751-1757 (1999).

237. Goldberg, Carey, Nicotine studied as possible remedy for mental impairment. *Boston Globe,* pp. A1-A4, Nov. 12 (2003).

238. Thoreau, Henry David, *Cape Cod* (Orleans: Parnassus, 1984; orig. 1864), pp. 47-48.

239. Editorial, Cigars and health: the National Cancer Institute Reports. *Harvard Men's Health Watch,* vol. 3, no. 8, p.4 (1999).

240. National Cancer Institute. Cancer Facts. Questions and answers about cigar smoking and cancer. *National Cancer Institute, Fact Sheet 3.65,* pp. 1-6, March 7 (2000).

241. Baker, Frank, Ainsworth, Stuart R., Dye, Joseph T., *et al.*, Health risks associated with cigar smoking. *JAMA*, vol. 284, pp. 735-740 (2000).

242. *J. Natl. Cancer Inst.*, vol. 92, pp. 333-337 (2000). A summary appears in *CA- A Cancer J. for Clinicians*, vol. 50, no. 3, pp.138-139 (2000).

243. Feeney, Mark. Gone in a puff of smoke. *The Boston Globe*, pp. C1-C7, Aug. 5 (1998).

244. Rice, John, Castro warns Cubans of the risks of alcohol, smoking. *Boston Globe*, p. A45, December 2 (2002).

245. Horowitz, Janice M. Sweet as candy, deadly as cigarettes. Teens are flocking to a hip form of smokes. There are hidden dangers. *Time*, vol. 160, no. 25, p. 85(2002).

246. Editorial, Are clove cigarettes a safe option? *UC Berkeley Wellness Letter, p. 7*, vol. 15, no. 5 (1999).

247. AMA Council on Scientific Affairs, Evaluation of the health hazard of clove cigarettes. *JAMA*, vol. 260, pp. 3641-3644 (1988).

248. Berestein, Leslie, Healthy or not, the hookah habit is hot. The latest student craze is smoking the ancient Middle Eastern water pipe. *Time*, vol. 161, no. 4, p. 10 (2003).

249. National Cancer Institute, Questions and answers about smokeless tobacco and cancer. Cancer Facts, pp. 1-5, Oct. 23 (1998). See http://cis.nci.nih.gov/fact/3_63.htm

250. Cullen, Joseph W., Smokeless tobacco use as a cause of cancer. In: *Cancer Prevention*, DeVita, Vincent T., Jr., Hellman, Samuel, and Rosenberg, Steven A., eds., pp. 1-11 (1990).

251. Ernster, Virginia L., Grady, Deborah G., and Greene, John C. Use of smokeless tobacco in major-league baseball. *New Engl. J. Med.*, vol. 319, p.1015 (1988).

252. Connolly, Gregory N., Orleans, Tracy C., and Kogan, Michael, Use of smokeless tobacco in major-league baseball. *New Engl. J. Med.*, vol. 318, pp. 1281-1285 (1988).

253. Barnes, Deborah E., and Bero, Lisa A. Why review articles on the health effects of passive smoking reach different conclusions. *JAMA*, vol. 279, pps. 1566-1570 (1998).

254. Harris, Gardiner. Pfizer to pay $430 million over promoting drug to doctors. *New York Times*, p. 1-6, May 14 (2004).

255. Fontham, E. T. H., Correa, P., Reynolds, P., *et al.*, Environmental tobacco smoke and lung cancer in nonsmoking women: a multicenter study. *JAMA*, vol. 271, pps. 1752-1759 (1994).

256. Boffetta, P., Agudo, A., Ahrens, W, *et al.*, Multicenter case-control study of exposure to environmental tobacco smoke and lung cancer in Europe. *J. Natl. Cancer Inst.*, vol. 90, pps. 1440-1450 (1998).

257. Brennan, Paul, Buffler, Patricia A., Reynolds, Peggy, *et al.*, Secondhand smoke exposure in adulthood and risk of lung cancer among never smokers: A pooled analysis of two large studies. *Internat. J. Cancer*, vol. 109, pp. 125-131 (2003).

258. National Institute for Occupational Safety and Health, Environmental Tobacco Smoke in the Workplace. Lung Cancer and Other Health Effects. U.S. Department of Health and Human Services, Public Health Service, Centers for Disease Control, National Institute for Occupational Safety and Health, DHHS (NIOSH) Publication no. 91-08 (1991).

259. Kamins, Heather, The exiled smoker. First at the desk, then to smoking rooms, then outside, now away from entrances. *The Boston Globe*, p. F1, June 12 (1999).

260. Glantz, Stanton, A., and Parmley, William W., Passive Smoking and Heart Disease. Mechanisms and Risk. *JAMA*, vol. 273, pps. 1047-1053 (1995).

261. Howard, George, Wagenknecht, Lynne E., Burke, Gregory L., *et al.*, Cigarette smoking and progression of atherosclerosis. The atherosclerosis risk in communities (ARIC) study. *JAMA*, vol. 279, pps. 119-124 (1998).

262. Glantz, Stanton A., and Parmley, William W., Even a little secondhand smoke is dangerous. *JAMA*, vol. 286, pps. 462-463 (2001).

263. NNAL is (4-(Methylnitrosamino)-1-(3-pyridyl)-1-butanol) and is a potent lung carcinogen, according to Xia, Yang, McGuffey, James E., Wang, Lanqing *et al.*, Centers for Disease Control and Prevention, Atlanta, GA (2004).

264. Hecht, Stephen S., Carmella, Steven G., Murphy, Sharon E., *et al.*, A tobacco-specific lung carcinogen in the urine of men exposed to cigarette smoke. *New Engl. J. Med.*, vol. 329, pps. 1543-1546 (1931).

265. Anderson, Kristin E., Carmella, Steven G., Ye, Ming, *et al.*, Metabolites of a tobacco-specific lung carcinogen in non-smoking women exposed to environmental tobacc smoke. *J. Natl. Cancer Inst.*, vol. 93, pps. 378-381 (2001).

266. Everson, Richard B., Randerath, Erika, Santella, Regina M., *et al.* Quantitative associations between DNA damage in human placenta and maternal smoking and birth weight. *J. Natl. Cancer Inst.*, vol. 80, pps. 567-576 (1988).

267. Chilmonczyk, Barbara A., Salmun, Luis M., Megathlin, Keith N., *et al.* Association between exposure to environmental tobacco smoke and exacerbations of asthma in children. *New England J. Med.*, vol. 328, pp. 1665-1669 (1993).

268. Reif, Arnold E., Allergy to tobacco smoke: a new understanding. New evidence gives boost to campaign to restrict smoking in public places. *Environmental Action Bulletin*, Nov. 27 (1976).

269. Eisner, Mark D., Smith, Alexander K., and Blanc, Paul D., Bartender's respiratory health after establishment of smoke-free bars and taverns. *JAMA*, vol. 280, pp. 1909-1914 (1998).

270. Domino, Edward F., Hornbach, Erich, and Demana, Tsenge, The nicotine content of common vegetables. *New Engl. J. Med.*, vol. 329, p. 427 (1993).

271. Editorial, "Thank for not smoking." When you smoke, every-one near you smokes. *JAMA*, vol. 280, p. 1968 (1996).

272. Committee to Assess the Science Base for Tobacco Harm Reduction, *Clearing the Smoke: Assessing the Science Basis for Tobacco Harm Reduction*, eds. Stratton, K., Shetty, P., Wallace, R., *et al.* (Washington: Institute of Medicine, National Academy, 2000).

273. Reif, Arnold E., High level wellness and low level wellness: an overview. *Health Values: Achieving High Level Wellness*, vol. 2, no. 4, pp. 200-210 (1978).

274. Benowitz, Neal L., Health and public policy. Implications of the "low yield" cigarette. *New Engl. J. Medicine*, vol. 320, pp. 1619-1621 (1989).

275. Herning, Ronald ., Jones, Reese T., Bachman, John B., *et al.*, Puff volume increases when low-nicotine cigarettes are smoked. *Brit. Med. J.*, vol. 283, pp. 187-189 (1981).

276. Palmer, Julie R., Rosenberg, Lynn, and Shapiro, Samuel, "Low-yield" cigarettes and the risk of nonfatal myocardial infarction in women. *New Engl. J. Medicine*, vol. 320, pp. 1569-1573 (1989).

277. Nickerson, Colin. Canada to ban 'light' labels on cigarettes. *The Boston Globe*, p. A1, August 13 (2001).

278. Jaffe, Greg, and Chipello, Christopher J., A boom in home-made smokes. *The Boston Globe*, pp. 1-4, May 11 (1999).

279. Cherner, Joseph W., New York issues fire-safe cigarette standards. Tobacco manufacturers have until June 28 to comply. Joe@smokefree.org, Dec. 31 (2003).

280. Fontham, E. T., Protective dietary factors and lung cancer. *Internat. J. Epidemiology*, vol. 19, Suppl. 1, pp. S32-S43 (1990).

281. Mayne, S. T., Handelman, G. J., and Beecher, G., Beta-carotene and lung cancer promotion in heavy smokers—a plausible relationship? *J. Natl. Cancer Inst.*, vol. 88, pp. 1513-1515 (1996).

282. Knekt, P. Vitamin E and smoking and the risk of lung cancer. *Annals New York Acad. Sci.*, vol. 686, pp. 280-288 (1993).

283. Bal, Dileep G., Commentary on "European Consensus Statement on Lung Cancer." *CA- A Cancer J. for Clinicians*, vol. 48, no. 3, pp. 164-166 (1998).

284. Steinmetz, K. A., Potter, J. D., and Folsom, A. R. Vegetables, fruit, and lung cancer in the Iowa Women's Health Study. *Cancer Research*, vol. 53, pp. 536-543 (1993).

285. Wynder, E. L., Hebert, J. R., and Kabat, G. C., Association of dietary fat and lung cancer. *J. Natl. Cancer Inst.*, vol. 79, pp. 631-637 (1987).

286. McAllister, J. F. O., Once upon a time, there was a pot-smoking prince. *Time*, vol. 159, no. 4, Jan. 28 (2002).

287. McAllister, J. F. O., Europe goes to pot. *Time*, vol. 158, no. 7, Aug. 20 (2001).

288. News releases of December 24, 2003, from www.washingtonpost.com.

289. Fishburne, P. M., Abelson, H. I., and Cisin, I., *National Survey on Drug Abuse: Main Findings, 1979*. Washington, D.C.: U.s. Government Printing Office (1980).

290. Annas, George J., Reefer madness- the Federal response to California's Medical-Marijuana law. *New Engl. J. Med.*, vol. 337, pp. 435-439 (1997).

291. Denniston, Lyle, Court bars marijuana as medicine. *The Boston Globe*, p. A1-A6, May 15 (2001). July 31 (2001).

292. Roosevelt, Margot, A setback for medipot. *Time*, vol. 157, no. 21, p.50, May 28, (2001).

293. Nickerson, Colin, Canada OK's medical marijuana. *The Boston Globe*, p. A1-A12, July 31 (2001).

294. News releases of December 8, 2003, from Health Canada online.

295. Surgeon General, The Surgeon General's warning on marijuana. Centers for Disease Control and Prevention (CDC), Morbidity and Mortality Weekly Report, vol. 31, no. 31, pp. 428-429 (1982).

296. Wu, Tzu-Chin, Tashkin, Donald P., Djahed, Behnam, *et al.*, Pulmonary hazards of smoking marijuana as compared with tobacco. *New Engl. J. Medicine*, vol. 318, pp. 347-351 (1988).

297. Pope, Harrison G., and Yurgelun-Todd, Deborah, The residual cognitive effects of heavy marijuana use in college students. *JAMA*, vol. 275, pp. 521-527 (1996).

298. Block, R. I., and Ghoneim, M. M., Effects of chronic marijuana use on human cognition. *Psychopharmacology*, vol. 110, pp. 219-228 (1993).

299. Lambert, Craig, Marijuana's aftermath. *Harvard Magazine*, vol. 93, no. 3, pp. 13-15 (1995).

300. National Institute on Drug Abuse, *Marijuana: Facts for Teens*. Rockville: National Institute on Drug Abuse (1998 update of 1995 release).

301. CDC, Restricted activity days and other problems associated with use of marijuana or cocaine among 18 to 44 year olds:

United States, 1991. Hyattsville: CDC, National Center for Health Statistics, (1991).

302. Zimmer, Lynn, and Morgan, John P., *Marijuana Myths, Marijuana Facts: A Review of the Scientific Evidence*. New York: The Lindesmith Center (1997).

303. Lynskey, Michael T., Heath, Andrew C., Bucholz, Kathleen K., *et al.*, Escalation of drug use in early-onset cannabis users vs co-twin controls. *JAMA*, vol. 289, pp. 427-433 (2003).

304. Kandel, Denise B. Does marijuana use cause the use of other drugs? *JAMA*, vol. 289, pp. 482-483 (2003).

305. Di Chiara, Gaetano, Marijuana addiction. *Science*, vol. 277, pp. 750-751 (1997).

306. Greenspoon, Lester, Bakalar, James B., Zimmer, Lynn, *et al.*, Marijuana addiction. *Science*, vol. 277, pp. 749-750 (1997).

307. Tanda, Gianluigi, Pontieri, Francesco E., and Di Chiara, Gaetano. Cannabinoid and heroine activation of mesolimbic dopamine transmission by a common mu1 opioid receptor mechanism. *Science*, vol. 276, pp. 2048-2049 (1997).

308. Wickelgren, Ingrid, Marijuana: harder than thought? *Science*, vol. 276, pp. 1967-1968 (1997).

309. Childers, Steven R., How cannabis acts. *Science*, vol. 288, p. 1972 (2000).

310. Barinaga, Marcia, How cannabinoids work in the brain. *Science*, vol. 291, pp. 2530-2531 (2001).

311. Huestis, Marilyn A., *et al.*, Blockade of effects of smoked marijuana by the CB1-selective cannabinoid receptor antagonist SR141716. *Arch. Gen. Psychiatry*, vol. 58, pp. 322-328 (2001).

312. O'Brien, Charles, *et al.* Their study in *Nature Medicine* of October, 2001 is reported under Marijuana, cocaine share circuitry, *Science*, vol. 294, p. 297 (2001).

313. Solowij, Nadia, Stephens, Robert S., Roffman, Roger A, *et al.*, Cognitive functioning of long-term heavy cannabis users seeking treatment. *New Engl. J. Med.*, vol. 287, pp. 1123-1131 (2002).

314. Pope, Harrison G., Jr., Cannabis, cognition, and residual confounding. *New Engl. J. Med.*, vol. 287, pp. 1172-1174 (2002).

315. CDC. Health objectives for the nation. Current tobacco, alcohol, marijuana, and cocaine use among high school students- United States, 1990. *MMWR Weekly*, vol. 40, no. 38, pp. 659-663 (1991).

316. CDC. 1997 Youth risk behavior surveillance system (YRBSS). *MMWR*, vol. 47, no. SS-3 (1999).

317. McShane, Larry, Marijuana use by teens declines, survey finds. *The Boston Globe*, p. A3, Nov. 27 (2000).

318. Morrow, Lance. Kids & pot. *Time*, pps.26-31, December 9 (1996).

319. Johnston, Lloyd, New battle against marijuana. *National Education Assoc. Health*, p.24, February (1998).

320. Graff, James L., High times at New Trier High. *Time*, pps.33-38, December 9 (1996).

321. Knox, Richard A., Marijuana hook found in troubled youths. *The Boston Globe*, p. A3, April 7 (1998).

322. Golden, Frederic, Smoking gun for the young. A cancer study shows that tobacco poses more of a risk the earlier it's used. *Time*, vol 153, no. 15, April 19 (1999).

323. Gold, Diane R., Wang, Xiaobin, Wypij, David, *et al.*, Effects of cigarette smoking on lung function in adolescent boys and girls. *New Engl. J. Med.*, vol. 335, pps. 931-937 (1996).

324. Koh, Howard K., Kannler, Christine, and Geller, Alan C., Cancer prevention: preventing tobacco-related cancers. In DeVita, Vincent T., Jr., Hellman, Samuel, and Rosenberg,

Steven A., eds., *Cancer. Principles & Practice of Oncology*, 6th edn. (Philadelphia: Lippincott Williams & Wilkins, 2001), pp. 549-560.

325. Lowry, Richard, Kann, Laura, Collins, Janet L., The effect of socioeconomic status on chronic disease risk behaviors among US adolescents. *JAMA*, vol. 276, pps. 792-797 (1996).

326. Anda, Robert F., Croft, Janet B., Felitti, Vincent J., *et al.*, Adverse childhood experiences and smoking among adolescents and adulthood. *JAMA*, vol. 282, pps. 1652-1658 (1999).

327. Sargent. James D., *et al.*, *Pediatrics*, vol. 108: 1256-1262 (2001). Reported in *CA. A Cancer Journal for CLinicians*, vol. 52, no.2., pp. 64-65 (2002).

328. Maloney, Jennifer, Saving teens from smoking. *Your Health, Harvard Pilgrim Health Care*, pp. 4-7, Winter (2000).

329. CDC, Cigarette smoking among high school students- 11 states, 1991-1997. *JAMA*, vol. 282, pps. 935-936 (1999).

330. Gansler, Ted, and Eyre, Harmon J., What's new and what's not. *CA: A Cancer J. for Clinicians*, vol. 52, no. 6, p. 318-319 (2002).

331. CDC, Decline in cigarette consumption following implementation of a comprehensive tobacco prevention and education program- Oregon, 1996-1998. *JAMA*, vol. 281, pps. 1483-1484 (1999).

332. Mays, Patricia J., Smoking by youths falls in Fla. *Associated Press*, reported in *The Boston Globe*, p. A8, April 2 (1999).

333. Vaishnav, Anand, Fewer younger Mass. teens smoking. *The Boston Globe*, p. B2, Jan. 18 (2002).

334. Editorial on CDC report on smoking. *CA Cancer J. Clin.* vol.52, p. 319 (2002).

335. Smith, Stephen, Cigarette sales to teens up sharply. Trend is blamed on Budget cut. *The Boston Globe*, p. B1, May 1 (2003);

see also pp. A1-B5, March 16 (2004), and p. A11, March 22 (2004).

336. Virginia Slims ad, *Time*, p.25, April 22 (1996).

337. Farley, John, and Bland, Elizabeth, L., C'mon baby, light my fire. *Time*, p.66, Jan. 27 (1997).

338. Charles King, III, Siegel, Michael, Celebucki, Carolyn, *et al.*, Adolescent cigarette advertising in magazines. An evaluation of brand-specific advertising in relation to youth readership. *JAMA*, vol. 279, pps. 516-520 (1998).

339. Pierce, John P., Choi, Won S., Gilpin, Elizabeth A., *et al.*, Tobacco industry promotion of cigarettes and adolescent smoking. *JAMA*, vol. 279, pps. 511-515 (1998).

340. Natives, Selling caution or hedonism in a world of no smoking. *New York Times*, p. C1-C5, July 7 (2004).

341. Lewis, Diane E., New York Times drops cigarette, tobacco advertising. *The Boston Globe*, p. D3, April 19, (1999).

342. Leonard, Mary, US defends Mass. limits on cigarette ads. *The Boston Globe*, pp. A1-A6, March 31 (2001).

343. Leonard, Mary, Limits on tobacco ads lifted. High court strikes Mass. regulations. *The Boston Globe*, pp. A1-A13, June 29 (2001).

344. Goldstein, Adam O., Sobel, Rachel A., and Newman, Glen R., Tobacco and alcohol use in G-rated children's animated films. *JAMA*, vol. 281, pps. 1131-1136 (1999).

345. Tickle, J.J., Sargent, J.D., Dalton, M.A., *et al.*, Favorite movie stars, their tobacco use in contemporary movies, and its association with adolescent smoking. *Tobacco Control*, vol. 10, pp. 16-22 (2001).

346. Waxman, Sharon, Competing studios claim rights to the same film. *New York Times*, p. B2, Sept. 13 (2005).

347. Emma Ross. Smoking in movies entices youths, study says. *The Boston Globe*, p. A16, June 10 (2003).

348. Editorial, Smoke screen, *UC Berkeley Wellness Letter*, vol. 18, no. 12, p. 5 (2002).

349. Orey, Michael, *Assuming the Risk: the Mavericks, the Lawyers, and the Whistle-Blowers Who Beat Big Tobacco* (Boston: Little, Brown, 1999).

350. Phillips, Frank, Tobacco anti-ads rapped as weak. 16 states crtiticize Phillip Morris blitz. *The Boston Globe*, pp. B1-B8, April 7 (1999). See also Hohler, Bob, State targets cigarette ads. Says companies again luring youthful smokers. *The Boston Globe*, pp. B1-B5, May 18 (2000).

351. Editorial, Tobacco ads still aimed at kids; experts advise stronger protections. *CA. A Cancer Journal for Physicians*, vol 51, no. 6, pp. 324-326 (2001).

352. For instance, in June 2005 there were full-page Philip Morris ads in Psychology Today, and in the New York Times Magazine of mid June.

353. Stewart, Rhonda, Controls on teen smoking tighten. Town tightens tobacco rules. *The Boston Globe*, p. West 1, March 9 (2003).

354. Wechsler, Henry, Rigotti, Nancy A., Gledhill-Hoyt, Jeana, *et al.*, Increased levels of cigarette use among college students. A cause for national concern. *JAMA*, vol. 280, pps. 1673-1678 (1998).

355. Core Institute, Southern Illinois University Carbondale, Fall 2004 Survey, www.siu.edu/~coreinst/home.htm.

356. Stodghill, Ron, No smoking allowed in the ivory tower. U.S. colleges are cutting up places where students can light up. *Time*, vol. 160, no. 23, p.8 (2002).

357. American Cancer Society, *A Resource Guide to Youth Tobacco Cessation Programs* (1999). Free from the American Cancer Society Tobacco Control Program, 1599 Clifton Road, NE, Atlanta, GA 30329. Phone 404-329-5792.

358. U.S. Department of Health and Human Services, *Preventing Tobacco Use Among Young People. A Report of the Surgeon General.* HHS, CDC, Office on Smoking and Health, Atlanta, see p. 10 (1994).

359. Tobacco Research Implementation Group, *Tobacco Research Implementation Plan. Priorities for Tobacco Research Beyond the Year 2000* (Bethesda: National Cancer Institute, 1998).

360. Reif, Arnold E. Public Information on Smoking (1997), pp. 125-126

361. Koker, J. Kelly, Four-fold prevention: Strategies to prevent substance abuse among elementary school-aged children. *Am. School Counselor Assoc., Professional School Counseling*, vol. 5, no. 1, pp. 70-74 (2001).

362. Jacobson, Peter D., Lantz, Paula M., Warner, Kenneth E., et al., *Combating Teen Smoking: Research and Policy Strategies* (Ann Arbor: University of Michigan, 2001).

363. Campaign for Tobacco-Free Kids, 1707 L Street, NW, Suite 800, Washington, D.C. 20036 (www.tobaccofreekids.org).

364. Positive Promotions, 40-01 168th Street, Flushing, NY 11358 (www.positivepromotions.com) .

365. Jones, E. Stanley, *Abundant Living* (New York: Abingdon-Cokesbury, 1942; orig. publ. 1922), pp. 136-137.

366. Morgan, Oliver J., and Jordan, Merle, eds., *Addiction and Spirituality. A Multidisciplinary Approach* (Chalice, 1999).

367. Cairns, J., Lyon, J. L., and Skolnick, M., eds., *Banbury Report 4: Cancer Incidence in Defined Populations* (Cold Spring Harbor: Cold Spring Harbor Laboratory, 1980).

368. MacMahon, B., *et al.*, Populations at low risk of cancer. *J. Natl. Cancer Inst.*, vol. 65, pp. 1049-1195 (1980).

369. Women and Smoking. A Report of the Surgeon General (1998), p.81.

370. Special Report, Big Tobacco still targeting kids. *Campaign for Tobacco-Free Kids News Release,* updated Sept. 19 (2005).

371. Pitofsky, Robert, Pepared statement of the FDC presented before the Committee on Commerce, Science, and Transportation, United States Senate, March 3 (1998). Website: www.ftc.gov/os/1998/9803/tobacco98.tes.htm

372. Brown and Williams Company, Statement on Health Warnings. Download date: May 1 (2002). Website: www. bw.com

373. *Report of the Surgeon General, 1989. Reducing the Health Consequences of Smoking,* p. 496.

374. Reif, Arnold E., Public education and the health professional's role. *Tufts Health Science Review,* vol. 1, no. 4 – vol. 2, no. 1, Winter-Spring (1971).

375. Canadian Cancer Society release, April 1 (2002), posted on their web site.

376. Health Canda. Proposed New Labeling Requirements for Tobacco Products. Consultation Paper. Ottawa, Health Canada (1999). Carried on their web site.

377. Federal Trade Commission release, FTC announces settlements requiring disclosure of cigar health risks, June 26 (2000), posted on their web site.

378. Myers, Matthew L., Comments of the Campaign for Tobacco-Free Kids to the FDC on Proposal Regarding Smokeless Tobacco Warning Labels, July 21 (2000).

379. Studlar, Donley T., *Tobacco Control: Comparative Politics in the United States and Canada* (Peterborough: Broadview Press, 2002).

380. Mansfield, Melissa, Cigarette giveaways get mixed reviews. *The Boston Globe*, p. A28, December 26 (2002).

381. von Zielbauer, Paul. New York's statewise smoking law adds insult to inhaling. State limits on smoking in bars and restaurants are even tougher than New York City's. *New York Times*, p. A17, July 23 (2003).

382. Wolinsky, Howard. The AMA tackles tobacco subsidiary funding. *ACSH's Priorities*, pp. 39-43, Fall/Winter (1993).

383. Whelan, Elizabeth M., ACSH's president responds. *ACSH's Priorities*, p. 43, Fall/Winter (1993).

384. Robinson, David, *Cancer Clusters: Findings vs Feelings* (New York: American Council on Science and Health, March 2002).

385. Warner, Kenneth E., Goldenhar, Linda M., and McLaughlin, Catherine G., Cigarette advertising and magazine coverage of the hazards of smoking. A statistical analysis. *New Engl. J. Medicine*, vol. 326, pp. 305-309 (1992).

386. Editorial, *BMJ fumes over tobacco grant.* Science, vol. 292, p. 1055 (2001).

387. Whitby, William T., *The Smoking Scare De-bunked* (St. Louis: Fireside, 1986).

388. Grimm, David, Is tobacco research turning over a new leaf? *Science*, vol. 307, pp. 36-37 (2005).

389. *Associated Press*, Smoking danger reaffirmed *Middlesex News*, May (1982); International Medicine News Service, Research group affirms smoking, lung ca link. *Internal Medicine News*, vol. 15, no. 13, p. 16, July 1-14 (1982).

390. Daynard, Richard D., Tobacco liability litigation as a cancer control strategy. *J. Natl. Cancer Institute*, vol. 80, pp. 9-13 (1988).

391. Hilts, Philip J., *Protecting America's Health: The FDS, Business, and One Hundred Years of Regulation* (New York, Knopf, 2003).

392. Kessler, David, The Food and Drug Administration's regulation of tobacco products. *New Engl. J. of Medicine*, vol. 335, pp. 988-994 (1996).

393. Kessler, David, *A Question of Intent: A Great American Battle with a Deadly Industry* (Public Affairs, 2001).

394. Glantz, Leonard H., and Annas, George J., Tobacco, the Food and Drug Administration, and Congress. *New England J. Med.*, vol. 343, pp. 1802-1806 (2002).

395. The U.S. Act is referred to as 21 USC 321 (g)(l)(C).

396. Myers, Matthew L., Protecting the public health by strengthening the Food and Drug Administration's authority over tobacco product. *New England J. Med.*, vol. 343, pp. 1806-1809 (2002).

397. Friedman, Michael A., Strengthening the FDA. *Science*, vol. 298, p.2332 (2002).

398. Kaufman, Marc. Official backs tobacco ban. Surgeon general a staunch critic. *The Boston Globe*, p. A5, June 4 (2003).

399. Harris, Gardiner, Study on nicotine levels stirs calls for new controls. *New York Times*, p. A14, Jan. 19 (2007).

400. Glantz, Stanton, Slade, John, Bero, Lisa A., *et al.*, *The Cigarette Papers* (Berkeley: University of California, 1996).

401. Hilts, Philip J. *Smokescreen. The Truth Behind the Tobacco Industry Cover-Up* (Reading: Addison-Wesley, 1996).

402. Kluger, Richard, *Ashes to Ashes. America's Hundred-Year Cigarette War, the Public Health, and the Unabashed Triumph of Philip Morris* (New York: Knopf, 1996).

403. Merzer, Martin, Tobacco executives changing their tune. Heads of big companies acknowledge cigarettes are addictive and harmful. *The Boston Globe*, p. A22, June 18 (2000).

404. Schroeder, Steven A. Tobacco control in the wake of the 1998 Master Settlement Agreement. *New Engl. J. Med.*, vol. 350, pp. 293-301 (2004).

405. Smolowe, Jill. Sorry, pardner. Big Tobacco fesses up and pays up- $368.5 billion, but Congress must approve the deal. *Time*, pp. 24-29, June 30 (1997).

406. American Heart Association, Tobacco news from Capitol Hill. *The Advocacy Pulse*, vol. 6, issue 6, p. 1, Oct. 17 (2003), found at advocacydc@heart.org.

407. Reuters, Jury orders Philip Morris to pay $28b to cancer patient. *The Boston Globe*, p. A5, October 5 (2002).

408. Glaberson, William, After a death, revenge isn't so sweet. Brooklyn widow wins tobacco company suit. *New York Times*, p. A23, January 6 (2004).

409. herner, Joseph W., NY jury orders tobacco cartel to pay $20 million, joe@smokefree.org, Jan. 11 (2004).

410. Associated Press, Judge OK's pursuit of US tobacco case. *New York Times*, p. A5, March 18 (2004).

411. Editorial, Government presents strong case against tobacco companies but proposed remedies fall short. *Campaign for Tobacco-Free Kids News Release*, June 7 (2005).

412. Kaufman, Marc, Racketeering case against tobacco industry to begin. Suit alleges public was misled on risks, *Boston Globe*, p. A2, Sept. 20 (2004).

413. Janofsky, Michael, Prosecutors open case against tobacco firms. *New York Times*, p. A16, Sept. 22 (2004).

414. U.S. Department of Justice, Litigation against tobacco companies. Order #600 dated July 21 (2004). www.usdoj.gov/civil/cases/tobacco2/index.htm.

415. Janofsky, Michael, Appellate court backs companies in tobacco case. Setback for government. Ruling rejects U.S. effort to make industry pay record $280 billion. *New York Times*, p. A1-A13, Feb. 5 (2005).

416. Janofsky, Michael, Remedies emerging as issue in Federal tobacco case. *New York Times*, p. A11, April 2 (2005).

417. Editorial, Justice Department civil lawsuit. *Campaign for Tobacco-Free Kids Special Report*, updated Nov. 10 (2005).

418. Janofsky, Michael, Tobacco trial ends, but the arguing does not. *New York Times*, p. A14, June 10 (2005).

419. Janofsky, Michael, On smoking, Surgeon General favors tailored efforts to national campaign. *New York Times*, p. A18, May 4 (2005).

420. Lichtblau, Eric, Political leanings were always factor in tobacco suit. *New York Times*, p. A17, June 19 (2005).

421. Leonnig, Carol D., Witness in tobacco trial alleges pressure. Says official urged him to tone down penalties. *Boston Globe*, p. A3, June 20 (2005).

422. Fiore, Michael C., Keller, Paula A., and Baker, Timothy B., The Justice Department's case against the tobacco companies. *New England J. Med.*, vol. 353, pp. 972-975 (2005).

423. Janofsky, Michael, U.S. requests $14 billion in tobacco rackets case. *New York Times*, p. A17, June 29 (2005).

424. Associated Press. G.M. and tobacco shares help lead moderate rally. *New York Times*, p. C11, Oct. 18 (2004).

425. Greenhouse, Linda. Justices reject appeal in tobacco case. *New York Times*, p. A14, Oct. 18 (2004).

426. Shenon, Philp, New limits set by Federal judge on marketing of cigarettes. *New York Times*, p. A1-A12, August 18 (2006).

427. Natives, Kool cigarettes in new flavors draw criticism. *New York Times*, pp. C1-C11, March 9 (2004).

428. Glantz, Stanton A., and Charlesworth, Annemarie, Tourism and hotel revenues before and after passage of smoke-free restaurant ordinances. *JAMA*, vol. 281, pp. 1911-1918 (1999).

429. Eisner, M. D., Smith, A. K., and Blanc, P. D. Bartenders' respiratory health after establishment of smoke-free bars and taverns. *JAMA*, vol. 280, pp. 1909-1914 (1998).

430. Perez-Pena, Richard, A city of quitters? In strict New York, 11% fewer smokers. *New York Times*, p. A1-C17, May 12 (2004).

431. Gupta, A Montana ordinance has a surprising effect- and triggers a CDC warning. *Time*, vol. 163, no. 19, p. 82, May 10 (2004). The original study was authored by Robert Shepard and published in the *British Medical Journal*.

432. Parmet, Wendy E., Daynard, Richard A., and Gottlieb, Mark A. The physician's role in helping smoke-sensitive patients to use the Americans with Disabilities Act to secure smoke-free workplaces and public spaces. *JAMA*, vol. *JAMA*, vol. 276, pp. 909-1913 (1996).

433. Editorial, The tobacco bailout. *New York Times*, p. A220, Sept. 15 (2003).

434. Schroeder, Steven A., The tobacco buyout and the FDA. *New Engl. J. Med.*, vol. 381, pp. 1377-1380 (2004).

435. Romero, Simon, In tobacco country, growers keep their fingers crossed for a windfall. *New York Times*, p. A10, July 26 (2004).

436. USDA Fact Sheet, Tobacco Transition Payment Program (also called the "Tobacco Buyout"). www.fsa.usda.gov/pas/publications/facts/html/ttpp05.htm.

437. Editorial, Campaign for Tobacco-Free Kids newsletter, June 6 (2005).

438. Markel, Howard, Why America needs a strong FDA, *JAMA*, vol. 294, pp. 2489-2491 (2005).

439. Marcus, Donald M., What ails the FDA? *New Engl. J. Med.*, vol. 352, p. 2554 (2005).

440. Ribisl, Kurt M., Williams, Rebecca S., and Kim, Annice E., Internet sales of cigarettes to minors. *JAMA*, vol. 290, pp. 1356-1359 (2003).

441. Mohl, Bruce. Cigarette shoppers turn to the Internet. *The Boston Globe*, p. A1, February 16 (2001).

442. Reagan, K. A., Hong, T., Cohen, E. L., *et al.*, Blocking access to online tobacco sales sites, *Tobacco Control*, vol. 11, p. 164 (2002).

443. Healy, Patrick, New law bans New Yorkers from buying cigarettes online. *The New York Times*, p. A29, June 13 (2003).

444. Galvin, James C., *et al.*, *God's Little Devotional Bible*, Walking the talk, July 14 (Tulsa: Honor, 1997).

445. Cushman, John H., Jr., Big tobacco pays this foundation to bash tobacco. *New York Times*, p. E10, Nov. 17 (2003).

446. Skolnick, Andrew A., Judge rules diversion of antismoking money illegal, victory for California Tobacco Control Program. *JAMA*, vol. 273, p.610 (1995).

447. Klein, Rick, House hit on tobacco money. Antismoking funds diverted, critics say. *The Boston Globe*, pp. B1-B4, April 25 (2001).

448. Gross, Cary P., Soffer, Benny, Bach, Peter B., *et al.*, State expenditures for tobacco-control programs and the tobacco settlement. *New Engl. J. Med.*, vol. 347, pp. 1080-1086 (2002).

449. Schroeder, Steven A., Conflicting dispatches from the tobacco wars. *New Engl. J. Med.*, vol. 347, pp. 1107-1109 (2002).

450. Zuckerbrod, Nancy, Report says states rely on tobacco funds. *The Boston Globe*, p. A12, Oct. 10 (2003).

451. Levin, Myron, Cigarette makers targeted on smuggling. *The Boston Globe*, p. A14, August 10 (2000).

452. Surgeon General: 25 years of progress, DHS (1989).

453. Shane, Scott, Limited success seen in tobacco pact. Smoking drops; youths still enticed. *The Boston Sunday Globe*, p. A6, November 26 (2000).

454. McClam, Erin, High prices said to cut teen smoking. CDC also credits education efforts. *The Boston Globe*, p. A2, May 17 (2002).

455. O'Connor, Anahad, States fail to meet no-smoking goals for women. *New York Times*, p. D6, Sept. 30, 2003.

456. Fonda, Daren, Why tobacco won't quit. Legal costs and taxes haven't choked the industry. Profits are rising. And the feds are off the case. *Time*, vol. 157, no. 26, pp. 38-39, July 2, (2001).

457. Jackson, Derrick Z., Big tobacco's big lie about smokers. *The Boston Globe*, p. A27, May 10 (2002).

458. Kawahara, M., Ushijima, S., Kamimori, T., *et al.*, Second primary tumours in more than 2-year disease-free survivors of small-cell lung cancer in Japan: the role of smoking cessation. *Brit. J. Cancer*, vol. 78, pp. 409-412 (1998).

459. Leshner, Alan I., Science-based views of drug addiction and its treatment. *JAMA*, vol. 282, pp. 1314-1316 (1999).

460. USDHHS, *Nicotine Addiction. A* Report of the Surgeon General (1988).

461. Saal, D., Dong, Y., Monci, A., and Malenka, R. C., Drugs of abuse and stress trigger a common synaptic adaptation in dopamine neurons. *Neuron*, vol. 37, pp. 577-582 (2003).

462. Abrams, David B., *et al.*, *The Tobacco Dependence Treatment Handbook: A Guide to Best Practices* (New York: Guilford, 2003).

463. National Cancer Institute, *Those who continue to smoke: is achieving abstinence harder and do we need to change our interventions?* Smoking and Tobacco Control Monograph; 15 (Bethesda, MD: National Cancer Institute, 2003).

464. Fiore, M.C., Bailey, W. C., Cohen, S. J., *et al.*, Treating *Tobacco Use and Dependence. Quick Reference Guide for Clinicians* (Rockville, MD: U.S. Department of Health and Human Services, Public Health Service, October 2000). Available free by calling 800-358-9295.

465. Singleton, Mary G., and Pope, Mark, A comparison of successful smoking cessation interventions for adults and adolescents. *J. of Counseling and Development*, vol. 78, pp. 448-453 (2000).

466. Tashkin, D. P., Kanner, R., Bailey, W., *et al.*, Smoking cessation in patients with chronic obstructive pulmonary disease: a double-blind, placebo-controlled, randomised trial. *The Lancet*, vol. 357, pp. 1571-1575 (2001).

467. USDHHS, Public Health Service, *Reducing Tobacco Use*. A Report of the Surgeon General (2000).

468. Zhu, Shu-Hong, Anderson, Christopher M., Tedeschi, Gary J., *et al.*, Evidence of real-world effectiveness of a telephone quitline for smokers. *New Engl. J. Med.*, vol. 347, pp. 1087-1093 (2002).

469. Goldman, Lisa K., and Glantz, Stanton A., Evaluation of antismoking advertising campaigns. *JAMA*, vol. 279, pp. 772-777 (1998).

470. Fichtenberg, Caroline M., , and Glantz, Stanton A., Association of the California tobacco control program with declines in cigarette consumption and mortality from heart disease. *New Engl. J. Med.*, vol. 343, pp. 1772-1777 (2000).

471. Vastag, Brian, Teenage smoking continues to decline. *JAMA*, vol. 289, p. 163 (2003).

472. Reuters, Study finds antismoking success in 4 states. *New York Times*, p. A16, Sept. 19 (2003).

473. American Cancer Society, Anti-smoking efforts cut lung cancer deaths. *CA A Cancer J. for Clinicians*, vol. 53, no. 6, pp. 317-318 (2003).

474. Koh, Eun Lee, Best intentions up in smoke. Tobacco-control programs are cut along with budget. *The Boston Globe*, p. West1, June 29 (2003).

475. National Cancer Institute, *Risks Associated with Smoking Cigarettes with Low Machine-Measured Yields of Tar and Nicotine.* Smoking and Tobacco Control Monograph No. 13, NIH Pub. No. 92-5074 (Bethesda: National Cancer Institute, National Institutes of Health, 2001).

476. Gottlieb, S., New York's war on tobacco produces record fall in smoking. *Brit. Med. J.*, vol. 328, p.1222 (2004).

477. American Cancer Society, Quitting smoking. *CA A Cancer J. for Clinicians*, vol. 53, no. 6, pp. 327-375 (2003).

478. Editorial, Quitting smoking adds years to your life regardless of age. *CA. A Cancer J. for Clinicians*, vol. 52, no. 6, p. 319 (2002). The study referred to is in *Am. J. Publ. Health*, vol. 92, pp. 990-996 (2002).

479. Vaupel, James W., Carey, James R., and Christensen, Kaare, It's never too late. *Science*, vol. 301, pp. 1679-1680 (2003).

480. Djordjevic, M. V., Fan, J., Ferguson, S., *et al.*, Self-regulation of smoking intensity. Smoke yields of the low-nicotine, low-'tar' cigarettes. *Carcinogenesis*, vol. 16, pp. 2015-2021 (1995).

481. Jorenby, Douglas E., Leischow, Scott J., Nides, Mitchell A., A controlled trial of sustained-release bupropion, a nicotine patch, or both for smoking cessation. *New Engl. J. Med.*, vol. 340, pp.685-691 (1999).

482. Gatt, Moshe E., and Heyman, Samuel N., Treatment of tobacco use and dependence. *New Engl. J. Med.*, vol. 347, p. 294 (2002).

483. Editorial, Quitting for good: find what works for you. *UC Berkeley Wellness Letter*, vol. 17, no. 5, p. 5 (2001).

484. Editorial, If you are trying to quit smoking, beware of two new nicotine-delivery "systems". *UC Berkeley Wellness Letter*, vol 20, no. 5, p. 8 (2004).

485. Antonuccio, David O., Why the nicotine patch results may not stick. *Arch. Int. Med.*, vol. 154, pp. 923-927 (1994). See also *JAMA*, vol. 288, p. 3108 (2002).

486. Pierce, John P., and Gilpin, Elizabeth A., Letters: Effectiveness of over-the-counter nicotine replacement therapy. *JAMA*, vol. 288, p. 3110 (2002).

487. Rigotti, Nancy A., Treatment of tobacco use and dependence. *New Engl. J. Med.*, vol. 346, pp.506-512 (2002).

488. Abrams, Michael, The end of craving. A controversial new drug seems to stop addiction cold. *Discover*, vol. 24, no. 5 (2003).

489. Shamasunder, Bhavna, and Bero, Lisa, Financial ties and conflicts of interest between pharmaceutical companies and tobacco companies. *JAMA*, vol. 288, pp. 738-744 (2002).

490. Stevens, Lise M., Lynm, Cassio, and Glass, Richard M., Kicking the habit. *JAMA*, vol 288, p. 532 (2002).

491. See the *US Surgeon General's Reports* of 1988 and 1990 referenced above.

492. Reif, Arnold E. The Causes of Cancer (1981), Fig. 2, p. 440.

493. Brodish, Paul H., and Ross, Golbert L., *The Irreversible Health Effects of Cigarette Smoking*. (New York: American Council on Science and Health 1998).

494. HVMA, Smoking. Web: www.hvma.org/reference/systems/epiccare/PIsmoking.asp

495. Williamson, David F., Giovino, Gary A., Madans, Jennifer, *et al.*, Smoking cessation and the severity of weight gain. *New Engl. J. Med.*, vol. 325, pp.517-518 (1991).

496. Reuters, Death rate from obesity gains fast on smoking. *New York Times*, p. A19, March 18 (2004).

497. Editorial, Wellness made easy. *UC Berkeley Wellness Letter*, vol. 16, no. 4, p. 8 (2000).

498. Cromwell, Jerry, Bartosch, William J., Fiore, Michael C., *et al.* Cost-effectiveness of the clinical practice recommendations in the AHCPR guideline for smoking cessation. *JAMA*, vol 278, pp. 1759-1766 (1997).

499. McLellan, A. Thomas, Lewis, David C., O'Brien, Charles P., *et al.*, Drug dependence, a chronic medical illness. Implications for treatment, insurance, and outcomes evaluation. *JAMA*, vol. 284, pp. 1689-1695 (2000).

500. Editorial, If you are trying to quit smoking, you can now claim certain costs as medical expenses on your income tax. *UC Berkeley Wellness Letter*, vol. 16, no. 1, p.8 (1999).

501. Morra, Marion, and Potts, Eve, *Choices* (New York: Quill/HarperCollins, 2001).

502. Fisher, Edwin B., Jr., with Goldfarb, Toni L., *American Lung Association. 7 Steps to a Smoke-Free Life* (New York: John Wiley, 1998).

503. USDHHS, Public Health Service, *You Can Quit Smoking* (2000).

504. Carmelli, Dorit, Swan, Gary E., Robinette, Dennis, *et al.*, Genetic influence on smoking- a study of male twins. *New Engl. J. Med.*, vol. 327, pp. 829-833 (1992).

505. Blum, Kenneth, Cull, John G., Braverman, Eric R., *et al.*, Reward deficiency syndrome. Addictive, impulsive and compulsive disorders- including alcoholism, attention deficit disorder, drug abuse and food bingeing- may have a common genetic basis. *American Scientist*, vol. 84, pp. 132-144 (1996).

506. Editorial, Quitting and mental illness. *The Harvard Mental Health Letter*, pp. 3, June (1997).

507. Holden, Constance, 'Behavioral' addictions: do they exist? *Science*, vol. 294, pp. 980-982 (2001).

508. Glynn, Thomas J., *How to help your patients stop smoking: a National Cancer Institute manual for physicians* (Bethesda: National Cancer Institute, 1989).

509. Sloan, Frank A., Smith, V. Kerry, and Taylor, Donald H., Jr., *The Smoking Puzzle: Information, Risk Perception, and Choice* (Cambridge: Harvard University, 2003).

510. Fiore, M.C., Bailey, W. C., Cohen, S. J., *et al.*, *Smoking Cessation* (Rockville, MD: U.S. Department of Health and Human Services, Public Health Service, April 1996).

511. Fiore, M.C., Epps, R. P., and Manley, M. W., A missed opportunity: teaching medical students to help their patients successfully quit smoking. *JAMA*, vol. 271, pp. 624-626 (1994).

512. Ernster, Virginia L, and Croughan-Minihane, Mary S., Smoking cessation curriculum for first-year medical students. *JAMA*, vol. 272, pp. 659-660 (1994).

513. Ferry, Linda Hyder, Grissino, Linda M., and Runfola, Pamela Sieler, Tobacco dependence curricula in US undergraduate medical education. *JAMA*, vol. 282, pp. 825-829 (1999).

514. Hughes, John R., New treatments for smoking cessation. *CA, A Cancer J. Clin.*, vol. 50, pp. 143-155 (2000).

515. Sargent, James D., and DiFranza, Joseph R., Tobacco control for clinicians who treat adolescents. *CA, A Cancer J. Clin.*, vol. 53, pp. 102-125 (2003).

516. Mason, Abner. Cautious optimism on global AIDS battle. *The Boston Globe*, p. D7, July 7 (2002).

517. Steinbrook, Robert, Beyond Barcelona- The global response to HIV. *New Engl. J. Med.*, vol. 347, pp. 553-554 (2002).

518. Stephenson, Joan, Snuffing out tobacco ads. *JAMA*, vol. 286, p, 2801 (2001).

519. Peto, Richard, Chen, Zhengming, and Boreham, Jillian, Tobacco- The growing epidemic in China. *JAMA*, vol. 275, pp. 1683-1684 (1996).

520. Centers for Disease Control and Prevention, Cigarette smoking (2000).

521. Wong, Mitchell D., Shapiro, Martin F., Boscardin, W. John, *et al.*, Contribution of major diseases to disparities in mortality. *New Engl. J. Med.*, vol. 347, pp. 1585-1592 (2003).

522. Epstein, Helen, Enough to make you sick? *New York Times Magazine*, pp. 75-79, Oct. 12 (2003).

523. Cohen, Bernard L., Catalog of risks extended and updated. *Health Physics*, vol. 61, pp. 317-335 (1991).

524. Kane, Thomas J., The long road to race-blindness. *Science*, vol. 302, pp. 571-572 (2003).

525. Ghafoor, A. Jemal, Cokkinides, V., Cardinez, C. Murray, *et al.*, Cancer Statistics for African Americans, *CA Cancer J. Clin.*, vol. 52, pp. 326-341 (2002), see Fig. 8B, p.341.

526. Lenkowsky, Leslie, Book review: Minority report. Thernstrom, Abigail and Stephan, *No Excuses: Closing the Racial Gap in Learning* (New York: Simon & Schuster, 2003). *Commentary*, vol. 116, no. 4, pp. 66-68 (2003).

527. McDonough, Siobhan, Survey. Student behavior, teacher morale among concerns. *The Boston Globe*, p. A28, April 23 (2003).

528. Dillon, Sam, Houston's school violence data under a cloud. *New York Times*, pp. A1-A16, Nov. 7 (2003).

529. Gootman, Elissa, and Herszenhorn, David M., New York school overhaul shows growing pains. *New York Times*, p. A16, Jan. 5 (2004).

530. Wallis, Claudia, Does kindergarten need cops? *Time*, vol. 162, no. 24, pp. 52-53, Dec. 15 (2003).

531. Dillon, Sam, For children left behind, private tutors face rocky start. *New York Times*, pp. A1-A16, April 16, 2004.

532. Herbert, Bob, Failing teachers. *New York Times*, p. A23, Oct. 24 (2003).

533. Herszenhorn, David M., Union urges faster removal of incompetent teachers. *New York Times*, p. A27, Jan. 15 (2004).

534. *Time* of August 23, 2003, reported that all federal support for TFA had been eliminated, and that the AmeriCorps program, which also includes programs in policing and social casework, was cut by over one-third for the 2003-04 year. Since then, the funding for TFA for 2003-2004 seems to have been restored.

535. Klein, Joe, How teachers killed a dream. *Time*, vol. 162, no. 14, p. 27, Nov. 3 (2003).

536. Goldberg, Carey, The promise of preschool. Social science offers some hints- but not a firm answer- about the benefits of programs now being considered by the legislature. *The Boston Globe*, pp. C1-C2, March 23 (2004).

537. Richmond, Julius B., Entering the Arena of Head Start. In: *Project Head Start. A Legacy of the War on Poverty*, Zigler, E., and Valentine, J., eds. (New York: The Free Press, 1979).

538. Palmer, Francis, and Anderson, Lucille, Long-term gains from early intervention: finding from longitudinal studies. In: *Project Head Start. A Legacy of the War on Poverty*, Zigler, E., and Valentine, J., eds. (New York: The Free Press, 1979).

539. Jacobson, Linda, Head Start Programs back on track in Denver under new management. *Education Week on the Web*, p. 1, September 17 (1997).

540. Richmond, Julius B., and Palfrey, Judith. Keeping Head Start strong and successful. *The Boston Globe*, p. A15, July 19 (2003).

541. U.S. HHS Advisory Committee on Head Start Research and Evaluation, Evaluating Head Start: A Recommended Framework for Studying the Impact of the Head Start Program (Washington: U.S. Government Printing Office, 2000).

542. Editorial, Tinkering with Head Start. *The New York Times*, p. A22, June 16 2003).

543. U.S. HHS, Administration of Children and the Head Start Bureau, Making a Difference in the Lives of Infants and Toddlers and Their Families: The Impact of Early Head Start. Vol. I: Final Technical Report (Washington: Head Start Bureau, 2002).

544. Calvan, Bobby Caina, Classroom size limits are in jeopardy in Calif. *The Boston Globe*, p. A2, April 19 (2003).

545. Winerip, Michael, Miracles of small class size unfold ouch day in California. *New York Times*, p. A23, Oct. 29 (2003).

546. Editorial, Rescuing education reform. *New York Times*, p. A26, March 2 (2004).

547. Schemo, Diana Jean, and Clemetson, Jynette, Domestic spending: gains for Education but not much else. *New York Times*, pp. A1-A15, Feb. 3 (2004). See also Schemo, Kennedy demands full funding for school bill. *New York Times*, p. A18, April 7 (2004).

548. Mervis, Jeffrey, 2005 Bush budget pulls NSF schools funding. *Science*, vol. 303, p. 295 (2004).

549. Dillon, Sam, 1 in 4 schools fall short under Bush law. *New York Times*, p. A21, Jan. 27 (2004).

550. Ripley, Amanda, Beating the bubble test. How one Iowa school became a No Child Left Behind success story- and what it cost to do it. *Time*, vol. 163, no. 9, p. 52, March 1 (2004).

551. Heath, Marlene, A failure policy that succeeds. *New York Times*, p. A23, March 30 (2004).

552. Bachman, J. G., Wallace, J. M., O'Malley, P. M., *et al.*, Racial/ethnic differences in smoking, drinking, and illicit drug use among American high school seniors, 1976-1989, *Am. J. Public Health*, vol. 81, p. 372 (1991).

553. Koh, Howard K., Kannler, Christine, and Geller, Alan C., Cancer prevention: Preventing tobacco-related cancers. In *Cancer*, ed. by DeVita *et al.*, 6th edn. (2001), p. 551.

554. Rosenwald, Michael, Not all agree that jobs can cut crime. Specialists see little direct proof. *The Boston Globe*, pp. A1-B6, July 10 (2002).

555. Herbert, Bob, L.A.'s streets of death. *The New York Times*, p. A33, June 12 2003).

556. Herbert, Bob, Locked out at a young age. *New York Times*, p. A19, Oct. 20 (2003).

557. O'Connor, Anahad, Rise in income improves children's behavior, *New York Times*, p. D5, Oct. 21 (2003).

558. Malcolm, Mark. After-school sites target 'tweens.' Schools, libraries add activities to meet youngsters' ideal of 'cool.' *The Boston Globe*, p. West 1-11, May 23 (2003).

559. Bernstein, Nina. Daily choice turned deadly: children left on their own. *New York Times*, pp. A1-A28, Oct. 19 (2003).

560. Protherow-Stith, Deborah, and Spivak, Howard, A focus on preventing youth violence. *The Boston Globe*, p. A19, May 20 (2004).

561. Schemo, Diana Jean, Chapel Hill campus to cover all costs for needy students. *New York Times*, p. A18, Oct. 2 (2003).

562. Winter, Greg, Tens of thousands will lose college aid, report says. *New York Times*, p. A13, July 18 (2003).

563. Lewis, Diane E. Throwing cold water on summer jobs. State budget woes, economic malaise mean many teens won't have work. *Boston Globe*, p. E1-E4, May 9 (2003).

564. McCarthy, Kelly, LIFT violence out of schools. *Psychology Today*, vol. 33, no. 5, p.18 (2000).

565. Blumstein, Alfred, Violence: A new frontier for scientific research. *Science*, vol. 289, p.545 (2000).

566. Shafii, Mohammad, and Shafii, Sharon Lee, eds., *School Violence: Assessment, Management, Prevention* (Washington: American Psychiatric, 2001).

567. CDC, Prevalence of cigarette smoking among adults and changes in prevalence of current and some day smoking-United States, 1996-2001. *JAMA*, vol. 289, pp.2355-2356 (2003).

568. Heymann, Jody, Families on the edge. Overcoming untenable choices on work, health, childcare, and education. *Harvard Magazine*, vol. 105, no. 6, July-August (2003), pp. 48-53.

569. Jackson, Derrick Z., How Big Tobacco is rising from the ashes. *The Boston Globe*, p. A19, May 2 (2003).

570. Zuckerbrod, Nancy, Cigarette sales fall despite marketing. *Boston Globe*, p. A12, Oct. 23 (2004).

571. WHO, New WHO Director-General urges countries to sign Tobacco Convention. www.who.int/mediacentre/releases/2003/pr63/en/, p. 1, Aug. 4 (2003).

572. Sloan, Frank A., Ostermann, Jan, Picone, Gabriel, *et al.*, *The Price of Smoking* (Cambridge: MIT Press, 2004).

573. Feldman, Eric A., and Bayer, Ronald, eds., *Unfiltered: Conflicts over Tobacco Policy and Public Health* (Cambridge: Harvard University Press, 2004).

574. Brown, Charles C., and Kessler, Larry G., Projections of lung cancer mortality in the United States, 1985-2025. *J. Nat. Cancer Inst.*, vol. 80, pp. 43-51 (1988).

575. McElvaney, N. Gerry, Smoking ban- Made in Ireland, for home use and for export. *New Engl. J. Med.*, vol. 350, pp. 2231-2233 (2004).

576. Cherner, Joe. Washington State implements Smokefree Workplace Law. www.Joe@smokefree.org, December 8 (2005).

577. Cunningham, Rob, *Smoke and Mirrors: The Canadian Tobacco War* (Ottawa: International Development Research Center, 1996).

578. Cherner, Joe. Nova Scotia becomes Canada's 9th Smokefree Province/Territory. www.Joe@smokefree.org, Nov. 7 (2005).

579. U.S. Department of Health and Human Services, *Smoking and Health in the Americas. A 1992 Report of the Surgeon General in collaboration with the Pan American Health Organization* (Atlanta, U.S. Department of Health and Human Services,

Public Health Service, DHHS Publication No. (CDC) 92-8421 (1992).

580. Cherner, Joe, Uruguay begins smokefree future today. Joe@ smokefree.org, March 1 (2006).

581. Forey, Barbara, Ed., *International Smoking Statistics: A Collection of Historical Data from 30 Economically Developed Countries* (Oxford New York: Oxford University, 2002).

582. Simonato, L., Agudo, A., Ahrens A., *et al.*, Lung cancer and cigarette smoking in Europe: an update of risk estimates and an assessment of inter-country heterogeneity. *Internat. J. Cancer*, vol. 91, pp. 876-887 (2001).

583. Seigel, Jessica, Inhaling their food. *New York Times*, p. A21, February 21 (2005).

584. Sciolino, Elaine, No longer tres chic, smoking loses favor in France. *New York Times*, p. A4, October 6 (2006).

585. Cherner, Joe, England passes smokefree workplace law. Protection of worker health most important priority. Joe@ smokefree.org, February 14 (2006).

586. McLean, Renwick, After 500 years, can Spain end cigarette binge? *New York Times*, p. A10, December 29 (2005).

587. Cherner, Joe. Northern Ireland to go smokefree. www.Joe@ smokefree.org, October 17 (2005).

588. Jackson, Derrick Z., When death is the bottom line. *The Boston Globe*, p. A19. July 25, 2001.

589. World Health Organization. The world health report 1999- making a difference. Combating the tobacco epidemic (Geneva: World Health Organization, 1999).

590. Centers for Disease Control. Prevalence of cigarette smoking among secondary school students- Budapest, Hungary, 1995 and 1999. *JAMA*, vol. 283, pp. 3190-3191 (1999).

591. Vutuc, Christian, Waldhoer, Thomas, and Haidinger, Gerald, Cancer mortality in Austria: 1970-2002. *Wien Klin. Wochenschr.*, vol. 116, no. 19-20, pp. 669-675 (2004).

592. Associated Press, EU to ban tobacco ads in 2005. *The Boston Globe*, p. C2, December 3 (2002).

593. Zagorin, Adam. Inside Saddam. The Iraqi leader is not only a despot but one of the world's richest swindlers. Here's how he does it. *Time*, vol. 161, no. 9, pp. 36-37, March 10 (2003).

594. Myers, Steven Lee, The Great Russian Smoke-Out, fit for seventh graders. *New York Times*, p. A4, April 23 (2004).

595. Yang, Gonghuan, Fan, Lixin, Tan, Jian, *et al.*, Smoking in China. Findings of the 1996 National Prevalence Study. *JAMA*, vol. 282, pp. 1247-1253 (1999).

596. He, Jiang, Gu, Dongfeng, Wu, Xigui, *et al. New Engl. J. Med.*, vol. 353, pp. 1124-1134 (2005).

597. Editorial, Tobacco epidemic in China's future. *Science*, vol. 293, p. 1761 (2001). The editorial summarizes the article by Tai Hing Lam and coauthors in the *British Medical Journal* of 18 August (2001).

598. Sellers, Edward M., Pharmacogenetics and ethnoracial differences in smoking. *JAMA*, vol. 280, pp. 179-180 (1998).

599. Hughes, Jason, *Learning to Smoke: Tobacco Use in the West* (Chicago: University of Chicago, 2003).

600. Ohida, Takashi, Sakurai, Hideya, Mochizuki, Yumiko, *et al.*, Smoking prevalence and attitudes toward smoking among Japanese physicians. *JAMA*, vol. 285, pp. 2643-2648 (2001).

601. Jenkins, Christopher N. H., Dai, Pham Xuan, Ngoc, Do Hong, *et al.*, Tobacco use in Vietnam. Prevalence, predictors, and the role of transnational tobacco corporations. *JAMA*, vol. 277, pp. 1726-1731 (1997).

602. Bartecchi, Carl E., MacKenzie, Thomas D., and Schrier, Robert W., The human costs of tobacco use (First of two parts). *New Engl. J. Med.*, vol. 330, pp. 907-912 (1994).

603. MacKenzie, Thomas D., Bartecchi, Carl E., and Schrier, Robert W., The human costs of tobacco use (Second of two parts). *New Engl. J. Med.*, vol. 330, pp. 975-980 (1994).

604. Ruder, Debra, Glorian Sorensen takes a global view of *tobacco* use. *Paths of Progress*, Spring/Summer (2005).

605. Cherner, Joe, India implements smokefree workplace legislation. Joe@smokefree.org, May 2 (2004).

606. Jha, Prabhat, and Chaloupka, Frank J., eds., *Tobacco Control in Developing Countries* (Oxford: Oxford University, 2000).

607. Satcher, David, International tobacco control: An update. *JAMA*, vol. 286, p. 296 (2001).

608. Bitton, Asaf, Fichtenberg, Caroline, and Glantz, Stanton, Reducing smoking prevalence to 10% in five years. *JAMA*, vol. 286, p. 3733-3734 (2001).

609. Myers, Matthew L., and Wilkenfeld, Judith P., The Worldwide Tobacco Treaty. *JAMA*, vol. 286, p. 3736 (2001).

610. At that time, I was asked to serve as chairman of the Massachusetts Interagency on Smoking and Health, a collaboration of the American Cancer Society, the American Heart Association and the American Lung Association.

611. Koop, C. Everett, Pearson, Clarence E., and Schwarz, M. Roy, *Critical Issues in Global Health* (San Francisco: Jossey-Bass, 2001).

612. World Health Organization, *Tobacco and health. A global status report* (Geneva: World Health Organization, 1997).

613. Waxman, Henry A., The future of the global tobacco treaty negotiations. *New England J. Med.*, vol. 346, pp. 936-939 (2002).

614. Stephenson, Joan, Global antismoking measures. *JAMA*, vol. 287, p, 1255 (2002).

615. Stephenson, Joan, Global Antitobacco Treaty. *JAMA*, vol. 293, no. 3, p. 286 (2005).

616. Blum, Alan, Solberg, Eric, and Wolinsky, Howard, Precious little progress in war on smoking. *Chicago Sun-Times*, January 11 (2004).

617. Goodman, Ellen, A world safe for Big Tobacco. *The Boston Sunday Globe*, p. H1, May 4 (2003).

618. American Lung Association, Action letter: The time is now to ratify the Tobacco Treaty. www.lungaction.org/campaign/RatifyFCTC/, Oct. 25 (2005).

619. The Framework Convention Alliance for Tobacco Control, Toward global ratification. www.fctc.org/treaty/ratification.php, October 19 (2006).

620. American Cancer Society, Global tobacco treaty set to take effect; American Cancer Society urges swift U.S. ratification. Unice.Lieberman@cancer.org, Nov. 30 (2004).

621. Tobacco Free Initiative (TIF) of WHO, World No Tobacco Day 2004. www.who.int/tobacco/wntd/2004/en/, pp. 1-2 (2004).

622. Editorial, A treaty against tobacco. *The Boston Globe*, p. A22, May 22 (2003).

623. Bettcher, Douglas, and Subramaniam, Chitra, The necessity of global tobacco regulations. *JAMA*, vol. 286, p. 3737 (2001).

624. Steinbrook, Robert, Beyond Bareclona- The global response to HIV. *New Engl. J. Med.*, vol. 347, pp. 553-554 (2002).

625. Reif, Arnold E., Synergism in carcinogenesis. *J. Natl. Cancer Inst.*, vol. 73, pp. 25-39 (1985).

626. Stocks, P., The relation between atmospheric pollution in urban and rural localities and mortality from cancer, bronchi-

tis, and pneumonia, with particular reference to 3:4-benzo-pyrene, beryllium, molybdenum, vanadium, and arsenic. *Brit. J. Cancer*, vol. 14, pp. 397-418 (1960).

627. Richmond, J. B., Smoking and Health: A Report of the Surgeon General. DHEW Publ. No. PHS 79-50066 (Washington, D.C.: Government Printing Office, 1979).

628. Pyne, Solana, Small particles add up to big disease risk. *Science*, vol. 295, p. 1994 (2002).

629. Pope, C. Arden, III, Burnett, Richard T., Thun, Michael J., *et al.*, Lung cancer, cardiopulmonary mortality and long-term exposure to fine particulate air pollution. *JAMA*, vol. 287, pp. 1132-1141 (2002).

630. Seelye, Katherine Q., and Lee, Jennifer, Court blocks U.S. effort to relax pollution rule. *New York Times*, p. A1-A10, Dec. 25 (2003).

631. NASA, Scientists say soot is one of the biggest factors in global warming. *New York Times*, p. A17, Dec. 25 (2003).

632. Fettner, Ann Giudici, Dying in disgrace? *Harvard Health Letter*, vol. 20, no. 10, pp. 4-6 (1995). Green, Mark. Lung cancer among nonsmokers. *Cancer*, Jan. 1 (1995).

633. Alleman, James E., and Mossman, Brooke T., Asbestos revisited. Once considered safe enough to use in toothpaste, this unique substance had intrigued people for more than 2,000 years. *Scientific American*, vol. 277, no. 1, pp. 70-75 (1997).

634. Suzuki, Yasunosuke, and Yuen, Steven R., Asbestos fibers contributing to the induction of human malignant mesothelioma. *Ann. N.Y. Acad. Sci.*, vol. 982, pp. 160-176 (2002).

635. Reif, Arnold E., and Baker, Helen S., Inhalation studies with toluidine blue aerosol in rats. *A.M.A. Archives of Industrial Health*, vol. 14, pp. 560-568 (1956).

636. Associated Press. Halliburton agrees to $4 billion asbestos claim settlement. *The Boston Globe*, p. D2, December 19 (2002).

637. Treaster, Joseph B. Hartford to pay $1.5 billion to settle asbestos claims. *New York Times*, p. B4, Dec. 20 (2002).

638. Berenson, Alex, Senate panel approves bill to establish asbestos trust. New York Times, p. C1-C2, July 11 (2003).

639. Glater, Jonathan D., Suits on silica being compared to asbestos cases. *New York Times*, p. B1-B4, Sept. 6 (2003).

640. Chatzis, Christos, Danaka, Georgia, Linos, Athena, *et al.*, Lung cancer and occupational risk factors in Greece. *J. of Envir. Med.*, vol. 41, pp. 29-35 (1999).

641. Editorial, Radon risk for lung cancer back in the spotlight. *CA. A Cancer J. for Clinicians*, vol. 55, no. e, pp. 139-140 (2005).

642. Nero, Anthony V., Jr., Indoor radon exposure and lung cancer. In *Cancer Prevention*, ed. by DeVita, Vincent T., Jr., Hellman, Samuel, and Rosenberg, Steven A., pp. 1-12, December (1989).

643. Harley, Naomi H., and Harley, John H., Potential lung cancer risk from indoor radon exposure. *CA- A Cancer Journal for Clinicians*, vol. 40, no. 5, pp. 265-275 (1990).

644. Editorial, Indoor radon: A little less to worry about. *Science*, vol. 251, p. 1019 (1991).

645. Guimond, Richard J., Radon risk and EPA. *Science*, vol. 251, pp. 724-725 (1991).

646. Pershagen, G., Akerblom, G., Axelson, O., *et al.*, (On radon, smoking, and the risk of lung cancer). *New Engl. J. Med.*, vol. 330, pp. 159-164 (1994).

647. Darby, S., Whitley, E., Silcocks, P., *et al.*, Risk of lung cancer associated with residential radon exposure in south-west

England: a case-control study. *Brit. J. Cancer*, vol. 78, pp. 3394-408 (1998).

648. Neuberger, John S., and Gesell, Thomas F., Residential radon exposure and lung cancer: risk in non-smokers. *Health Phys.*, vol. 83, pp. 1-18 (2002).

649. In part compiled from data from www.bt.cdc.gov/radiation/

650. Stigum, Hein, Strand, Terje, and Magnus, Per. Should radon be reduced in homes? A cost-effect analysis. *Health Phys.*, vol. 84, pp. 227-235 (2003).

651. United States Nuclear Regulatory Commission, www.nrc.gov/reading-rm/doc-collections/fact-sheets/

652. Socolow, Robert H., and Pacala, Stephen W., A plan to keep carbon in check. *Scientific American*, vol. 295, no. 3, pp. 76-83 (2006).

653. Deutch, John M., and Moniz, Ernest J., The nuclear option. *Scientific American*, vol. 295, no. 3, pp. 50-57 (2006).

654. Loewwen, Eric P., Heavy-metal nuclear power. *American Scientist*, vol. 92, pp. 522-531 (2004).

655. Wald, Matthew L., Casks gain favor as method for storing nuclear waste. *New York Times*, p. A22, June 5 (2005).

656. Wald, Matthew L., Agency is seen as unfazed on atom waste. *New York Times*, p. A12, June 12 (2004).

657. Deutch, John M., and Moniz, Ernest J., The nuclear option (2006).

658. Kintisch, Eli, DOE outlines two roads to recycling spent fuel. *Science*, vol. 313, p. 746 (2006).

659. Normile, Dennis, Proton guns set their sights on taming radioactive wastes. *Science*, vol. 302, pp. 379-381 (2003).

660. U.S. Nuclear Regulatory Commission, Fact Sheet on Dirty Bombs. Feb. 25 (2004), www.nrc.gov/reading-m/doc-collections/fact-sheets/dirty -bombs.html.

661. FAS, Public Interest Report. Dirty Bombs: Response to a Threat. April (2002), www.fas.org/faspir/2002/v55n2/dirty-bomb.htm.

662. Johnson, Raymond H., Jr., Dealing with the terror of nuclear terrorism. *Radiation Safety J.*, vol. 87, suppl. 1, pp. S3-S7 (2004).

663. Center for Defense Information (CDI), Pacal's new wager: The dirty bomb threat heightens. Sept. 29 (2005), last updated Feb. 4 (2003), www.cdi.org/terrorism/dirty-bomb.cfm.

664. Slack, Donovan, and Smalley, Suzanne, 6 sought after tip alleging 'dirty bomb.' *Boston Globe*, pp. 1-14, Jan. 20 (2005).

665. Sanger, David E. 10 plots foiled since Sept. 11, Bush declares. *New York Times*, p. A1-A10, Oct. 7 (2005).

666. International Atomic Energy Agency, Inadequate Control of World's Radioactive Sourves, *Press Release*, June 24 (2004).

667. Stone, Richard, New efforts aim to thwart dirty bombers. *Science*, vol. 296, pp. 2117-2118 (2002).

668. Center for Defense Information (CDI), What if terrorists go nuclear? Sept. 29 (2005), last updated Oct. 1 (2001), www.cdi.org/terrorism/nuclear.cfm.

669. Whitehouse, David, Analysis: Making a 'dirty bomb.' *BBC News*, UK Edition, June 10 (2002); http://news.bbc.co.uk/1/hi/world/americas/2037056.stm.

670. Lipton, Eric, Democrats want all ship containers inspected. *New York Times*, p. A17, April 26 (2006).

671. Ritter, Ken, Homeland Security tests nuclear sensors at Nevada test site. Looks to perfect tools that detect 'dirty bombs.' *Boston Globe*, p. A16, Jan. 29 (2006).

672. Flynn, Stephen E., and Wein, Lawrence M., Think inside the box. *New York Times*, p. A31, Nov. 29 (2005).

673. Kouzes, Richard T., Detecting illicit nuclear materials. *American Scientist*, vol. 93, pp. 422-427 (2005).

674. Martyny, John, Glazer, Craig S., and Newman, Lee S., Respiratory protection. *New Engl. J. Med.*, vol. 347, pp. 824-830 (2002(=),

675. Markoff, John, This is only a drill: In California, testing technology in a disaster response. *New York Times*, p. C1-C8, August 28 (2006).

676. Petroff, Dale M., Responding to 'dirty bombs.' *Occupational Health & Safety*, vol. 72, pp. 82-88 (2003).

677. Moulder, J. E., Post-irradiation approaches to treatment of radiation injuries in the context of radiological terrorism and radiation accidents: a review. *Int. J. Radiation Biol.*, vol. 80, pp. 3-10 (2004).

678. Schlesinger, Robert, A threat to nuclear plants. Warning fueling debate on safety, federal regulation. *Boston Globe*, p.A4, May 14 (2002).

679. National Council on Radiation Protection and Measurements, *Evaluation of the Linear-Nonthreshold Dose-Response Model for Ionizing Radiation.* NCRP Report no. 136, June 4 (2001).

680. Tokarskaya, Z. B., Scott, B. R., Zhuntova, G. V., *et al.*, Interaction of radiation and smoking in lung cancer induction among workers at the Mayak nuclear enterprise. *Health Phys.*, vol. 83, pp. 833-846 (2002).

681. United Nations Scientific Committee on the Effects of Atomic Radiation. UNSCEAR 2000 Report to the General Assembly, with Scientific Annexes. *Sources and Effects of Ionizing Radiation.* Vol. II: Effects, Annex I, p. 425 (2000).

682. UK National Physical laboratory. Ionising Radiation. *Metromina*, issue 12, www.npl.co.uk/publications/metromania/issue12, autumn (2001).

683. Australian Government Radiation Protection and Nuclear Safety Agency. Ionizing Radiation and Health. *Fact Sheet 17*, www.arpansa.gov.au in transmission, August (2006).

684. Ron, Elaine, Cancer risks from medical radiation. *Health Physics*, vol. 85, pp. 47-59 (2003).

685. United States. Congress. Senate. Committee on Foreign Relations, *Dirty bombs and basement nukes: the terrorist threat: hearing before the Committee on Foreign Relations, United States Senate, One Hundred Seventh Congress, second session, March 6, 2002* (Washington: U.S.G.P.O., 2002).

686. Reif, Arnold E., and Triest, William E, Effects of strontium-90 plus external irradiation in C57BL/6J mice. *Health Phys.*, vol. 42, pp. 891-904 (1982).

687. Associated Press, Military is called unprepared for attack. *New York Times*, p. A18, Feb. 1 (2008).

688. Sanger, David E., 10 terror plots have been foiled since 9/11, Bush declares. *New York Times*, p. A1-A10, Oct. 7, 2007.

689. Varmus, H. Klausner, R., Zerhouni, E., *et al.*, Grand challenges in global health. *Science*, vol. 302, pp. 398-399 (2003).

690. Flanagin, Annette, and Winker, Margaret A., Global health- Targeting problems and achieving solutions. A call for papers. *JAMA*, vol. 290, pp. 1382-1384 (2003).

691. Gates, Bill, *The Road Ahead*, 2nd edn. (New York: Penguin, 1996).

692. Glanz, James, Scientists say administration distorts facts. Accusations include suppressing reports and stacking committees. *New York Times*, p. A21, February 19 (2004).

693. Drew, Christopher, and Oppel, Richard A., Jr., How industry won the battle of pollution control at E.P.A. *New York Times*, pp. A1-A10, March 6 (2004).

694. Bal, Dileep G., Cancer statistics 2001: *Quo vadis* or Whither goest thou? *CA Cancer J. Clin.*, vol. 51, pp. 11-14 (2001).

695. Editorial, Early action on early education. *Boston Globe*, p. A14, Dec. 5 (2006).

696. Breyer, Stephen G., 50 years after Brown. A decision that changed America also changed the court. *New York Times*, p. A25, May 17 (2004).

697. Bell, Derrick, The failed legacy of Boston school desegregation. *Boston Sunday Globe*, p. E11, May 16 (2004).

698. Gates, Henry Lois, Jr. Breaking the silence. *New York Times*, Week, p. 11, Aug. 1 (2004).

699. Herbert, Bob. Dad's empty chair. *New York Times*, p. A27, July 7 (2005).

700. Butterfield, Fox. 2 studies find laws on felons forbid many blacks men to vote. *New York Times*, p. A21, Sept. 23 (2004).

701. Thernstrom, Abigail, and Thernstrom, Stephan, Have we overcome? *Commentary*, vol. 118, no. 4, Nov. (2004).

702. Stocks, P., The relation between atmospheric pollution in urban and rural localities and mortality from cancer, bronchitis, and pneumonia, with particular reference to 3:4-benzopyrene, beryllium, molybdenum, vanadium, and arsenic. *Brit. J. Cancer*, vol. 14, pp. 397-418 (1960).

703. Richmond, J. D., Smoking and Health: A Report of the Surgeon General. DHEW Publ. No. PHS 79-50066 (Washington, D.C.: Government Printing Office, 1979).

704. Pyne, Solana, Small particles add up to big disease risk. *Science*, vol. 295, p. 1994 (2002).

705. Pope, C. Arden, III, Burnett, Richard T., Thun, Michael J., *et al.*, Lung cancer, cardiopulmonary mortality and long-term exposure to fine particulate air pollution. *JAMA*, vol. 287, pp. 1132-1141 (2002).

706. Seelye, Katherine Q., and Lee, Jennifer, Court blocks U.S. effort to relax pollution rule. *New York Times*, p. A1-A10, Dec. 25 (2003).

707. NASA, Scientists say soot is one of the biggest factors in global warming. *New York Times*, p. A17, Dec. 25 (2003).

708. Fettner, Ann Giudici, Dying in disgrace? *Harvard Health Letter*, vol. 20, no. 10, pp. 4-6 (1995). Green, Mark. Lung cancer among nonsmokers. *Cancer*, Jan. 1 (1995).

709. Alleman, James E., and Mossman, Brooke T., Asbestos revisited. Once considered safe enough to use in toothpaste, this unique substance had intrigued people for more than 2,000 years. *Scientific American,* vol. 277, no. 1, pp. 70-75 (1997).

710. Suzuki, Yasunosuke, and Yuen, Steven R., Asbestos fibers contributing to the induction of human malignant mesothelioma. *Ann. N.Y. Acad. Sci.*, vol. 982, pp. 160-176 (2002).

711. Reif, Arnold E., and Baker, Helen S., Inhalation studies with toluidine blue aerosol in rats. *A.M.A. Archives of Industrial Health*, vol. 14, pp. 560-568 (1956).

712. Associated Press. Halliburton agrees to $4 billion asbestos claim settlement. *The Boston Globe*, p. D2, December 19 (2002).

713. Treaster, Joseph B. Hartford to pay $1.5 billion to settle asbestos claims. *New York Times*, p. B4, Dec. 20 (2002).

714. Berenson, Alex, Senate panel approves bill to establish asbestos trust. New York Times, p. C1-C2, July 11 (2003).

715. Glater, Jonathan D., Suits on silica being compared to asbestos cases. *New York Times*, p. B1-B4, Sept. 6 (2003).

716. Chatzis, Christos, Danaka, Georgia, Linos, Athena, *et al.*, Lung cancer and occupational risk factors in Greece. *J. of Envir. Med.*, vol. 41, pp. 29-35 (1999).

717. Editorial, Radon risk for lung cancer back in the spotlight. *CA. A Cancer J. for Clinicians*, vol. 55, no. e, pp. 139-140 (2005).

718. Nero, Anthony V., Jr., Indoor radon exposure and lung cancer. In *Cancer Prevention*, ed. by DeVita, Vincent T., Jr., Hellman, Samuel, and Rosenberg, Steven A., pp. 1-12, December (1989).

719. Harley, Naomi H., and Harley, John H., Potential lung cancer risk from indoor radon exposure. *CA- A Cancer Journal for Clinicians*, vol. 40, no. 5, pp. 265-275 (1990).

720. Editorial, Indoor radon: A little less to worry about. *Science*, vol. 251, p. 1019 (1991).

721. Guimond, Richard J., Radon risk and EPA. *Science*, vol. 251, pp. 724-725 (1991).

722. Pershagen, G., Akerblom, G., Axelson, O., *et al.*, (On radon, smoking, and the risk of lung cancer). *New Engl. J. Med.*, vol. 330, pp. 159-164 (1994).

723. In part compiled from data from www.bt.cdc.gov/radiation/

724. Darby, S., Whitley, E., Silcocks, P., *et al.*, Risk of lung cancer associated with residential radon exposure in south-west England: a case-control study. *Brit. J. Cancer*, vol. 78, pp. 3394-408 (1998).

725. Neuberger, John S., and Gesell, Thomas F., Residential radon exposure and lung cancer: risk in non-smokers. *Health Phys.*, vol. 83, pp. 1-18 (2002).

726. Stigum, Hein, Strand, Terje, and Magnus, Per. Should radon be reduced in homes? A cost-effect analysis. *Health Phys.*, vol. 84, pp. 227-235 (2003).

727. Socolow, Robert H., and Pacala, Stephen W., A plan to keep carbon in check. *Scientific American*, vol. 295, no. 3, pp. 76-83 (2006).

728. Deutch, John M., and Moniz, Ernest J., The nuclear option. *Scientific American*, vol. 295, no. 3, pp. 50-57 (2006).

729. Loewwen, Eric P., Heavy-metal nuclear power. *American Scientist*, vol. 92, pp. 522-531 (2004).

730. Wald, Matthew L., Agency is seen as unfazed on atom waste. *New York Times*, p. A12, June 12 (2004).

731. Wald, Matthew L., Casks gain favor as method for storing nuclear waste. *New York Times*, p. A22, June 5 (2005).

732. Kintisch, Eli, DOE outlines two roads to recycling spent fuel. *Science*, vol. 313, p. 746 (2006).

733. Normile, Dennis, Proton guns set their sights on taming radioactive wastes. *Science*, vol. 302, pp. 379-381 (2003).

734. U.S. Nuclear Regulatory Commission, Fact Sheet on Dirty Bombs. Feb. 25 (2004), www.nrc.gov/reading-m/doc-collections/fact-sheets/dirty -bombs.html.

735. FAS, Public Interest Report. Dirty Bombs: Response to a Threat. April (2002), www.fas.org/faspir/2002/v55n2/dirty-bomb.htm.

736. Johnson, Raymond H., Jr., Dealing with the terror of nuclear terrorism. *Radiation Safety J.*, vol. 87, suppl. 1, pp. S3-S7 (2004).

737. Center for Defense Information (CDI), Pacal's new wager: The dirty bomb threat heightens. Sept. 29 (2005), last updated Feb. 4 (2003), www.cdi.org/terrorism/dirty-bomb.cfm.

738. Slack, Donovan, and Smalley, Suzanne, 6 sought after tip alleging 'dirty bomb.' *Boston Globe*, pp. 1-14, Jan. 20 (2005).

739. Sanger, David E. 10 plots foiled since Sept. 11, Bush declares. *New York Times*, p. A1-A10, Oct. 7 (2005).

740. International Atomic Energy Agency, Inadequate Control of World's Radioactive Sourves, *Press Release*, June 24 (2004).

741. Stone, Richard, New efforts aim to thwart dirty bombers. *Science*, vol. 296, pp. 2117-2118 (2002).

742. Center for Defense Information (CDI), What if terrorists go nuclear? Sept. 29 (2005), last updated Oct. 1 (2001), www.cdi. org/terrorism/nuclear.cfm.

743. Whitehouse, David, Analysis: Making a 'dirty bomb.' *BBC News*, UK Edition, June 10 (2002); http://news.bbc.co.uk/1/ hi/world/americas/2037056.stm.

744. Lipton, Eric, Democrats want all ship containers inspected. *New York Times*, p. A17, April 26 (2006).

745. Ritter, Ken, Homeland Security tests nuclear sensors at Nevada test site. Looks to perfect tools that detect 'dirty bombs.' *Boston Globe*, p. A16, Jan. 29 (2006).

746. Flynn, Stephen E., and Wein, Lawrence M., Think inside the box. *New York Times*, p. A31, Nov. 29 (2005).

747. Kouzes, Richard T., Detecting illicit nuclear materials. *American Scientist*, vol. 93, pp. 422-427 (2005).

748. Martyny, John, Glazer, Craig S., and Newman, Lee S., Respiratory protection. *New Engl. J. Med.*, vol. 347, pp. 824-830 (2002(=),

749. Markoff, John, This is only a drill: In California, testing technology in a disaster response. *New York Times*, p. C1-C8, August 28 (2006).

750. Petroff, Dale M., Responding to 'dirty bombs.' *Occupational Health & Safety*, vol. 72, pp. 82-88 (2003).

751. Moulder, J. E., Post-irradiation approaches to treatment of radiation injuries in the context of radiological terrorism and radiation accidents: a review. *Int. J. Radiation Biol.*, vol. 80, pp. 3-10 (2004).

752. Schlesinger, Robert, A threat to nuclear plants. Warning fueling debate on safety, federal regulation. *Boston Globe*, p.A4, May 14 (2002).

753. National Council on Radiation Protection and Measurements, *Evaluation of the Linear-Nonthreshold Dose-Response Model for Ionizing Radiation.* NCRP Report no. 136, June 4 (2001).

754. Tokarskaya, Z. B., Scott, B. R., Zhuntova, G. V., *et al.*, Interaction of radiation and smoking in lung cancer induction among workers at the Mayak nuclear enterprise. *Health Phys.*, vol. 83, pp. 833-846 (2002).

755. United Nations Scientific Committee on the Effects of Atomic Radiation. UNSCEAR 2000 Report to the General Assembly, with Scientific Annexes. *Sources and Effects of Ionizing Radiation.* Vol. II: Effects, Annex I, p. 425 (2000).

756. UK National Physical laboratory. Ionising Radiation. *Metromina*, issue 12, www.npl.co.uk/publications/metromania/issue12, autumn (2001).

757. Australian Government Radiation Protection and Nuclear Safety Agency. Ionizing Radiation and Health. *Fact Sheet 17*, www.arpansa.gov.au in transmission, August (2006).

758. Ron, Elaine, Cancer risks from medical radiation. *Health Physics*, vol. 85, pp. 47-59 (2003).

759. Reif, Arnold E., and Triest, William E, Effects of strontium-90 plus external irradiation in C57BL/6J mice. *Health Phys.*, vol. 42, pp. 891-904 (1982).

760. Sanger, David E., 10 terror plots have been foiled since 9/11, Bush declares. *New York Times*, p. A1-A10, Oct. 7, 2007